T0248870

Data Mining: Concepts and Algorithms

Data Mining: Concepts and Algorithms

Edited by Mick Benson

MURPHY & MOORE
www.murphy-moorepublishing.com

Murphy & Moore Publishing,
1 Rockefeller Plaza,
New York City, NY 10020, USA

Copyright © 2022 Murphy & Moore Publishing

This book contains information obtained from authentic and highly regarded sources. Copyright for all individual chapters remain with the respective authors as indicated. All chapters are published with permission under the Creative Commons Attribution License or equivalent. A wide variety of references are listed. Permission and sources are indicated; for detailed attributions, please refer to the permissions page and list of contributors. Reasonable efforts have been made to publish reliable data and information, but the authors, editors and publisher cannot assume any responsibility for the validity of all materials or the consequences of their use.

Trademark Notice: Registered trademark of products or corporate names are used only for explanation and identification without intent to infringe.

ISBN: 978-1-63987-150-6

Cataloging-in-Publication Data

Data mining : concepts and algorithms / edited by Mick Benson.
  p. cm.
Includes bibliographical references and index.
ISBN 978-1-63987-150-6
1. Data mining. 2. Database searching. I. Benson, Mick.
QA76.9.D343 D38 2022
006.312--dc23

For information on all Murphy & Moore Publications
visit our website at www.murphy-moorepublishing.com

 **MURPHY & MOORE**

Contents

Preface

Data mining is a process which deals with discovering patterns in large data sets. It incorporates approaches from machine learning, statistics and database systems. Data mining is a subfield of computer science and statistics. The goal of data mining is to extract information patterns and knowledge from large amounts of data and transform the information into a comprehensible structure. The term is frequently applied to any form of large-scale data or information processing, as well as any application of computer decision support system (DSS). In data mining, large quantities of data is analyzed to extract previously unknown, interesting patterns such as groups of data records, unusual records, and dependencies. This book elucidates the concepts and innovative models around prospective developments with respect to data mining. It will also provide interesting topics for research which interested readers can take up. The book aims to equip students and experts with the advanced topics and upcoming concepts in this area.

This book unites the global concepts and researches in an organized manner for a comprehensive understanding of the subject. It is a ripe text for all researchers, students, scientists or anyone else who is interested in acquiring a better knowledge of this dynamic field.

I extend my sincere thanks to the contributors for such eloquent research chapters. Finally, I thank my family for being a source of support and help.

Editor

Data mining for decision making in engineering optimal design

A. Mosavi

University of Debrecen, Faculty of Informatics, Hungary.

*Corresponding author: a.mosavi@math.unideb.hu (A. Mosavi).

Abstract

Often in modeling the engineering optimization design problems, the value of objective function(s) is not clearly defined in terms of design variables. Instead it is obtained by some numerical analysis such as finite element structural analysis, fluid mechanics analysis, and thermodynamic analyses. Yet, the numerical analyses are considerably time consuming to obtain the final value of objective function(s). For the reason of reducing the number of analyses as few as possible, our methodology works as a supporting tool to the meta-models. The research in meta-modeling for multi-objective optimization are relatively young and there is still much research capacity to further explore. Here is shown that visualizing the problem on the basis of the randomly sampled geometrical big-data of computer aided design (CAD) and computer aided engineering (CAE) simulation results, combined with utilizing classification tool of data mining could be effective as a supporting system to the available meta-modeling approaches.

To evaluate the effectiveness of the proposed method, a case study in 3D wing optimal design is proposed. Discussion focusing on how effective the proposed methodology could be in further practical engineering design problems is presented.

Keywords: *Data Mining, classification, Multi-objective Optimization, Engineering Optimization, Meta-Modeling.*

1. Introduction

The research field of considering decision problems with multiple conflicting objectives is known as multiple criteria decision making (MCDM) [1]. Solving a multi-objective optimization problem has been characterized as supporting the decision maker (DM) in finding the best solution for the DM's problem. DM and optimization typically create an interactive procedure for finding the most preferred solutions. Yet, despite the increasing level of complexity, it has been often tried to pay attention to improving all the defined objective functions instead of reducing or ignoring some of them. Although due to the increased complexity, this would apply complications where objective functions are visualized by trade-off analysis methods as well studied in [9, 10, 25, 26, 35, 37].

According to [1], the general form of the multi-objective optimization problems can be stated as;

Minimize $\mathbf{f}(x) = \{f_1(x), ..., f_m(x)\}$, Subjected to $x \in \Omega$, where $\mathbf{x} \in \mathbb{R}^n$ is a vector of n decision variables; $\mathbf{x} \subset \mathbb{R}^n$ is the feasible region and is specified as a set of constraints on the decision variables; $\mathbf{f} : \Omega \rightarrow \mathbb{R}^m$ is made of objective functions subjected to be minimization. Objective vectors are images of decision vectors written as $\mathbf{z} = \mathbf{f}(x) = \{f_1(x), ..., f_m(x)\}$. Yet an objective vector is considered optimal if none of its components can be improved without worsening at least one of the others. An objective vector $\mathbf{z}$ is said to dominate $\mathbf{z}'$, denoted as $\mathbf{z} \prec \mathbf{z}'$, if $z_k \leq z_k'$ for all k and there exists at least one h that $z_h \leq z_h'$. A point $\hat{x}$ is Pareto optimal if there is no other $x \in \Omega$ such that $\mathbf{f}(x)$ dominates $.\mathbf{f}(\hat{x})$. The set of Pareto optimal points is called Pareto set (PS). And the corresponding set of Pareto optimal objective vectors is called Pareto front (PF).

Solving a multi-objective optimization problem would be done by providing the DM with the optimal solution according to some certain utility criteria allowing to choose among competing PF. Such utility criteria are often inconsistent, difficult to formalize and subjected to revision.

The complete process of MCDM has two parts (1) multi-objective optimization process which tries to find the PF solutions (2) decision making process which tries to make the best decision out of the possible choices. In dealing with increased complexity, this paper focuses on the first part which mostly deals with variables, constraints and objective functions.

1.1. Computational intelligence and multi-objective optimization

Developing the methods for multi-objective optimization using computational intelligence along with real applications appeared to be quite young. However it has been observed that techniques of computational intelligence are indeed effective [3, 7, 15, 27]. On the other hand, the techniques of multi-objective optimization by themselves can also be applied to develop and to improve the effective methods in computational intelligence [2].

Currently there are many computational intelligence-based algorithms available to generate PF [1, 16, 17, 30]. However, it is still difficult to generate and visualize the PF in the cases with more than three objectives. In this situation, methods of sequential approximate optimization of computational intelligence with meta-modeling are recognized to be very effective in a series of practical problems [1, 4].

1.2 Meta-modeling and multi-objective optimization in shape optimization

Meta-modeling is a method for building simple and computationally inexpensive models, which replicate the complex relationships. However the research in meta-modeling for multi-objective optimization is relatively young and there is still much to do. So far there existed only a few standards for comparisons of methods, and little is yet known about the relative performance and effectiveness of different approaches [4, 15].

The most famous methods of Meta-modeling are known as response surface methods (RSM) and design of experiments (DOE). Although it is concluded in previous studies [16, 18, 19, 20], in the future research, scalability of MCDM models in terms of variables' dimension and objective space's dimension will become more demanding.

This is because the models have to be capable of dealing with higher computation cost, noise and uncertainties.

According to [18], the application of meta-modeling optimization methods in industrial optimization problems is discussed. Some of the major difficulties in real-life engineering design problems counted: (1) there are numerous objective functions to be involved, (2) the function form of criteria is a black box, which cannot be explicitly given in terms of design variables, and (3) there are a huge number of unranked and non-organized input variables to be considered. Additionally in engineering design problems, often the value of objective functions is not clearly defined in terms of design variables. Instead it is obtained by some numerical analyses, such as FE structural analysis [34, 37], fluid mechanics analysis [7, 16, 17, 32], thermodynamic analysis [30], chemical reactions [3]. These analyses for obtaining a single value for an objective function are often time consuming. Considering the high computation costs, the number of CAE evaluations/calculations are subjected to minimization with the aid of meta-models [18]. In order to make the number of analyses as few as possible, sequential approximate optimization is one of the possible methods, utilizing machine learning techniques for identifying the form of objective functions and optimizing the predicted objective function. Machine learning techniques have been applied for approximating the black-box of CAE function in many practical projects [1, 9, 10 ,25 ,37]. Although the major problems in these realms would be (1) how to approach an ideal approximation of the objective function based on as few sample data as possible (2) how to choose additional data effectively. The objective functions are modeled by fitting a function through the evaluated points. This model is then used to help the prediction value of future search points. Therefore, those high performance regions of design space can be identified more rapidly. Moreover the aspects of dimensionality, noise and expensiveness of evaluations are related to method selection [32]. However, according to Bruyneel et al. [18] for the multi-objective capable version of meta-modeling algorithms further aspects such as the improvement in a Pareto approximation set and modeling the objective function must be considered.

Today, numerical methods make it possible to obtain models or simulations of quite complex and large scale systems [7, 8, 20, 22]. But there are still difficulties when the system is being modeled numerically. In this situation, modeling the simplified models is an effective method, generating a simple model that captures only the relevant input and output variables instead of modeling the whole design space [3, 20, 22].

The increasing desire to apply optimization methods in expensive CAE domains is driving forward the research in meta-modeling. The RSM is probably the most widely applied to meta-modeling. The process of a meta-model from big data is related to classical regression methods and also to machine learning [4, 37]. When the model is updated using new samples, classical DOE principles are not effective. In meta-modeling, the training data sets are often highly correlated, which can affect the estimation of goodness of fit and generalization performance. Yet Meta-modeling brings together a number of different fields to tackle the problem on optimizing the expensive functions. On the other hand the classical DOE methods with employing evolutionary algorithms have delivered more advantages in this realm. Figure 1 describes the common arrangement of meta-modeling tools in multi-objective optimization processes of engineering design. It is worth mentioning that the other well-known CAD-Optimization integrations for shape optimization e.g. [24, 29, 31] would also follow the described scheme.

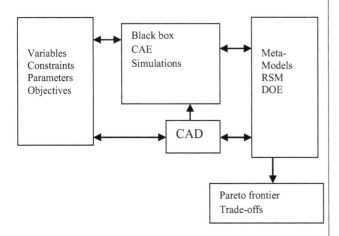

Figure 1. Meta-modeling tools in multi-objective optimization process.

2. Data mining classification in engineering design applications

The particular advantage of evolutionary algorithms (EAs) [11] in the multi-objective optimization (EMO) applications [19] is that they work with a population of solutions. Therefore, they can search for several Pareto optimal solutions providing the DM with a set of alternatives to choose from [14]. EMO-based techniques have an

application where mathematical-based methods have difficulties with. EMO are also helpful in knowledge discovery related tasks in particular for mining the data samples achieved from CAE and CAD systems [29, 31]. Useful mined information from the obtained EMO trade-off solutions have been considered in many real-life engineering design problems.

2.1. Classifications

Finding useful information in large volumes of data drives the development of data mining procedure forward. Data mining classification process refers to the induction of rules that discriminate between organized data in several classes so as to gain predictive power [5]. There are some example applications of data mining classification in evolutionary multi-objective optimization available in the literature of [1, 6, 12, 19] where the goal of the classification algorithms is to discover rules by accessing the training sets. Then the discovered rules are evaluated using the test sets, which could not be seen during the training tasks [5].

In the classification procedures, the main goal is to use observed data to build a model, which is able to predict the categorical or nominal class of a dependent variable given the value of the independent variables [5]. Obayashi [12] for the reason of mining the engineering multi-objective optimization and visualization data applied self-organizing maps (SOM) along with a data clustering method. Moreover Witkowski et al. [13] and Mosavi [7, 20, 22] used classification tools of data mining for decision making supporting process to multi-objective optimization.

2.2. Modeling the problem

According to [1], before any optimization takes place, the problem must first be accurately modeled. In this case, identifying all the dimensions of the problem, such as formulation of the optimization problem with specifying decision variables, objectives, constraints, and variable bounds is an important task. Here the methodology proposes that mining the available sample data before actual modeling will indeed help to better model the problem as it delivers more information about the importance of input variables and could in fact rank the input variables. The proposed method of classification, also earlier utilized in [7, 20, 22], presented in Figure 2, is set to mine the input variables which are in fact associated with the final CAE data.

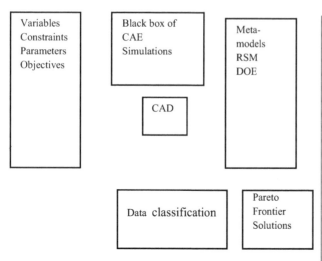

Figure 2. Supporting the meta-modeling process by mining the data

a)   b)

Figure 3. Airfoil geometry, modeled by S-plines [12, 14, 33, 34]

The airfoil of Figure 3 part (a) is subjected for shape improvement. The shape needs to be optimized in order to deliver *minimum displacement distribution* in terms of applied pressure on the surface. Figure 3, part (b) shows the basic curves of the surface modeled by S-plines. Here the proposed S-pline geometrical modeling methodology of Albers et al. [36] is successfully adapted and utilized. In the study case for modeling the 3D wing surface, four curve profiles have been with 42 points utilized. The coordinates of all points are supplied by a digitizer in which each point includes three dimensions of X, Y, and Z. Consequently the case, by adding the variable constraints, would include 126 columns plus three objectives which are going to highly increase the complexity. In fact, an optimal configuration of 42 variables supposed to satisfy the following three described objectives.

The objectives are listed as follow:
    Objective 1: Minimizing the displacement distribution in the airfoil for constant pressure value of α.
    Objective 2: Minimizing the displacement distribution in the airfoil for constant pressure value of 2α.
    Objective 3: Minimizing the displacement distribution in the airfoil in constant pressure value of 4α.

3. Study case; three-objective and 42-variale optimization problem

The applications in engineering optimal design have numerous disciplines to bring into the consideration. In mechanical engineering, the structural simulation is tightly integrated more than one discipline [18, 21, 22, 23, 24, 36]. Meanwhile, the trend nowadays is to utilize independent computational codes for each discipline [32]. In this situation, the aim of MCDM tools is to develop methods in order to guarantee that all physical variables are involved in the model. Bo et al. [28] in aerodynamic optimization of a 3D wing has tried to utilize the multi-objective optimization techniques in a multidisciplinary environment.

In the similar cases [20, 24, 29, 32] in order to approach the optimal shape in an aerospace engineering optimization problem, the mul objective optimization techniques are necessary to deal with all important objectives and variables efficiently. Here the optimization challenge is to identify as many optimal designs as possible to provide a choice of better decision. However with an increased number of design variables the modeling task, in a multidisciplinary environment, is getting even ever complicated. Therefore the multi-objective optimization tasks become more difficult with the increasing number of variables [20, 35]. Although the recent advances in parametric CAD/CAE integrations [24, 29, 31] have reduced the complexity of the approach in some levels.

In the described multi-objective optimization problem the number of variables is subjected to minimization before the multi-objective optimization modeling process takes place in order to evolve a large scale design space to the smaller and much more handy design space. Here the proposed and utilized model reduction methodology differs from the previous study Filomeno et al. [35] in terms of applicability and ease of use in general multi-objective optimization design applications.

Table 1. Training dataset including five CAE calculations' results

	Variables Configuration : V1-V42	CAD Model	Displacement Distribution	Objective Results
1	0,1,1.2,1,0.8,0.4,0.2,0,-0.4,-0.48, 0.6,-0.8,-0.72, 0,0.84,0.99,0.84,0.62,0.26,0,-0.20,-0.40,-0.36,-0.70,-0.58, 0,0.59,0.78,0.56,0.30,0,-0.21,-0.24,-0.38,-0.38 0,0.26,0.50,0.39,-0.03,-0.10,-0.12,			O1=c O2=c O3=c
2	0,1,1,1.21,.9,0.82,0.42,0.18,.1,-0.41,-0.46,-0.62,-0.81,-0.70, 0,0.86,0.1,0.82,0.60,0.25,0.01,-0.20,-0.39,-0.39,-0.70,-0.58, 0,0.58,0.76,0.57,0.32,0,-0.21,-0.23,-0.37,-0.39 0,0.26,0.54,0.40,-0.03,-0.1,-0.1,			O1=b O2=c O3=d
3	0,1,1.2,1,0.8,0.4,0.2,0,-0.4,-0.48,-0.6,-0.8,-0.72, 0,.88,0.99,0.84,0.62,0.26,0,-0.23,-0.35,-0.37,-0.70,-0.54, 0,0.58,0.76,0.58,0.31,0,-0.23,-0.23,-0.37,-0.37 0,0.24,0.50,0.40,-0.03,-0.13,-0.10,			O1=b O2=c O3=b
4	0,1.3,1.23,1.06,0.83,0.41,0.28,0.07,-0.41,-0.48,-0.6,-0.8,-0.78,0,0.84,.92,0.84,0.62,0.26,0,-0.23,-0.39,-0.37,-0.70,-0.54,0,0.58,0.76,0.58,0.31,0,-0.24,-0.22,-0.36,-0.38, 0,0.24,0.52,0.38,-0.02,-0.12,-0.12,			O1=d O2=c O3=b
5	0,1.01,1.21,1,0.8,0.4,0.21,0,-0.41,-0.47,-0.59,-0.79,-0.69, 0,0.80,1.01,0.86,0.64,0.26,-0.01,-0.20,-0.40,-0.40,-0.72,-0.56, 0,0.58,0.76,0.58,0.31,0,-0.23,-0.23,-0.37,-0.37 0,0.24,0.52,0.38,-0.06,-0.10,-0.10,			O1=c O2=d O3=e

The dataset of big data for data mining is supplied from the Table I. The table has gathered a collection of initial dataset including shapes' geometries and simulation results from five CAE calculations, based on random initial values of variables, which in the proposed method will be mined. In the next section, the discussion of how the dataset of five random CAE calculations are being utilized for creating the smaller design space for a multi-objective optimization model is made.

4. Methodology and experimental results

The effectiveness of data mining tools in multi-objective optimization problems presented by Coello et al. [2] and earlier in [5] the classification rules for evolutionary multi-objective algorithms were well implemented, in which along with the research work of Witkowski et al. [13] forms the proposed methodology working via a novel workflow. The workflow of data mining procedure methodology is described in Figure 4. In this method, the classification task is utilized to create several classifiers or decision trees. In the next steps, the most important variables, which have more effects on the objectives, are detected.

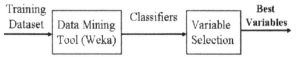

Figure 4. Proposed methodology workflow

Regressions and model trees are constructed by a decision tree building an initial tree. However, most decision tree algorithms choose the splitting attribute to maximize the information gain. It is appropriate for numeric prediction to minimize the intra subset variation in the class values under each branch.

The splitting criterion is used to determine which variable is better to split the portion T of the training data. Based on the treating the standard deviation of the objective values in T as a measure of the error and calculation the expected reduction in error as a result of testing each variable is calculated. Meanwhile the variables, which maximize the expected error reduction, are chosen for splitting. The splitting process terminates when the objective values of the instances vary very slightly, that is, when their standard deviation has only a small fraction of the standard deviation of the original instance set. Splitting also terminates when just a few instances remain. Experiments show that the obtained results are not very sensitive to the exact choice of these thresholds. Data mining classifier package of Weka provides implementations of learning algorithms and dataset which could be preprocessed and fed into a learning scheme, and analyze the resulting classifier and its performance. The workbench includes methods for all the standard data mining problems such as regression, classification, clustering, association rule mining, and attribute selection. Weka also includes many data visualization facilities and data preprocessing tools. Here three different data mining classification algorithms i.e. J48, BFTree, LADTree are applied and their performance is compared to choose attribute importance. The mean absolute error (MAE) and root mean squared error (RMSE) of the class probability is estimated and assigned by the algorithm output. The RMSE is the square root of the average quadratic loss and the MAE is calculated in a similar way using the absolute instead of the squared difference.

The comparison between importance ranking results is obtained by our experiments listed in Table II. It is concluded that in the worst case, more than 55% variable reduction is achieved. As one can see, BFTree and J48 algorithms have classified the datasets with less number of variables. While in LADTree algorithms, at least seven variables have utilized to classify dataset. The variables number 15 and 24 play much more important role in effecting the first objective (O_1).

Variables number 41 and 35 also have the more effects on third objective (O_3) as well. According to the experimental results, it is possible to optimize the model by reducing the 45% number of variables. In Table II, two types of classification error (MAE, RMSE) are shown for all algorithms corresponding to different class of objectives.

Table 2. Variables importance ranking for three classification methods

Classification Method	MAE	RMSE	Effective Variables	Objectives
BFTree	0.370	0.517	15	O_1
	0.412	0.519	23	O_2
	0.418	0.555	41	$O3$
J48	0.309	0.514	15,24	O_1
	0.482	0.642	13	$O2$
	0.378	0.590	35,41	O_3
LAD Tree	0.277	0.500	15,24,2,32,41,39,3 23,22,18,15,42,2,17,	$O1$
	0.604	0.769	20	O_2
	0.365	0.584	41,35,9,17,11,38,37, 16	O_3

5. Conclusions

In order to extract more information from the optimization variables in a reasonable way, the classification task of data mining has been applied. Variables were ranked and organized utilizing three different classification algorithms. The results show the reduced number of variables speeds up and scales up the process of optimization within a preprocessing step. The utilized data mining tool has found to be effective in this regard. Additionally, it is evidenced that the growing complexity can be handled by a preprocessing step utilizing data mining classification tools. The modified methodology is demonstrated successfully in the framework and the author believes that the process is simple and fast.

Future research should focus on the effectiveness of the proposed data reduction process. Also, trying other data mining tasks such as clustering, association rules, and comparison could be beneficial. Although in real-life applications where the optimal design problem has to be considered by inclusion of multiple criteria, a combination of the proposed method with the other developed MCDM tools [38-46] would be effective.

References

[1] J. Branke, K. Deb, K. Miettinen, R. Słowinski, Multiobjective, Optimization (Springer, Berlin, Heidelberg New York, 2008)

[2] C. Coello, S. Dehuri, S. Ghosh, Swarm Intelligence for Multi-objective Problems in Data Mining (Springer, Berlin, Heidelberg New York, 2009)

[3] A.Mosavi, "Applications of Interactive Methods of MOO in Chemical Engineering Problems," Global Journal of Researches in Engineering, Vol. 10, No. 3, p.8. (2010).

[4] J. Knowles, H. Nakayama, Meta-Modeling in Multiobjective Optimization (Springer, Berlin, Heidelberg New York, 2008)

[5] K. K. Kshetrapalapuram, M. Kirley, Mining Classificationm Rules Using Evolutionary Multi-objective Algorithms, Knowledge-Based Intelligent, Information and Engineering Systems. 3683 (Springer Berlin, Heidelberg, 2005).

[6] Alex A. Freitas, On Objective Measures of Rule Surprisingness, Principles of Data Mining and Knowledge Discovery. 1510, (2008).

[7] A. Mosavi, "The Large Scale System of Multiple Criteria Decision Making; Pre-Processing," Large Scale Complex Systems Theory and Applications, Vol. 9, 2010, pp. 354- 359.

[8] A. Adejuwon and A. Mosavi, "Domain Driven Data Mining; Application to Business," International Journal of Computer Science Issues, Vol. 7, No 2, 2010, pp. 41-44.

[9] Mosavi, M.Azodinia Abbas S. Milani, Kasun N. Hewage and M.Yeheyis, "Reconsidering the Multiple Criteria Decision Making Problems of Construction Workers with the Aid of Grapheur," International ANSYS and EnginSoft Conference, Verona, Italy, 2011.

[10] E. Foldi, A. Delavar, A. Mosavi, K. N. Hewage, A. S. Milani, A. A. Moussavi and M. Yeheyis, "Reconsidering the Multiple Criteria Decision Making Problems of Construction Projects; Using Advanced Visualization and Data Mining Tools," Conference of PhD Students in Computer Science, Szeged, Hungary, 28-30 June 2012.

[11] X. Llor, D.E. Goldberg, I. Traus, E.Bernad, Generalisation and Model Selection in Supervised Learning with Evolutionary Computation, Applications of Evolutionary Computing. 2611, (2003).

[12] S.Obayashi, evolutionary multiobjective optimization and Visualization, new developments in computational fluid dynamics (Springer, 2005)

[13] K. Witkowski, M. Tushar, Decision making in multiobjective optimization for industrial application-Data mining and visualization of Pareto, In Proceedings of 7th European LS-DYNA Conference, 416-423 (2009).

[14] K. Deb, Current Trends in Evolutionary MultiObjective Optimization, International Journal for Simulation and Multidisciplinary Design Optimization. 2, 1–8 (2007).

[15] A.Mosavi, "The Multiobjective Optimization Package of IOSO; Applications and Future Trends," In: CSCS, Conference of PhD Students in Computer Science, University of Szeged, Szeged, Hungary, 2010, p. 55.

[16] A.Mosavi, "Computer Design and Simulation of Built Environment; Application to Forest," Proceeding of ICECS'09, The Second IEEE International Conference on Environmental and Computer Science, Dubai, 28-30 December 2009, pp. 81-85.

[17] A.Mosavi, "Parametric Modeling of Trees and Using Integrated CAD/CFD and Optimization Tools: Application to Creating the Optimal Planting Patterns for New Forests," Proceedings of 2nd International Conference Wind Effects on Trees, Albert-Ludwigs-University of Freiburg, Freiburg, 2009.

[18] M. Bruyneel, B. Colson, P. Jetteur, C.Raick, A. Remouchamps, S. Grihon, Recent progress in the optimal design of composite structures: industrial solution procedures on case studies, Int. J. Simul. Multidisci. Des. Optim. 2, 283-288 (2008).

[19] S. E. Bedingfield, K. A. Smith, Evolutionary Rule Generation Classification and its Application to Multiclass Data, Computational Science, Springer. 2660, (2003).

[20] Mosavi, Multiple Criteria Decision-Making Preprocessing Using Data Mining Tools, International Journal of Computer Science Issues. 7, 26-34 (2010).

[21] V. Arularasan, Modeling and simulation of a parallel plate heat sink using computational fluid dynamics, Int J Adv Manuf Technol. 5, 172-183(2008).

[22] M. Esmaeili and A. Mosavi, "Variable Reduction for Multi-Objective Optimization Using Data Mining Tech-niques; Application to Aerospace Structures," Proceeding of ICCET, the 2nd IEEE International Conference on Computer Engineering and Technology, Vol. 5, Chengdu, 16-18 April 2010, pp. 333- 337.

[23] I. Olcer, a hybrid approach for multi-objective combinatorial optimization problems in ship design and shipping, Computers & Operations Research. 35, 2760 – 277(2007).

[24] L. Toussaint, N. Lebaal, D. Schlegel, S. Gomes, Automatic Optimization of Air Conduct Design Using Experimental Data and Numerical Results, Int. J. Simul. Multidisci. Des. Optim. 4, 77-83 (2010).

[25] A.Mosavi, M. Hoffmann and A. S. Milani, "Optimal Design of the NURBS Curves and Surfaces Utilizing Multiobjective Optimization and Decision Making Algorithms of RSO," Conference of PhD Students in Mathematics, Szeged, Hungary, Jnue 2012.

[26] Mosavi, M. Hoffmann and A. S. Milani, "Adapting the Reactive Search Optimization and Visualization Algorithms for Multiobjective Optimization Problems; Application to Geometry," Conference of PhD Students in Computer Science, Szeged, Hungary, June 2012.

[27] Mosavi, A. S. Milani, M. Hoffmann and M. Komeili, "Multiple Criteria Decision Making Integrated with Mechanical Modeling of Draping for Material Selection of Textile Composites," ECCM15, 15th Eeuropean Conference on Composite Materials, Venice, Italy, 24-28 June, 2012.

[28] Y. Bo, X. ANY, Aerodynamic optimization of 3D wing based on iSIGHT, Appl. Math. Mech. -Engl. Ed. 5, 603–610 (2008).

[29] J. B. Bluntzer, S. Gomes, D.h. Bassir, A. Varret and J.c. Sagot, Direct multi-objective optimization of parametric geometrical models stored in PLM systems to improve functional product design, Int. J. Simul. Multidisci. Des. Optim. 2, 83-90(2008).

[30] A.Mosavi, "Application of Multiobjective Optimization Packages in Design of an Evaporator Coil," World Academy of Science, Engineering and Technology, Vol. 61, 2010, pp. 25-29.

[31] P. Vik, D. Luís, P. Guilherme, J. Oliveira, Automatic Generation of Computer Models through the Integration of Production Systems Design Software Tools, Int. J. Simul. Multidisci. Des. Optim. 4, 141-148 (2010).

[32] Mosavi, "Hydrodynamic Design and Optimization: Application to Design a General Case for Extra Equipments on the Submarine's Hull," Proceeding on IEEE International Conference on Computer Technology and Development, ICCTD'09, Vol. 2, Kota Kinabalu, 13-15 November 2009, pp. 139-143.

[33] Mosavi, "Multiobjective Optimization of Spline Curves Using modeFrontier," Proceedings of Internaional Conference on Engineering Optimization

and In-ternational Mode Frontier users' Meeting, Trieste, 2010.

[34] Mosavi, "On Engineering Optimization the Splined Profiles," Proceedings of International Conference on Engineering Optimization and International modeFrontier Users' Meeting, Trieste, 2010.

[35] R. Filomeno, C. Coelho, P. Breitkopf, C. Knopf-Lenoir, Model reduction for multidisciplinary optimization - application to a 2D wing, Struct Multidisc Optim, 7, 29–48 (2008).

[36] Albers, N. Leon-Rovira, Development of an engine crankshaft in a framework of computer-aided innovation, Computers in Industry, 60, 604–612 (2009).

[37] Mosavi, A.Vaezipour, "Reactive Search Optimization; Application to Multiobjective Optimization Problems." Applied Mathematics, 3, no.30 (2012): 1572-1582.

[38] Mosavi, "A MCDM Software Tool for the Automated Design Environments," 26th Europian Conference on Operational Research, Rome 2013, EURO - INFORMS XXVI.

[39] A.Vaezipour, A.Mosavi, U.Seigeroth, "Machine learning integrated optimization for decision making," 26th Europian Conference on Operational Research, Rome 2013, EURO - INFORMS XXVI.

[40] Mosavi, "Multiobjective Optimization package of IOSO," Mini EURO Conference EUROPT, Izmir, 2010.

[41] Vaezipour, A.Mosavi, "Managing Decision Making Within Enterprise," International CAE Conference, Verona, Italy, 22-23 Oct 2012.

[42] Vaezipour, A.Mosavi, "Enterprise Decision Management With the Aid of Advanced Business Intelligence and Interactive Visualization Tools," International CAE Conference, Verona, Italy, 22-23 Oct 2012

[43] Mosavi, "Data Mining for Business Applications," OGIK_ISBIS, Hungary, 2010.

[44] Mosavi, "Data Mining for Business Applications and Business Decision-Making: Challenges and Future Trends," OGIK_ISBIS, Hungary, 2010.

[45] Mosavi, Nage Peter, Miklos Hoffmann, "Automatic multi-objective surface design optimisation using modeFRONTIER's CAD/CAE integrated system: Application to military submarine sail," EnginSoft International Conference, CAE Technologies for Industry, Italy, 2009.

[46] Mosavi, "Recent developments and innovations in engineering optimization," Spring Wind Conference, Pecs, Hungary, 2010.

2

A multi-objective approach to fuzzy clustering using ITLBO algorithm

P. Shahsamandi Esfahani[*] and A. Saghaei

Department of Industrial engineering, Science and Research Branch, Islamic Azad University, Tehran, Iran.

Corresponding author: parastoushahsamandi@yahoo.com (P. Shahsamandi).

Abstract
Data clustering is one of the most important research areas in data mining and knowledge discovery. Recent research works in this area has shown that the best clustering results can be achieved using multi-objective methods. In other words, assuming more than one criterion as objective functions for clustering data can measurably increase the quality of clustering. In this work, a model with two contradictory objective functions based on maximum data compactness in clusters (the degree of proximity of data) and maximum cluster separation (the degree of remoteness of cluster centers) is proposed. In order to solve this model, the multi-objective improved teaching-learning–based optimization (MOITLBO) algorithm is used. This algorithm is tested on several datasets, and its clusters are compared with the results of some single-objective algorithms. Furthermore, with respect to noise, the comparison of the performance of the proposed model with another multi-objective model shows that it is robust to noisy datasets, and thus it can be efficiently used for multi-objective fuzzy clustering.

Keywords: *Fuzzy Clustering, Cluster Validity Measure, Multi-objective Optimization, Meta-heuristic Algorithms, Improved Teaching-learning–based Optimization.*

1. Introduction

Data clustering is an important topic in data mining and knowledge discovery. The main objective of any clustering technique is to group a set of objects into a number of clusters in such a way that the objects in one cluster are very similar and the objects in different clusters are quite different [1-3]. One measure of similarity for data in K clusters is the distance between the data and their cluster center (e.g. the Euclidean distance in the fuzzy c-means (FCM) algorithm proposed by [4]). In fact, this unsupervised classification produces a $K \times m$ optimum partition matrix $U^*(x)$ of the given dataset X that consists of m data samples $X = \{x_1, x_2, x_3, \ldots, x_m\}$, where each x_i in universe X is a p-dimensional vector of m elements or m features, where $i = 1, 2, \ldots, m$. The partition matrix can be represented as $\{u_{ki}\}$, $k = 1, 2, \ldots, K$. For fuzzy data clustering, $0 \le u_{ki} \le 1$ (where u_{ki} denotes the degree to which object i belongs to the kth cluster). Finding the optimum matrix U^* is difficult for practical problems.

Hence, the application of advanced optimization techniques is required. As clustering is an NP-hard problem (since the number of data and clusters increases), the application of meta-heuristics is necessary for partitioning data [5]. Meta-heuristic algorithms can be classified into different groups depending on the criteria being considered. Evolutionary algorithms (e.g. genetic algorithms (GAs) and differential evolution) and swarm intelligence algorithms (e.g. particle swarm optimization (PSO), ant colony optimization, and artificial bee colonies) are based upon the population criteria. In addition to these algorithms [6], there are some other algorithms that work based on the principles of different natural phenomena such as harmony search [7], gravitational search [8], and teaching-learning–based optimization (TLBO) [28, 29].

Meta-heuristic algorithms can solve large problems quickly. Moreover, these algorithms can be simply designed and implemented [5, 6]. A large number of such algorithms have been introduced to solve single-objective clustering problems [26, 27, 35, 41], in most of which, the fitness function is based on maximizing the compactness of the data in a cluster. Recent research works have shown that more efficiency may be obtained by using more than one objective function for clustering. Therefore, it is necessary to optimize several cluster validity measures, simultaneously. There are some related studies that have applied multi-objective techniques to data clustering [13-23].

Different meta-heuristic algorithms require similar control parameters such as the population size and the number of generations as well as the algorithm-specific control parameters (e.g. mutation rate and cross-over rate for GA [26] or inertia weight, social, and cognitive parameters for PSO [27]). However, TLBO requires merely common controlling parameters. Thus TLBO can be said to be an algorithm-specific parameterless algorithm [39]. The TLBO algorithm has been designed based upon a teaching-learning process of several students and one teacher in a classroom. The learners are considered to be the population, and the best solution in the population is the teacher. Different subjects that have been suggested to the learners are comparable to different design variables of an optimization problem. TLBO is effective in terms of computational effort and consistency. This algorithm has been improved by introducing more than one teacher for the learners (i.e. increasing the collective knowledge) and some other modifications [24].

In this paper, we use the multi-objective improved TLBO (MOITLBO) [33] for the proposed multi-objective fuzzy clustering model. Two objective functions have been proposed in order to cluster data in a manner better than single objective algorithms. Measure of FCM algorithm (j_m) [4], partition coefficient and an exponential separation (PCAES) validity index [32] have been proposed to minimize the proximity of data in clusters and maximize the differentiation of clusters. The proposed objectives optimize the compactness and separation of the clusters independently.

Sometimes there can be noise in datasets, and as some validity indices are sensitive to noisy data, they cannot determine a good clustering. Therefore, we chose the PCAES validity index that was not sensitive to noise [25] so as to achieve more advantageous clustering results.

Clustering results have been reported for a number of real-life datasets as well as two artificial ones. The performance of this algorithm was compared with those of the single-objective improved TLBO (ITLBO) and FCM clustering algorithms. In order to demonstrate the robustness of the model to noise, it was compared with another multi-objective clustering model.

This paper is organized as what follows. The next section discusses the multi-objective optimization concept, and provides a brief literature review of multi-objective clustering. In Section 3, the proposed multi-objective clustering method and some validity measures are discussed. In Section 4, the MOITLBO algorithm for data clustering is described. Section 5 presents the experimental results of this method on several datasets. Finally, Section 6 concludes the study.

2. Multi-objective clustering optimization

In most practical situations, there are several objectives that must be optimized simultaneously to solve a problem. A multi-objective optimization problem deals with more than one objective function. It is typical that no unique solution exists in multi-objective optimization problems but a set of equally good mathematical solutions can be identified. These solutions are known as non-dominated or Pareto-optimal solutions. The best solution is often subjective, and depends on the needs of the decision-makers (DMs). The multi-objective problem can be categorized into three main methods. If the DMs state some considerations before starting to optimize the problem, the techniques are called priori; if the DMs make some decisions during the process of solving the multi-objective problem, they are called progressive or interactive; and if after solving the problem, some subsets of effective solutions are presented to the DMs to select the most satisfying solution, they are called posteriori.

However, it is not possible to use exact methods to solve real multi-objective problems that have large and complex dimensions. Therefore, approximate methods are often used to solve these problems. Regarding the approximate methods, considerable research works have focused on the multi-objective meta-heuristic algorithms [14]. Multi-objective optimization can be formally stated as follows:

$$\begin{cases} \max f(x) \\ s.t \, x \in X = \left\{ x \in R^n | g(x) \le b, \, x \ge 0 \right\} \end{cases} \quad (1)$$

where, $f(x)$ represents n conflicting objective functions, $g(x) \le b$ represents m constraints, and is an n-vector of decision variables, $x \in R^n$. Solution x^* is said to be a Pareto-optimal solution if and only if there does not exist another $x \in X$,

Such that $f_i(x) \geq f_i(x^*)$ for all i and $f_i(x) \neq f_i(x^*)$ for at least one i.

The use of multi-objective optimization has been gaining popularity since the last few years, and there are some instances in the related literature that have applied multi-objective techniques for data clustering. One of the earliest approaches to multi-objective clustering can be found in [13]. A bi-criterion clustering algorithm has been proposed, in which the objective functions representing homogeneity and separation of the clusters are optimized in a crisp clustering context using a deterministic method. The theoretical advantages of multi-objective clustering have been described in [15] but this paper is limited to an exclusive proof of the concept. A series of related studies on multi-objective clustering can be found in [14, 16, 18-21], in which the authors have developed the first multi-objective clustering algorithm [15]. The Voronoi-initialized evolutionary nearest-neighbor algorithm (VIENNA), which is based upon the Pareto envelope–based selection algorithm II (PESAII) [17], and employs a straightforward encoding of a clustering with a gene for each data item such that its allele value specifies the cluster to which the data item should belong. In [18], the authors have developed a method for selecting solutions from the Pareto front based on a null model, and also determining a better encoding that does not fix the number of clusters. These developments have been incorporated into a new algorithm called multi-objective clustering with automatic K-determination (MOCK). A brief summary of MOCK has been given in [19], where the authors have used a canonical problem to demonstrate that the best solution to some clustering problems is a trade-off between two objectives, and cannot be reached by methods that optimize these objectives individually. MOCK has been further extended in [20] to improve its scalability to large, high-dimensional datasets and data with a large number of clusters.

Most clustering algorithms may not be able to find the global optimal cluster that fits the dataset; these algorithms will stop if they find a locally-optimal partition of the dataset. The algorithms in the family of search-based clustering algorithms can explore the solution space beyond local optimality to find a globally-optimal clustering that fits the dataset [1]. In [22], a metaheuristic search procedure based on two well-known methodologies, Tabu search and Scatter search, has been proposed for multi-objective clustering problems.

A new multi-objective differential evolution-based fuzzy clustering technique has been developed in [23]. The authors have presented a new model that encodes the cluster centers in its vectors and optimizes multiple validity measures simultaneously. For this reason, the Xie-Beni (XB) index [12] and FCM [4] measures (j_m) are considered to be the two objective functions that must be minimized simultaneously. The tendency of the XB index is to increase monotonically when the number of clusters becomes very large and close to the number of patterns. In addition, this index is sensitive to noise (here, the term noise refers to the points that are separated from the other clusters but do not have enough potential to form a distinct cluster) [25]. The main characteristics of the aforementioned multi-objective clustering methods are summarized in table 1.

Table 1. Some main characteristics of related works in multi-objective clustering.

Researcher(s) (Year) – [Ref.]	Multi-objective clustering environment	Optimization methods	Objective functions
Delattre, M., Hansen, P., (1980)-[13]	Crisp	Exact method	Homogeneity and separation based on Single link clustering algorithm and graph-theoretic algorithm
Ferligoj, A., Batagelj, V., (1992)-[15]	Theoretical advantages of multi-criteria clustering		
Caballero, R., Laguna, M., Marti, R., Molina, J., (2006)-[22]	Fuzzy	Approximation method/Tabu search algorithm and Scatter search	A combination of the four functions: Partition diameter, Unadjusted within-cluster dissimilarity, Adjusted within-cluster dissimilarity, and Average within-cluster dissimilarity.
Handl, J., Knowles, J., (2004, 2005, 2006)-[18-21]	Fuzzy	Approximation method/ Multi-objective Clustering with automatic K-determination (MOCK) algorithm	Overall deviation(compactness) and connectivity
saha, I., Maulik, U., Plewczynski, D., (2011)-[23]	Fuzzy	Approximation method/ Differential Evolution algorithm	Compactness and separation- measure of FCM algorithm (J_m) and validity index (XB)

3. Proposed Multi-objective clustering model

The goal of a partitioned clustering algorithm is to find clusters, that the data that is assigned to the same cluster are similar (i.e. homogenous), while the data that is assigned to different clusters is different (i.e. heterogeneous) [1, 2].

The proposed multi-objective model is based upon two criteria, compactness and separation [21]. Compactness indicates the sameness of data, and separation indicates the dissimilarity among all data. Let $X_{m \times p}$ be the profile data matrix with m rows (for a set of m objects) and p columns (p-dimensional), in most cases, the data is in the form of real value vectors. The Euclidean distance is derived from the Minkowski metric, and is a suitable measure of similarity for these datasets [1]. Equation (2) is the Euclidian distance between the two points x and y.

$$d(x,y) = (\sum_{i=1}^{m} |x_i - y_i|^2)^{\frac{1}{2}} \tag{2}$$

Fuzzy c-means (FCM) is a widely-used technique that allows an object to belong to more than one cluster [4]. It is based on the minimization of the J_m measure, as shown in (3).

$$\text{Min } J_m = \sum_{i=1}^{m} \sum_{k=1}^{K} u_{ki}^{m'} d_{ki}^2 \tag{3}$$

where m is the number of data objects, K represents the number of clusters, and u is the fuzzy membership matrix. Furthermore, m' ($m' > 1$) is the weighting exponent that controls the fuzziness of the resulting clusters, and d_{ki} is the Euclidian distance from data $_i$ to the center of the kth cluster. The first objective function of the proposed model is J_m, and this criterion is based on increasing the compactness of data in clusters by minimizing the degree of proximity of data [4].

The second objective is based on the partition coefficient and an exponential separation (PCAES) [31], and it seeks to calculate the global cluster variance (i.e. to maximize the separation between one cluster to the other $c - 1$ clusters) and the intra-cluster compactness.

$$\text{Max } V_{PCAES} = \sum_{k=1}^{K} PCAES_k =$$

$$\sum_{i=1}^{m} \sum_{k=1}^{K} u_{ki}^2 \Big/ u_M - \sum_{k=1}^{K} \exp\left(-\min_{l \neq k}\left\{\frac{v_k - v_l^2}{\beta_T}\right\}\right) \tag{4}$$

where, u_M and β_T are defined as follow:

$$u_M = \min_{1 \leq k \leq K} \sum_{i=1}^{m} u_{ik}^2, \beta_T = \frac{1}{K} \sum_{k=1}^{K} v_k - \bar{v}^2 \tag{4a}$$

$$\bar{v} = \frac{1}{K} \sum_{k=1}^{K} v_k \tag{4b}$$

A large V_{PCAES} value means that each one of these K clusters is compact, and separated from the other clusters. In addition, under the proposed PCAES objective, a noisy point will not have enough potential to be a cluster; hence, the algorithm will be robust in a noisy environment [32]. Under the proposed multi-objective model, the constraints are as follow:

$$\sum_{k=1}^{K} u_{ki} = 1 \qquad i = 1, 2, \ldots, m \tag{5a}$$

$$0 \leq u_{ik} \leq 1 \qquad i = 1, \ldots, m \quad k = 1, \ldots, K \tag{5b}$$

$$\sum_{i=1}^{m} u_{ik} > 0 \qquad k = 1, 2, \ldots, K \tag{5c}$$

As mentioned in [35], the maximum possible number of clusters that one should consider for a dataset is $\sqrt{m}$ ($2 \leq k \leq \sqrt{m}$). The performance of multi-objective clustering highly depends on the choice of objectives, which should be as contradictory as possible. A further important aspect to be considered when choosing two objective functions is their potential to balance each other's tendency to increase or decrease the number of clusters. While the objective value associated with compactness is necessarily improved with an increasing number of clusters, the opposite is the case for separation among the centers of clusters. The interaction of the two is crucially important to keep the number of clusters dynamic and to explore interesting areas of the solution space.

3.1. Validity measures in clustering

In general, internal and external cluster validations determine the goodness of the partitions as well as the possibility of better partitioning. In addition, if the number of classes within the data is not known beforehand, a validation index may help to determine the optimal number of classes [11, 25]. Therefore, the role of a validity index is very important. In this research work, to evaluate the performance of the proposed multi-objective clustering algorithm, the partition coefficient (PC) [4, 9], Pakhira-Bandyopadhyay-Maulik (PBM) [34], and Davies-Bouldin (DB) [37] indices were used. Furthermore, the performance of the XB [12] index, as one of the objective functions in the MOITLBO algorithm, was compared with the PCAES index.

3.1.1. PC index

The PC index [4, 9] is based on minimizing the overall content of pairwise fuzzy inter-sections in partition matrix U. This index indicates the average relative amount of membership sharing done between pairs of fuzzy subsets in partition matrix U by combining into a single number the average contents of pairs of fuzzy algebraic products. The index is defined as:

$$V_{PC} = \frac{1}{m}\sum_{i=1}^{m}\sum_{k=1}^{K}u_{ki}^2 \qquad (6)$$

A larger V_{PC} indicates a better clustering performance for dataset X.

3.1.2. DB index

This index is a function of the ratio of the sum of the within-cluster scatter to the between-cluster separation [37]. The scatter within the kth cluster may be computed as:

$$S_k = \frac{1}{|C_k|}\sum_{x \in C_k}\{x - v_k\} \qquad (7)$$

The Euclidian distance between the centers of the kth and lth clusters is denoted by d_{kl}. This index is then defined as:

$$DB = \frac{1}{k}\sum_{k=1}^{K}R_{k,qt} \qquad (7a)$$

where:

$$R_{k,qt} = \max_{1, l \neq k}\left\{\frac{S_{kq} + S_{lq}}{d_{kl}}\right\} \qquad (7b)$$

Lower values for the DB index indicate better clustering.

3.1.3. PBM index

The PBM index [34] is a composition of three factors, namely $\frac{1}{k}$, $\frac{E}{J_m}$, and D_k.

$$V_{PBMF} = \left(\frac{1}{k} \times \frac{E}{J_m} \times D_k\right)^2 \qquad (8)$$

In (8), the first factor indicates the divisibility of a k cluster system that decreases with increasing k. However, in this research work, its value is specified. Equation (8a) is factor E, the sum of the distances of each sample to the geometric center v_0, the centroid of the dataset, and is a measure of the compactness of a k cluster system.

$$E = \sum_{i=1}^{m}u_{ki}x_i - v_0 \qquad (8a)$$

The third factor, as shown in (8b), is the maximum inter-cluster separation in a k cluster system, which is based on the maximum cluster separations.

$$D_k = \max_{1 \leq i, k \leq K} v_k - v_i \qquad (8b)$$

Hence, while the first factor decreases, the other two increase for increasing k.

Based on the above analysis, the maximum value for V_{PBMF} indicates the best clustering performance for dataset X.

3.1.4. XB index

Validity index V_{XB} focuses on compactness and separation [11].

$$V_{XB} = \frac{\sum_{k=1}^{K}\sum_{i=1}^{m}u_{ik}^{m'}x_i - v_k^2}{m \min_{k,i} v_k - v_i^2} \qquad (9)$$

As indicated in (9) for V_{XB}, the numerator indicates the compactness of the fuzzy partition, and the denominator indicates the strength of the separation between clusters. A small value for the compactness and a high value for the separation indicate a good partition

4. MOITLBO-based fuzzy clustering

The ITLBO algorithm proposed in [24] is a version of the basic TLBO algorithm with enhanced exploration and exploitation capacities. The TLBO algorithm simulates the teaching-learning process in which every individual tries to learn something from another individual to improve him/herself. The algorithm simulates two fundamental modes of learning, teacher phase and learner phase. A group of learners are considered to be the population of the algorithm, and the results of a learner are the fitness value of the optimization solution, which indicates its quality [28, 29]. In the teacher phase, learning of a learner through a teacher is simulated. The teacher is the most experienced person (the best learner) in the algorithm. During this phase, the teacher conveys knowledge to the learners and makes an effort to increase the mean results of the class. At any iteration of the algorithm, there are n number of learners (population size) and m number of subjects. Let $M_{j,i}$ be the mean result of learners in the jth subject. The difference between the result of the teacher and the mean result of the learners in each subject is given by:

$$\text{Difference}_{\text{Mean } j,i} = r_i\left(X_{j,\text{lbest},i} - T_F M_{j,i}\right) \qquad (10)$$

where, $X_{j,\text{lbest},i}$ is the result of the teacher (best learner) in subject j, T_F is the teaching factor that decides the value of the mean to be changed, and r_i is a random number in the range $[0, 1]$. Based on the calculated difference, the existing solution is updated in the teacher phase and accepted if it gives a better function value. These accepted values become the input for the learner phase.

The learner phase of the algorithm simulates the learning of the learners through interaction among themselves. One learner interacts randomly with other learners who have more information than itself; hence, in this way, it can increase its knowledge. Randomly, two learners P and Q are selected such that $X'_{total-P,i} \neq X'_{total-Q,i}$ (where these values are the updated values at the end of the teacher phase), the following equations are for the maximization problem:

$$X''_{j,P,i} = X'_{j,P,i} + r_i \left(X'_{j,P,i} - X'_{j,Q,i} \right) \ ,$$

$$\text{if} \quad X'_{total-P,\,i} > X'_{total-Q,\,i}$$

$$X''_{j,P,i} = X'_{j,P,i} + r_i \left(X'_{j,Q,i} - X'_{j,P,i} \right), \qquad (11)$$

$$\text{if} \quad X'_{total-Q,\,i} > X'_{total-P,\,i}$$

According to (11), we accept $X''_{j,P,i}$ if it returns a better function value. The algorithm stops according to criteria such as the maximum number of iterations allowed or a minimum change in the objective function. In [24], the algorithm is improved by introducing more than one teacher for the learners to avoid premature convergence, and some other modifications such as the adaptive teaching factor that can automatically tune itself, and self-motivated learning. This algorithm is named ITLBO. In this work, MOITLBO [33] was used to optimize the multi-objective fuzzy clustering. At every iteration of the algorithm, the solutions are maintained in a fixed-size archive. If the solution is dominated by at least one member of the archive, it is not added to the archive; otherwise, the solution is added to the archive. The ε-dominance method is used to refine the solutions in the external archive [33]. In the ε-dominance method, the algorithm uses a grid. The size of each box in the grid is ε, and only one non-dominated solution is placed in each box [10].

Based on these statements, the steps of the MOITLBO algorithm for fuzzy clustering are described, in detail, as follows:

Step 1. Defining objective functions: Define the optimization problem as minimizing the overall deviation of partitioning and maximizing the separation among the centers of each cluster. The first objective is simply computed as the overall summed distances between the data items and their corresponding cluster center (i.e. the objective function of the FCM algorithm). The weighting exponent m' is set to two, which is a common choice for fuzzy clustering. The second objective calculates the global cluster variance and the intra-cluster compactness. However, the TLBO algorithm does not require any algorithm-

specific parameter; therefore, setting the control parameter value is not necessary.

Step 2. Initialization: Initialize the external archive and population (N learners). To solve clustering, each candidate solution in the population consists of N $U_{k \times m}$ matrices, where each element of the matrix represents the degree of belonging of the mth object to the kth cluster. The fuzzy matrix U is generated randomly according to the population size, then the center of each cluster is computed to find the distance between each data and the centroids of the clusters. In the experiment, we set the population size or number of learners to 100.

Step 3. Evaluation: To evaluate the population, rank the evaluated solutions (in ascending order for the minimization problem, and descending order for the maximization problem), then select and assign the best solution as the chief teacher to the first rank.

$$(X_{teacher})_1 = f(x^1), \text{ where } f(x^1) = f(x)_{best}$$

Select the other teachers based on the chief teacher, and rank them:

$$f(x^s) = f(x^1)) \pm \text{ rand} \times f(x^1),$$

where s is the number of teachers selected. (If the equality cannot be met, select the $f(x^s)$ closet to the value calculated above.) We selected four teachers in this algorithm.

Step 4. Assignment: Assign the learners to the teachers according to their fitness values, as:

$$(X_{teacher})_s = f(x^s) \text{ , where } s = 1, 2, ..., T$$

For l= 1: (n-s)
if $f(x^1) \leq f(x^l) < f(x^2)$
assign learner $f(x^l)$ to teacher 1
else if $f(x^2) \leq f(x^l) < f(x^3)$
assign learner $f(x^l)$ to teacher 2
else if $f(x^3) \leq f(x^l) < f(x^4)$
assign learner $f(x^l)$ to teacher 3
else
assign learner $f(x^l)$ to teacher 4
end if
end for

In this work, the number of teachers T is 4.

Step 5. Updating: Calculate the mean result of each group of learners in each subject (i.e. $(M_j)_s$), where $f(x^l)$ is the result of any learner l associated with group s at iteration i, and $f(x^s)$ is the result of the teacher of the same group during the same iteration i. Evaluate the difference given by (10). For each teacher, the adaptive teaching factor is:

$$(T_F)_i = (\frac{f(x^1)}{f(x^s)})_i \quad 1 = 1,2,\ldots,n \quad ; \text{if } f(x^s) \neq 0$$
$$(12)$$
$$(T_F)_i = 1, \quad\quad ; \text{if } f(x^s) = 0$$

According to (13), for each group, update the learners' knowledge with the help of a teacher's knowledge or fellow classmates during tutorial hours.

$$(X'_{j,l})_s = (X_{j,l} + Difference_{Mean\,j})_s$$
$$+rand(X_h - X_l)_s , \quad if \ f(x^h) < f(x^l)$$
$$(X'_{j,l})_s = (X_{j,l} + Difference_{Mean\,j})_s$$
$$(13)$$
$$, \ if \ f(x^l) < f(x^h) \ +rand \ (X_l - X_h)_s$$

Here, $h \neq l$. According to (14), update the learner's knowledge for each group by utilizing the knowledge of some other learners as well as by self-learning.

$$(X''_{j,l})_s = X'_{j,l,i} rand(X'_{j,l} - X'_{j,p})_s$$
$$+rand \ (X_{teacher} - E_f \ X'_{j,l})_s$$
$$if \ f(x^{l}) < f(x^{p})$$
$$(14)$$
$$(X''_{j,l})_s = X'_{j,l,i} + rand(X'_{j,p} - X'_{j,l})_s$$
$$+rand \ (X_{teacher} - E_f \ X'_{j,l})_s ,$$
$$if \ f(x^{p}) < f(x^{l})$$

where, E_f = Exploration Factor = round(1 + rand).
Step 6. Elimination: Eliminate duplicate solutions. It is necessary to modify the duplicate solutions to avoid becoming trapped in local optima. These solutions are modified by random selection.
Step 7. Combination: Combine all groups.
Step 8. External archive: Check the archive. If the archive is not full, add the new solution to it; otherwise, select a victim solution to be removed from the archive. The ε-dominance is used to maintain the archive; each dimension of the objective space is divided into segments of width ε. Initialize the grid on the archive. For each box in the grid, if any box dominates the other boxes, remove the dominated box and its related solutions. For the remaining boxes in the grid, if the box contains more than one solution, remove the dominated solution(s) from the box. If the box still contains more than one solution, keep the solution closest to the lower left corner of the box (for the minimization problem) and remove the others.
Step 9. Checking: Check the termination criteria. If neither termination criteria is satisfied, repeat steps 3–8; otherwise, stop the algorithm and output the external archive as a Pareto-optimal set. In this experiment, the maximum number of iterations was 300 and the minimum improvement of the objective function was 10^{-6}.

5. Results

The performance of multi-objective fuzzy clustering based on the MOITLBO algorithm was tested on four different real-life datasets (Iris, Thyroid, Wine, and Red Wine) and four artificial datasets [40]. The artificial datasets are shown in figure 1.

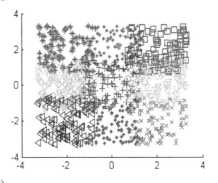

(a)

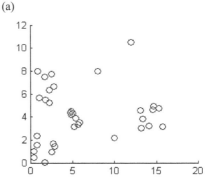

(b)

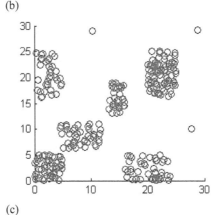

(c)

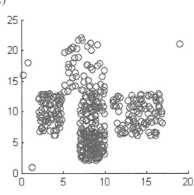

(d)

Figure 1. (a) Artificial dataset 1, (b) Artificial dataset 2, (c) Artificial dataset 3, (d) Artificial dataset 4.

The performance of the algorithm was also compared with FCM [4] and ITLBO [24]. The well-known datasets are described below.

Artificial dataset 1: This is a 2D data set consisting of 900 points. The dataset has nine classes.

Artificial dataset 2: There are 35 points in this dataset. It contains some noise and four classes.

Artificial dataset 3: The dataset contains 483 sample points and some random noise. There are five categories in the data.

Artificial dataset 4: This dataset contains 554 points with five classes and some random noise.

Iris dataset: This dataset contains 3 clusters of 150 objects, where each cluster refers to a type of Iris plant, Setosa, Virginica, or Versicolor. The data represents four dimensions (sepal length, sepal width, petal length, and petal width). There are no missing attribute values.

Wine dataset: This dataset contains 178 data points along with 13 continuous features derived from chemical analysis (e.g. Alcohol, Malic Acid, and Ash). It is divided into three clusters.

Thyroid dataset: This dataset contains 215 samples of patients suffering from three human thyroid diseases. Each individual was characterized by five features from laboratory tests.

Red Wine dataset: This dataset is related to red Vinho Verde wine samples from the north of Portugal. The number of instances is 4,898 and the number of attributes is 12. There are some outliers (noise) in this dataset. We refer the reader to [38] for more information about this dataset.

The algorithms were implemented in MATLAB, and the PC, DB, and PBM validity indices were calculated according to their definitions. Several runs of the algorithms were executed. The data in this work was crisp but their memberships were fuzzy. Table 2 shows the comparative results for all the 6 datasets. For the FCM algorithm, the fuzzy exponent m' was set to 2. The population size used for ITLBO algorithms was 100, and did not require any algorithm-specific parameters. Four teachers were used. The objective function in ITLBO I is to minimize j_m, the objective function in ITLBO II is to maximize V_{PCAES}, and the objective functions in MOITLBO I are to minimize j_m and XB. The objective functions in the proposed multi-objective model, namely, MOITLBO II are j_m and PCAES indices.

The low values of the PC and DB indices indicate that the multi-objective clustering performance for all datasets is better than that of single-objective clustering. Parameter m' in the PBM index was set to 2. Larger results of this value indicate a better clustering performance.

Table 2. Cluster index values for some algorithms on different datasets (averaged over 40 runs).

cluster validity indices	Algorithm name	Artificial dataset 1	Artificial dataset 2	Artificial dataset3	Artificial dataset4	Iris dataset	Wine dataset	Thyroid dataset	Red Wine dataset
PC	FCM	0.3210	0.2513	0.3343	0.5012	0.7833	0.5322	0.6510	0.2899
	ITLBOI	0.8864	0.3428	0.7061	0.6229	0.8770	0.7012	0.7943	0.3015
	ITLBO II	0.9032	0.3771	0.7187	0.6953	0.8992	0.7923	0.7734	0.3567
	MOITLBO I	0.9322	0.6105	0.8854	0.7402	0.9114	0.8714	0.8979	0.5188
	MOITLBO II	**0.9767**	**0.7127**	**0.9016**	**0.8916**	**0.9346**	**0.8809**	**0.9106**	**0.7931**
DB	FCM	0.4916	0.7892	0.6669	1.3944	0.9643	1.3944	2.0316	1.0231
	ITLBOI	0.3567	0.6690	0.4660	0.9915	0.8660	1.0975	1.9965	0.8041
	ITLBO II	0.3064	0.6721	0.4732	0.8920	0.8732	0.9962	1.4490	0.7569
	MOITLBO I	0.2031	0.5323	0.3661	0.4318	0.5165	0.7388	1.2338	0.5537
	MOITLBO II	**0.1908**	**0.3206**	**0.1980**	**0.2987**	**0.5089**	**0.7097**	**1.2531**	**0.2438**
PBM	FCM	14.3862	10.9359	54.0640	111.2321	32.4641	204.6350	78.9321	132.7210
	ITLBOI	23.4142	12.8471	40.0558	134.1657	38.3021	231.4027	86.3508	158.8721
	ITLBO II	28.8915	16.0113	42.3727	135.9878	40.9561	309.1602	87.0755	160.4215
	MOITLBO I	33.2092	20.5988	54.6849	167.6579	63.9981	318.0650	98.2698	162.0358
	MOITLBO II	**35.1470**	**26.1943**	**57.5101**	**172.1079**	**67.5482**	**322.8770**	**99.7463**	**181.1477**

A Wilcoxon's rank sum test [31] for independent samples was conducted at the 5% level. This method is a non-parametric statistical hypothesis test that is used when the data does not meet the requirements for a parametric test. It is appropriate for analyzing data from any distribution. Therefore, we used this test to assess whether the difference between the performances of the algorithms could have occurred merely by chance.

It is obvious from table 3 that the median values for MOITLBO II are better than those of the other algorithms. To show that these values are statistically significant, table 4 lists the P-values produced by Wilcoxon's rank sum test for MOITLBO II with respect to the FCM, ITLBOI, and ITLBO II algorithms. All the P-values reported in the table are less than the 5% significance level. As a null hypothesis, it is assumed that there are no significant differences between the median values of MOITLBO II and other algorithms. The alternative hypothesis states that there is a significant difference in the median values of the two groups. The P-values in table 3 indicate the rejection of the null hypothesis. For example, the rank sum test between algorithms

MOITLBO II and ITLBO II for the Red Wine dataset provides a P-value of 0.0007, which is very small. This strongly indicates that the better median values of the performance metrics produced by MOITLBO II are statistically significant, and have not occurred by chance. Similar results were obtained for all the other indices and algorithms with respect to MOITLBO II.

Table 3. PBM index values of each algorithm for datasets (median over 40 runs).

Algorithm	Artificial dataset 1	Artificial dataset 2	Artificial dataset 3	Artificial dataset 4	Iris dataset	Wine dataset	Thyroid dataset	Red Wine dataset
FCM	13.8654	10.9774	53.2229	113.7129	32.3081	204.6352	77.8350	132.7231
ITLBOI	23.7221	13.0125	39.5157	134.9650	39.2355	228.1093	86.3491	151.9906
ITLBO II	25.0907	16.1056	42.3488	133.2571	43.6159	303.0045	86.9788	160.4251
MOITLBO I	33.1834	22.3780	56.1294	168.0878	64.0621	316.5639	94.0913	163.1189
MOITLBO II	34.8099	27.1834	58.7861	171.4372	67.4508	321.7338	100.3428	184.0602

Table 4. P-values of Wilcoxon's rank sum test for tested algorithms.

Algorithms	Artificial dataset 1	Artificial dataset 2	Artificial dataset 3	Artificial dataset 4	Iris dataset	Wine dataset	Thyroid dataset	Red Wine dataset
FCM	2.536×10^{-4}	2.789×10^{-4}	1.380×10^{-4}	2.055×10^{-4}	3.700×10^{-4}	1.675×10^{-4}	1.224×10^{-4}	1.532×10^{-4}
ITLBOI	0.0081	0.0038	0.0022	0.0075	0.0023	0.0055	0.0068	0.0022
ITLBO II	0.0023	0.0009	0.0024	0.0070	0.0044	0.0018	0.0038	0.0007
MOITLBO I	0.0015	0.0011	0.0010	0.0035	0.0030	0.0025	0.0014	0.0009

6. Conclusion

This paper proposed a multi-objective approach for fuzzy clustering based on two objective functions, namely the J_m and V_{PCAES} indices. An important aspect to be considered when choosing the two objective functions, is their potential to balance each other's tendency to increase or decrease the number of clusters. This interaction between the two objectives is crucially important to keep the number of clusters dynamic and explore interesting areas of the solution space. In order to optimize the model, the MOITLBO algorithm was applied. This algorithm modeled the process of teaching-learning, where every individual learned something from the other individuals in order to improve themselves. In clustering, the role of validity indices are very important, and these indices help determining the validity of the clustering. We used the PC, PBM, and DB indices to evaluate the performance of the clustering algorithms. To evaluate the clustering performance of the MOITLBO algorithm, a statistical test was performed to compare it with some single-objective algorithms, FCM and ITLBO. In addition, the performance of this model with respect to noise was compared using MOITLBO based on the two objectives, namely $_m$ and XB indices. The experimental results showed that the proposed MOITLBO algorithm based on the J_m and $PCAES$ indices achieved the best performance.

Although we introduced a multi-objective clustering model that can be used to generate research insights, there are some limitations that need to be addressed. These limitations clearly point to the potential future developments.

The proposed model in this study was tested on some real-life and artificial datasets; if the technique is applied on more big datasets and real life domains, the results may or may not be as valid.

Since the Euclidean measure was used as distance metric to measure similarity and dissimilarity between clusters, future research works could involve examination and evaluation using different distance measures (e.g. Mahalanobis distance measure) to determine the performance of the clustering model introduced in this paper.

Comparing and evaluating the proposed multi-objective clustering based on MOITLBO to other multi-objective meta-heuristic approaches will help further evaluation of the robustness of the model.

References

[1] Gan, G., Ma, C., & Wu, J. (2007). Data Clustering: Theory, Algorithms, and Applications. ASA-SIAM Series on Statistics and Applied Probability, Philadelphia, Alexandria: SIAM.

[2] Everitt, B. S. (1993) Cluster Analysis. (3rd ed.), New York, Toronto: Halsted Press.

[3] Mosavi, A. (2014). Data mining for decision making in engineering optimal design, Journal of AI and Data Mining, vol. 2, no. 1, pp.7-14.

[4] Bezdek, J. C. (1981), Pattern Recognition with Fuzzy Objective Function Algorithms. New York: Plenum Press.

[5] Brucker, P. (1978). On the Complexity of Clustering Problems. In M. Beckmenn, & H. P. Kunzi (Eds.), Optimisation and Operations Research, Lecture Notes in Economics and Mathematical Systems), Berlin: Springer, vol. 157, pp. 45–54.

[6] EL-Ghazali, T. (2009). Metaheuristics: From Design to Implementation. (1st ed.), John Wiley and Sons.

[7] Geem, Z. W., Kim, J. H., & Loganathan, G. V. (2001). A New Heuristic Optimization Algorithm: Harmony Search. Simulation, vol. 76, pp. 60–70.

[8] Rashedi, E., Nezamabadi-pour, H., & Saryazdi, S. (2009). GSA: A Gravitational Search Algorithm. Information Sciences, vol. 179, pp.2232–2248.

[9] Jardin, N., & Sibson, R. (1971), Mathematical Taxonomy. (1st ed.), John Wiley and Sons.

[10] Deb, K., Mohan, M., & Mishra, S. (2005). Evaluating the Epsilon-Domination Based Multi-Objective Evolutionary Algorithm for a Quick Computation of Pareto-optimal Solutions. Evolutionary Computations, vol. 13, no. 4, pp.501–525.

[11] Rezaee, M. R., Lelieveldt, B. P. F., & Reiber, J. H. C. (1998). A New Cluster Validity Index for the Fuzzy c-mean. Pattern Recognition Letters, vol. 19, pp. 237–246.

[12] Xie, X. L., & Beni, G. (1991). A Validity Measure for Fuzzy Clustering. IEEE Transactions on Pattern Analysis and Machine Intelligence, vol. 13, pp.841–847.

[13] Delattre, M., & Hansen, P. (1980). Bicriterion Cluster Analysis. IEEE Transactions on Pattern Analysis and Machine Intelligence, vol. 2, no. 4, pp. 277–291.

[14] Handl, J., & Knowles, J. (2007). An Evolutionary Approach to Multiobjective Clustering. IEEE Transactions on Evolutionary Computation, vol. 11, pp. 56–76.

[15] Ferligoj, A., & Batagelj, V. (1992). Direct Multicriterion Clustering. Journal of Classification, vol. 9, pp. 43–61.

[16] Handl, J., & Knowles, J. (2004). Evolutionary Multiobjective Clustering. In Proceedings 8th International Conference on Parallel Problem Solving from Nature, pp. 1081–1091.

[17] Corne, D. W., Jerram, N. R., Knowles, J. D., & Oates M. J. (2001). PESA-II: Region-based Selection in Evolutionary Multiobjective Optimization. In Proceedings of the Genetic and Evolutionary Computation Conference, pp. 283–290.

[18] Handl, J., & Knowles, J. (2004). Multi-objective Clustering with Automatic Determination of the Number of Clusters. Technical Report TR-COMPSYSBIO, Institute of Science and Technology, University of Manchester.

[19] Handl, J., & Knowles, J. (2005). Exploiting the Tradeoff—The Benefits of Multiple Objectives in Data Clustering. In Proceedings 3rd International Conference on Evolutionary Multi-Criterion Optimization, pp. 547–560.

[20] Handl, J., & Knowles, J. (2005). Improvements to the Scalability of Multiobjective Clustering. In Proceedings 2005 IEEE Congress on Evolutionary Computation, vol. 3, pp. 2372–2379.

[21] Handl, J., & Knowles, J. (2006). Multiobjective Clustering and Cluster Validation. Computational Intelligence, vol. 16, pp.21–47.

[22] Caballero, R., Laguna, M., Marti, R., & Molina, J. (2006). Multiobjective clustering with metaheuristic optimization technology. Technical Report, Leeds School of Business at the University of Colorado at Boulder.

[23] Saha, I., Maulik, U., & Plewczynski, D. (2011). A New Multi-objective Technique for Differential Fuzzy Clustering. Applied Soft Computing, vol. 11, pp. 2765–2776.

[24] Rao, R. V., & Patel V. (2013). An Improved Teaching-Learning-Based Optimization Algorithm for Solving Unconstrained Optimization Problems. Scientia Iranica, vol. 20, no. 3, 710–720.

[25] Wang, W., & Zhang, Y. (2007). On Fuzzy Cluster Validity Indices. Fuzzy Sets and Systems, vol. 158, pp. 2095–2117.

[26] Mualik, U., & Bandyopadhyay, S. (2002). Genetic Algorithm Based Clustering Technique. Pattern Recognition, vol. 33, pp.1455–1465.

[27] Kao, Y.-T., Zahara, E., & Kao, I.-W. (2008). A Hybridized Approach to Data Clustering. Expert Systems with Applications, vol. 34, no. 3, pp.1754–1762.

[28] Rao, R. V., Savsani, V. J., & Vakharia, D. P. (2011). Teaching-learning-based optimization: A Novel Method for Constrained Mechanical Design Optimization Problems. Computer-Aided Design, vol. 43, no. 3, pp. 303–315.

[29] Rao, R. V., Savsani, V. J., & Vakharia, D. P. (2012). Teaching-learning-based optimization: A Novel Optimization Method for Continuous Non-Linear Large Scale Problems. Information Sciences, vol. 183, no. 1, pp.1–15.

[30] Van Veldhuizen, D. A. (1999). Multi-objective Evolutionary Algorithms: Classifications. Analysis and New Innovations. Evolutionary Computation, vol. 8, no. 2, pp. 125–147.

[31] Hollander, M., & Wolfe, D. A. (2014), Nonparametric Statistical Methods (3rd ed.), John Wiley and Sons.

[32] Wu, K. L., & Yang, M. S. (2005). A Cluster Validity Index for Fuzzy Clustering. Pattern Recognition Letters, vol. 26, pp.1275–1291.

[33] Rao, R. V., & Patel, V. (2014). A Multi-Objective Improved Teaching Learning Based Optimization Algorithm for Unconstrained and Constrained Optimization Problems. International Journal of Industrial Engineering Computation, vol. 5, pp. 1–22.

[34] Pakhira, M. K., bandyopadhyay, S., & Maulik, U. (2004). Validity Index for Crisp and Fuzzy Clusters. Pattern Recognition, vol. 37, pp. 481–501.

[35] Murty, M. R., et al. (2014). Automatic Clustering Using Teaching Learning Based Optimization. Applied Mathematics, vol. 5, pp. 1202–1211.

[36] Pal, N. R., & Bezdek, J. C. (1995), On Cluster Validity for the Fuzzy c-means Model, IEEE Transactions on Fuzzy Systems, vol. 3, no. 3, pp. 370–379.

[37] Davies, D. L., & Bouldin, D. W. (1979). A Cluster Separation Measure, IEEE Transactions on Pattern Analysis and Machine Intelligence, vol. 1, pp. 224–227.

[38] Cortez, P., Cerdeira, A., Almeida, F., Matos, T., & Reis, J. (2009). Modeling Wine Preferences by Data Mining from Physicochemical Properties, In Decision Support Systems, vol. 47, no. 4, pp. 547–553.

[39] Rao, R. V., & Patel, V. K. (2012). An elitist teaching-learning-based optimization algorithm for solving complex constrained optimization problems, International Journal of Industrial Engineering Computations, vol. 3, pp. 535–560.

[40] These datasets, Available: (http://www.ics.uci.edu/~mlearn/MLResponsitory.html), (ftp://ftp.ics.edu/pub/machine-learning-databases).

[41] Gaffari, A., & Nobahar, S. (2015). FDMG, Fault detection method by using genetic algorithmin clustered wireless sensor networks, Journal of AI and Data Mining, vol. 3, no. 1, pp. 47–57.

3

Plagiarism checker for Persian (PCP) texts using hash-based tree representative fingerprinting

Sh. Rafieian[1*] and A. Braani Dastjerdi[2]

1. Computer Engineering Department, Sheikh Bahaii University, Isfahan, Iran.
2. Computer Engineering Department, University of Isfahan, Isfahan, Iran.

*Corresponding author: shima.rafieian@gmail.com (Sh. Rafieian).

Abstract
With due respect to the authors' rights, plagiarism detection is one of the critical problems in the field of text-mining, in which many researchers are interested. This issue has been considered as a serious one in high academic institutions. There exist language-free tools that do not yield any reliable results since the special features of every language are ignored in them. Considering the paucity of works in the field of Persian language due to the lack of reliable plagiarism checkers in Persian, there is a need for a method to improve the accuracy of detecting plagiarized Persian phrases. An attempt is made in this work to present the PCP solution. This solution is a combinational method, in which, in addition to the meaning and stem of words, synonyms and pluralization are dealt with by applying the document tree representation based on manner fingerprinting the text in the 3-grams words. The grams obtained are eliminated from the text, hashed through the BKDR hash function, and stored as the fingerprint of a document in fingerprints of the reference document repositories in order to check the suspicious documents. The proposed PCP method here is evaluated by eight experiments on seven different sets, which include the suspicions documents and the reference document from the Hamshahri newspaper website. The results obtained indicate that the accuracy of this proposed method in detecting similar texts, in comparison with the "Winnowing" localized method, has a 21.15% average improvement. The accuracy of the PCP method in detecting the similarities, in comparison with the language-free tool, reveals a 31.65% average improvement.

Keywords: *Text-Mining, Natural Language Processing, Plagiarism Detection, External Plagiarism Detection, Persian Language.*

1. Introduction
Nowadays plagiarism has become a cancer cell in the literary world. This important global issue is considered as a serious crisis for high academic institutions even in freelance writing. Accessibility of different digital documents in Worldwide Web makes it easy for the swindlers to copy explicit subjects from students and academicians by allowing them to be promoted to high academic levels or grades in life without any required scientific background [1].
Plagiarism may include:

- Replacing the original author's name
- Copying ideas, phrases, concepts, research proposals, articles, reports, computer program designs, websites, and the internet and other electronic resources without citing the author's name
- Lack of citation regarding quotation
- False referencing or referencing the non-existing resources
- Translation plagiarism, where the translated text is submitted without reference to the original text
- Artistic plagiarism, where different media including images and videos are used for other works without (a) proper reference(s) to the resource(s) [2,4].

There are two major methods that can be used to reduce literary pirating: plagiarism detection and plagiarism prevention [3,4]. An attempt is made in this work to adapt the detection method.

The path and status of this work are presented in figure 1, with their hierarchical sequence in gray boxes. According to this tree diagram, plagiarism detection methods include manual methods and software tools that are simple to be implemented, and can be applied in plagiarism [3].

Software plagiarism detection is categorized based on text homogeneity regarding monolingual plagiarism detection and cross-lingual plagiarism detection [2].

Detecting plagiarism in monolingual environments refers to a homogeneous and congruent environment like English to English, and nearly all systems that are developed to detect it and are divided into the inherent and external types [2,4].

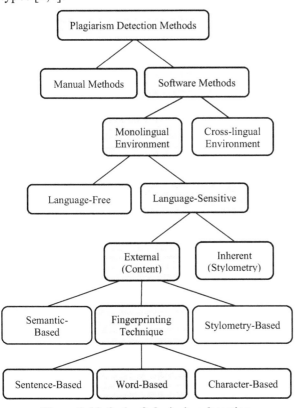

Figure 1. Methods of plagiarism detection.

Detecting cross-lingual plagiarism refers to detecting texts that encompass multi-languages like English and Arabic. In this method, the document recovery process is similar to the suspicious documents in a cross-lingual environment [5].

In detecting inherent plagiarism, named the stylometry-based method as well, there is no reference document, and just the suspicious document is controlled [2]. The objective of inherent plagiarism detection is to identify the potential pirate(s) with analyzing changes in writing style [6].

For detecting external plagiarism, named the content-based method, a suspicious document is compared with a number of documents, and the text contents are analyzed based on the logical structure and detection of similarities among texts [2]. In this method, a text investigation is made through textual features including removing stop words from the text [7].

The common techniques that act based on the content-based method rely on the explicit comparison of the document contents. Most detection methods use stop word deletions [3]. The objective of this work is to improve the accuracy of detecting the similarities among the pirated phrases in Persian texts through the stem of current words and document tree representation, and applying the fingerprinting technique according to the word-based 3-grams.

The innovation aspects of this proposed method consist of preprocessing operation(s) in more accuracy in comparison with the previous works, and replacement of pluralization or broken words.

Applying the document tree representing and its fingerprinting introduces a new tree-nodes with a key volume that contains the hash value of its children trio. Therefore, in copy detection, only branches with the same hash values are considered, which prevent excessive search.

The rest of this article is organized as follows: A literature review is presented in section 2. The solution and operation used for pre-processing the text and document tree representation, text fingerprinting, and detecting the suspected phrases are presented in section 3. The presented combinational method (PCP) is discussed in section 4, and, finally, the conclusion is presented in section 5.

2. Literature review

Using language-free plagiarism detection tools are inefficient on texts like Persian and Arabic, and the outputs of these tools are imprecise and unreliable because they do not consider their special features and structural complexities [3]. Hence, the language-sensitive tools should be used. Despite the endeavors in this field in the recent years, no updated and efficient tool has been presented for Persian texts.

ZiHayat and Basiri have presented a tool that makes the detection of copying scale of phrases possible in the Persian electronic documents through a native-user interface based on the grand algorithm "Winnowing" [8]. The average accuracy of this total is 64%, which is relatively low. It is possible to adapt more updated algorithms for document categorization and natural language processing in order to improve the accuracy of this system [9].

Kamran et al. have also presented a tool for detecting plagiarism in Persian documents using "Simhash" algorithm which, despite its low accuracy, is fast in detecting pirates in a large collection of texts. There exist 300 reference articles and 25 suspicious articles as the inputs of the system, which are used to detect phrase similarities of the word-based grams and "Simhash" and "Shingling" algorithms. The developers have concluded that in large sets of Persian documents, using the "Simhash" algorithm (despite its low accuracy) is a more proper method [10].

Mahmoodi and MahmmodiVarNamkhasti has proposed another tool for plagiarism detection; a precise tool for detecting plagiarism in short paragraphs [1]. It is impossible to detect plagiarism in documents with multiple paragraphs because the inputs of this tool are both a suspicious document and a reference document, where each one of them includes one paragraph by itself. Assuming the high level of accuracy in the plagiarism detection for short paragraphs, it is not possible to detect plagiarism in multiple paragraphs, and if either of these documents contain more than one paragraph considered as an input, the results would be of low accuracy, and unreliable.

Mahdavi et al. have adapted the vector space model to detect external plagiarism in Persian texts. In their article, 41 reference documents and 84 suspicious documents were created by the developers, and using the vector space model and cosine similarity among them, more accurate document processings s were selected as the candidates. Next, the similarity coefficient shows the overlapping features of 3-grams comprising each document, where the probable similarities are discovered. For every feature, the vector of a document requires both more memory and a long time in the processing of finding similar documents. Therefore, the size and number of features of this vector depend on the length and expression of the documents [11].

Rakian at al. have used the new method of a fuzzy algorithm to consider the different levels of a hierarchical text and use the synonyms necessary in determining the degree of similarity between two sentences in Persian texts, and hence, the external plagiarism detection in Persian texts. Here, 1,000 reference documents and 400 suspicious documents were established, where the structural change in sentences and then being rewritten are recognizable. In order to select the candidate documents related to the keywords of the text offer recovery and divide their constituent sentences, the potential similarities are detected by the fuzzy methods [12]. An increase in the sentence divisions can slow down the processing time and accelerate the memory consumption.

3. Proposed combinational method (PCP)

Implementing this combinational method includes text preprocessing, document tree representation, text fingerprinting, and copy detection (see Figures 2).

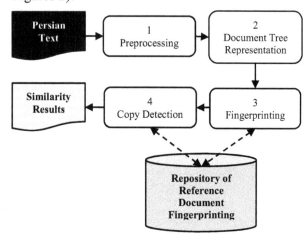

Figure 2. Steps of detecting similarities in PCP method.

In this study, the fingerprints were based upon 3-grams of the text created by different levels of the document tree representation. This representation can be obtained by traversing the bottom-up tree. The final fingerprint of a document created by the hash of the paragraph level will be less than the volume of the hash made at the level of the 3-grams words. The fingerprint of a document is compressed and improves the fault memory-consumption presented in [3, 7] and similar works with respect to another language. Since in their fingerprint idea, the hashes in the level of words were copied into their father, they created a high volume of hash word levels in the fingerprint of a document. Moreover, the fingerprint idea in the PCP method causes a difference in the similarity detection approach towards the proposed method in [3,7].

3.1. Text preprocessing measure

Text preprocessing is run in order to clean and delete useless information from the text, causing a rise in the accuracy and a reduction in the time required for a possible similarity detection.

According to figure 3, this measure includes the following steps:

1. Text segmentation: here, the text is separated into its constituent paragraphs.

2. Sentence tokenization: here, the constituent sentences of a paragraph are separated by the punctuation marks "?, ! , .", and the excess spaces in each paragraph are removed and replaced by one empty space; therefore, it is assumed that all sentences are separated with an empty space.

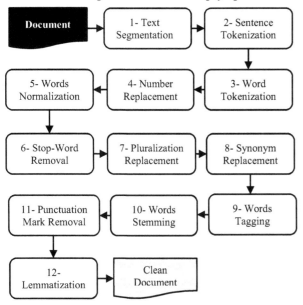

Figure 3. Text preprocessing measure.

3. Word tokenization: here, for every specified sentence in the previous step, word ranges and punctuation marks are determined in a sense that each sentence would be broken into its constituent words.

4. Number replacement: here, the number character is replaced by the "#" sign, which makes finding similarity among the number in the text independent.

5. Words normalization: here, operations like removing three points from the text, putting half-space between the prefixes and postfixes including "می،نمی،تر،ترین،ها", and finally, replacing the excessive spaces with one space are applied to the normalized words.

6. Stop word removal: words like relation words including "و، از، را، ولی، اما، به" are among the frequent words in the Persian language, which are applied to all texts, and must be ignored in order to assess the similarity in texts because they have no special meaning weight.

7. Fragmented pluralization or broken word replacements: in the Persian language, there are words that have the same stem but their pluralization is irregular, like the word "اخبار", which is a pluralization summation of the word "خبر". It is worth mentioning that this step is being presented for the first time in the Persian language.

The input function is a word processing of the document (see Figure 4). If this word is pluralized and replaced by its singular term, then the homogenization of this class of words is accomplished. This step requires pluralized lexicon in the Persian language. For this purpose, the Persian Gate 6.0 plug-in, which is applied in natural language processing in [13], is applied.

```
Pluralization Replacing Algorithm
1.   Input: The word of Document
2.   Output: The Singular_word of Clean Document
3.   Begin
4.        While (! Pluralization _Lexicon.EndOfFile)
5.          If (word = = Pluralization _Token)
6.          {
7.              Singular_word = Singular_Token
8.          Break
9.          }
10.  End
```

Figure 4. Pseudo-code of pluralization replacement.

8. Synonym replacement: in the Persian language, there are words that have the same meaning but different stems such as the word "پند" that has the synonyms "اندرز، موعظه، رهنمون، عبرت، نصیحت، وعظ". If there are such words in a sentence, all of them are replaced with their stems, The word "پند" is followed by homogenization of this kind of words in the text.

The input function is a word-processing of the document (see Figures 5). If this word is in a series of synonymous words, replaced by their root words, this class of words is homogenized. This step is required to be lexicon synonyms in the Persian language. Here, a comprehensive synonymous and antonyms lexicon in the Persian language has used name as Raghoumi version [14].

```
Synonym replacement Algotithm
1.   Input: The word of Document
2.   Output: The Root_word of Clean Document
3.   Begin
4.        While (! Synonym_Lexicon.EndOfFile)
5.          If (word = = Syn_Token)
6.          {
7.              Root _word = Root_Token
8.          Break
9.          }
10.  End
```

Figure 5. Pseudo-code of synonym replacement.

9. Part-of-speech (POS) tagging: here, the reminded basic words of the text are tagged, and their types are specified on grammatical parts like the noun, verb, adverb, adjective, and punctuation marks [15]. This step is impressive in determining the stem of the words.

10. Stemming: here, the words are stemmed based on a specified tag given to them in the previous

step followed by removal of prefixes, postfixes, and infixes from the word, respectively.

In the manner, different derivative and inflectional states of words in similarity detection are not affected. For example, the words "رفته بود", "می‌رود" are verbs with the stems "رفت" in past and "رو" in the present. This process becomes possible through the trained model in NHazm [16], which is a tool for processing Persian natural language in Visual Studio environment.

11. Punctuation removal: in this step, ignore all the writing signs and available punctuation marks in the text.

12. Lemmatization: in the final step, words are replaced with stems in their dictionaries. This step proceeds with each word tag and its stem.

3.2 Fingerprinting

A document tree representation is applied in order to fingerprint a text. The PCP approach is to determine the fingerprint of the document at words level in the text, which is divided into 3-grams, and after applying the hash function on them, a fingerprint of the document is generated in the 3-grams words. In the next step, to produce a fingerprint of the document in sentences, the generated hashes in the 3-grams are broken into the next 3-grams, as well, where the hash function would be applied on them. Finally, to create the final fingerprint of the document (at the paragraph level), the hashes generated in sentences are broken into the 3-grams again, and then the hash function is applied to them. The final fingerprint of a document created based on tree representation and applied the hash function would generate the hashed 3-grams at each level, whose volume is smaller than the approach presented in [3,7].

As shown in figure 6, the stem consists of the tree basic document, the second level consists of all refined text paragraphs, and the third level of the tree encompasses the sentences of the paragraph.

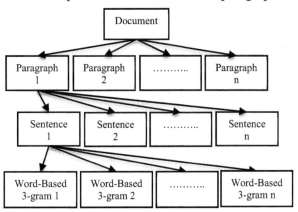

Figure 6. Document tree representation.

Then sentences are divided into word-based 3-grams, and using a proper hash function, they are converted into a number. In this manner, the processing speed is increased in the copy detection operation.

In figure 7, there is a tree representation of the single sentence paragraph " امروز هوای اصفهان ابری و بارانی است.".

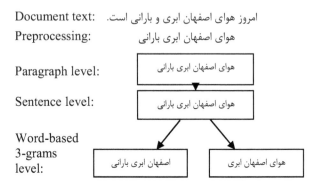

Figure 7. An example of a document tree representation.

It is important to select a hash function that minimizes the collisions due to mapping different chunks to the same hash [6, 10]. In this implementation, the BKDR hash function is used. This function is the sum of each character's multiplication in a certain value named "seed" that usually has the value of 31. The seed value must be an odd number because odd numbers are unique, and multiplication of a number in an odd number creates a unique hash value [6, 10].

The steps for the above example of fingerprinting are shown in figure 8. The fingerprint of this single sentence paragraph is 25319069.

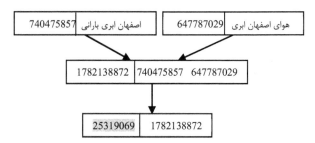

Figure 8. A fingerprinting example.

According to figure 8, after breaking all the words contained in sentences into 3-grams, it is time to hash operations at sentence-level. Through this procedure, the hashes obtained from words-based 3-grams are broken into 3-grams in tree sentence-level, and a hash operation is run on them.

In the final step, the hashed 3-grams will be converted from sentence-level into paragraph-level 3-grams. Therefore, the document fingerprints obtained contain paragraph-level hashes of the document.

3.3 Copy detection

The main objective of the document tree representation is time-saving during similarity investigation and preventing excessive comparisons.

In the PCP method, the similar detection approach is based upon the membership fingerprint in each level of suspicious document fingerprint and the corresponding level of reference document fingerprint. For example, if a hash value of fingerprint (at paragraph level) in the suspicious document exists in the hash fingerprint collection (at paragraph level) of the reference document, each one of the 3-grams that here created this hash (each one of the three hash of manufacturer this hash) at the sentence levels is checked separately. Similarly, if existed similarity in sentences, the hashes of the suspicious document at sentences level checked more precisely at the 3-grams words. In other words, the generated hashes of sentences in the 3-grams words level are examined separately. Therefore, if there exists a similarity, the 3-grams words in the tree leaf are displayed to the user for final decisions.

According to the pseudo-code in figure 9, a tree is surveyed by a top-down traverse, and the fingerprints of two texts in the document level are evaluated. Due to the lack of injective hash function and generation of equal hashes for different phrases with these, in order to ensure the final result, the star-tagged parts are added to the code that can generally be deleted from the algorithm.

```
Copy Detection Algorithm
1.     Input: Fingerprinting of Doc suspect,
       Fingerprinting of Doc source,
2.     Output: Similarity
3.     Begin
4.        For each hash_ paragraph _suspect
5.           If (suspect_ paragraph  in source_ paragraph)
6.              For each hash_ sentence _suspect
7.    *          If (suspect_ sentence  in source_ sentence)
8.                 For each hash_ words _suspect
9.    *               If (suspect_ words  in source_ words)
10.                       Similarity = True
11.   *               Else
12.                       Similarity = False
13.   *            Else
14.                   Similarity = False
15.              Else
16.                 Similarity = False
17.    End
```

Figure 9. Pseudo-code of copy detection.

1. The fingerprints of the reference document and the suspicious document are considered as the algorithm inputs.
2. If there is any similarity/dissimilarity in each one of the steps, the algorithm output or

"Similarity" variable is determined by "True" or "False".
3. Similarity detection operation begins.
4. Following steps will continue for all the current document paragraph-level hashes.
5. If the following paragraph-level hashes of the suspicious document are the subsets of paragraph-level hashes of the reference document, evaluate the comparison process in sentence-level.
6. For each hash in sentence-level of the suspicious document, the comparison process continues at the level of current word.
7. If sentence-level hashes of the suspicious documents are the subsets of the sentence-level hashes of the reference document, then the comparison process continues in their word-level.
8. For each hash at word-level of the suspicious document, the comparison process continues at their 3-grams level.
9. If the 3-grams level hashes of the suspicious document are the subsets of the 3-grams level hashes of reference document,
10. Possible similarity is detected.
11, 12. Otherwise, the comparison process continues at the sentence-level hashes of the suspicious document.
13, 14. According to line 9, if the sentence-level hashes of the suspicious document are not the subsets of sentence-level hashes of the reference document, then the comparison operation continues at the paragraph-level hashes of the suspicious document.
15, 16. According to line 7, if the paragraph-level hashes of the suspicious document are not a subset of paragraph-level hashes of the reference document, then the comparison operation stops.
17. Operation of similarity detection ends.

4. Method evaluation

The implementation is run using the C# programming language, where the features, functions, and classes are used.

The evaluation process proceeds once with similarity parameters and their comparison with the native algorithm in "Winnowing" [9], and once, by using the Duplicate Content Checker tool, which implements text similarity detection, and is placed in the language-free categories [17].

4.1. Datasets

Evaluation of the performance of the proposed PCP method requires a standard textual dataset. Therefore, seven sets of texts consisting of one suspicious and one reference text in each are collected from the standard dataset of Persian language and Hamshahri newspaper sources [18].

The specification of these texts is tabulated in table 1.

Table 1. Randomly-created document sets.

Document Number	Word counts	Construction type
1	119	Random
2	117	Document 1
3	537	Random
4	907	Random + Document 3
34	575	Document 3 + Document 4
5	827	Random
6	497	Random + Document 3 + Document 5
7	5392	Document 1 + Document 3 + Document 4 + Random
8	3003	Document 7

4.2. Parameters

Evaluation through Recall, Precision, and F-measure scales are the three important measures in the efficiency of the plagiarism detection algorithms in addition to Jaccard Similarity Coefficient (1) to (4), and all of these algorithms are calculated as follow [10]:

$$Recall = \frac{TP}{TP+FN} \quad (1)$$

$$Precision = \frac{TP}{TP+FP} \quad (2)$$

$$F\text{-measure} = 2 \cdot \frac{Recall.Precision}{Recall+Precision} \quad (3)$$

$$Jaccard\ Similarity\ Coefficient = \frac{TP}{TP+FP+TN} \quad (4)$$

where, TP is the number of cases that are detected True as a copy, FN is the number of cases that are detected False as the original, and FP is the number of cases that is detected False as a copy [10].

3.4. Evaluation results

With respect to table 2, this proposed combinational method is examined through seven random datasets created by documents, tabulated in table 1 with eight tests.

To illustrate the improved accuracy in similarity detection in Persian phrases, the similarity rate of each pair in the tested document is assessed by the "Winnowing" algorithm and PCP method, and hence, the desired parameters are provided.

Table 2. Suspicious and reference created document sets.

Document Set	Suspicious Document	Reference document	Used in
I	Doc2	Doc1	Test 1 , 2
II	Doc34	Doc3	Test 3
III	Doc34	Doc4	Test 4
IV	Doc6	Doc3	Test 5
V	Doc6	Doc5	Test 6
VI	Doc5	Doc6	Test 7
VII	Doc8	Doc7	Test 8

Then to compare the proposed combinational method with the language-free tools, the similarity rate of any suspicious and reference document acquired using the Duplicate Content Checker tool are calculated. The results obtained for these tests are tabulated in table 3.

The results shown in figure 10 show that by using this combinational method, where the meaning of each word and replacement of proper pluralization and synonyms are of concern, the average values for Recall, Precision, and F-measure are improved in the order of 19.26%, 23.61% and 20.58%, respectively, and according to the accuracy in the plagiarism detection evaluated by these parameters, the improved accuracy average is 21.15%. The similarity coefficient improvement of the two texts by 21.13% has gained more safety factor. Since the PCP method is used as a combination of word stems and the tree representation of documents, the effectiveness of all the hashes generated in the fingerprint of any document, which can increase accuracy in the similar detection process, is improved.

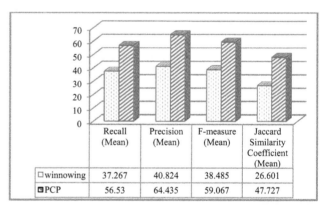

	Recall (Mean)	Precision (Mean)	F-measure (Mean)	Jaccard Similarity Coefficient (Mean)
winnowing	37.267	40.824	38.485	26.601
PCP	56.53	64.435	59.067	47.727

Figure 10. Comparison of PCP method and localized Winnowing algorithm.

This similarity scale in comparison with the similarity that is obtained from language-free tools is reliable by 31.65% (see Figures 11).

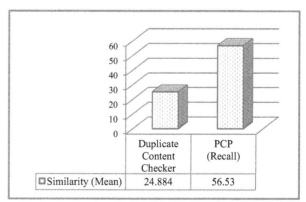

	Duplicate Content Checker	PCP (Recall)
Similarity (Mean)	24.884	56.53

Figure 11. Comparison of PCP method and Duplicate Content Checker tool.

Since language-free tools do not consider the appearance of words and the specific characteristics of the Persian language in the text, they are not accurate enough in detecting similarity or dissimilarity in the Persian texts. To the contrary, this proposed method makes it possible to obtain more accurate results in relation to the language-free method.

Since there exists a direct relation between the document-length and the time-consumed, and since accurate preprocessing and tree representations are applied in this method, naturally, the time-consumption is increased, and this might be considered as a drawback, something that no new method can be without.

Table 3. Evaluating the proposed combinational method using eight tests.

		Test 1	Test 2	Test 3	Test 4	Test 5	Test 6	Test 7	Test 8
Suspicious Document		Doc 2	Doc2	Doc34	Doc34	Doc6	Doc6	Doc5	Doc8
Reference document		Doc 1	Doc1	Doc3	Doc4	Doc3	Doc5	Doc6	Doc7
Recall	Winnowing	76.67	53.55	38.64	27.56	44.7	9.74	15.45	32.06
	PCP	100	100	52.26	36.98	57.14	22.53	36.93	46.4
Precision	Winnowing	76.67	55.17	38.93	47.33	47.9	15.45	9.74	55.41
	PCP	100	100	50.73	61.68	63.07	36.93	22.53	80.54
F-measure	Winnowing	76.67	54.24	38.78	34.83	46.27	11.59	11.95	40.61
	PCP	100	100	51.48	46.24	59.96	27.99	27.99	58.88
Jaccard coefficient Similarity	Winnowing	62.16	37.21	24.06	21.09	30.1	6.35	6.35	25.48
	PCP	100	100	34.66	30.07	42.82	16.27	16.27	41.72
Duplicate Content Checker		56.56	36.59	23.54	20.64	29.63	4.9	4.9	22.31
PCP (Recall)		100	100	52.26	36.98	57.14	22.53	36.93	46.4

With respect to the nature of fingerprinting, this needs a repository for reference. The bigger the repository, the bigger is the memory storage. This issue, on its own, can be considered as a drawback.

In addition, due to the nature of the fingerprinting technique, the restructuring of the text and the changes thereof, word ordering is not possible.

5. Conclusion and future work

A combinational method based on the semantic of current words in text and tree representation of the document, accompanied with the fingerprinting technique according to words-based 3-grams and improvements made in similarity detection accuracy of plagiarized phrases in Persian texts is proposed in the PCP method.

The results obtained indicate that this combinational method improved the similarity coefficient of two texts by 21.13% because the word meanings and replacing proper pluralization and synonyms are of concern.

The calculated similarity scale has an improved rate of 31.65%, and is more reliable, in comparison with the similarity obtained from the language-free tool. This indicates the lack of accuracy in the language-free tools in relation to the language-sensitive methods, especially the proposed combinational method.

The data-mining algorithms in categorizing documents automatically are among the proposals to improve this method, which prevents excess-comparison between texts with different themes.

References

[1] Mahmoodi, M. & Mahmoodi Varnamkhasti, M. (2014). Design a Persian Automated Plagiarism Detector (AMZPPD). International Journal of Engineering Trends and Technology (IJETT), vol. 8, no. 8, pp. 465-467.

[2] Alzahrani, S. M., Salim, N. & Abraham, A. (2012). Understanding Plagiarism linguistic patterns, textual features, and detection methods. IEEE Transaction on Systems, Man, and Cybernetics, Part C: Applications and Reviews, vol. 42, no. 2, pp. 133-149.

[3] Menai, M. E. B. (2012). Detection of Plagiarism in Arabic Documents. International Journal of Information Technology and Computer Science, vol. 4. no.10, pp. 80-89.

[4] Bin-Habtoor, A. S. & Zaher, M. A. (2012). A Survey on Plagiarism Detection Systems. International Journal of Computer Theory and Engineering, vol. 4, no. 2, pp. 185-188.

[5] Ceska, Z. (2008). Plagiarism Detection Based on Singular Value Decomposition. 5th International Conference on Advances in Natural Language Processing. Berlin, Heidelberg, New York: Springer-Verlag.

[6] Potthast, M., Barron-Cedeno, A., Stein, B. & Rosso, P. (2011). Cross-language Plagiarism Detection. Language Resources and Evaluation, vol. 45, no. 1, pp. 45-62.

[7] Menai, M. E. B. & Bagais, M. (2011). APlag: A Plagiarism Checker for Arabic Texts. 6th International Conference on Computer Science & Education (ICCSE), SuperStar Virgo, Singapore, 2011.

[8] Schleimer, S., Wilkerson, D. S. & Aiken, A. (2003). Winnowing: Local Algorithms for Document

Fingerprinting. The 2003 ACM SIGMOD International Conference Management of Data, New York, 2003.

[9] Zihayat, M. & Basiri, J. (2009). Controlling Similarities and Copying in Persian E-documents Received from Danesh Pajohan for Virtual Lessons. International Conference of E-learning, Tehran, Iran, 2009.

[10] Kamran, K., Mohammadi, A. & Mohsenzadeh, M. (2012). Plagiarism Detection in Persian Texts with SimHash Algorithm. 11th Conference of Intelligent Systems, Iran science and industry-university, Iran, 2012.

[11] Mahdavi, P., Siadati, Z. & Yaghmaee, F. (2014). Automatic External Persian Plagiarism Detection Using Vector Space Model. 4th International Conference on Computer and Knowledge Engineering (ICCKF), Ferdowsi University of Mashhad, Iran, 2014.

[12] Rakian, Sh., Safi Esfahani, F. & Rastegari, H.(2015). A Persian Fuzzy Plagiarism Detection Approach. Journal of Information Systems and Telecommunication (JIST), vol. 3, no. 3, pp. 182-190.

[13] Academic Homepage of Majid Sazvar (2015), Available: http://sazvar.student.um.ac.ir/index.php.

[14] The Marjae Dadegan website (2015), Available: http://dadegan.ir/catalog/D3911124a.

[15] Pakzad, A. & Minaei Bidgoli, B.(2016). An improved joint model: POS tagging and dependency parsing. Journal of AI and Data Mining (JAIDM), vol. 4, no. 1, pp. 1-8.

[16] The Github website (2015), Available: https://github.com/mojtaba-khallash/NHazm.

[17] The Search Engine Optimization tool (2015), Available: http://www.seomastering.com/similar-text-checker.php.

[18] The Hamshahri Collection website (2015), Available: http://ece.ut.ac.ir/dbrg/hamshahri.

4

The application of data mining techniques in manipulated financial statement classification: The case of turkey

G. Özdağoğlu[1]*, A. Özdağoğlu[2], Y. Gümüş[3] and G. Kurt-Gümüş[4]

1. Dept. of Business Administration, Faculty of Business, Dokuz Eylül University, Tınaztepe Campus, Buca, İzmir, Turkey.
2. Dept. of Business Administration, Faculty of Business, Dokuz Eylül University, Tınaztepe Campus, Buca, İzmir, Turkey.
3. Dept. of Tourism Management, Reha Midilli Foça Tourism Faculty, Dokuz Eylul University, Foça, İzmir, Turkey.
4. Dept. of International Business and Trade, Faculty of Business, Dokuz Eylül University, Tınaztepe Campus, Buca, İzmir, Turkey.

*Corresponding author: guzin.kavrukkoca@deu.edu.tr (G.Özdağoğlu).

Abstract
Predicting financially false statements to detect frauds in companies has an increasing trend in recent studies. The manipulations in financial statements can be discovered by auditors when related financial records and indicators are analyzed in depth together with the experience of auditors in order to create knowledge to develop a decision support system to classify firms. Auditors may annotate the firms' statements as "correct" or "incorrect" to add their experience, and then these annotations with related indicators can be used for the learning process to generate a model. Once the model is learned and tested for validation, it can be used for new firms to predict their class values. In this research, we attempted to reveal this benefit in the framework of Turkish firms. In this regard, the study aims at classifying financially correct and false statements of Turkish firms listed on Borsa İstanbul, using their particular financial ratios as indicators of a success or a manipulation. The dataset was selected from a particular period after the crisis (2009 to 2013). Commonly used three classification methods in data mining were employed for the classification: decision tree, logistic regression, and artificial neural network, respectively. According to the results, although all three methods are performed well, the latter had the best performance, and it outperforms other two classical methods. The common ground of the selected methods is that they pointed out the Z-score as the first distinctive indicator for classifying financial statements under consideration.

Keywords: *Classification, Data Mining, Manipulated Financial Statements, Audit Opinion, Borsa İstanbul.*

Introduction
Financial statement fraud is recently an important issue in the related research. Particularly, Enron crisis emerged the financial statement fraud and earnings management concepts. Fraud causes falsifications in elements of financial statements, and gradually financially false statements are generated by manipulating assets, liabilities, revenue, expenses, profit or losses [2]. Period shifting, changing accounting methods, fiddling with managerial estimates of costs, manipulating documents, changing test documents and preparing false work reports are the other common techniques for fraud and manipulation of profits [3,4]. In this regard, American Institute of Certified Public Accountants (AICPA) Auditing Standards group the red flags, i.e. undesired and risky indicators in financial activities, into three categories: management characteristics, industry conditions, and operating characteristics and financial stability [5]. Recently, frauds over falsified financial statements (manipulated financial statements) got firms into a scrape during auditing processes. This kind of institutional behavior and the undesired financial activities, i.e. the red flags, increased the importance of financial audit process and directly affected the auditor's opinion at the end of the process. Audit opinions are also categorized with respect to the criteria defined in red flags. According to the International Standards on Auditing [1] there are four types of an audit opinion: unmodified opinion, adverse opinion, disclaimer of opinion, and qualified opinion according to the completeness and the correctness of the financial records. All types of the opinions,

except unmodified, carry some suspicious situations and risks from the auditor's perspective. In auditing, a number of articles have been published in order to provide decision support to detect suspicious situations through financial indicators such as ratios. Data mining techniques which have made a significant contribution to the field of decision science, are also used to develop this kind of decision support tools with the help of information technologies. Hence, the manipulations originated from red flags can be discovered by auditors when related financial statements and indicators are analyzed in depth together with their audit experience. This knowledge can be used to develop a decision support system in order to classify financial statements as true or false through financial indicators. Once auditors annotate the firms' statements as "true" or "false", this knowledge with the other indicators can be used for the supervised learning process of classification techniques in data mining. After training and testing for validation, the learned model can be beneficially used as a decision support tool or system to predict the status of new statements.

In this research, we attempted to reveal this benefit in the framework of Turkish firms. In this regard, the study aims at classifying financially correct and false statements of Turkish firms listed on Borsa İstanbul, using their particular financial ratios as indicators of a success or a manipulation. An annotated term dataset was selected from a particular period after the crisis (2009 to 2013). Commonly used three classification methods in data mining were employed for the classification: decision tree, logistic regression, and artificial neural network. According to the results, although all of three methods performed well, the latter had the highest performance and it outperforms other two classical methods. The common ground of the selected methods is that they pointed out the Z-score as the first distinctive indicator for classifying financial statements under consideration.

The rest of the paper is organized as follows. First of all, a theoretical framework is discussed, and then the methodology is explained. Thirdly, the analysis results are given, and the final section concludes.

1. Related work

Data mining methods are frequently implemented for financial forecasting to identify market trends [6]. Dhar [7] discussed the real value of data mining, particularly in the field of finance, and a framework was constructed to decide when the results of a data mining effort, the patterns are usable for decision support.

Koyuncugil and Ozgulbas [8] proposed an early warning system model based on data mining for financial risk detection through Turkish central bank database. Financial data from balance sheets were used to calculate financial indicators. Zhou et al. [9] investigated the performance of different financial distress prediction models with feature selection approaches based on domain knowledge or data mining techniques. Zhang et al. [10] used the information fusion technique to build a finance early-warning model based on data mining methods. In the paper, the respective strengths of different data mining methods were integrated to improve the prediction accuracy rate. The model based on Support Vector Machines, and Logistic and Dempster-Shafer theory was used for firm's financial risk prediction. Liu [11] constructed a data mining process with discriminant analysis, logistic regression and neural network to predict financial distress.

Predicting financially false statements to detect frauds in companies has an increasing trend in recent studies. Some studies discuss the theoretical framework and indicators or metrics of fraud where others focus on obtaining significant prediction models. Rezaee [12] explained causes and consequences of financial statement and discussed fraud prevention and detection strategies theoretically. Phua et al. [13] analyzed the fraud detection studies for defining the adversary, the types and subtypes of fraud, the technical nature of data, performance metrics, and the methods and techniques. Omar et al. [14] proposed M-Score, Beneish Model, and Z-Score based ratio analysis for detecting fraud in small market cap companies.

Several learning algorithms and other data mining techniques are used to develop classification models; the learned patterns are then used to predict unlabeled testing data sets. Bai et al. [15] used Classification and Regression Tree (CART) statistical technique for identifying and predicting the impacts of false financial statements in China stock market and the findings obtained from CART were also compared with Logit regression. They concluded that CART model achieved better accuracy in identifying fraud cases and making predictions. Pai et al. [16] integrated sequential forward selection (SFS), support vector machines (SVM), and CART for reducing unnecessary information, detecting fraudulent financial statements and providing optimum resource allocation. The features used in the study were leverage, liquidity, efficiency, corporate governance and probability features which were also divided into several related sub features. Amara et al. [17] analyzed the theoretical foundations of fraud in the financial statements and the impact of the elements of "fraud triangle" on the detection of fraud in the financial statements. Logistic regression was used for the empirical model. The variables of the logistic regression model in this study were ratios of current assets to current liabilities, income before extraordinary items to total assets and the number of outside directors to the total number of directors. Wuerges and Borba [18] used logit and probit models for estimating frauds in US companies. Factor analysis was performed for classifying the companies accused of fraud by the Securities and Exchange Commission (SEC). Kotsiantis et al. [19] designed an artificial neural network (ANN) model) to predict fraudulent financial statements and corporate bankruptcy. Fraud and non-fraud Greek firms in the recent period 2001-2002 were used for training ANNs in the first part. Failed and solvent Greek firms in the recent period 2003-2004 were used for training ANNs in the second part. The main research variable categories in the study are profitability variables, liquidity/leverage variables, efficiency variables, growth variables and the size variable.

Based on these related research, this paper presents such a research aiming at classifying financially true and false statements of Turkish firms with the help of financial ratios which are important for the audit process. Audit opinions are used as the basic criteria to divide financial statements as financially false or correct. Decision tree, logistic regression, and artificial neural network are employed for the detection process.

2. Methodology
2.1. Term dataset
The term dataset covers firms listed on Borsa İstanbul and the period from 2009 to 2013. The dataset for classification was constructed by categorizing the firms into two, as the firms with financially correct statements which have received unmodified opinion (coded as 1) and the firms with financially false statements which have not received unmodified opinion (coded as 0)[1]. For

the selected term to collect data, only 110 records could be classified in the risky class coded as 1 (Table 1), then to make a balanced dataset for classification 114 additional records having successful audit reports were added to the dataset to form the entire dataset and conduct the analyses. Financial statements were collected from Finnet (an online platform providing financial data), and related indicators were then calculated.

Table 1. Frequency of audit opinions of firms with financially false statements.

Type of Audit Opinion	Frequency
Qualified Opinion	97
Disclaimer of Opinion	13
Adverse Opinion	0
Total	**110**

2.2. Variables
The below-mentioned ratios are a new mix inspired by the previous studies [2, 20] which emphasized the distinctive characteristics of these ratios to detect a potentially falsified statement. Referring to those studies, 13 variables are chosen as possible indicators of financially false statements, i.e. Net Working Capital/Total Assets, Retained Earnings/Total Assets, Earnings Before Interest and Taxes/Total Assets, Net Sales/Total Assets, Total Debt/Total Equity, Net Profits After Taxes/Net Sales, Receivables/Net Sales, Net Profits After Taxes/Total Assets, Gross Profit/Total Assets, Inventory/Total Assets, Total Debt/Total Assets, Market Value of Equity/Book Value of Debt, Z-Score.

Net working capital/Total assets (R1): Net Working Capital is calculated by taking the difference between current assets and current liabilities. The difference is divided by Total Assets.

Retained earnings/Total assets (R2): Retained Earnings is not shown as one specific amount in Turkish financial statements, contrarily it is shown by two indicators: previous year's losses if the firm had a loss, previous year's profits if the firm had profit. The related amount is divided by total asset value of the companies.

Earnings before Interest and taxes/Total assets (R3): Since Turkish financial statements are having some differences with international financial statements; operating profit value is used as an indicator of Earnings before Interest and Taxes. This amount is divided by total asset value.

Net sales/Total assets (R4): Net sales values is used instead of gross sales value to show the exact sales amount of the companies. Net sales ratio is calculated by subtracting the sales returns and

---

[1] Although according to the definitions of International Standards on Auditing, adverse opinion is the best indicator of financially false statements, none of the firms received adverse opinion during the analysis period. Thus, the firms which received qualified opinion and disclaimer of opinion were included into the dataset.

allowances from gross sales. The calculated amount is divided by total assets.

Total debt/Total equity (R5): It is a capital structure indicator. Total debt value (current liabilities and long-term liabilities) is divided by total equity value.

Net profits after taxes/Net sales (R6): It is a profitability indicator. Net Profit or loss is divided by net sales value.

Receivables/Net sales (R7): It shows sales in credit. Only trade sales are considered since they are directly related to operations of the firm. Both short and long-term trade receivables are taken into consideration. The total is divided by net sales.

Net profits after taxes/Total assets (R8): It is a profitability indicator. Also referred as Return on Assets. Net profit or loss is divided by total assets.

Gross profit/Total assets (R9): This profitability indicator also gives information about asset profitability. Gross profit is divided by total asset value.

Inventory/Total assets (R10): This indicator shows the ability of the firm to convert its inventory into sales. Inventory is divided by total asset value.

Total debt/Total assets (R11): It is another indicator of debt/capital structure and shows how much of the assets are financed by external funds. Total debt amount is divided by total asset value.

Market value of equity/Book value of total debt (R12): It shows how much the firm's assets can decline in value before the liabilities exceed the assets and the firm faces with insolvency.

Z-Score: It is an insolvency indicator used firstly by [21].

Z=1.2*(Net Working Capital/Total Assets) +1.4*(Retained Earnings/Total Assets) + 3.3*(Earnings Before Interest and Taxes/Total Assets+0.06*(Market Value of Equity/Book Value of Total Debt) +1.0*(Net Sales/Total Assets).

2.3. Classification algorithms used in analysis

Classification techniques are used to predict a particular output based on defined set of input variables or attributes. The attribute that is supposed to be predicted is defined as a class label or attribute. Data set covers the class labels and other attributes that are assumed to have an impact on the selected class label.

There exist many classification algorithms adopting supervised learning that have been developed for different data types and purposes. In general, a classification algorithm processes a training set including a set of attributes and the corresponding output, i.e., the class attribute, generally called prediction attribute. The selected algorithm tries to find out relationships between the attributes that would provide predictions for the outcome through the training set. In the next phase, the learned relationships are applied a test set that includes the same attributes, except for the class attribute, and therefore, predictions are generated [22]. Finally, those predictions are compared with the real class values to analyze the performance of the algorithm through a test set. Performance levels depend on both the structure of algorithms and their parameter values. Performances are measured on the confusion matrix by many formulations, e.g., accuracy, precision, recall, f-measure, Kappa statistics, and so forth [23].

From the financial perspective, classification techniques can classify a firm as low, medium, or high risky category based on a set of attributes related to financial statements and movements [20]. In this study, similarly, particular classification algorithms are used for predicting financially false statements through financial ratios. Financial statements of the firms in the data set are classified as true or false and then this attribute is labeled as a class attribute for the analysis phase. Among the common classification algorithms, artificial neural network, logistic regression, and decision tree are selected for classifying the firm's financial statement.

Decision tree algorithms work based on a divide-and-conquer approach to classifying a target attribute by seeking an attribute at each stage to split on that best separates the classes; then recursively processing the following branches that result from the split. This algorithm generates a decision tree, which can be converted into a set of classification rules. Decision tree classification method is an effective method due to its simplicity in understanding and interpreting. ID3 and C 4.5 or 5.0 are the most common algorithms of decision tree induction [24].

Logistic regression builds a linear model based on a transformed output variable, i.e. target class or class attribute. Logistic regression is used for binary classification problems where the target class consists of only two values such as yes/no, true/false, 0/1. It is also possible to obtain multiple classes by executing this model for each class. Suppose that there are only two classes. Logistic regression replaces the original target variable which cannot be approximated accurately using a linear function, with a log transformation of odd ratio. The resulting values are no longer constrained to the interval from 0 to 1 but can lie anywhere between negative infinity and positive infinity. These values are converted into the desired interval using logit transformation. The final model is obtained by using maximization of log-likelihood via a standard optimization approach. Once the parameters have been learned, then these parameters are used to predict the class values in testing dataset [25].

Artificial Neural Networks (ANNs) are computing technology whose fundamental purpose is to recognize patterns in data. Based on a computing model, ANNs use the simulated brain's ability to learn or adapt in response to external inputs. When exposed to a stream of training data, neural networks can discover previously, unknown relationships and learn complex nonlinear mappings in the data. ANNs behave like a black box, in other words, it is difficult to understand the inside of the network. Each arc has a weight, and these weights are summed up in each layer considering a particular policy for propagation. These networks are iteratively improved until they reach a state where the error term is minimum [26]. Parameters are assigned to the inputs of the neurons; the output of the neuron is a nonlinear combination of the inputs, weighted by the parameters similar to the synaptic weights of biological neurons. Calculations are often performed based on the weighted sum of inputs and parameters plus a constant called bias.

Execution of a neural network is initialized by activation, and this can only happen when the other neurons are activated through the edges that are connected to it. The neurons within a neural network are usually arranged in layers. The number of layers, number of neurons in each layer, learning rate, momentum values are important parameters for the design of such networks. Neural networks and related data mining algorithms are widely used for financial applications. Predicting fraudulent credit transactions, interest rates, and exchange rate fluctuations in currency markets, bankruptcy; managing portfolios; assessing risks [27].

2.4. The application platform

The classification model development and implementation were performed using RapidMiner Studio 6.4, i.e. an open-source data mining tool, based on the data and variable set. The selected parameters of each classifier were optimized by embedding the model into "optimize parameters" operator. This operator is a collapsed process in which a set of parameters in a wide range can be tested iteratively to discover the best ones. Figure 1 explains the general flow of the modeling process.

Decision tree method embedded into RapidMiner is similar to C 4.5. In each node, the split variable is selected by iterating all variables for finding the best split for each variable with respect to the splitting criterion. Finally, the method uses the variable that maximizes the criterion and continues until all branches end up with a class decision. For nominal variables, one branch for each value is created whereas for numerical attributes a binary split is performed to achieve the best split value by trying all possible values in the training set. Pre-pruning conditions can be used and considered during the splitting period, and then optionally post-pruning can also be added to improve the structure of the tree.

In this research, the decision tree was executed at different pruning levels, and the tree that has given the best performance was selected. Then linear and quadratic logistic regression models were run comparatively, and the linear model was found to have higher performance. As the last classification algorithm, the artificial neural network model was executed based on the optimized values for its two important parameters, i.e., learning rate and momentum. Thus, the predictions having the highest performance were tried to obtain based on the given input set. Finally, these results were compared to indicate the method that gave the better results. For all of the learning algorithms, training, and testing datasets were determined based on 10-fold cross validation.

3. Analysis and results

The current status of the firm categories in the data set was compared regarding their ratios to see the preliminary differences between them. Table 2 illustrates the mean values of the variables both for firms with financially false and correct statements separately. It is remarkable that all profit related variables of the statements that could not have an unmodified opinion (coded as 0) are negative except gross profit/total asset ratio, conversely all have positive values for the statements having an unmodified opinion (coded as 1).

The other striking point is debt-related ratios: Net working capital/total assets, total debt/total equity and market value of equity/book value of debt.

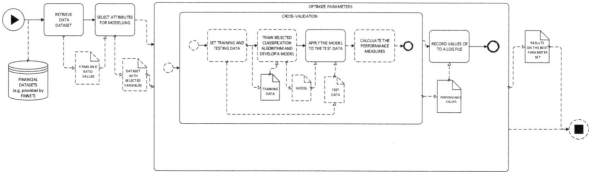

Figure 1. General flow of modelling process.

Table 2. Mean values of the variables.

Ratio Definition		Class-0 (mean)	Class-1 (mean)
Net Working Capital/Total Assets	R1	-0,34418	0,200973
Retained Earnings/Total Assets	R2	-1,19817	0,037748
Earnings Before Interest and Taxes/Total Assets	R3	-0,02042	0,056646
Net Sales/Total Assets	R4	0,603963	0,953397
Total Debt/Total Equity	R5	3,191075	1,835819
Net Profits After Taxes/Net Sales	R6	-0,25488	0,162205
Receivables/Net Sales	R7	0,496203	0,249811
Net Profits After Taxes/Total Assets	R8	0,006841	0,032273
Gross Profit/Total Assets	R9	0,098115	0,183753
Inventory/Total Assets	R10	0,093032	0,14989
Total Debt/Total Assets	R11	0,922455	0,472218
Market Value of Equity/Book Value of Debt	R12	1,823368	5,322425
Z-Score		-1,44449	1,753689

The first one is negative for the class-0 by contrast with the class-1, showing current liabilities exceed current assets; according to the second one both classes are predominantly financed with debt instead of equity, but the class-0 relies on debt more; because of the second debt related ratio and most probably high stock prices of the companies, the class-1 has extremely high market value of equity/book value of debt ratio. Finally, the Z-score is negative for the class-0 and on the other hand positive for the class-1.

In the light of these distinctive indicators, the selected firms were classified with the help of above-mentioned classification techniques in data mining and a general classification modeling scheme was developed for this purpose. The classification process started with a training set to learn the pattern in the dataset in the first partition within a validation operator, therefore, the learned pattern was applied to the testing set and the selected performance indicators, i.e. accuracy, f-measure, area under ROC curve, were calculated using the related performance indicators (Figure 1). Training and testing steps were embedded in 10-fold cross-validation, and for the training part, the classifier related to the classification method

was placed where each training group was selected with respect to stratified sampling.

In this regard, the decision tree algorithm was firstly executed at different pruning levels, and the tree that has given the best performance was selected. The overall accuracy rate of this classifier was calculated as 82.5% with a tolerance value where the f-measure is 78.22%. The AUC gave values that are close to "1". These performance measures (see Table 3) indicate a good prediction model. Especially the accuracy values close to one may imply an overestimation where low values, generally less than fifty percent, imply underestimation. The differences in performances of the classes were also measured by using recall and precision measures. These measures in class-1 were greater than the same values in class 0, indicating that the decision tree model could predict true class-1 better than class-0.

Appendix 1 presents the decision tree indicating the important attributes that have higher impact on the false statements. According to this tree, Z-score is the most important attribute to distinct true and false statements. In the second level, from the top edge of the tree, R11 (Total Debt/Total Assets), then R2 (Retained Earnings/ Total Assets), R8 (Net Profits After Taxes/ Total Assets), R1 (Net Working Capital/ Total Assets) and R7 (Receivables/Net Sales) are the important factors on the decomposition at the successive levels of the tree as well, respectively. Some conditional statements can be generated by following the branches given in the decision tree[2]. For the same dataset, linear and quadratic logistic regression models were executed and reported comparatively. Parameter optimization process was performed based on kernel-type and kernel-gamma parameters, i.e., important parameters of logistic regression.

---

[2] For example, "if z-score < 0.368 and R11 < 0.198 and R2 > -1.261, then the statement is true" (Appendix 1).

Table 3. Results based on the selected performance measures.

Classification Model		true Class-1	true Class-0	class precision	Accuracy	AUC	f_measure
Decision Tree	pred. Class-1	102	30	77.27%	82.25% +/- 9.78%	0.984	78.22% +/- 12.03%
	pred. Class-0	8	74	90.24%			
	class recall	92.73%	71.15%				
Logistic Regression	pred. Class-1	102	30	77.27%	82.34% +/- 7.45%	0.870 +/- 0.066	79.41% +/- 8.90%
	pred. Class-0	8	74	90.24%			
	class recall	92.73%	69.23%				
Artificial Neural Network with one hidden layer	pred. Class-1	99	25	79.84%	83.29% +/- 7.89%	0.874 +/- 0.089	80.96% +/- 10.34%
	pred. Class-0	11	79	87.78%			
	class recall	90.00%	75.96%				

Finally, the linear model was found to have higher performance. As implemented in the model based on the decision tree, training, and testing steps were embedded in the cross-validation operator in which the logistic regression operator was placed as a classifier in the training partition (Figure 1). Similar results were obtained from the linear logistic regression model as indicated in Table 3Error! Reference source not found.. The accuracy of the model was obtained as 82.34% with some tolerance and f-measure was 79.41% which is also close the results obtained from decision tree, however, AUC on logistic regression is worse than AUC calculated on the decision tree. These values could be observed a bit above the values of the decision tree model. Logistic regression could detect two more false statements. However, logistic regression model underestimated false statements (class-0) if compared with the performance of the true (class-1) statements. Appendix 3Error! Reference source not found. gives the weights of the variables in the logistic regression model to predict future values. As seen from this list, z-score has the highest effect on the classification; R2, R1, and R8 are the other attributes following the Z-score.

As the last classifier, ANNs model was executed based on the values for its three important parameters (learning rate, the number of learning cycles, and momentum). The infrastructure of the model was developed in a similar manner to the models presented in the previous sections, only the classifier operator and related parameters change (Figure 1). The related ANN algorithm was executed on the normalized dataset via the optimized number of training cycles, learning rate, and momentum with sigmoid function and one hidden layer to use for predictions. This classifier with one layer ended up with a better performance than multiple hidden layers. Thus, only the findings of the one-layer model were presented. The best performance was obtained via learning rate=0.14; momentum=0.22 with 170 training cycles. Table 3Error! Reference source not found. shows the performance level and parameter set of improved neural network with the same metrics. It can be inferred from the table that both class recall and precision values were improved and balanced. The ANNs model which predicted "false" statements through the selected attributes or variables resulted in more than 80% accuracy which means that a correct prediction with a relatively higher probability is possible by adopting this classifier. The details about the neural network model, network scheme, and numerical values on neurons and edges are given in Appendix 2 for prediction. Each column of this table corresponds to weight list of the arcs incoming from the input layer to the hidden layer or outgoing from the hidden layer to the output layer. Weighted sums plus bias value activates the further phases until the network achieves a class value.

Gray and Deprecency [20] investigated the use of data mining techniques to classify firms with respect to their statements and proposed a taxonomy to detect manipulations. Data mining targets in the audit environment were tabulated according to data classes, target datasets, signaling, data types, semantic representations, and score. Data mining applications were classified according to account scheme and evidence scheme combinations. At the last phase of that study, fraud and evidence schemes and application of data mining were integrated into a relationship matrix. In the light of Gray and Deprecency [20], our study performed particular classification methods in data mining to the term dataset gathered from Borsa Istanbul by evaluating their suggestion and also considering additional ratios used in the previous studies.

Spatis [2] applied only logistic regression on the relatively smaller dataset and analyzed firms with and without Z-score to show the effect of this indicator. The study also compared the impact of the ratios with the previous studies. Our analyses produced the results compatible with this study providing that z-score is very distinctive to detect falsified financial record. Furthermore, our study applied additional classification methods with additional ratios in order to present the comparative performances of different methods. Bai et al. [15] compared CART and Logit Regression methods and found that CART gave better results for fraud detection. Pai et al. [16] compared over data mining techniques on eighteen financial ratios and obtained different model accuracies lying between 73% and 92%. Our findings and the findings of the previous studies revealed that the performance of the model is very dependent on the data set, the selected algorithm, and the variables, i.e. selected financial ratios.

4. Conclusion and policy implications

Fraud on falsified financial statements got firms into a scrape during auditing processes. This potential negative situation has a critical impact on the auditing process and increases the stress on auditors because of the responsibility to reveal the situation over the financial records and statements. Although the related auditing standards try to make the process easier by defining undesired manipulations (red flags) that can be performed by firms, additional decision support tools are necessary to detect these negative situations efficiently and immediately. There exist many studies as mentioned in "the related work" section proposing various approaches and case studies which benefitted from data mining techniques in order to detect false statements over the particular financial indicators such as ratios through the selected classification techniques.

In this context, this paper presented research that aims at classifying financially true and false statements with the help of financial ratios which are important indicators for the auditors through particular classification techniques in data mining. The analysis was conducted on the group of 214 records gathered from 136 different Turkish firms listed on Borsa İstanbul for the period between 2009 and 2013. The dataset for classification was constructed by categorizing the firms into two, as the firms with financially correct statements which have received unmodified opinion (coded as 1) and the firms with financially false statements which have not received unmodified opinion (coded as 0). For the selected term to collect data, only 110 records could be classified in the risky class coded as 1, then to make a balanced dataset for classification 114 additional records having successful audit reports were added to the dataset in order to form the entire dataset. Although the adverse opinion is the best indicator of financially false statements, none of the firms received adverse opinion during the analysis period. Thus, the firms which received qualified opinion and disclaimer of opinion were included in the dataset.

This study originally combined distinctive financial ratios that were handled in the previous studies and analyzed as a whole through the selected classification methods. Twelve financial ratios and one combination of financial ratios were calculated from the firms' balance sheets and income statements to construct the dataset for the classification process: Net Working Capital/Total Assets, Retained Earnings/Total Assets, Earnings before Interest and Taxes/Total Assets, Net Sales/Total Assets, Total Debt/Total Equity, Net Profits after Taxes/Net Sales, Receivables/Net Sales, Net Profits after Taxes/Total Assets, Gross Profit/Total Assets, Inventory/Total Assets, Total Debt/Total Assets, Market Value of Equity/Book Value of Total Debt, and Z-Score.

For the purpose of indicating the difference between the record groups in terms of the selected ratios, class means were calculated and based on these preliminary results, a valuable finding was obtained over debt ratios, i.e. net working-capital/total assets, total debt/total equity and market value of equity/book value of debt. The first one was negative for the class-0 by contrast with the class-1, showing current liabilities exceeded current assets; according to the second one both classes were predominantly financed with debt instead of equity, but the class-0 relied on debt more. Because of the second debt related ratio and most probably high stock prices of the companies, the class-1 had an extremely high market value of equity/book value of debt ratio. In addition to the findings on the debt ratios, another important point was that the Z-score was negative for the class-0 and positive for the class-1. These results were the preliminary signs of the distinctive characteristics of the selected ratios used for classification.

The classification model development and implementation were performed by using RapidMiner 6.4. The parameters of each classifier were optimized through its "optimize parameters" operator to obtain the best prediction model on the classifier for the given dataset. The classification process started with a training set to learn the pattern in the dataset; therefore, the learned pattern was applied to the testing set and the selected performance indicators. Training and testing stages were carried out over 10-fold cross validation where ten training data were selected in each iteration with respect to stratified sampling and trained through the selected classifier and then tested on the selected test data. In this regard, decision tree, logistic regression, and artificial neural networks were employed for the classification process. The results indicated that the artificial neural network had the highest prediction accuracy. Furthermore, Z-score which is a combination of different financial ratios is a better indicator to classify financially false or correct statements than the individual ratios. Thus, auditors might start using this kind of ratio combinations while they are auditing the financial statements of the companies.

Consecutively, this paper presented a study that developed a classification modeling framework for categorizing the selected Turkish firms' financial statements as "correct" or "incorrect" regarding their financial indicators in order to use the framework for predicting the status of new firms or upcoming statements of the existing firms. The optimized values of the parameters and the performance of the selected classifiers may change depending on the data set and the selected financial indicators. The main idea is developing such a decision support system for auditors to provide some clues for a potential manipulation before inspecting the other accounting data in detail. Various classifiers can easily be added to the modeling framework to extend the scope of classification process, and even non-experts can use it as a reference by only changing the dataset.

References

[1] IAASB. (2015). Handbook of International Quality Control, Auditing, Review, Other Assurance, and Related Services Pronouncements, The International Auditing and Assurance Standards Board (IAASB).

[2] Spathis, C. T. (2002). Detecting false financial statements using published data: some evidence from Greece. *Managerial Auditing Journal*, *17*(4), 179-191.

[3] Worthy, F. S. (1984). Manipulating profits: how is it done? Fortune, 25, 50-54.

[4] Comer, J. M. (1998). Corporate Fraud (3 ed.). Aldershot: Gower.

[5] AICPA. (2016, 01 15). Statements on Auditing Standards. Retrieved from AICPA: www.aicpa.org/Research/Standards/AuditAttest/Pages/SAS.aspx

[6] Kovalerchuck, B., & Vityaev, E. (2000). Data Mining in Finance: Advances in Relational and Hybrid Methods. Norwell, Massachusetts: Kluwer Academic Publishers, ISBN 0-7923- 7804-0.

[7] Dhar, V. (1998). Data Mining In Finance: Using Counterfactuals To Generate Knowledge From Organizational Information Systems. Information Systems, 23(7), 423-437.

[8] Koyuncugil, A. S., & Ozgulbas, N. (2012). Financial Early Warning System Model and data mining application for risk detection. Expert Systems with Applications, 39, 6238–6253.

[9] Zhou, L., Lu, D., & Fujita, H. (2015). The performance of corporate financial distress prediction models with feature selection guided by domain knowledge and data mining approaches. Knowledge-Based Systems, 85, 52–61

[10] Zhang, L., Zhang, L., Teng, W., & Chen, Y. (2013). Based on information fusion technique with data mining in the application of finance early-warning. Procedia Computer Science, 17, 695 – 703. doi:10.1016/j.procs.2013.05.090

[11] Liu, M. (2004). A data mining method for forecasting financial distress of Chinese listed companies. Proceedings of The 2004 International Conference on Management Science & Engineering (pp. 370-374). , Harbin, Peoples R China, Vol: 1- 2.

[12] Rezaee, Z. (2005). Causes, consequences, and deterrence of financial statement fraud. Critical Perspectives on Accounting, 16(3), 277-298.

[13] Phua, C., Lee, V., Smith, K., & Gayler, R. (2010). A comprehensive survey of data mining-based fraud detection research. arXiv preprint arXiv:1009.6119.

[14] Omar, N., Sanusi, Z. M., Johari, A., & Mohamed, I. S. (2014). Predicting financial stress and earning management using ratio analysis. Predicting financial stress and earning management using ratio analysis, 8(8), Predicting financial stress and earning management using ratio analysis.

[15] Bai, B., Yen, J., & Yang, X. (2008). False financial statements: characteristics of China's listed companies and CART detecting approach. International Journal of Information Technology & Decision making, 7(2), 339-359.

[16] Pai, P. F., Hsu, M. F., & Wang, M. C. (2011). A support vector machine-based model for detecting top management fraud. Knowledge-Based System, 24(2), 314-321.

[17] Amara, I., Amar, A. B., & Jarboui, A. (2013). Detection of fraud in financial statements: french companies as a case study. International Journal of Academic Research in Accounting, Finance and Management Sciences, 3(3), 40-51.

[18] Wuerges, A. F., & Borba, J. A. (2011). Accounting Fraud: an estimation of detection probability.

[19] Kotsiantis, S., Koumanakos, E., Tzelepis, D., & Tampakas, V. (2006). Financial application of neural networks: two case studies in Greece. Artificial Neural Networks–ICANN 2006 (pp. 672-681). Springer Berlin Heidelberg.

[20] Gray, G. L., & Debreceny, R. S. (2014). A taxonomy to guide research on the application of data mining to fraud detection in financial statement audits.

International Journal of Accounting Information Systems, 15(4), 357-380.

[21] Altman, E. I. (1968). Financial ratios, discriminant analysis and the prediction of corporate bankruptcy. The Journal of Finance, 23(7), 423-437.

[22] Witten, I. H., & Frank, E. (2005). Data Mining: Practical machine learning tools and techniques. Morgan Kaufmann.

[23] Han, J., & Kamber, M. (2006). Data Mining: Concepts and Techniques. Data Mining: Concepts and Techniques.

[24] Siciliano, R., & Conversano, C. (2006). Decision tree induction. In J. Wang, Encyclopedia of Data Warehousing and Mining (p. 353). Idea Group, USA.

[25] Panik, M. (2009). Regression Modeling Methods, Theory, and Computation with SAS. CRC Press.

[26] Dreyfus, G. (2005). Neural Networks: An Overview. In Neural Networks (pp. 1-83). Springer Berlin Heidelberg.

[27] Bigus, J. P. (1996). Data Mining with Neural Networks: Solving Business Problems from Application Development to Decision Support. McGraw-Hill, Inc.

Appendix 1: Decision Tree Representation

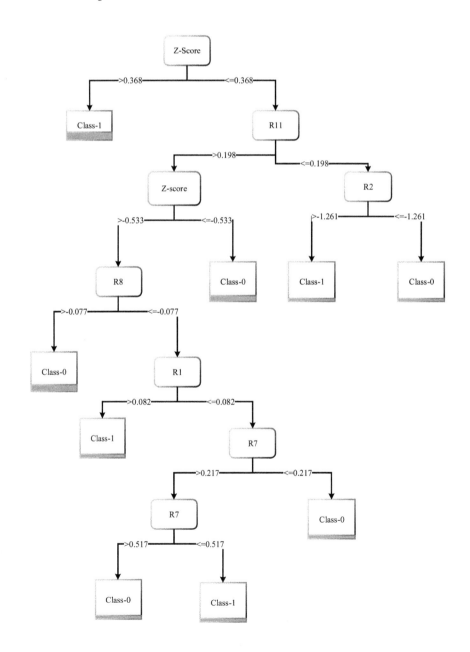

Appendix 2: Weights on the Arcs of the ANN

HIDDEN LAYER

Node 1 (Sigmoid)	Node 2 (Sigmoid)	Node 3 (Sigmoid)	Node 4 (Sigmoid)	Node 5 (Sigmoid)
R1: -0.902	R1: 1.665	R1: 0.666	R1: 0.369	R1: -1.333
R2: -1.431	R2: 3.214	R2: 1.253	R2: 0.792	R2: -5.081
R3: 0.545	R3: -0.052	R3: 0.082	R3: 0.062	R3: -3.527
R4: 0.064	R4: 0.273	R4: 0.375	R4: 0.342	R4: -1.590
R5: -0.139	R5: 0.694	R5: 0.353	R5: 0.243	R5: -0.357
R6: -0.279	R6: 0.932	R6: 0.591	R6: 0.446	R6: -1.214
R7: -0.321	R7: 0.761	R7: 0.571	R7: 0.429	R7: 0.894
R8: 0.053	R8: 0.282	R8: 0.299	R8: 0.248	R8: 0.244
R9: 0.066	R9: 0.480	R9: 0.239	R9: 0.176	R9: -2.091
R10: 0.273	R10: 0.182	R10: -0.444	R10: -0.110	R10: -2.599
R11: 0.626	R11: -1.031	R11: -0.379	R11: -0.240	R11: 0.724
R12: -0.599	R12: 1.825	R12: 1.044	R12: 0.739	R12: -2.182
Z Score: -1.326	Z Score: 3.185	Z Score: 1.420	Z Score: 0.955	Z Score: -4.727
Bias: 0.472	Bias: -1.506	Bias: -0.784	Bias: -0.581	Bias: 1.884

	HIDDEN LAYER			OUTPUT LAYER	
Node 6 (Sigmoid)	Node 7 (Sigmoid)	Node 8 (Sigmoid)	Node 9 (Sigmoid)	Class '1.0' (Sigmoid)	Class '0.0' (Sigmoid)
R1: -1.534	R1: -0.077	R1: 1.601	R1: -0.988	Node 1: -1.287	Node 1: 1.245
R2: -2.797	R2: 0.029	R2: 3.066	R2: -1.614	Node 2: 1.870	Node 2: -1.867
R3: 0.438	R3: 0.088	R3: -0.026	R3: 0.408	Node 3: 0.828	Node 3: -0.793
R4: 0.026	R4: 0.335	R4: 0.271	R4: -0.016	Node 4: 0.529	Node 4: -0.498
R5: -0.614	R5: 0.196	R5: 0.731	R5: -0.167	Node 5: -4.113	Node 5: 4.100
R6: -0.681	R6: 0.218	R6: 0.936	R6: -0.367	Node 6: -2.082	Node 6: 2.129
R7: -0.536	R7: 0.313	R7: 0.757	R7: -0.226	Node 7: -0.027	Node 7: 0.020
R8: -0.150	R8: 0.217	R8: 0.297	R8: -0.048	Node 8: 1.772	Node 8: -1.787
R9: -0.191	R9: 0.184	R9: 0.469	R9: -0.036	Node 9: -1.322	Node 9: 1.379
R10: -0.013	R10: 0.176	R10: 0.171	R10: 0.161	Threshold: -0.606	Threshold: 0.583
R11: 0.934	R11: 0.149	R11: -0.999	R11: 0.620		
R12: -1.344	R12: 0.402	R12: 1.688	R12: -0.717		
Z Score: -2.641	Z Score: 0.229	Z Score: 3.089	Z Score: -1.500		

Appendix 3: Coefficients of the Linear Logistic Regression Model

Bias (offset): 0.779

Weight	Value	Weight	Value
w[R1]	-1.163	w[R7]	0.163
w[R2]	-1.522	w[R8]	0.846
w[R3]	-0.446	w[R9]	-0.160
w[R4]	-0.138	w[R10]	0.265
w[R5]	-0.012	w[R11]	-0.029
w[R6]	-0.234	w[R12]	-1.576

5

A New Ontology-Based Approach for Human Activity Recognition from GPS Data

A. Mousavi[1*], A. Sheikh Mohammad zadeh[2], M. Akbari[3] and A. Hunter[1]

1. Department of Geomatics, University of Calgary, Calgary, Canada.
2. Department of Geomatics, Civil Engineering Faculty, Shahid Rajaee Teacher Training University, Tehran, Iran.
3. Department of Civil Engineering, University of Birjand, Birjand, Iran.

*Corresponding author: mousavia@ucalgary.ca (A. Mousavi).

Abstract
Mobile technologies have deployed a variety of internet-based services via location-based services. The adoption of these services by users has led to mammoth amounts of trajectory data. To use these services effectively, the analysis of this kind of data across different application domains is required in order to identify the activities that users might need to do in different places. Researchers from different communities have developed models and techniques to extract activity types from such data but they have mainly focused on the geometric properties of trajectories, and do not consider the semantic aspect of moving objects. The current work proposes a new ontology-based approach so as to recognize human activity from GPS data for understanding and interpreting mobility data. The performance of the approach was tested and evaluated using a dataset acquired by a user over a year within the urban area in the city of Calgary in 2010. It was observed that the accuracy of the results obtained was related to the availability of the points of interest around the places that the user had stopped. Moreover, an evaluation experiment was carried out, which revealed the effectiveness of the proposed method with an improvement of 50% performance with complexity trend of an O(n).

Keywords: Ontology, Data Mining, Activity Recognition, Semantic, GPS.

1. Introduction
The development of location technologies in mobile devices and wireless communication has led to deploying a variety of internet-based services such as Location-Based Services (LBS) [1]. The application domain for these types of services are typically transportation management, location-aware advertising, and tourism [2]. The widespread use of these applications and services in our daily activities has led to a large number of positioning data that can be represented as trajectories [3]. Moreover, spatially distributed networked systems with thousands of energy- and resource-limited mobile devices (i.e. "thin" devices, e.g. smartphones, PDAs, tablets, RFIDs), all capable of acquiring and communicating in real time, cause an ever-increasing volume of heterogeneous data streams [4]. With such an increase in the trajectory data, there is a need for improving the existing methods to efficiently handle and investigate user activity types out of such a large amount of data. In this regard, some researchers have investigated some analytical techniques [5,6] and computational methods [7,8,9] for the analysis of movement data; yet, they mainly concentrate on the study of the geometric view of raw trajectory data and do not consider the semantic aspect of moving objects. Therefore, the extracted patterns are classified based on a set of geometric properties. For example, when considering only the geometric properties, one could discover a dense area where trajectories meet. However, without semantics, it is hard to find out why the trajectories meet, and consequently, what might attract the users. Furthermore, mined results can be made more meaningful when the nature of movement data is considered as a context within the recognition process [3]. Geographic data recognized as

context can provide the possibility of activity identification based on GPS trajectories. Therefore, trajectory data is required to be reconsidered not only from the geometric view but also from the meaningful semantic view in order to interpret and understand their meanings.

The main idea of this paper is to propose a new ontology-based approach to recognize human activity types by considering ontology in order to explore and interpret the extracted semantic patterns. This study investigates various extracted features and background information based on the model ontology to extract different activity types. To accomplish this, it is required to define a semantic conceptual data model and a number of computing techniques to integrate various sources of data and reconstruct meaningful trajectories from the movement data. The remainder of the paper is organized as what follows. Section 2 presents a summary of various research studies in particular studies on analyzing mobility data. Section 3 describes the proposed methodology and illustrates each component. First the proposed conceptual data model is described in order to develop an ontology based model and then the activity recognition process is presented. Section 4 illustrates the experiment conducted on a dataset. Moreover, a summary of the results is presented and the implications of the evaluation outcomes are discussed. Finally, section 5 concludes the paper and describes the future research works regarding further developments.

2. Related works

Activity recognition studies usually use spatial distance-based and statistics-based methods. The basic idea of spatial distance-based method is to assign the closest POIs to the stops where activities have happened. Bohte et al. [10] have defined rules to restrict the candidate POIs and possible activity types, and then they have detected the POIs with the smallest distance to the activity centers in trajectories. Xie et al. [11] have proposed the influence and influence duration of POIs on trajectories. This method actually selects the POIs closest to the polyline geometry of the trajectory. Some researchers have extracted regular activity patterns in trajectories to identify the activity types. For instance, Huang and Li [12] have introduced a multivariate analysis approach to identify activities using vehicles trajectories. Time constraints, network distance, activity chains, and POIs were used as four inputs. Scores for candidate POIs were selected around the locations where vehicles stopped were calculated

using a neural network framework. Some works [13,14] used Markov networks to classify activities into six pre-defined types. This technique was an extension of the Markov networks for sequence matching. Moreover, Liao et al., in [15], have proposed machine learning and probabilistic reasoning methods in particular conditional random field method to identify daily activities using the GPS data.

Studies like Alvares et al. [16], Xie et al. [11], and Moreno et al. [17] have designed relevant spatiotemporal join methods to infer activities from trajectories by computing the topological relationships between the trajectory data and a small set of predefined activity hotspots together with the time constraints. Spinsanti et al. [18] have proposed a series of rules to detect the overall activity of the trajectory. Considering a trajectory whose stops are annotated with possible activities and common sense IF-THEN rules, the authors annotated the trajectory with the most probable global activity. A similar approach has been proposed by Renso et al. [19]. This work annotated trajectories with activities such as tourist, home-to-work commute using an ontology, and an inference engine.

The majority of the mentioned activity recognition works still have unresolved questions. The key idea of these approaches is to extract the location history of the individual, in conjunction with knowledge about the semantics of the locations, in order to infer the activity of a person. Therefore, they only discover the stops and moves of moving objects and annotate them with contextual data. However, it can still be difficult to identify the activity type of the moving object [20]. For instance, if two stops are identified for a moving object, one on a residential land use and the other on a commercial land use, it is difficult to determine whether the residential stop is the residence of the moving object or if the commercial stop is a work place. The moving object could, for example, be visiting a friend or shopping. To draw stronger inferences, one needs not only to identify stops but also extract some associated semantic features such as stop begin time, stop duration, and also stop frequency from the trajectory data.

3. Methodology

This section illustrates the proposed ontology-based approach to recognize human activity types. As depicted in figure 1, it consists of two main parts, namely semantic trajectory ontology modelling and activity recognition.

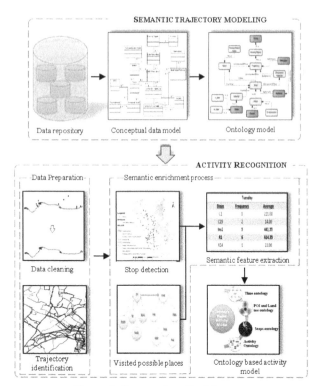

Figure 1. Proposed methodology.

The first part contains raw trajectory data, maps/layers, and an application domain. In this part, a conceptual data model is defined, and based on that, a semantic trajectory ontology model is designed. In the activity recognition step, first the raw trajectory data is cleaned and the trajectories are reconstructed. In the semantic enrichment process, stops are identified and annotated with the probable visited places. Next some semantic features are extracted from the annotated stops. Then the model ontology is populated with the extracted features and some predefined axioms. Finally, the ontology inference engine is executed and the axioms are interpreted to classify the ontology instances using the appropriate concepts on the activity types.

3.1. Semantic trajectory modelling
In this research work, an application was developed to gather the user's trajectory data [21]. The background knowledge database includes land use, road network, and POI layers.

3.1.1. A conceptual data model for semantic trajectories
Figure 2 describes a conceptual model that addresses the modelling requirements with the goal of analysis of semantic trajectory data. The aim of this model is to represent the concepts and relations of the movement domain, where the trajectory data and semantic movement patterns are to be interpreted along with the activity types.

This model is an extended version (green colored box) of the conceptual framework introduced in Spaccapietra et al. [22], which relies on the conceptualization of stops and moves in trajectories. The conceptual model contains information related to moving object, raw trajectory, sub-trajectory, semantic sub-trajectory, semantic trajectory, semantic place, stop, move, activity type, and behavior type.

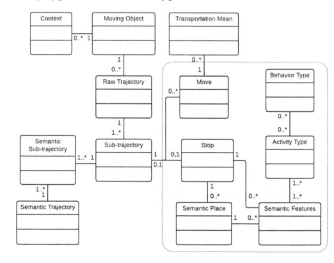

Figure 2. Extended conceptual model of semantic trajectory used in this work.

A moving object generates raw trajectory that, based on different criteria, can be divided into sub-trajectories. By giving meaning to these sub-trajectories, the semantic trajectory becomes a combination of different semantic sub-trajectories. Each sub-trajectory is composed of stops and moves. Every stop is connected to an interval that represents the time of the stop. It includes the start time and end time concepts, which anticipate when the trajectory starts and ends. Each stop, as shown in figure 2, could have different semantic features, as what follow.

Definition 1 (Semantic features): Semantic features are extracted from the stops, and are divided into five different types including stop frequency, average duration, stop land use type, stop POI category type, and stop start time.

Definition 2 (Semantic place): A semantic place consists of a set of positions where a stop is located. It includes land use type and POI type, which would cover environmental information related to a stop.

Definition 3 (Activity): An activity is what the moving objects are going to do during their movement. In other words, it is the objective of the movement, which has a start time and an end time, and it can be relative to the entire trajectory or part of the trajectory (the semantic sub-trajectory). Activities can be represented as taxonomy, from the more specific to the more general. It is classified into four different major activities including recreation, profession, shopping, and other activity types.

Profession activity types could be working, getting involved into different jobs, etc. Shopping refers to the time spent at different stores for buying food, drinks or groceries required, in general, for one's daily needs. Recreation might include going to the theatre, pub, gyms, and other places related to leisure. Other activity types might include relaxing at home, cultural or religious activities, etc.

The inference of the activity types is based on the semantic features. Activity types are highly influenced by the users' location. For instance, if a person is close to a university, the most probable activity types would be studying, teaching or working. In order to capture this dependency, first it is needed to model which activity types can be performed or hosted within or nearby every place (e.g. eating is possible in a restaurant, while shopping is possible in a mall). Therefore, there is an association between places and activity types and, according to the conceptual model, an activity is typically performed in a place.

For example, the restaurant is both a place for eating and a working place expressing the fact that a restaurant may be a kind of work place for people working there (the cook, the waiter, etc.) or a place to represent the fact that typically restaurants are attended by people for dining. Therefore, activity types are also correlated to time and, in particular, to the time of day and the duration that a user spends at each place. Different activity types might have different timetables and durations.

For instance, if the place is a restaurant, different time periods may be interpreted as different activity types. As an example, the period of 15 to 30 minutes would be interpreted as a delivery since there is not enough time to stay in and eat. If the time period is between 30 minutes and 3 hours, it would be interpreted as dining, and if the time period is between 3 hours and 8 hours, it would be interpreted as working.

Also stop frequency and average duration are important features to find out the type of activity. As a general example, if the stop frequency is more than five days a week and the average duration is more than eight hours, it could be inferred that the place would be either where the person works or lives. Therefore, this research work hypothesizes a functional relationship (1) for Activity Types (AT) based on different features, as shown below:

$$AT = f(P, L, S_f, T_b, S_d) \tag{1}$$

where:

- P is the POI type that is around the stop
- L is the land use type where the stop has occurred
- S_f is the frequency of the stop in a week
- T_b is the start time of the stop in the place
- S_d is the average duration of the stop in a week

For instance, for a specific stop, if the land use type is residential, the POI type is null, the begin time is evening, stop frequency per week is more than six, and the average duration is more than ten hours per week, then the moving object is 'spending time at home', i.e. AT= Return Home. At this step, some rules can be defined on the captured data in order to extract different activity types.

3.1.2. Semantic trajectory ontology model

Semantic Trajectory Ontology Model (STOM) is built based on the proposed conceptual data model. Figure 3 shows a very partial version of this ontology with only the most important concepts and relationships. Shapes represent the main concepts, whereas arrows represent relationships between two concepts.

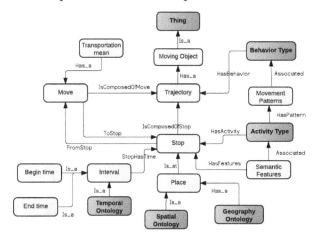

Figure 3. Semantic trajectory ontology model.

The main concepts of STOM are listed below:
- Moving object is a user object, who is equipped with an enabled-GPS device;
- Trajectory is a logical form to represent a set of stops and moves;
- Stop is the spatial part in trajectory ontology;
- Move is defined as the maximal subsequence between two consecutive stops;
- Place is a description of the location that user visited/stopped;

- Transportation mean refers to the type of transportations that objects use to move from one stop to another;
- Start time is the time when the activity starts, the time when user arrived at the location;
- End time is the time when the activity is finished, the time when the user leaves the location;
- Activity is the semantic part representing user activity types for a stop;
- Movement patterns are the regularities and common things that happen in the movement data;
- Behavior is a pattern among different activity types.

STOM consists of different ontologies such as spatial ontology, temporal ontology, geographic ontology, and thematic ontology. The spatial ontology holds generic concepts for the description of the geometric component of a trajectory. The temporal ontology is another source of information that integrates time concepts and rules for modelling semantic trajectories. OwlTime ontology [23], which is being developed by the World Wide Web Consortium (W3C) is chosen. Geographic ontology describes the places where people move through, and includes a variety of land use types, road networks, and POIs layer. POI represents the specific categories such as shopping center, park, etc. The road network represents the interconnections of different road types designed within urban areas. The land use represents different regions and their utilization such as agricultural, residential, recreational or other types. Therefore, this ontology is used to aid potential interpretation of each stop, i.e. why the moving object stopped. The thematic ontology model gathers a wide range of application-dependent concepts. The understanding of trajectories profoundly depends on their relationships to application objects and not just the moving object itself. The model describes the concept of activity type that includes the stop, trajectory, semantic features, movement patterns, activity type, and behavior type concepts. The activity type is composed of stops and their features. Therefore, integrating these ontologies together provides the semantic description of application-relevant trajectories with their domain specific semantic meaning. These ontologies are integrated into a unique ontology by setting up rules between them.

3.2. Activity recognition

As shown in figure 4, the activity recognition consists of three steps. The first step is the data preparation, where the GPS data is cleaned and the daily and weekly basis trajectories are identified. The second step is the semantic enrichment process, which includes stop detection, finding probable visited places and extracting semantic features. Once stops are detected, they are annotated with the POI and land use types. Next, several semantic features such as the stop start time, stop frequency, and average duration are extracted. The final step is the ontology-based activity model. The information retrieved from the previous steps is used to populate STOM for reasoning the activity type. Each step is explained in more details in the following sub-sections.

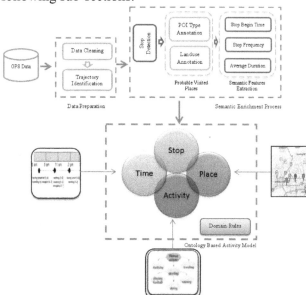

Figure 4. Activity recognition process.

3.2.1. Data preparation

Due to the problems in GPS data collection and sampling errors from mobile devices, the recorded positions usually contain errors [24]. Therefore, data has to be cleaned from any inconsistencies such as empty values, duplicates, and outliers. Moreover, in order to index the data, semantic indexing technique, introduced in [25], which is a suitable method for ontology data, was applied in this research work. Generally, this step helps eliminate unrealistic attributes such as trajectories with a travel time that is too short (e.g. 10 seconds duration) and also improbable speed (by defining thresholds). Next, trajectory identification is applied for dividing the cleaned GPS data into daily and weekly basis trajectories. Time constraint is used to identify these two types of trajectories.

3.2.2. Semantic enrichment process

The enrichment process aims at extracting stops from the cleansed trajectory data and annotating them with the environmental information around them, in particular, by exploiting nearby POIs and land use types.

3.2.2.1. Stop detection

As mentioned earlier, stops are the portion of trajectories where people stop for a given time duration and where it is assumed that they are performing activities. In this research work, the GPS data, which was collected by users using our application contains temporal gaps (the application was turned off automatically or manually when users did not move for a certain time or when they entered a building).

Therefore, considering the format of the GPS data, the TVB algorithm is used to extract stops. Algorithm 1 provides pseudo-code for determining stops. Given the speed threshold Δ_{speed} and time interval $\Delta_{duration}$, for any two consecutive GPS records $p_i(x_i, y_i, t_i)$ and $p_{i+1}(x_{i+1}, y_{i+1}, t_{i+1})$, if the speed of p is lower than Δ_{speed} and the temporal gap $t_{i+1} - t_i > \Delta_{duration}$, then p_i is the end point of the current trajectory, while p_{i+1} is the starting point of the next trajectory. Therefore, p_i is considered as a stop.

Algorithm 1. TVB

Input:
Cleaned raw trajectory $T_{raw} = \{p_1, p_2, ..., p_n\}$

Speed threshold Δ_{speed}

Time gap $\Delta_{duration}$

Output:
Stops $T_{stops} = \{s_1, s_2, ..., s_m\}$

1 *begin*
2   *for all* $p_i = (x_i, y_i, v_i, t_i)$ *do*
3   *if* $(v_i < \Delta_{speed} \ AND t_{i+1} - t_i > \Delta_{duration})$ *then*
4          $T_{stops} = p_i(x_i, y_i, t_i, t_{i+1}, \Delta_{duration})$
5   *return* T_{stops}
6 *end*

3.2.2.2. Probable visited places

The objective of this step is to find probable places that can be visited by a user at a stop. This step utilizes available third party data sources such as Open Street Map (OSM) to gather contextual data for each stop. Two different algorithms are applied to annotate stops with the land use types (Algorithm 2) and the POI category types (Algorithm 3).

(1) Annotation with land use types

Algorithm 2 shows the pseudo-code for the annotation procedure, which annotates stops with semantic regions. For this purpose, the topological correlation is measured using the spatial join between each stop and the semantic regions. If a stop either intersects with or is nearby any region, the stop is annotated with that region. If a stop is located out of the boundary of the city, it is annotated as an unknown area.

Algorithm 2. Select Landuse Type

Input:
Stops $T_{stops} = \{s_1, s_2, ..., s_m\}$,

Land use layer $A_{landuse} = \{r_1, r_2, ..., r_q\}$

Output:
Land use type for each stop $L_{Region} = \{l_1, l_2, ..., l_n\}$

1 *begin*
2   *for all* $s_i = (x_i, y_i, t_i, t_{i+1}, \Delta_{duration})$ *do*
3   *if* T_{stops} *intersects* $A_{landuse}$ *then*
4          $L_i = (x_i, y_i, t_i, t_{i+1}, \Delta_{duration}, r_i)$
5   *else*
6   *find nearest* $A_{landuse}$ *to* T_{stops}
7          $L_i = (x_i, y_i, t_i, t_{i+1}, \Delta_{duration}, r_i)$
8   *return* L_{region}
9 *end*

The different land use types in this research work are Residential, Parks and recreation, Urban development, Commercial, Institution, Industry and Transportation.

(2) Annotation with probable visited POI category types

The following list provides POIs and their category types. The POIs were divided into 9 category types.

- Food: bar, café, pub, dining restaurant, bakery, fast food restaurant, food court
- Recreation: park, sports center, cinema, concert hall, gym, museum, night club, spa, stadium, zoo, bar, casino, theater
- Religious: church, mosque
- Education: school, college, university, library
- Shopping: shopping mall, strip mall, plaza, book store, clothing store, electronics' store, furniture store, pet store
- Daily shopping: grocery store, wholesale store, department store, supermarket, bakery, butcher's shop
- Business services: post office, car rental, gas station, ATM, industrial place, personal business

- Health services: dental office, pharmacy, clinic, hospital
- Accommodation: hotel, hostel

The pseudo-code in Algorithm 3 shows the detailed procedure of retrieving the probable visited POI category types for a given stop. The inputs of the algorithm are a set of stops, a set of POIs, Maximum Walking Distance (MWD), and User Walking Speed (UWS).

Algorithm 3. POI Type Annotation

Input:
Stops $T_{stops} = \{s_1, s_2, ..., s_m\}$,

POI layer $A_{poi} = \{a_1, a_2, ..., a_u\}$

MWD
UWS

Output:
POI category type probability for each stop
$Prob_{cat} = \{c_1, c_2, ..., c_n\}$

1 generalPOIs=[]
2 probablePOIs=[]
3 prob=[]
4 **begin**
5   **for all** $s_i = (x_i, y_i, t_i, t_{i+1}, \Delta_{duration})$ **do**
6   **if** $dis\tan ce(s_i, A_{poi}) \leq MWD$ *and*
7          $s_i, time \subset A_{poi}, H_i$ **then**
8   generalPOI $\leftarrow A_{poi}$

9   **for all** POI_i in generalPOIs
10   **if** $TE \leq duration_i$ **then**
11   probablePOIs $\leftarrow poi$

12   **for all** probablePOIs **do**
13         $POI_{cat} = \{p \in probablePOIs : \mu(p) = cat\}$
14         $dist = dis\tan ce(s, p)$ for each $p \in probablePOIs$
15         $mass = length(POI_{cat})$
16         $prob \leftarrow (POI_{cat}, \frac{mass}{dist^2})$

17   **return** POI_{cat}
18 **end**

In order to extract the POI category type for each stop, three steps are required. First, general POIs are selected; second, probable POIs are extracted, and finally, gravity model is used to calculate the probability for each POI category type.

To detect the general POIs, two conditions are taken into account, as seen in lines 5-8.

First, each POI has to be within a certain spatial range, which is defined by the MWD (the distance likely to be accepted for a walk from a stop to a POI). Dijkstra algorithm is used to compute the distance between each stop and the POIs on a road network. Second, the time period of each stop has to be compatible with the opening hours of the POIs. A stop during the closure of a POI cannot be matched with that POI, so, for example, a stop at 11 p.m. can be matched with a restaurant or a pub but not with a museum. In order to find the probable POIs, users need to have enough time to go and visit the POI based on the Minimum Service Time (MST), and return to the stop (lines 9-11). Therefore, TE (2) is the time that a person needed to reach the POI, visit the POI based on the MST, and come back to the stop again.

$$TE = 2 * TP + MST \qquad (2)$$

TP (3) is the time a person needs to cover the distance, where d is the distance between the stop and the POI, and UWS is the user's speed on a road network.

$$TP = \frac{d}{UWS} \qquad (3)$$

Once the probable visited POIs are selected, the algorithm measures the probability for each POI category type (lines 12-16). A method based on the gravity model is considered for this purpose. The gravity model (4) is a model derived from Newton's Law of Gravitation, and is used to predict the degree of interaction between a stop and each POI.

$$Gravity\, law = \frac{mass_1 * mass_2}{dis\tan ce^2} \qquad (4)$$

The definition for the gravity model is represented using the principle of bodies' attraction, where $mass_1$ represents a stop, $mass_2$ represents the number of the probable visited POIs in each category, and the distance is the sum of all the distances of POIs associated with the same category type. It means that the POIs associated with the same category type are assigned the same probability of being visited. More formally, for every stop s the probability p of a category type is determined as:

$$P(s_i, c_i) = \sum \frac{\left|\{p_i \in probable\, POIs(s_i) \mid \mu(p_i) = c_i\}\right|}{(d_i(s_i, p_i)^2)} \qquad (5)$$

where, s_i is the stop, c_i indicates the category of POI p_i, and d_i is a function returning the distance between each stop and the POIs associated with the same category type. Thus using formula (5), a probability is associated to each possible category type relative to the stops.

3.2.2.3 Semantic features extraction

The last step of the semantic enrichment process is to extract the semantic features from the annotated stops with the land use types. As shown in Algorithm 4, stops are first divided on a weekly basis, and then different semantic features such as the stop frequency, average duration, and start time for each stop are extracted.

Algorithm 4. Semantic Features Extraction

Input:
Selected land use type $L_i = (x_i, y_i, t_i, t_{i+1}, \Delta_{duration}, r_i)$

Output:
Stop frequency S_f, average duration of a stop S_d, and begin time T_e

1 begin
2   for all L_i *do*
3   compute stop frequency per week (S_f)
4   compute average duration of stop per week (S_d)
5   extract begin time of a stop (T_e)
6   return $S_f, S_d,$ *and* T_e
7 end

3.2.3. Ontology-based activity model

In this section, STOM is used to perform an inference on the most probable activities occurring by users during their trip. Given the extracted features from the previous sub-sections, the ontology model is populated and integrated in a formalism that is capable of reasoning the activity type of users. The activity types are defined as axioms using the domain knowledge. The model is composed of four ontologies: Time ontology, Place ontology, Stops ontology, and Activity ontology.

Activity ontology contains user activity type classes. Description logic is used to formalize the hierarchy of activities with axioms.

Place ontology contains various classes of POIs and the land use types. Each of them denotes a geo-referenced object such as a restaurant, a shop, a lake or other objects. Time ontology contains temporal references, in which the activity types can occur. It is designed for the modelling of time in qualitative terms (e.g. morning, evening). Stop ontology contains places where a user would stay for a period of time including the semantic features such as stop frequency, average duration, and begin time.

3.2.3.1. User activity type axioms

The activity types are defined using axioms based on different semantic features included in the ontology model to express relations between the ontologies (see table 1). For instance, in rule number one, if the land use type is residential, the POI type is null, the start time is evening, the stop frequency per week is more than 5, and the average duration is more than 10 hours per week,

then the moving object is 'spending time at home', i.e. AT= Return home.

Table 1. Axioms associated to activity types.

Land use Type	POI Category Type	Features			Activity Type
		T_b	S_f	S_d	
Residential	-	Evening or night	≥ 5	≥ 9 hours	Return home
Residential	-	Evening or night	≥ 1	≥ 30 minutes	Socializing
Commercial	Shopping	Evening or night	≥ 1	≥ 30 minutes	Shopping
Commercial	Daily Shopping	Evening or night	≥ 1	≥ 30 minutes	Daily Shopping
Any Type	Any Type	Morning	≥ 5	≥ 8 hours	Work Full-Time

Another example is rule number 2: if the moving object stops once within a residential land use type per week, with an average stop duration of more than 30 min and the start time is evening or night, then the moving object is 'visiting a friend', i.e. AT= Socializing. Therefore, applying the axioms outlined above, different activity types can be inferred. The added value of having such an ontology-based approach allows us to define axioms in terms of high-level semantic concepts, abstracting away from the geometry coordinates of the geographical features. Indeed, in this approach, each stop is treated as a semantic concept instead of using spatial coordinates. The assertion of these relationships is an existential restriction, which is specified using the following example axiom expressed in the Web Ontology Language (OWL) syntax as semantic rule number one specifies a typical home activity (Table).

Table 2. Definition of home activity ontology rule.

Concept	Definition in Description Logic
Return	$\equiv Stop \sqcap$
home	$HasLanduseType. Residential \sqcap$
Activity	$HasBeginTime. Evening \sqcap$
	$HasPoiType. null \sqcap$
	$\exists \geq 5\ Frequency \sqcap$
	$\exists \geq 600\ Duration$

4. Experiment and results

The performance of the approach was evaluated using a dataset, which was captured by a user, who had installed an application (developed based on the prototype for this research work) on his phone, and carried the phone with him while driving a car in the city of Calgary for a year in 2010. The experiment includes 862046 GPS records and 8050 landuse polygons and 17307 POI points. As it can be seen in figure 5, the last six months of the year had more data recorded than the first six months.

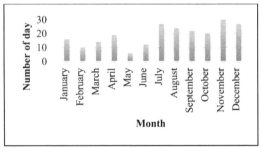

Figure 5. Raw GPS data acquired over a year.

It has a total of 862,046 GPS records. The attributes collected include user id, date, speed, heading, mode, and location of the user as shown in table 3. The x and y coordinates are transformed to an attribute called geometry (geometry column).

Table 3. Attributes of collected data.

User Id	Date	Speed	Heading	Mode	Geometry
1	2010-07-06 07:51:18	25.74	24.3	Car	"POINT(-114.133044 50.940534)"
1	2010-07-06 07:51:19	30.19	22.7	Car	"POINT(-114.132991 50.940454)"

Figure 6 shows the routes that the user used to complete the various activity types.

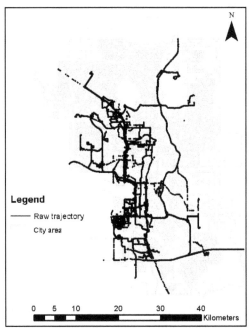

Figure 6. Routes used by user in his history data.

4.1. Data sources

(1) Land use data of Calgary
As shown in figure 7, the land use data includes different types such as commercial, urban development, residential, institutional, industrial, parks, major infrastructure, and transportation.

The land use is predominantly residential, with most industrial uses in the eastern half of the city. Commercial and green space land use types are spread throughout the city. Around 35% of the city is covered by residential types, 30% is covered by parks, and 25% is covered by commercial types.

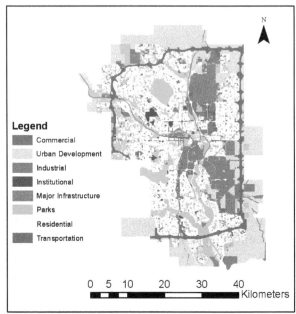

Figure 7. Land use of city of Calgary.

(2) POI data of Calgary
POIs were downloaded from OSM. There are 17,307 POIs, which were divided into nine category types: 2,304 food, 2,213 recreation, 407 religious, 281 education, 1,072 shopping, 996 daily shopping, 1,721 business services, 312 health services, and 7,749 accommodation. Since some of the opening hours were not currently included in the POIs' data, a time table (see table 4) was manually created based on the typical openings of different POIs. Note that the days of the week were divided into Monday-Friday, Saturday and Sunday. Moreover, MST was also added to the table.

4.2. Data preparation

The data preparation procedure was applied to the described collected data. First, the trajectories that were not in the monitored area were removed. Next, the dataset was cleaned from the inconsistencies such as empty values, duplicates, and outliers. In the trajectory identification, 239 daily basis trajectories were extracted. Unrealistic attributes such as trip durations that were too short were removed. Moreover, 28 Weekly basis trajectories were extracted.

Table 4. Opening hours of POIs in different days.

POI	Mon-Fri Opening Hours	Sat Opening Hours	Sun Opening Hours	Category	MST
Bank	9:30 – 17:00	9:00 – 16:00	Closed	Business service	15 min
Shopping mall	9:30 – 21:00	9:30 – 20:00	11:00 – 18:00	Shopping	30 min
Restaurant	11:00 – 23:00	11:00 – midnight	11:00 - midnight	Food	20 min
Post office	9:00 – 18:00	10:00 – 17:00	Closed	Business service	20 min
....	....	....	....	....	....

4.3. Semantic enrichment process

Stop detection

Figure 8 shows the number of stops, which were extracted with different parameters for the dataset. With higher $\Delta_{duration}$ (from two to ten minutes), the number of stops decreased when given a low Δ_{speed}; whilst with a higher Δ_{speed}, the stop number goes up and saturates because stops computed with a higher coefficient Δ_{speed} usually have a longer duration. Therefore, the number of stops decrease as some stops join together. Nevertheless, it is observed that the total percentage of time duration for stops always increases when the minimal stop time $\Delta_{duration}$ becomes smaller or the speed threshold Δ_{speed} increases. Empirical evaluations suggested to use $\Delta_{speed} < 15km/h$ and $\Delta_{duration} \geq 4 min$ to obtain the best accuracy.

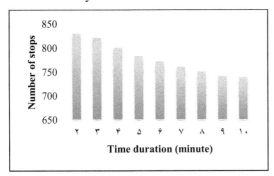

Figure 8. Number of stops based on different time durations (similar graph for speed).

As a result of the stop detection, 1,237 sub-trajectories with 832 moves and 801 stops over the dataset were produced.

Land use Type Annotation

Figure 9 shows the detailed land use type distribution over the trajectories.

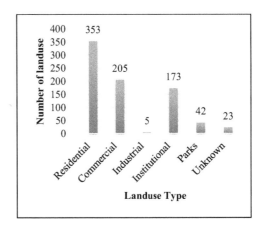

Figure 9. Land use type distribution for user trajectory.

Most of the stops were observed in the residential areas (44.1%), commercial areas (25.6%), and institutional areas (21.6%); and the others were industrial (0.6%), parks (5.2%), and unknown (2.9%).

Figure 10 shows all the stops annotated with different land use types including residential, park, institutional, commercial, out of town, and industrial. As it can be seen, most of the stops have happened in the area where the user lives.

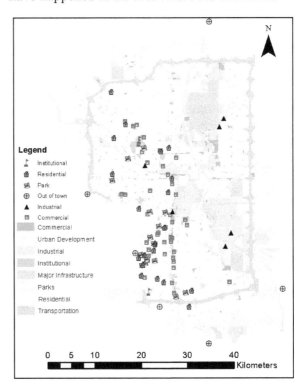

Figure 10. All detected stops in different land use types.

POI Category Type Annotation

In Algorithm 4, UWS and UWD were considered 5 km/h and 100 meters, respectively. As shown in figure 11, most of the stops belonged to the shopping (30.1%), business services (18.9%), and food (17.7%) categories.

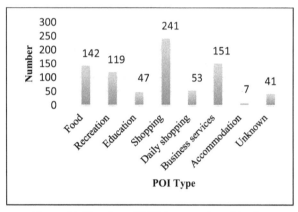

Figure 11. Number of POI types assigned to stop trajectories.

Table 5 represents the POI category type annotation in which a probable activity is returned using the gravity formula. For instance, for the stop S_1, two different category types were computed; food category type with the probability of 0.65 and the business service category type with the probability of 0.35.

Table 5. Most probable POI category type.

Stop	POI Category Type	Probability
S_1	Food	0.65
S_1	Business service	0.35
S_2	-	-
S_3	Recreation	1

4.4. Ontology-based activity model

STOM was populated using the extracted information in the previous steps. The time ontology contained the temporal discretization such as absolute intervals, as shown in table 6.

Table 6. Temporal discretization of time ontology.

Semantic time	Time period
Morning	4:00 AM - 11:59 AM
Afternoon	12:00 PM - 4:59 PM
Evening	5:00 PM - 8:59 PM
Night	9:00 PM - 3:59 AM

The stop ontology included the semantic features, as shown in table 7. For instance, the user had stopped six times a week in a residential land use type named "Residential 1" in the evenings with the average of 614 minutes per week. The place ontology contained the POIs and the land use types, as shown in table 8. For instance, for the stop S1, commercial was assigned as land use type and two different category types were computed; the food category type with the probability of 0.65 and the business service category type with the probability of 0.35.

Table 7. Some semantic features in stop ontology.

Stops	Frequency	Begin time	Average (min)
Commercial1	1	Evening	221
Commercial29	2	Night	14
Institutional1	**5**	**Morning**	**441**
Residential1	6	Evening	614
Residential14	1	Evening	22

Table 8. POI and land use in place ontology.

Stop	Land use Type	POI Category Type	Probability
S_1	Commercial	Food	0.65
S_1	Commercial	Business service	0.35
S_2	Residential	-	-
S_3	Parks	Recreation	1

4.5. Activity inference

The reasoning step was executed by the reasoner using the axioms that had been defined in sub-section 3.2.4.1 for some activity type. Table 9 shows some of the inferred activity types.

Table 9. Some inferred activity types.

Land use Type	POI Category Type	Features			Activity Type
		T_b	S_f	S_d	
Residential	-	Evening	6 days per week	10.2 hours	Return Home
Residential	-	Evening	1 day per week	45 min	Visiting
Commercial	Shopping	Afternoon	2 days per week	41 min	Shopping
Institutional	-	Morning	5 days per week	8.2 hours	Go to work

4.6. Activity type evaluation

Figure 12 illustrates a web interface application to visualize daily semantic trajectories and collecting users' feedback to validate the proposed methodology for activity recognition in this research work. At the bottom of the box, the user is asked to verify if the inferred activity type is correct or not.

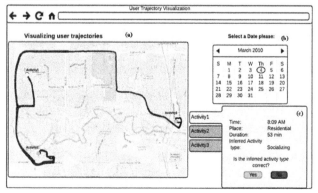

Figure 12. User interface to visualize user's trajectories in order to get his/her feedback.

As shown in figure 12, for instance, a user on March 4th, 2010 had 3 different activity types displayed with green circles on the map. Therefore, the inferred activity types using the proposed method are compared with the collected feedback of the users. The accuracy, as seen in (6), is the number of correctly inferred activity types over the number of total inferred activity types from the dataset.

$$Accuracy = \frac{No.\,of\ correctly\ inferred\ activity\ type}{No.\,of\ total\ inferred\ activity\ type\ from\ dataset} \qquad (6)$$

The experimental outcome and the evaluation results are depicted in table 10. It shows the accuracies per activities i.e. the percentage of activities correctly identified w.r.t. the number of declared activities (of the same type). For example, good results for activities of type "business services" (the method recognized 97.3% of them) were obtained, while the method was unable to identify "daily shopping" (the method recognized 35.9% of them). It was observed that these results were related to the availability of the POIs around the stops.

Table 10. Accuracy of extracted activities using user's feedback.

Activity Type	Accuracy (%)
Eating	88.4
Recreational	86.1
Education	69.5
Shopping	91.3
Daily shopping	35.9
Business services	97.3
Go to work	93.8
Trip	88.6
Socializing	90.6
Return home	89.1

4.7. Evaluation
To assess the performance of the proposed method, two different evaluations were performed. First, a reasoning evaluation was performed to show the impact of sematic enrichment of data. Second, a space/time sensitivity analysis was performed to evaluate the performance of the proposed method.

4.7.1. Reasoning evaluation
To measure the impact of the ontology axioms in the reasoning process, two experiments were performed. For this purpose, two sets of data were considered: GPS data and semantically enriched data. For the experiments, as described in table

12, the axiom named "return home" was considered. Figures 13 and 14 show the experimental results for the computation time in seconds and the storage space in triples needed by the inference calculation. The evolution curves are given by the number of stops.

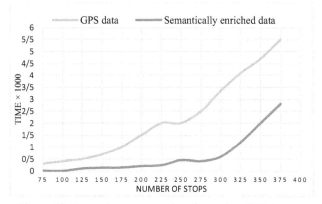

Figure 13. Reasoning computation time using GPS data and semantically enriched data.

The first experiment, which used the real GPS data shows the reasoning result with poor characteristics in terms of the computation time and space storage. For example, for 375 stops, the reasoning takes around 5,500 seconds ($\simeq$1.5 hours) and generates 220,000 triples.

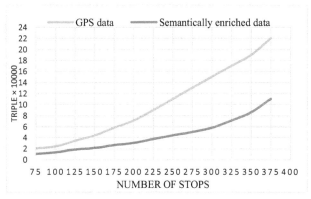

Figure 14. Reasoning storage space taken using GPS data and semantically enriched data.

In experiment 2, semantically enriched data was considered. The computation time and space storage results show the improvement made on the reasoning calculation compared to the first experiment. For example, for 370 stops, the reasoning takes less than 2,800 seconds ($\simeq$ 46 minutes) and generates around 110,000 triples. This reveals a reduction about 49% in processing time and 50% in storage space by applying ontology enrichment.

4.7.2. Performance evaluation
To evaluate the performance of the proposed method, a space/time sensitivity analysis was performed. A desktop computer used for the

testing and its configuration (i.e. hardware and software) is shown in table 11.

Table 11. Test system configuration.

Specification	Value
Operating System	Windows 7 Professional- 64 bit
RAM	4.00 GB
Processor	Inter® Core™2 Duo CPU 2.99 GHz
HDD	160 GB (7200 rpm) 8 MB Cache

In this experiment, different values were considered for the Maximum Walking Distance (MWD); from 50m-125m by 25m steps, while the rest of the parameters were left unchanged. The result of this evaluation is shown in figure 15.

As shown in figure 15, the fitted regression model almost follows a linear model, and it can be concluded that the performance trend of the proposed method has an O(n). Of course, due to the dependency of the proposed method on the other parameters, it does not show a complete linear regression.

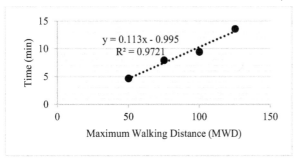

Figure 15. Performance evaluation.

5. Conclusions

This research work proposed a new ontology-based approach to recognize human activity type using GPS data. In comparison with other approaches, the proposed method for activity recognition considered several semantic constraints to annotate stops with the POI category types and the land use types. One constraint was added to relate the duration of the stop to the typical duration of the visits (e.g. a duration of 10 minutes is not compatible with dining in a restaurant). For each POI, a MST was defined to express the minimum amount of time that a person needs to spend to visit the place. Moreover, another constraint was that the amount of time a person could spend in a place is not the complete stop duration but the time needed to cover the distance between the POI and the stop must be taken into account.

With regard to the needs and challenges facing a research work, which is trying to establish an ontology-based approach for computing and understanding human activity types, this paper formulated two major contributions. The first contribution of this study was developing a semantic conceptual data model in order to recognize different activity types. In this respect, several semantic features were added to the model in order to enrich the relationship between the objects in the model. The second contribution was to propose an ontology-based activity model to infer different activity types. The semantic conceptual data model was used to develop the model. In this study, we investigated various extracted features and background information based on the model ontology to extract the activity types. Different axioms were defined using common sense rules so as to recognize the activity types. Finally, two experiments were performed to show the effectiveness of the proposed method. Moreover, a space/time sensitivity analysis was performed to evaluate the performance of the proposed method. In the future works, we shall investigate the usefulness of geo-social network data in the activity recognition process.

References

[1] Steiniger, S., Neun, M., & Edwardes, A. (2006). Foundations of location based services. CartouCHe1 Lecture Notes on LBS. vol. 1.

[2] Jensen, C. S. (2002). Research Challenges in Location-enabled M-services. Third International Conference on Mobile Data Management. pp. 3–7.

[3] Ong, R., Wachowicz, M., Nanni, M., & Renso, C. (2010). From Pattern Discovery to Pattern Interpretation in Movement Data. Proceedings of the IEEE International Conference on Data Mining Workshops. pp. 527–534.

[4] Baccarelli, E. u. a. (2016). Energy-efficient dynamic traffic offloading and reconfiguration of networked data centers for big data stream mobile computing. review, challenges, and a case study. IEEE Network. vol. 30, no. 2, pp. 54–61.

[5] Galton, A. (2005). Dynamic collectives and their collective dynamics. Spatial Information Theory. pp. 300–315.

[6] Miller, H. J. (2005). A measurement theory for time geography. Geographical analysis. vol. 37, no. 1, pp. 17–45.

[7] Dodge, S. (2011). Exploring Movement Using Similarity Analysis. PhD thesis, Universitaet Zuerich.

[8] Laube, P. (2005). Analysing Point Motion, Spatio-Temporal Data Mining of Geospatial Lifelines. PhD thesis, Universitz of Zurich.

[9] Mesrikhani, A., & Davoodi, M. (2017). Non-zero probability of nearest neighbor searching. Journal of AI and Data Mining. vol. 5, no. 1, pp. 101–109.

[10] Bohte, W., & Maat, K. (2009). Deriving and validating trip purposes and travel modes for multi-day GPS-based travel surveys: a large-scale application in the Netherlands. Transportation Research Part C: Emerging Technologies. vol. 17, no. 3, pp. 285–297.

[11] Xie, K., Deng, K., & Zhou, X. (2009). From trajectories to activities. a spatio-temporal join approach. Proceedings of the International Workshop on Location Based Social Networks. ACM. pp. 25–32.

[12] Huang, L., & Li, Q. (2010). Automatic activity identification from raw GPS vehicle tracking data. Proceedings of the Canadian Geomatics Conference.

[13] Liao, L., Fox, D., & Kautz, H. (2006). Location-based activity recognition. Advances in Neural Information Processing Systems. vol. 18, pp. 787.

[14] Patterson, D. J., Liao, L., Fox, D., & Kautz, H. (2003). Inferring high-level behavior from low-level sensors. UbiComp 2003: Ubiquitous Computing. Springer. pp. 73–89.

[15] Liao, L., Fox, D., & Kautz, H. (2007). Extracting places and activities from gps traces using hierarchical conditional random fields. The International Journal of Robotics Research. vol. 26, no. 1, pp. 119–134.

[16] Alvares, L.O. u. a. (2007). A model for enriching trajectories with semantic geographical information. Proceedings of the 15th annual ACM international symposium on Advances in geographic information systems. pp. 162-169.

[17] Moreno, B., Times, V. C., Renso, C., & Bogorny, V. (2010). Looking Inside the Stops of Trajectories of Moving Objects. Geoinfo. pp. 9_20.

[18] Spinsanti, L., Celli, F., & Renso, C. (2010). Where you stop is who you are: understanding peoples' activities. Proceedings of the 5th workshop on behaviour monitoring and interpretation—user modelling. Karlsruhe, Germany.

[19] Renso, C. u. a. (2013). How you move reveals who you are: understanding human behavior by analyzing trajectory data. Knowledge and information systems. vol. 37, no. 2, pp. 331–362.

[20] Mousavi, A., & Hunter, A. J. S. (2012). Pointers Extraction of Trajectory Data for Semantic Knowledge Discovery. Gehalten auf der GIScience - Seventh International Conference on Geographic Information Science , Columbus, Ohio.

[21] Mousavi, A., & Hunter, A. J. S. (2012). Using Ontology Based Knowledge Discovery in Location Based Services. Gehalten auf der The 2012 AutoCarto International Symposium on Automated Cartography , Columbus, Ohio September 18.

[22] Spaccapietra, S. u. a. (2008). A conceptual view on trajectories. Data & Knowledge Engineering. vol. 65, no. 1, pp. 126–146.

[23] The time ontology website (2006) Available: http://www.w3.org/2006/time.

[24] Zhang, J., & Goodchild, M. F. (2002). Uncertainty in geographical information. CRC press.

[25] Gani, A., Siddiqa, A., Shamshirband, S., & Hanum, F. (2016). A survey on indexing techniques for big data: taxonomy and performance evaluation. Knowledge and Information Systems. vol. 46, no. 2, pp. 241–284.

6

Fuzzy clustering of time series data: A particle swarm optimization approach

Z. Izakian[*] and M. S. Mesgari

Department of Geodesy & Geomatics & Geoinformation Technology Center of Excellence, K. N. Toosi University of Technology, Tehran, Iran.

Corresponding author: zahedeh_izakian@yahoo.com (Z. Izakian).

Abstract

Developing information gathering technologies and getting access to a large amount of data, we always require methods for data analyzing and extract useful information from large raw dataset. Thus, data mining is an important method for solving this problem. Clustering analysis as the most commonly used function of data mining, has attracted many researchers in computer science. Because of different applications, the problem of clustering the time series data has become highly popular and many algorithms have been proposed in this field. Recently Swarm Intelligence (SI) as a family of nature inspired algorithms has gained huge popularity in the field of pattern recognition and clustering. In this paper, a technique for clustering time series data using a particle swarm optimization (PSO) approach has been proposed, and Pearson Correlation Coefficient as one of the most commonly-used distance measures for time series is considered. The proposed technique is able to find (near) optimal cluster centers during the clustering process. To reduce the dimensionality of the search space and improve the performance of the proposed method, a singular value decomposition (SVD) representation of cluster centers is considered. Experimental results over three popular data sets indicate the superiority of the proposed technique compared with fuzzy C-means and fuzzy K-medoids clustering techniques.

Keywords: *Clustering, Time Series, Particle Swarm Optimization, Singular Value Decomposition, Pearson Correlation Coefficient.*

1. Introduction

A time series is a sequence of data points, measured on a successive time space through a uniform interval. Meteorologists use time series for displaying climate change and forecasting weather. Demographers use time series for Anticipating population changes within a specified period of time. In Economics time series are used for analyzing and predicting stock price. Further analysis of time series in science, such as bioinformatics, geology, marine science, medicine and engineering are frequently used. Because of time series applications in various sciences, the interest to analyze these data has been increased. Challenges related to the analysis of these data (time series), is because of its not only size and volume, but also the complexity of this type of data. Time series clustering provides a way for reducing the complexity by categorizing time series in few groups. Grouping should be done in such a way that patterns in the same group should likely be similar to each other while maximizing the dissimilarity of different clusters. In general, the purpose of clustering is representing large datasets by a fewer number of cluster centers. It brings simplicity for large datasets and thus is an important step in the process of knowledge discovery and data mining. So far, different algorithms have been proposed for solving the problem of clustering spatio-temporal data such as time series. Recently, a family of nature inspired algorithms, known as Swarm Intelligence (SI), has attracted the attention of researchers working on clustering field and Particle Swarm Optimization (PSO) is a popular optimization algorithm, which is based on swarm intelligence [1].

Fuzzy C-Means (FCM) [2] is a popular clustering technique and there is a membership degree in unit interval instead of assigning each object to one cluster. This clustering algorithm has been employed successfully in many applications but there are some challenges in using this technique for clustering time series data. FCM is sensitive to initialization and may get trapped in a local optimum. Since time series are high-dimensional data, it is actually more probable that results fall into local optima. Moreover the most commonly used similarity measure in FCM is Euclidean distance but sometimes in time series data, using another similarity/dissimilarity measures is more appropriate. To deal with the above-mentioned challenges, in this paper, a particle swarm optimization approach for time series data clustering has been proposed. In this method, PSO is applied to find optimal cluster centers based on the selected objective function and the selected similarity measure. For this purpose, a singular value decomposition (SVD) representation of time series is considered and PSO estimates SVD coefficients of cluster centers.

This study is organized as follows: In section 2, a brief literature review is presented. In section 3 we describe the fuzzy C-means technique. Section 4 focuses on PSO algorithm. In section 5, we briefly explain time series representation methods. In section 6, we focus on similarity measures. In section 7, the proposed method for clustering time series is explained, and in section 8, experimental studies are reported. Finally, section 9 concludes this work.

2. Literature review

In this section, we present some PSO based clustering methods. Niknam et al. [3] introduced a new clustering method based on combination of the Ant Colony Optimization and the Particle Swarm Optimization called PSO-ACO. They used ACO algorithm for decision making process of particle movement. This combination makes the particles search the surrounding area better. Results show that the proposed PSO-ACO optimization algorithm has much potential in allocating N objects to k clusters. Ahmadyfard and Modares [4] proposed a hybrid clustering method based on combination of the particle swarm optimization (PSO) and the k-mean algorithm to cluster dataset into a user specified number of cluster. They used the property of PSO in fast convergence during the initial stages of a global search and the fast convergence around global optimum property of k-means algorithm in their method. The performance of their method was compared to K-means and PSO clustering algorithms using five datasets. Hwang and Huang [5] presented a clustering algorithm based on

particle swarm optimization (PSO) and fuzzy theorem. Their proposed algorithm can compute appropriate number of clusters and find cluster centers in a dataset. The result of comparing their algorithm with PSO clustering and fuzzy c-means on three datasets, showed good performance of the method in determining the number of clusters and clustering of data. Rana et al. [6] offered a new Hybrid Sequential clustering approach based on PSO and K-Means that overcomes the drawback of both algorithms. They used PSO in sequence with K-Means algorithm for data clustering. Their method improved the slow convergence of PSO near optimal solution. The obtained results of comparing presented method with K-Means, PSO and Hybrid K-Means-Genetic algorithms showed better performance of the method.

Premalatha and Natarajan [7] proposed a new approach integrating Particle Swarm Optimization (PSO) and Genetic Algorithm (GA) for document clustering called HPSO. For convergence improvement, they applied the PSO algorithm capability in fast convergence and the genetic algorithm ability in exploiting previous solution. In this method, the crossover operation of GA is used in order to transmit information between two particles and the mutation operation is used to increase the population diversity. The results illustrated the efficiency of HPSO. Esmin and Matwin [8] presented a new clustering method based on particle swarm optimization and called it hybrid particle swarm optimization with mutation (HPSOM). This method was used to find the centroids of a user specified number of clusters. They applied mutation process of GA to improve the results obtained from PSO. Their approach was compared with K-means clustering method and the standard PSO algorithm on five benchmark datasets.

The results illustrated more efficiency of the proposed clustering method. Kamel et al. [9] proposed a new approach based on K means, PSO and Sampling algorithms for data clustering. Their proposed method was evaluated on four datasets and was compared with K means, PSO, Sampling+K means, and PSO+K means. The results showed that their approach generates the most compact clusters. Kamel and Gaikwad [10] proposed a new hybrid sequential clustering approach used for PSO algorithm in sequence with Fuzzy k means technique in data clustering. An experiment was done on standard datasets available online. The experimental studies showed the efficiency of the proposed method in detecting clusters.

This study used evolutionary algorithms for clustering datasets including short sequences in all methods provided in this section.

Applying evolutionary algorithms for long time series is time consuming and moreover with increasing the number of unknown elements, the efficiency of algorithm will be reduced. Therefore, we used time series dimensionality reduction technique to solve the problem of using evolutionary algorithms for long time series clustering.

3. Fuzzy C-means algorithm

Fuzzy C-Means is one of the commonly used fuzzy clustering methods proposed by Bezdek (1981) [2]. It is based on the minimization of the following objective function:

$$J(U,V) = \sum_{i=1}^{C} \sum_{j=1}^{n} u_{ij}^{m} d^2(v_i, x_j) \quad 1 \le m \le \infty \tag{1}$$

Where m is fuzziness parameter and determines the level of cluster fuzziness, C is the number of clusters, n is the number of objects in the data set, v_i is the prototype of the center of cluster i, u_{ij} is the degree of membership of x_j in the cluster i and $d^2(v_i, x_j)$ is the distance between object x_j and cluster center v_i. V is a matrix including C cluster centers and U is partition matrix. A solution of the object function can be obtained via a sequence of iterations, which is carried out as follows:

1. Set values for C (the number of clusters) and m (fuzziness parameter)
2. Initialize U (fuzzy partition matrix)
3. Calculate V (the cluster centers) by using U

$$v_i = \frac{\sum_{j=1}^{n} u_{ij}^m x_j}{\sum_{j=1}^{n} u_{ij}^m} \tag{2}$$

4. Calculate the new partition matrix by using V

$$u_{ij} = \frac{1}{\sum_{k=1}^{C} \left(\frac{d(x_j, v_i)}{d(x_j, v_k)} \right)^{2/(m-1)}} \tag{3}$$

5. Repeat step 3 and 4 until stopping condition is true

4. Particle swarm optimization

Particle swarm optimization [11,12] is a population-based optimization technique inspired by the social behavior of bird flocking or fish schooling.

In PSO algorithm, each particle represents a possible solution that moves randomly in the search space towards the optimal solution. Displacement of each particle in the search space is influenced by their own and their neighbors knowledge. PSO algorithm tries to combine the local search method (using their experience) and global search method (using the experiences of neighbors) to achieve good results.

Let is the position of particle i at time t .The particle at time t +1 will change its position according to (4).

$$X_i(t+1) = X_i(t) + V_i(t+1) \tag{4}$$

Where $V_i(t+1)$ is the particle's velocity vector at time $t+1$. From (4) we can find that the position of each particle changes based on its previous position and the velocity vector. $V_i(t+1)$ is calculated from (5).

$$V_i(t+1) = w.V_i(t) + c_1 R_1 (Pbest_i(t) - X_i(t)) + c_2 R_2 (Gbest_i(t) - X_i(t)) \tag{5}$$

In (5), $pbest_i(t)$ is the best known position of particle i since the beginning of the algorithm, and $nbest_i(t)$ is the best position found through its neighborhood.

c_1 and c_2 called acceleration constants and w is called inertia weight and increases the convergence speed. r_1 and r_2 are random positive numbers uniformly distributed in the range [0,1]. The personal best (pbest) of particle i is updated by:

$$pbest_i(t+1) =$$
$$\begin{cases} pbest_i(t) & \text{if } f(pbest_i(t)) \ge f(X_i(t+1)) \\ X_i(t+1) & \text{if } f(pbest_i(t)) < f(X_i(t+1)) \end{cases} \tag{6}$$

where, $f()$ is the fitness function. According to (6) if a particle's current position is better than its previous best position, it is to be updated. If $X_k(t+1)$ is the best particle in the neighborhood of particle i at time $t+1$, it needs to be updated Gbest using (7).

$$Gbest_i(t+1) =$$
$$\begin{cases} Gbest_i(t) & \text{if } f(Gbest_i(t)) \ge f(X_k(t+1)) \\ X_k(t+1) & \text{if } f(Gbest_i(t)) < f(X_k(t+1)) \end{cases} \tag{7}$$

The pseudocode for PSO algorithm is shown as table 1.

Table 1. Continuous PSO pseudocode (Elbeltagi et al. [13]).

```
Generate random population of P solutions (particles).
Repeat
for each particle i=1,...,P do
compute the fitness of particle i (Xi)
          if  fitness(Xi) > fitness(pbesti)  then
                           pbesti= Xi;
          end
          if  fitness(pbesti) > fitness(Gbesti)then
                           Gbesti = pbesti;
          end
end
for each particle i=1,...,P do
          update the velocity vector using Eq. (5)
          update the position vector using Eq. (4)
end
until stopping condition is true;
return Gbest and corresponding position
```

5. Time series representation methods

Time series representation methods are categorized into data adaptive, non data adaptive and sometimes statistical methods. Among the methods, Single Value Decomposition is one of the most efficient techniques that is explained in this section.

Assume that we have n time series and each has m points. According to [14], if we consider these time series in the form of a matrix $A_{n \times m}$ then, it can be expressed as (8).

$$A = U \times S \times V^T \qquad (8)$$

Where U is a $n \times n$ unitary matrix, S is $n \times m$ diagonal matrix and V is $m \times m$ orthogonal matrix called SVD-transform matrix. After calculating the SVD matrix, each time series x can be represented in the new space as follows:

$$y = xV \qquad (9)$$

In this equation, y is a vector with m point so that except for its first k ($k << m$) coefficients, the other coefficient are almost equal to zero. Therefore, having just the first k coefficients in y is enough to represent the time series in the new space. Also, reconstructing the original time series from its SVD transform, y, can be done by

$$x = yV^{-1} \qquad (10)$$

Notice that if y is a vector with length k, zero padding should be performed to convert y to a vector with length m. Usually the first few coefficients of SVD are enough to capture the most important features of time series and the original time series can be reconstructed using these first few coefficients with a little loss of information.

Because of facing real numbers in using singular value decomposition coefficients (SVD) as one of the time series representation methods, high speed, high efficiency and popularity among researchers, we have selected this method to define particles in our proposed method.

6. Similarity measures in working with time series data

Selecting a suitable similarity measure or distance function is one of the main steps in clustering. A distance function is the criterion used for determining the similarity in a dataset. Selecting the right distance function is application dependent. Some similarity measures used for time series are Euclidean distance [15], Pearson correlation coefficient [16], LCSS distance [17] and DTW distance [18]. The similarity measure used in our work is Pearson correlation coefficient.

Pearson product moment correlation is the most commonly used measure of correlation, which is called simply Pearson correlation. The Pearson correlation shows the degree of the linear relation between two varieties. For two time series x and y with mean $\bar{x}$ and $\bar{y}$ and length m the Pearson coefficient can be calculated as (11).

$$\rho_{x,y} = \frac{\text{cov}(x,y)}{\sigma_x \sigma_y} = \frac{\sum_{i=1}^{m}(x_i - \bar{x})(y_i - \bar{y})}{\sqrt{\sum_{i=1}^{m}(x_i - \bar{x})^2}\sqrt{\sum_{i=1}^{m}(y_i - \bar{y})^2}} \qquad (11)$$

Where $\rho_{x,y}$ is a number in range [-1, 1]. $\rho_{x,y} = 1$ means the two time series are in a perfect positive correlation. In other words, an increase seen in one time series will lead to a proportionate increase in the other time series. $\rho_{x,y} = -1$ means they are in a perfect negative correlation or an increase seen in one time series results in a proportionate decrease in the other time series and $\rho_{x,y} = 0$ means there is no correlation between them. One may use $D(x,y) = 1 - \rho_{x,y}$ as a distance function between two time series. One may use $D(x,y) = 1 - \rho_{x,y}$ as a distance function between two time series.

7. Clustering of time series data using a PSO technique

As mentioned earlier, using FCM for clustering high-dimensional data may result in some local optima. To deal with the above-mentioned problems, we considered using a particle swarm optimization for clustering time series data.

The PSO clustering algorithm that was explained in section 4, is appropriate for short time series clustering. In datasets including long time series, finding the elements of cluster centers by particles is time consuming and the large number of unknown parameters related to the cluster centers will reduce the efficiency of PSO algorithm. In the proposed method, the PSO algorithm finds the most important SVD coefficients of cluster centers instead of finding all elements of each cluster center. Then, all the cluster centers are reconstructed using corresponding SVD coefficients and with considering Pearson correlation coefficient as similarity measure, the objective function is calculated for each particle. This method significantly reduces the number of unknown parameters but increases the efficiency of the PSO algorithm.

In our proposed method for each particle, we have C cluster centers and every cluster center has k features, these features are the first k SVD coefficients of that cluster center. In this method, figure 1 shows each particle.

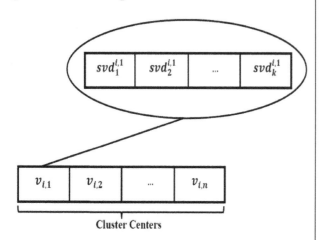

Figure 1. Particle scheme in the proposed method.

At the first step of the algorithm, a set of p particles including cluster center is generated randomly to comprise real numbers. The length of each cluster center is equal to the length of SVD representation of time series (the first k coefficients). Moreover, for each particle, a velocity vector is generated to include real numbers in a range. To evaluate a potential solution encoded by a particle, all the selected cluster centers are reconstructed to time series data using an inverse SVD. Next, (3) is used to estimate the membership degree of each trajectory to each cluster center and finally, the FCM objective function is considered as the fitness of each particle. FCM objective function is considered as the fitness of each particle.

Because of two reasons, we selected the objective function of FCM algorithm as our proposed method's objective function. First, this objective function takes into account compactness and

separation of clusters well and second, we are going to compare our method with FCM and FKM clustering algorithms which try to minimize this objective function as their fitness function.

To update a particle in each step of the algorithm based on the calculated fitness values of particles, *pbest* of each particle and *gbest* of the whole population is updated and then (5) has been used for velocity vectors updating. As the result, (4) is used to update cluster center part. After updating particles, if in a particle there was a cluster center located outside of boundaries of SVD coefficients of the data set, it has to be generated randomly again. Table 2 shows the pseudo-code of the proposed method.

Table 2. Proposed method pseudo-code.

1: Create and initialize P particles with C cluster centers
2: **FOR** iteration_count = 1 to maximum_iterations **DO**
3:     **FOR** each particle i **DO**
4:         reconstruct cluster centers using their SVD coefficients.
5:         Calculate partition matrix (U) using E.q. (3).
6:         Calculate the fitness function $f(Z_i)$ using E.q. (1).
7:         Update *pbest* for each particle using E.q. (6).
8:     **END**
9:     Update *Gbest* using E.q. (7).
10:    **FOR** each particle i **DO**
11:        Update velocity for cluster centers. E.q. (5).
12:        Update cluster centers of each particle using PSO algorithm. E.q. (4).
13:    **END**
14: **END**
15: Extract the cluster centers corresponding to Gbest.

8. Results and discussion
8.1. Dataset
We used three well-known [19, 20, 21] datasets including Cylinder Bell Funnel Data (CBF), Trace and Gun Point from the UCR Time Series Data Mining Archive [22]. The properties of each dataset were shown in table 3.

Table 3. The properties of datasets.

Data set	Dataset size	Time series length	Number of clusters
Cyliner Bell Funnel	900	128	3
Trace	200	275	4
Gun Point	200	150	2

8.2. Parameter setting
The parameters in the proposed method were set in table 4:

Table 4. The proposed method parameters.

Parameters	Value
m	2
p	30
itr	100
c_1	2
c_2	2
SVD	4

Where m is fuzziness parameter, p is the population size, Itr is number of iterations, c_1 and c_2 are inertia weight and SVD is the number of unknown SVD coefficients of clusters centers. A fine tuning has been performed to set the parameters of the proposed method for clustering time series data. In more data sets, the first four to five SVD coefficients are enough to capture the important features of time series; therefore, we use four coefficients for representing cluster centers in a particle.

8.3. Evaluation criteria

Precision, recall and f-measure are three most well-known validation techniques for clustering and classification. Precision (also called positive predictive value) is the fraction of retrieved instances that are relevant, while recall (also known as sensitivity) is the fraction of relevant instances that are retrieved. Both precision and recall are therefore based on an understanding and the measure of relevance. The harmonic mean of precision and recall is another validation technique called F-measure. In this study, for comparing our method with other clustering algorithms, Objective function, Precision and F-

Measure were considered as tools for evaluation. According to above explanations, the Precision is defined as (12).

$$P(i,j) = \frac{n_{ij}}{n_j} \qquad (12)$$

Where n_{ij} is the number of members of class i in cluster j, n_j is the number of members of cluster j and n_i is the number of members of class i. the F-Measure is computed using 13.

$$F(i,j) = \frac{2 \times P(i,j) \times R(i,j)}{P(i,j) + R(i,j)} \qquad (13)$$

Where

$$R(i,j) = \frac{n_{ij}}{n_i} \qquad (14)$$

Higher precision and F-Measure and lower objective function means that the performance of clustering algorithm was better and algorithm returned higher quality clusters.

8.4. Results

For evaluating the performance of the proposed method, we compared it with fuzzy C-means and fuzzy K-medoids clustering algorithms. By considering Pearson correlation coefficient as the similarity measurement, the following results were obtained. J, FM and PR respectively show the best value of fitness function, F measure and Precision achieved over 20 independent runs. Moreover, mean and standard deviation of run time over 20 runs are shown in table 5.

Table 5. Results of three clustering methods on three datasets.

Data set	method	J	FM	PR	Time (sec)
CBF	FCM	44.126	0.64	0.66	1.067±0.070
	FKM	67.138	0.59	0.60	6.827±0.052
	PSO	44.065	0.64	0.66	70.280±2.694
Trace	FCM	1.702	0.57	0.53	0.2450±0.130
	FKM	2.271	0.59	0.56	0.547±0.042
	PSO	1.664	0.59	0.57	69.365±0.607
Gun point	FCM	1.580	0.50	0.50	0.060±0.029
	FKM	1.963	0.50	0.50	0.333±0.018
	PSO	1.391	0.55	0.56	14.649±0.147

It is evident from table 5 that the proposed method has obtained the best fitness function value in all datasets. Also, in all cases, the F-Measure and Precision values obtained through the proposed method is one of the best. Comparing the run time of the methods, the evolutionary techniques in general are more time consuming than FCM and

FKM. The reasons for the superiority of the proposed clustering algorithm are, first, the efficiency of PSO algorithms in data clustering and second, SVD dimension reduction technique ability in time series reconstruction with a limited number of coefficients. If we use PSO algorithm for long time series clustering, the algorithm faces with many unknowns, thus the efficiency of that will be reduced and we cannot get the expected results.

9. Conclusion

In this study, a fuzzy clustering method based on PSO algorithm was proposed for clustering time series datasets. The main advantage of the proposed method is its ability to long time series data clustering. The main difference between our method and the existing time series clustering methods based on PSO algorithm is, how to define the particles. In the proposed method, the most important singular value decomposition coefficients (SVD) of the cluster centers that are limited number of real numbers, were recognized as the main unknown clustering problem and PSO algorithm tries to determine the unknowns by minimizing the selected objective function. This reduces the number of unknowns and increases the efficiency of the algorithm. By selecting fuzzy C-means objective function as the fitness function and with considering Pearson correlation coefficients as the similarity measure, we implemented our method and two other well-known algorithms on three datasets. By comparing with the obtained results of implementing three methods, we found out the best performance in our proposed method.

References

[1] Abraham, A., Das, S. & Roy, S. (2008). Swarm intelligence algorithms for data clustering. Soft Computing for Knowledge Discovery and Data Mining, Springer, pp. 279-313.

[2] Bezdek, J. C. (1981). Pattern Recognition with Fuzzy Objective Function Algorithms. Plenum Press.

[3] Niknam, T., Nayeripour, M. & Firouzi, B. B. (2008). Application of a New Hybrid optimization Algorithm on Cluster Analysis Data clustering, World Academy of Science, Engineering and Technology, vol. 36, pp. 598-604.

[4] Ahmadyfard, A. & Modares, H. (2008). Combining PSO and K-means to enhance data clustering, In: International symposium on telecommunications, Tehran, Iran, 2008.

[5] Hwang, J. & Huang, C. (2010). Evolutionary dynamic particle swarm optimization for data clustering, in: International Conference on Machine Learning and Cybernetics (ICMLC), Qingdao, China, pp. 3240 – 3245.

[6] Rana, S., Jasola, S. & Kumar, R. (2010). hybrid sequential approach for data clustering using K-means and particle swarm optimization algorithm, International Journal of Engineering, Science and Technology, vol. 2, no. 6, pp. 167-176.

[7] Premalatha, K. & Natarajan, A. M. (2010). Hybrid PSO and GA Models for Document Clustering, International Journal of Advances in Soft Computing and Its Applications, vol. 2, no. 3, pp. 302-320.

[8] Esmin, A. A. A. & Matwin, S. (2012). Data clustering using hybrid particle swarm optimization, in: 13th International Conference on Intelligent Data Engineering and Automated Learning (IDEAL 2012), Lecture Notes in Computer Science (Springer LNCS). Springer, Heidelberg, vol. 7435, pp. 159–166.

[9] Kamel, N., Ouchen, I. & Baali, K. (2014). A Sampling PSO-K-means Algorithm for Document Clustering, Advances in Intelligent Systems and Computing, Springer International Publishing Switzerland, pp. 45-54.

[10] Kamel, N. & Gaikwad, P. (2014). Hybrid Particle Swarm Optimization (HPSO) for Data Clustering, International Journal of Computer Applications, vol. 97, pp. 1-5.

[11] Kennedy, J. & Eberhart, R. C. (1995). Particle swarm optimization. , Proceedings of the IEEE International Conference on Neural Networks, Piscataway, NJ:IEEE Press, pp. 1942–1948.

[12] Kennedy, J. & Eberhart, R. C. (1997). A discrete binary version of the particle swarm algorithm. Proc. IEEE Int. Conf. on Systems, Man, and Cybernetics, pp. 4104-4108.

[13] Elbeltagi, E., Hegazy, T. & Grierson, D. (2005). Comparison among five evolutionary-based optimization algorithms, Advanced Engineering Informatics, vol. 19, pp. 43 -53.

[14] Korn, F., Jagadish, H. V. & Faloutsos, C. (1997). Efficiently Supporting Ad Hoc Queries in Large Datasets of Time Sequences, In Proceedings of the ACM SIGMOD Int'l. Conference on Management of Data, pp. 289–300.

[15] Zhang, Z., Huang, K. & Tan, T. (2006). Comparison of similarity measures for trajectory clustering in outdoor surveillance scenes, Proceedings of the 18th International Conference on Pattern Recognition, pp.1135 -1138.

[16] Junejo, I. N., Javed, O. & Shah, M. (2004). Multi Feature Path Modeling for Video Surveillance, Proc. Int\'l Conf. Pattern Recognition, vol. 2, pp.716 -719.

[17] Vlachos, M., Gunopulos, D. & Kollios, G. (2002). Discovering similar multidimensional trajectories, in ICDE, San Jose, CA, pp. 673 – 684.

[18] Berndt, D. & Clifford, J. (1994). Using Dynamic Time Warping to Find Patterns in Time Series, Proc. AAAI-94 Workshop Knowledge Discovery in Databases, pp. 359-370.

[19] Zhang, H., Ho, T. B., Zhang, Y. & Lin, M. S. (2006). Unsupervised Feature Extraction for Time Series Clustering Using Orthogonal Wavelet Transform, Informatica, pp. 305-319.

[20] Keogh, E. & Folias, T. (2002), The UCR Time Series Data Mining Archive, Available: http://www.cs.ucr.edu/»eamonn/TSDMA/index.html,2 002

[21] Chis, M., Banerjee, S. & Hassanien, A. E. (2008). Clustering Time Series Data: An Evolutionary Approach, Foundations of Computational Intelligence, Springer , vol. 206, pp.193-207.

[22] Keogh, E. & Smyth, P. (1997). A probabilistic approach to fast pattern matching in time series databases, in: Proceedings of the 3rd International Conference of Knowledge Discovery and Data Mining, pp. 24–20.

7

Evaluation of Classifiers in Software Fault-Proneness Prediction

F. Karimian and S. M. Babamir*

Department of Computer Engineering, University of Kashan, Kashan, Iran.

Corresponding author: babamir@kashanu.ac.ir (Babamir).

Abstract

Reliability of a software counts on its fault-prone modules. This means that the less the software consists of fault-prone units, the more we may trust it. Therefore, if we are able to predict the number of fault-prone modules of a software, it will be possible to judge its reliability. In predicting the software fault-prone modules, one of the contributing features is software metric, by which one can classify he software modules into the fault-prone and non-fault-prone ones. To make such a classification, we investigated 17 classifier methods, whose features (attributes) were software metrics (39 metrics), and the mining instances (software modules) were 13 datasets reported by NASA.

However, there are two important issues influencing our prediction *accuracy* when we use data mining methods: (1) selecting the best/most influential features (i.e. software metrics) when there is a wide diversity of them, and (2) instance sampling in order to balance the *imbalanced* instances of mining; we have two imbalanced classes when the classifier *biases* towards the majority class. Based on the feature selection and instance sampling, we considered 4 scenarios in appraisal of 17 classifier methods to predict software fault-prone modules. To select features, we used correlation-based feature selection (*CFS*), and to sample instances, we implemented the synthetic minority oversampling technique (*SMOTE*).The empirical results obtained show that suitable sampling software modules significantly influences the accuracy of predicting software reliability but metric selection does not have a considerable effect on the prediction. Furthermore, among the other data classifiers, *bagging*, *K**, and *random forest* are the best ones when we use the sampled instances for training data.

Keywords: *Software Fault Prediction, Classifier Performance, Feature Selection, Data Sampling, Software Metric, Dependent Variable, Independent Variable.*

1. Introduction

The software fault prediction methods use software *metrics* and *faulty* modules to guess *fault-prone* modules for the next software version. Hereafter, a *software module* indicates an *instance*, and a *software metric* does a *feature*. When we aim to classify software modules into the faulty and non-faulty ones, the software metrics are considered as *predictor* (*independent*) variables (features), and the faulty/non-faulty modules are done as the *outcome* (*dependent*) variable. *Software metrics* measure/quantify software characteristics such as *line of code* (LOC).

The software fault prediction models have been investigated since 1990s. According to [1], the probability of detection (PD) (71%) of the robust fault prediction models may be higher than that for *software reviews* (60%). According to [1], Fagan claimed that inspections can find 95% of defects before testing was not defended at the IEEE Metrics 2002 conference, and this detection ratio was about 60%.One member of the review team may examine 8-20 software lines of code in a minute. Thus, compared to the software reviews, the software fault prediction methods are more cost-effective to recognize software faults. The advantages of a robust software fault prediction are [2]:

- Reach a dependable system;
- Improving test process by concentrating on the fault-prone modules;

- Improving quality by improving test procedure.

Software quality engineering uses various methods and processes for producing high quality softwares. One efficient method is to apply the *data mining* techniques to software metrics for detection of the potential fault-prone modules. Through these techniques, we employed classification to predict program modules as fault-prone (*fp*) or not-fault-prone (*nfp*) [3-5], in which two noteworthy issues, the feature selection and class imbalance problems, were considered.

The class *imbalance* problem is raised if the *fp* instances are much less than the *nfp* ones. The imbalance problem can cause an undesirable conclusion; however, researchers often do not care about it [3, 5]. The efficiency of the software fault prediction models is affected by two significant numbers: (1) software metrics, and (2) software *fp* modules. The software quality prediction model without balancing up classes will not produce efficient fault predictors.

Before investigating the classifier methods to predict the fault proneness of software modules, we presented 4 scenarios consisting of an informed combination of two data preprocessing steps, feature selection (for selecting the important software metrics), and instance sampling (for the class imbalance problem), according to the Shepperd's work [6].

Some researchers have considered the *feature reduction* techniques such as principal component analysis (*PCA*) to improve the performance of the prediction models [7]. We used the correlation-based feature selection (*CFS*) [8] technique to obtain the relevant metrics, and the synthetic minority over-sampling technique (*SMOTE*) [9] for instance sampling (*fp*/*nfp* modules). We used (1) the *SMOTE* technique because it chooses samples through a non-random way [10, 11], and (2) *CFS* because, according to Catal et al. [12], it has a high performance. Considering the use of the *SMOTE* and *CFS* techniques for the selection of samples and features, figure 1 shows our approach.

The process of using feature (metric) selection and instance(module) sampling concurrently gives 4 scenarios, furnishing 4different training datasets for building the prediction models (classifiers).We made the software metric selection on the (1) *sampled* and (2) *original* modules, providing2 different metric subsets. Note that we will obtain *different metrics* if we use a feature selection method on the sampled or original modules. Having selected the features, we dealt with training the prediction model using the original or

sampled modules separately. Accordingly, 4 possible scenarios may be considered:

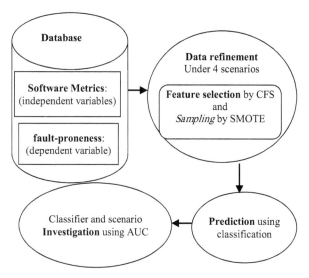

Figure 1. Our approach phases.

- First, to make use of the original modules for feature (metric) selection, and then training the classifiers based on the (**1**) original or (**2**) sampled instances.
- First, to make use of the sampled modules for feature (metric) selection, and then training the classifiers based on the (**3**) original or (**4**) sampled instances.

The research goal of our work was to compare the performance of the fault prediction models based on each of these scenarios, and to detect the best classification model. To this end, we exploited 13 public NASA datasets from PROMISE repository that were created in 2005 [13].

The remainder of this paper is organized as what follows. Section 2 discusses the related works. Section 3 explains the feature selection and sampling methods. Section 4 deals with the classifier methods and techniques applied in this paper. Section 5 deals with our empirical evaluation. Finally, in Section 6, we summarize our conclusions and provide suggestions for the future works.

2. Related works

Various methods have already been applied for software fault prediction. Catal et al. [12, 14, 15] have expanded and validated some artificial immune system-based models in the software fault prediction. Elish et al. [16] have compared the performance of support vector machines (*SVMs*) with the performance of logistic regression, multi-layer perceptron, Bayesian belief network, naive bayes (NB), random forests (RFs), and decision trees, and have finally concluded that the performance of *SVMs* is better than or (at least the same as) the other methods in the context of 4 NASA datasets. Kanmani et al. [17] have used probabilistic neural network (*PNN*) and back–propagation neural network (*BPN*) with a dataset obtained from the project of graduate students to compare their results with the results of statistical methods. They stated that *PNN* provided a better performance. Gondra [18] has shown that *SVM*s have a higher performance over the artificial neural networks (ANNs)in software fault prediction. Menzies et al. [1] have stated that although it is a very simple algorithm, naive Bayes is the best software prediction model. The area under the *ROC* (receiver operating characteristic) curve (called *AUC*, and explained in section 5.4) has been applied to evaluate the fault prediction models [3, 5]. Malhotra et al. [19] have shown that, based on *AUC*, LogitBoost is the highest method among the machine learning techniques *ANN*, *RF*, two boosting algorithms (*LogitBoost*, *AdaBoost*), NB, *KStar*, and *bagging* and *logistic regression*; their dataset was some open source software.

Catal et al. [2] have studied machine-learning methods such as RFs and artificial immune systems in the context of public NASA datasets, i.e. the PROMISE repository. They focused on the effects of dataset size, metrics set, and feature selection techniques. They showed (1) RFs had the best prediction performance for large datasets, (2) NB was the best prediction algorithm for small datasets based on *AUC*, and (3) the parallel implementation of artificial immune recognition systems (AIRS2Parallel) was the best artificial immune system paradigm-based algorithm when the method-level metrics were used.

A survey of the feature selection algorithms has been explained in [20]. Typically, the feature selection techniques fall into 2 categories, the *wrapper*-based and *filter*-based approaches. The former trains a learner during the feature selection process, whereas the latter does not depend on training a learner and applies the natural characteristics of instances (which is based on the given metrics) to the feature selection. The latter is computationally faster than the former.

Hall et al. [21] have validated 6 feature selection techniques producing ranked lists of features, and have applied them to 15 datasets in the UCI repository. The experimental results obtained showed that no one approach was the best for all situations. However, if computational complexity is eliminated as a factor, a wrapper-based approach has the best accuracy for a feature selection scheme.

Saeys et al. [22] have perused the use of an *ensemble* of feature selection techniques; this means that the multiple feature selection methods are combined for the feature selection process. They have stated that the ensemble approach provides subset of features more robust than a single feature selection technique.

Khoshgoftar et al. [23] have studied 2 types of feature selections for software defect prediction: (1) individual, and (2) repetitive and sampled with learning processes (boosting *vs.* plain learner).The former denotes that the feature ranking algorithm is used individually on the original data and once. The latter also uses only one feature ranking algorithm but it creates a sample dataset using an under-sampling or over-sampling technique. They applied 6 feature ranking techniques and 2 learners to build classification models (multi-layer perceptron and support vector machine). Their results have shown that the latter enjoys a better performance over the former. Moreover, the ensemble learning (boosting) approach enjoys a better classification performance over the plain learning process, which uses no boosting.

Gao et al. [24] have used 9 filter-based feature-ranking techniques for feature selection with random under-sampling data through 3 scenarios: (1) the features were selected based on the sampled data, and the training data was based on the original data, (2) the features were selected based on the sampled data, and the training data was based on the sampled data, and (3) the features were selected based on the sampled data, and the training data was based on the original data. The SVM classifier was applied to build the classification model, and the eclipse dataset of the PROMISE repository was used. The results obtained demonstrated that the first scenario was better than Scenarios 2 and 3, and the AUC feature-ranking technique performed better than the other approaches.

Similar to their earlier work, Gao et al. [25] applied the three scenarios but they used CFS for feature selection and 5 classifiers (SVM, MLP, LR, KNN, and NB) for constructing the model. The results showed that the 1st scenario performed better than the others, and SVM presented the best performance.

In [26], Gao et al. have applied (1) 6 filter-based feature-ranking techniques before and after the ensemble sampling methods RUSBoost and SMOTEBoost, and (2) 5 different classification algorithms for a group of datasets from real-world software systems. The results obtained demonstrated that feature selection after ensemble sampling was better, and RUSBoost performed better than SMOTEBoost. Among the 6 ranking techniques, RF (Random Forest) and RFW (random forest walk)enjoyed more performance over the others.

Wang et al. [27] investigated different feature-selection techniques consisting of filter-based and wrapper-based methods, and showed that the efficiency of the classification models improved; however, there was no efficiency when over 85% of the features were removed from the original datasets. The experiments carried out by Catal et al. [12] showed a high performance of the *CFS* method.

The class imbalance problem have been investigated in various areas [28-30], and various techniques have been developed to overcome the difficulties of learning from imbalanced data. In a binary classification, under-sampling the majority class and over-sampling the minority class [31-33] are the main approaches for solving the class imbalance problem. Since in this work, the majority and minority classes are non-faulty and faulty modules, respectively, we used under-sampling the non-faulty module class and over-sampling the faulty module one.

Riquelme et al. [11] have shown that the balancing techniques such as SMOTE improve the *AUC* parameter (see section 3.2.1). They applied the 2 balancing techniques *SMOTE* and resample, with 2 common classification algorithms, NB and J48, on 5 open public datasets from the PROMISE repository. In the current study, we considered the *SMOTE* method to resolve the class imbalance problem in fault prediction modeling.

Considerable works have been done on feature selection and data sampling separately but a few studies have been presented for considering both of them simultaneously, particularly in the software engineering field.

Chen et al. [34] considered data sampling and feature selection in the context of software cost/effort estimation but did not focus on the class imbalance problem, and used data sampling prior to feature selection. Furthermore, their classification model was for non-binary problems. Liu et al. [35] have introduced the *active* feature selection in their sampling approach. However, their goal of data sampling was dataset size reduction instead of addressing the class imbalance problem.

Khoshgoftaar et al. [36] presented feature selection and data sampling together for software fault prediction. They viewed 6 commonly used feature-ranking techniques [27] for feature selection and the random under-sampling [33]

technique for data sampling. However, they used just the *SVM* and *KNN* classifiers for building the software prediction models and their dataset; their results were different from ours. In this paper, we used 4 scenarios consisting of 4 significant synthesis of feature selection and data sampling. Each synthesis was used as a data preprocessing step for the training phase of 17 classifiers in the context of 13 public and cleaned NASA datasets from PROMISE repository.

3. Feature selection and sampling methods
In this section, we address the feature selection and sampling methods exploited in our work.

3.1. Correlation-based feature selection
In machine learning, feature selection is the process of selecting a subset of relevant features for the construction of a prediction model. Instances may contain *redundant* or *irrelevant* features, where the former does not provide additional information and the latter provides no useful information.

Elimination of redundant features from a set of features is called *filtering*. The filtering process may be considered for all or correlated features. For predict models that use machine learning techniques, it is important to determine relevant and significant features. In this work, we used a filter-based method called the correlation-based feature selection (*CFS*) to identify relevant metrics. This method begins with a null set, and at each stage, adds the features having the highest correlation with the class but not have high correlation with the already included features in the set.

3.2. Sampling methods
Sampling is a pre-processing method implemented to balance a given imbalanced dataset by increasing or decreasing the modules (cases) in the dataset before building the prediction model. Usually a dataset consists of a large number of "normal" (unconcerned) instances with just a small number of "abnormal" (concerned) ones. In this work, the normal and abnormal classes were the non-fault prone and fault-prone classes, respectively.

There are 2 types of samplings, *over-sampling* and *under-sampling*. In a binary classification, the former tries to increase the minority (abnormal) class, while the latter tries to decrease the majority (normal) one. Although under-sampling increases the sensitivity of a classifier to the minority class, a combination of over-sampling and under-sampling leads to a better performance over just under-sampling. Accordingly, prediction of the minority class is improved by correcting the imbalance problem.

Another sampling concern is that over-sampling may lead to over-fitting and under-sampling may lead to elimination of useful instances. Therefore, we used the synthetic minority over-sampling technique (*SMOTE*).

3.3. SMOTE

Chawla et al. [9] have proposed *SMOTE*, producing new instances based on K-nearest neighbor (KNN).To produce sample modules, we used *SMOTE* through the following steps:

1. Normalizing software metrics as the predictor variables. The normalization was used to fit a variable into a specific range. Among the others, the Min-Max normalization maps the metric value $mt_{i,j}$ to $nval(mt_{i,j})$, fitting in the range [0,1] "(1)". The $nval(mt_{i,j})$ value indicates the normalized value for metric mt_i of module j, where $val(mt_{i,j})$ is the current value for the metric of module j, and $min(mt_{i,j})$ and $max(mt_{i,j})$ indicate the max. and min. values for the metric of module j, respectively.

$$nval\left(mt_{i,j}\right)=\frac{val(mt_{i,j})-\min\left(mt_{i,j}\right)}{\max\left(mt_{i,j}\right)-\min\left(mt_{i,j}\right)} \quad (1)$$

2. Choosing a sample module, say m_s, from the fault-prone class.

3. Computing the KNN value for m_s based on the *similarity* (we considered K=5). Among 5 neighbors, the most similar module to m_s is the one that has the least Euclidian distance to m_s. Given that each module consists of n metrics, "(2)" shows the Euclidean distance between m_s and another module (similarity m_s to another module), say m_b, where n indicates the number of metrics of the module.

$$sim\left(m_s,m_b\right)=\sqrt{\sum_{i=1}^{n}[nval(mt_{i,s})-nval(mt_{i,b})]^2} \quad (2)$$

Having calculated the similarity of module m_s to others, we selected 5 modules having the minimum Euclidian distance to m_s. These modules are called the 5 NNs of module m_s.

4. Choosing one of the 5 neighbors randomly, say m_r, and adding to the minority (fault-prone) class.

5. Generating the *synthetic* module. (a) The difference between each m_s metric value and the corresponding m_r metric was computed as follows (n is the number of metrics):

$$d_{i,s} = val(mt_{i,s})-val(mt_{i,r}), \ i=1..n \quad (3)$$

(b) $d_{i,s}$ is multiplied by a random number between 0 and 1, and added to the corresponding m_s metric value.

$$val(mt_{i,s})=val(mt_{i,s})+rand[0,1]*d_{i,s}, \ i=1,n \quad (4)$$

Step 5 leads to the generality of the decision region of the fault-prone class.

4. Classifiers

We evaluated the statistical and machine learning classifiers [37-39] for software fault prediction. In what follows, we briefly explain them.

4.1. Logistic regression (LR)

LR is widely applied as a statistical technique. A detailed explanation of the LR analysis could be obtained from Hosmer et al. [34] and Basili et al. [11]. It is called *ridge* regression, which is the most commonly used regularization method for the not well-posed problems, meaning that the solution is highly sensitive to changes in data. In this work, we used the multinomial logistic regression model using the *ridge estimator* [40].

4.2. Bagging

Bagging (**b**ootstrap **agg**regat**ing**), introduced by Breiman [41], improves the classification performance using the *bootstrap aggregation*, meaning that it produces various similar sets of training data and applies a new method to each set. It is an *ensemble* classifier, and provides an aggregation of predictions of some independent classifiers with the goal of improving the prediction accuracy. An *ensemble* classifier uses the multiple classification algorithms and averages their predictions. To this end, it uses random samples with replacement and/or random predictor (feature) sets to generate diverse classifications. Therefore, each training set is a bootstrap sample because of using sampling with replacement. The ensemble methods are used to address the *class imbalance* problem.

The bagged classifier makes a decision by the majority of the prediction results returned by each classification. According to [41, 42], the benefits of bagging are (1) a better classification accuracy over the other classifiers,(2) the variance reduction, and (3) avoidance of over-fitting.

4.3. Random forest (RF)

RF was proposed by Breiman [43], and similar to *bagging*, it is an ensemble method. It produces a forest of decision trees at the training time. Each tree is produced based on the values for a random vector; these vectors are sampled with the same distribution and independently for all trees of the forest. The result of the output class is known as the mode of output classes obtained from the individual trees [42].

According to [41, 42, 44], the features of RF are: (1) simplicity and robustness against noises, (2) ability of accurate classification for various datasets, (3) ability of fast learning, (4) having efficiency on large datasets, (5) ability of estimation of important variables in the classification, (6) ability of estimating missing data and maintaining accuracy in missing a large proportion of the data, and (7) having methods for balancing unbalanced datasets.

4.4. Boosting techniques

Similar to *bagging* and *random forest*, *boosting* is a machine-learning ensemble meta-algorithm. It uses a decision tree algorithm for producing new models. Unlike *bagging*, which assigns an equal vote to each classifier, *boosting* assigns weights to classifiers based on their performance. The *boosting* methods use a training set for each classifier based on the performance of the earlier classifiers.

There are various *boosting* algorithms present in the literature. In this work, we used *AdaBoost(AB)* [45] and *LogitBoost(LB)* [46] for classification. The features of *boosting* are its ability to (1) reduce bias and variance in supervised learning, and (2) convert *weak learners* to *strong* ones[47]. A weak/strong learner is a classifier that is ill-correlated/well-correlated with the true classification.

4.5. DECORATE

DECORATE (diverse ensemble creation by oppositional relabeling of artificial training examples) is a meta-learner, exploiting a *strong* learner for constructing classes. To this end, *DECORATE* artificially builds random examples for the training phase. This is why *DECORATE* provides a high accuracy on the training data to build efficient various classes in a simple way. The class labels of these artificially constructed examples are in inverse relation to the current classes, and therefore, it increases diversity when a new classifier is trained on the additional data. The problem with the *boosting* and *bagging* classifiers is that they restrict the amount of the ensemble diversity they can get when the training set is small. This is because the *boosting* and *bagging* classifiers provide the diversity by re-weighting the existing training examples, while the *DECORATE* classifier ensures variety on a large set of additional artificial examples.

In the case of class imbalance, identifying samples from the minority class is usually more significant and dearer than the majority class. Therefore, some ensemble methods have been presented to resolve it. According to [48], adding variety to an ensemble method improves the performance of a learning method in case of the class imbalance. Haykin and Network have dealt with the influence of diversity on the performance of the minority and majority classes [48]. They have presented good and bad patterns in imbalanced scenarios, and have obtained 6 different situations of the influence of the diversity through theoretical analysis. Furthermore, they have carried out experimental studies on the datasets consisting of highly skewed class distributions. Then they have come into the conclusion that there is a strong correlation between diversity and performance, and that diversity has a good influence on the minority class.

4.6. Multi-layer perceptron (MLP)

MLP uses biological neurons to construct a model, and is applied to model complex relationships between inputs and outputs and search patterns in datasets [48]. *MLP* could be considered as a binary classifier with multiple layers. An *MLP feed forward* network includes one input layer, one or more hidden layers, and one output layer. Each layer consists of nodes that are connected to their immediate preceding layers as the input and the immediate succeeding layers as the output. The *back-propagation* method is the most commonly used learning algorithm in order to train the multi-layer feed forward networks, and includes 2 passes, forward and backward. Through the forward pass, a training input dataset is used, and a set of outputs is created as the actual response. In this pass, the network weights are fixed and their effect is propagated through the layers of the network [48]. Through the backward pass, an error, which is the difference between the actual and desired output of the network, is computed. The computed error is propagated backward through the network, and the weights are re-adjusted in order to reduce the gap between the actual and desired responses.

4.7. Radial basis function (RBF) network

RBF is a function whose value depends only on the distance (normally the *Euclidean* distance) from the origin. The *RBF* network, proposed by Broomhead and Lowe [49], is an artificial neural network (ANN) applying *RBF* as an activation function. Among others such as function approximation and time series prediction, the *RBF* networks could apply to the classification.

The RBF networks often consist of 3 layers: input layer, non-linear RBF hidden layer, and linear output layer, where the input layer is a vector of real numbers, $x \in \mathbb{R}^n$, and the output layer is a scalar function of the input vector (Relation 5). In fact, we have $\varphi : \mathbb{R}^n \longrightarrow \mathbb{R}$.

$$\varphi(x) = \sum_{i=1}^{N} a_i \rho(|x\text{-}c_i|) \qquad (5)$$

where, N is the number of neurons in the hidden layer, c_i is the center vector, and a_i is the weight of neuron i in the output layer. All inputs are connected to each hidden neuron. The RBF network consisting of enough hidden neurons can approximate any continuous function with a desired accurate [50]. The RBF networks could be normalized; in this work, we used the normalized Gaussian RBF network.

4.8. Naïve bayes (NB)

The NB classifier is a probabilistic classifier based on the Bayes theorem, assuming that there is a strong (naive) independency between the features [51]. When *NB* equips with an appropriate preprocessing, it classifies as well as some advanced methods such as the support vector machine (*SVM*).

Instead of the expensive iterative approximation, which is used by many classifiers, the *NB* classifier uses maximum-likelihood (i.e. without Bayesian methods), and training is performed through assessing a closed-form expression in the linear time.

A feature value is independent from the other feature values in the *NB* classifier. Accordingly, the *NB* classifier considers each feature independently in the sample classification, regardless of the correlations with other features of the sample.

The *NB* classifiers can be trained efficiently using the supervised learning for some types of probability models, and their advantage is that they require a small amount of training data for the classification process.

4.9. Bayes network (BN)

A Bayesian network is a probabilistic graphical model that shows relationships among the subsets of variables. Unlike the NB classifier, this method considers dependencies between variables, and determines joint conditional probability distributions. The advantages of a *BN* model are: (1) it easily handles the missing data because of representing dependencies between variables, (2)

it could provide a graphical model of causal relationships, and hence could be used to predict the consequences of intervention, and (3) since it has both the causal and probabilistic semantics, it is ideal for incorporating prior knowledge (which typically comes in the causal form) [52].

4.10. Support vector machines (SVM)

SVM, proposed by Vapnik [53], is a supervised learning method creating a hyper-plane or collection of hyper-planes, and can be used for classification and regression. When a hyper-plane has the largest distance to the nearest training data of any class (called functional margin) a good separation is obtained because a larger margin leads to a smaller error of the classifier. *SVM* could be used for the ill-posed problems, meaning that the solution is highly sensitive to the changes in a dataset.

The main problem with *SVM* is that it is not possible to separate the datasets linearly in a finite dimensional space. Accordingly, the original finite-dimensional space is mapped into a higher-dimensional space so that we can separate the datasets [54]. The hyper-planes in the higher-dimensional space are the set of points whose dot product with a vector in that space is constant. Another problem with *SVM* is that despite a good performance in the pattern, recognition field does not consider the problem domain knowledge; moreover, the classification speed is considerably slower than that of the neural networks.

4.11. K*

K* is an instance-based learning method, using the *entropy distance* to compute the distance between instances [55]. Learning based on instances means that the instance classification is carried out through comparing the instances with a dataset of pre-classified examples. Such a learning is based on the fact that similar instances have similar classifications. The similarity between 2 instances is determined according to a distance function, and a classification function is used to exploit the instance similarity for the classification of the new instances. The entropy distance manages (1) symbolic attributes, (2) real-valued features, and (3) missing values.

4.12. DecisionStump (DS)

DS is a binary classifier, and has a one-level decision tree with one root node connected to the terminal nodes (leaves) [56]. The prediction through DS is carried out based on the value for a single input attribute. *DS* is often used as a component of the ensemble methods such as bagging and boosting.

4.13. J48

J48 is a Java implementation of the C4.5 algorithm [57], and is a decision tree-based classifier. A decision tree is a machine-learning predictor that predicts the *dependent* variable value based on the attribute values of the existing data. The dependent variable is the attribute that should be predicted. The independent variables are other attributes, which are used to predict the dependent variable value.

A decision tree has internal nodes, indicating different attributes, where the attribute values for the observed samples are shown on branches between the nodes. The final values for the dependent variables are shown by the tree leaves. To classify a new sample, the *J48* decision tree classifier creates a decision tree based on the attribute values of the training dataset. Afterwards, the order of attribute selection is followed based on the tree. The target value of a new instance is predicted through checking values of all attributes against the corresponding values in the decision tree model.

4.14. AN alternating decision tree (ADTree)

The *ADTree* classifier combines decision trees with the prediction accuracy of the boosting classifier in a set of classification rules. The *ADTree* classifier consists of *decision* and *prediction* nodes [58], where the former is used to determine conditions and contains both the root and leaf nodes. The latter nodes have a single number. Classifying a sample by an *ADTree* is different from classifying it by the binary classification trees such as *C4.5* because a sample follows only one path in tree in *C4.5*, while in *ADTree*, a sample follows all paths for which the decision nodes are true; then all the prediction nodes visited in these paths were considered. A variation in *ADTree* is the multi-class *ADTree* [59].

4.15. PART

PART is a Java implementation of the C4.5 algorithm [60]. *PART* is a partial decision tree algorithm, applying the divide-and-conquer method, builds a partial C4.5 decision tree in a number of iterations, and adds the best leaf to a rule. The main feature of the *PART* classifier is that it needs no global optimization, while C4.5 does such an optimization.

5. Empirical evaluation

This section aims to represent the empirical study results to evaluate the ability of classifiers in predicting fault-prone software modules. We used the *weka* toolkit with default settings.

5.1. Datasets

We used cleaned versions of the datasets of 13 mission critical NASA software projects (Table 1) in this work; they were available from the PROMISE repository. The software metrics were considered as the *independent variables* (the predictor variables), and the faulty-prone and non-faulty-prone classes were considered as the *dependent variables* (the predicted variables).

Table 1. NASA PROMISE datasets.
Legends: NSM: #software metrics, NI: #instances,
%DI: %defective instances (modules).

	Dataset	Language	NSM	NI	%DI
1	CM1	C	21	439	10.47
2	JM1	C	22	7782	20.71
3	KC1	C++	22	1183	21.4
4	KC2	Java	22	334	27.84
5	KC3	Java	40	325	12.92
6	MC1	C & C++	39	1988	1.81
7	MC2	C	40	157	32.48
8	MW1	C	38	379	7.38
9	PC1		22	946	6.65
10	PC2		37	1391	1.50
11	PC3	C	38	1436	10.44
12	PC4		38	1287	13.67
13	PC5	C++	39	1711	26.82

5.2. Independent variables

We considered 39 software metrics as the independent variables. They were quantitative values indicating the software features. The metrics are explained briefly below, and are of 3 types: (1) *module-level* called *McCabe* metrics [61, 62], (2) *Halstead*, and (3) *enumerated* metrics.

The *module-level* metrics consisting of metrics 1-4, 24, 26, 28, 30, 31, 33, and 37 were considered using flow-graph of a module, the *Halstead* metrics consisting of metrics 6-12 and 32 were used for the experimental verifications of a module, and the *enumerated* metrics consisting of metrics 5, 13-23, 25, 27, 29, 34-36, 38, and 39 indicate the number of comments, instructions, delimiters, and blank lines of a module. The abbreviations used at the beginning of the metrics are used by the PROMISE dataset.

Loc: total number of lines

1. v(g): cyclomatic complexity= $p+1$, where p denotes the predicate (branch) of the module;

2. ev(g): essential complexity, denoting unstructured codes of a module, and used to compute the *effort* prediction for the module maintenance;

3. iv(g): design complexity: number of calls directly performed by a module or number of modules directly call a module;

4. n: parameter count: number of parameters of a module;

5. v:volume = length× $\log_2(\eta_1+\eta_2)$, where η_1 and η_2 denote the number of distinct operators and operands of a module, respectively;

6. l:length = $N_1 + N_2$, where N_1 and N_2 denote the total number of operands and operators of a module, respectively;

7. d: difficulty = $(\eta_1/2)*$ (N_2/η_2), parameters η_1, N_2, and η_2 were explained above. This metric denotes the module understanding;

8. i: content = level×volume, where program *level* ranges between zero and one, and *level*=1 denotes that a module has been composed at the highest possible level (i.e. with a minimum size);

9. e: effort = difficulty×volume; the effort estimated for development of a module; *difficulty* is computed as *D=1/level*. As the module volume increases, its level and difficulty decreases and increases, respectively;

10. error_est: error estimation=*(effort$^{2/3}$)/3000;* the number of errors is estimated to code a module;

11. prog_time: effort/18 seconds; the required time to program;

12. LOCode: number of instructions of a module;

13. LOComment: number of comment lines of a module;

14. LOBlan: number of blank lines of a module;

15. uniq_op:number of unique operators of a module;

16. uniq_opnd: number of unique operands of a module;

17. total_op: total number of operators of a module;

18. total_opnd: total number of operands of a module;

19. branch_count: number of branches of a module;

20. call_pairs: number of invocations by a module;

21. loc_code_and_comment: number of instructions and comment lines of a module;

22. condition_count: number of condition points of a module;

23. cyclomatic_density = $v(g)$ / (*LOCode* + *LOComment*);

24. decision_count: number of decision points of a module;

25. design_density:iv(g)/v(g);

26. e: edge_count: number of edge flow graph of a module;

27. essential_density: $(ev(g)-1)/(v(g)-1)$;

28. loc_executable: number of lines of executable code of a module;

29. gdv(g):global_data_complexity = $v(g)/n$ (see Parameter 4 for *n*);

30 global_data_density: $gdv(g)/v(g)$;

31. L: halstead_level = $2*\eta_2/(\eta_1*N_2)$;

32. maintenance_severity =$ev(g)/v(g)$;

33. modified_condition_count: effect of changing a condition on a decision outcome;

34. multiple_condition_count: number of multiple conditions of a module;

35. node_count: number of nodes of flow graph of a module;

36. normalized_cylomatic_complexity: $v(g)/loc$;

37. number_of_lines: number of lines of a module;

38. percent_comments: percentage of comment lines of a module.

The PROMISE calculated metrics 1-20 for datasets 1-4 and 9 in table 1, and all metrics for datasets 5-8 and 10-13. However, because some independent variables might be highly correlated, we used a correlation-based feature selection technique (CFS) [8] to select the best predictors of the original and sampled data (Table 2).

Table 2. Metrics selection using CFS method for original and sampled data.

#	Dataset	Selected metrics of original data	Selected metrics of sampled data
1	CM1	1-4-9-14-16-17	3-4-9-13-14-15-16
2	JM1	1-4-9-13-14-15-22-16-17	3-4-14-15-22-16
3	KC1	6-7-8-9-14-15-17-20	3-4-14-15-17
4	KC2	1-3-9-15-22-18-19	2-3-9-13-14-15-22-17-19
5	KC3	7-22-15	22-31-30-6-37-39
6	MC1	21-38-39	15-21-22-14-26-3-30-31-33-38-39
7	MC2	15-14-4-28-31-8-10-11-36-18	14-26-4-3-31-8-10-11-7
8	MW1	15-14-4-27-9-32-34-36-17	15-21-14-24-4-26-27-35-18-38
9	PC1	9-14-22-15-17	3-4-9-14-22-15-19
10	PC2	20-22-14-26-9-8-18-39	14-4-26-29-33-16-39
11	PC3	15-22-14-9-33-37-17	1-21-22-14-25-3-5-9
12	PC4	22-23-3-39	3-24-26-4-28-5-39
13	PC5	21-22-24-4-3-30-9-8-10-34-16-36-1	15-21-3-24-4-3-5-30-31

5.3. Dependent variable

This work focuses on the prediction of being fault-prone a module. Therefore, our dependent variable was a *boolean* variable consisting of true or false values, indicating that the module was fault-prone (*fp*) or non-fault-prone (*nfp*). Predicting the number of faults is a possible future work if such data is accessible.

5.4. Performance metrics

Since the area under the *ROC* (receiver operating characteristic) curve (called *AUC*) is used to evaluate the fault prediction models (classifier methods) [3, 5], we used *AUC* in this work. The *ROC* curve shows *sensitivity* against *specificity*, where the *sensitivity* and *specificity* denote the probability of true fault detection and the probability of false alarm, respectively. We did not have a good performance when the *AUC* value was less than 0.7. (1-.9 = excellent, .9-.8 = good, .8-.7 = fair, .7-.6 = poor, less than .6 = fail).

If the *fp* and *nfp* modules are regarded as the positive and negative cases, the *ROC* curve will show rates of the *true positive* (i.e. correct prediction in fault-proneness of a module) against the false positive (i.e. incorrect prediction of a non-fault-prone module as a fault-prone module). An *ROC* curve shows the classifier performance, lying between 0 and 1 (the value 1 indicates a *perfect* classifier) [47].

5.5. Environment setting

The parameters of the experimental environment were set for the classifiers, as follow:

Logistic Regression: (1) maxIts=-1 (maximum number of iterations to be performed. Value -1 means until convergence), (2) ridge=10^{-8} (ridge value in the log-likelihood).
Bagging: (1) classifier: RepTree, (2) bagSizePercent=100 (Size of each bag, as a percentage of the training set size).
Random Forest: (1) maxDepth=0 (maximum depth of the trees, 0 for unlimited), (2) numFeatures=0 (number of attributes to be used in random selection, zero means log_2 (number_of_attributes) + 1 is used), (3) numTrees=10 (number of trees to be generated).
Boosting: (1) classifier: DecisionStump, (2) likelihood Threshold=-1.7976931348623157E308 (threshold on likelihood improvement), (3) numRuns = 1 (number of runs for internal cross-validation), (4) weightThreshold=10 (weight threshold for weight pruning).
Decorate: (1) artificialSize=1.0 (number of artificial examples to use during training), (2) classifier: J48, (3) desiredSize=15 (number of classifiers in this ensemble. Decorate may terminate before the size is reached (depending on the value for num Iterations), (4) numIterations=50 (maximum number of iterations to be run).
Multilayer Perceptron: (1) hiddenLayers = (attribs+ classes)/2, (2) learningRate=0.3 (amount that the weights are updated), (3) momentum=0.2 (momentum applied to the weights during updating).
Radial Basis Function: (1) clusteringSeed=1 (random seed to pass to K-means), (2) minStdDev=0.1 (minimum standard deviation for clusters), (3) numClusters=2 (number of clusters for K-Means to be generated), (4) ridge=10^{-8} (ridge value for logistic or linear regression).
Naïve Bayes: (1) KernelEstimator=false (kernel estimator for numeric attributes rather than a normal distribution), (2) SupervisedDiscretization =false (supervised discretization to convert numeric attributes to the nominal ones).
Bayes Network: (1) Estimator= SimpleEstimator (Estimator algorithm for finding the conditional probability tables of the Bayes network), (2) search Algorithm=k_2 (selected method to search the network structures).
Support Vector Machine: (1) c=10 (complexity parameter C), (2) epsilon=0.001 (epsilon for round-off error), (3) kernel: radial basis function(kernel to be used).
K^*: (1) entropicAutoBlend=false (entropy-based blending is not used), (2) globalBlend=20 (parameter for global blending), (3) missingMode: average column entropy curves (to determine how missing attribute values are treated).
J48: (1) confidenceFactor=0.25 (confidence factor for pruning), (2) minNumObj=2 (minimum number of instances in per leaf), (3) subtreeRaising=true (subtree raising operation is considered in pruning).
ADTree: (1) numOfBoostingIterations=10 (number of boosting iterations to be performed), (2) saveInstanceData=false (tree does not save instance data), (3) searchPath: expand all paths (type of search to be performed when it builds the tree. It will do an exhaustive search).
PART: (1) minNumObj=2 (minimum number of instances per rule), (2) confidenceFactor=0.25.

5.6. Cross-validation

A 10-fold cross-validation [63] was used to validate the prediction models. Each dataset was randomly partitioned into 10 folds of the same size.

For 10 times, 9 folds were selected to train the models, and the remaining fold was used to test the models, with each time leaving out a different fold. All the preprocessing steps (feature selection and data sampling) were done on the training dataset. The processed training data was then applied to build the classification model, and the resulting model was used for the test fold. This cross-validation was repeated 10 times; each fold was used exactly once at the test data.

5.7. Discussion of results

In this section, we aim to show the effect of feature selection techniques in combination with data sampling using 4 scenarios. The scenarios (see Figure 2) include all the possible situations when feature selection and data sampling are used simultaneously to create the training dataset.

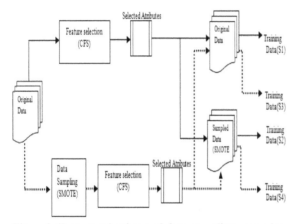

Figure2. Feature selection and data sampling scenarios.

Scenario 1 (S1): using CFS, we select features from the *original* data, and create the training dataset based on the *original* data;
Scenario 2 (S2): using CFS, we select features from the *original* data, and create the training dataset based on the *sampled* data;
Scenario 3 (S3): using CFS, we select features from the *sampled* data, and create the training dataset based on the *original* data;
Scenario 4 (S4): using CFS, we select features from the *sampled* data, and create the training dataset based on the *sampled* data.

5.7.1. Investigation using AUC performance

As stated in Section 5.4, the *AUC* value denotes the method performance. In other words, if h and g are 2 classifiers, then AUC(h) > AUC(g) means that classifier h has a better average performance over classifier g.

We classified the 13 datasets stated in table 1 using 17 classifiers and the 4 scenarios, and then calculated the *AUC* values. For brevity, we

showed just the results of classifying the datasets MC1, MC2, JM1, and KC2 (the datasets 6, 7, 2, and 4 in Table 1) obtained by 17 data classifiers under the 4 scenarios.

According to table 1, MC1 consists of the Min. percent of faulty modules (1.81%), many metrics (39 from 40), and comparatively many instances (1988).
Against MC1, MC2 consists of the max. percent of faulty modules (32.48%) and the min. number of instances (157). Similar to MC1, MC2 contains the max. number of metrics (40). Against MC2, JM1 has the max. number of instances (7782) and the nearly min. numbers of metrics (22 from 40).
Finally, KC2 lacks about half of the metrics (18) and comparatively, does not have many instances (324).

We then proceeded to evaluate the 17 classifiers for classifying the 4 datasets mentioned above. Figures 3-6 show the evaluation under the 4 scenarios for the datasets MC1, MC2, JM1, and KC2. The figures show two issues: (1) method performance with the 4 scenarios, and (2) comparison between the performances of the methods.
The 1st issue shows that with scenarios 2 and 4, we have a higher AUC (performance) than scenarios 1 and 3. The 2nd issue shows that there are agreements and disagreements on the performance of the methods (Table 3). This table shows that the figures agree on the best performance of the *random forest* and *LogitBoost* classifiers (predictors), and the worst performance of *SVM* and *LADTree*.
With the 4 scenarios, we obtained 4 different AUC performance values for each classifier in the classification of the 13 datasets. Then we calculated the *mean* (average) values for the 4 ACU values obtained and *standard deviation* of the scenarios from the mean (Relation 6, μ is the mean) for each classifier.

$$s = \sqrt{\frac{1}{4} \sum_{1}^{4} (\text{scenario}_i - m)^2} \qquad (6)$$

A low *mean* (less than 0.5) and a high *standard deviation* indicate inappropriate values.
A *low* standard deviation means that the data is very close to the mean, while a *high* standard deviation does that data scatter over a wider range of values.

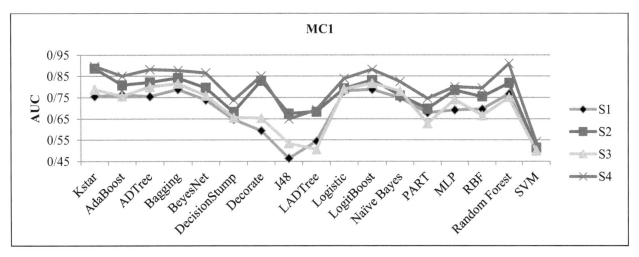

Figure 3. Performance evaluation of 17 data classifiers for MC1 dataset.

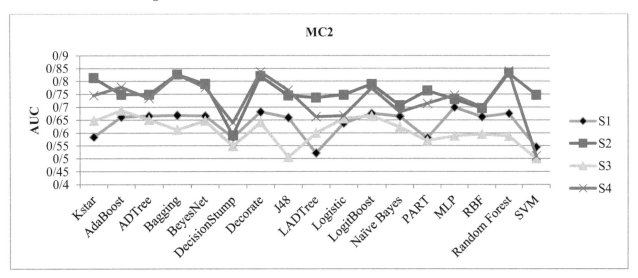

Figure 4. Performance evaluation of 17 data classifiers for MC2 dataset.

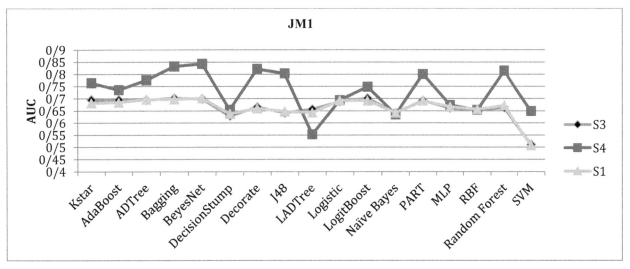

Figure 5. Performance evaluation of 17 data classifiers for JM1 dataset.

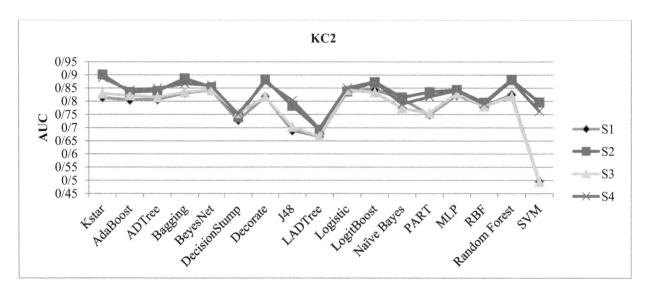

Figure 6. Performance evaluation of 17 data classifiers for KC2 dataset.

Table 3. Performance of classifiers under scenarios.

Dataset	Best classifier under scenario 2/4	Worst classifier under scenario 2/4
MC1	Random Forest, LogitBoost	SVM
MC2	Random Forest, logitBoost	SVM DecisionStump
JM1	BayesNet, Decorate, Random Forest	LADTree
KC2	KStar, Bagging, Decorate, LogitBoost, Random Forest	LADTree

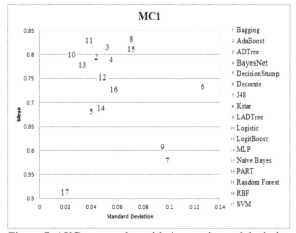

Figure 7. AUC mean value with 4 scenarios and deviation from mean value in *MC1* dataset classification.

Figure 7 shows (1) the mean AUC value obtained with 4 scenarios, and (2) standard deviation of scenarios from the mean for the 17 classifiers in the classification of the *MC1* dataset. According to figure 7, the *worst* (least) mean of the AUC value with the 4 scenarios is that of the *SVM* predictor; therefore, totally, it is not a good prediction method for the MC1 dataset, while the *best* (most) mean of the AUC value with the 4 scenarios is that of *LogitBoost*, *Bagging* and *Kstar*. However, the deviation in the *SVM*, *Logistic*, *Naïve Bayes*, *LogitBoost*, and *Bagging*

classifiers from the mean is the lowest; this means that they are stable against the *class imbalance* problem. By contrast, the deviation of the *Decorate*, *J48*, and *LADTree* classifiers from the mean is the *worst* (most). This means that they are more *unstable* for the *class imbalance* problem over others. Overall, figure 7 shows that *Logistic*, *Bagging*, and *LogitBoost* are better predictors than the others with view of the mean and deviation.

Figure 8 shows the mean AUC value obtained using the 4 scenarios, and the standard deviation of the scenarios from the mean for the 17 classifiers in the classification of the *MC2* dataset.

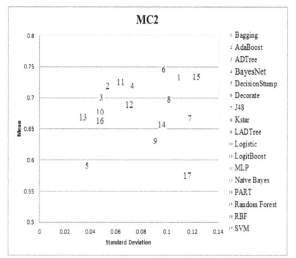

Figure 8. AUC mean value with 4 scenarios and deviation from mean in *MC2* dataset classification.

Similar to the classification used for the *MC1* dataset, Figure 8 shows that the *worst* (least) value of the mean AUC with the 4 scenarios is that of the *SVM* predictor; therefore, totally, it is not a good prediction method for the MC2 dataset; by contrast, the *best* (most) value of the mean AUC with the 4 scenarios is that of *Decorate*, *Bagging*, and *Random Forest*. However, the deviations in *Naïve Bayes* and *Decision Stump* from the mean are the least. This means that they are stable against *imbalanced* data. Overall, figure 8 shows that *ADTree* and *AdaBoost* predict better than the others with view of the mean and deviation.

Figure 9 shows the AUC mean value obtained with the 4 scenarios and standard deviation of scenarios from the mean for the 17 classifiers used for classification of the *JM1* dataset. Similar to the classification used for the *MC1* and *MC2* datasets, figure 9 shows that the *worst* (least) mean AUC value with the 4 scenarios is that of the *SVM* predictor. Therefore, totally, it is not a good prediction method for *JM1*; moreover, deviation in the *SVM* classifier from the mean value is the worst (most). By contrast, the *best* (most) mean AUC value with the 4 scenarios is that of the *BayesNet*, *Bagging*, and *Part* predictors.

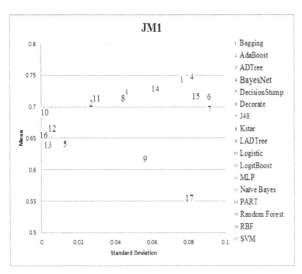

Figure 9. AUC mean value with 4 scenarios and deviation from mean in *JM1* dataset classification.

Deviation of the *Logistic*, *RBF*, *MLP*, *Naïve Bayes*, and *DecisionStump* predictors from the mean value is the least (best).This means that they are stable against the class *imbalance* problem.

Figure 10 shows the mean AUC value obtained with the 4 scenarios and standard deviation of scenarios from the mean for the 17 classifiers used for classification of the *KC2* dataset.

Again, similar to the three previous experiences, Figure 10 shows that the *worst* (least) mean AUC value with the 4 scenarios is that of the *SVM* predictor; therefore, totally, it is not a good prediction method for *KC2*; moreover, similar to the *JM1* dataset, deviation of *SVM* from the mean value is the worst.

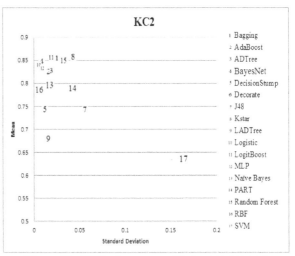

Figure 10. AUC value mean with 4 scenarios and deviation from mean value in *KC2* dataset classification.

However, the mean AUC value of about 10 classifiers is high, and their deviation from the mean value is low. Moreover, the deviation of all classifiers but *SVM* from the mean is *low*. This means that all predictors but *SVM* are stable against the *imbalanced* data.

5.8. Overall evaluations

Figures 11 and 12 show the AUC values obtained for the classifiers in classifying all the datasets with: (1) scenarios 2 and 4, and (2) all the scenarios, respectively.

Furthermore, the figures show the deviation of the classifiers from the mean value. With scenarios 2 and 4, figure 11 shows that the best performance is that of *Bagging* and *Random Forest*, while the worst performance is that of the *SVM* classifier.

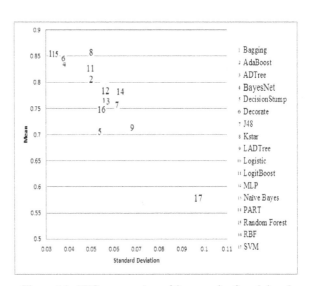

Figure 11. AUC mean value with scenarios 2 and 4 and deviation from mean for classification of *all* datasets.

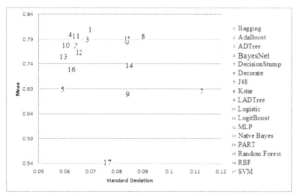

Figure 12. AUC mean of all scenarios and deviation from mean for classification of *all* datasets.

Based on all scenarios, figure 12 shows that the best performance is that of the *BayesNet*, *LogitBoost*, and *Bagging*, while the *worst* one is that of the *SVM* predictor. Moreover, the deviation of the *J48* classifier from the mean value is the *worst*. Based on Figs. 10 and 11, we came into this conclusion that the performance of the classifiers for software fault prediction is according to table 4.

Table 4. Software fault prediction performance of classifiers.

Scenario	Value	Method Performance
2 and 4	Mean	Kstar> Bagging > RF > Decorate >BayesNet
1,2,3,4	Mean	Bagging >BayesNet>LogitBoost>Kstar> RF
1,2,3,4	Standard Deviation	DecisionStump> Naïve Bayes >BayesNet

To show the impact of the 4 scenarios on the prediction models, we classified all of the 13 datasets to faulty and non-faulty modules using the 17 classifiers, and obtained the mean value of the classifiers for each scenario. Then we calculated the impact mean value of the scenarios and the deviation of each scenario from the mean value.

We used one-way analysis of variance (ANOVA) F-test [64] to determine the statistical difference between the 4 scenarios. There are 2 possible hypotheses: (1) null hypothesis, meaning that means of all groups of the population (scenarios) are the same, and (2) alternate hypothesis, meaning that at least one pair of mean values are different.

To show the statistical difference between the mean values of groups of population, the significance level (indicated by probability value or p-value) was computed by ANOVA. The difference between some of the means are statistically significant if p-value≤0.05. Otherwise, we have not enough evidence to reject the null hypothesis, meaning that the means are

equal. Therefore, for p-value≤0.05, we concluded that the alternate hypothesis should be accepted, and the means of at least 2 scenarios are significantly different from each other. We used MATLAB [65] to compute the p-value (Table 5).

Table 5. ANOVA results for 4 scenarios.

Source	sum of squares	degree of square	mean sum of squares	F-test	p-value
Scenario	0.08573	m-1= 4-1=3	0.08573/3 =0.02858	0.02858/ /0.00489 =5.84	P[F(3,64) ≥ 5.84] <0.0014
Error	0.31313	n-m= 68-4=64	0.31313/64 =0.00489		
Total	0.39886	64+3=67	0.00489 + 0.02858		

The p-value=0.0014 indicates that the scenarios are different. *Source* means "the source of the variation in the data" and *Scenario* shows groups of the population whose p-values to be compared. *Error* means "the variability within the groups" or "unexplained random error." Parameters $m=4$ and $n=68$ denote the number of scenarios and data, respectively.

After rejecting the null hypothesis, a multiple comparison called Tukey's test was used to compare the difference between the mean values pair wise. Figure 13 displays the multiple comparisons for the 4 scenarios with 95% confidence interval. As the figure shows, these intervals have no overlap; therefore, the mean values are significantly different. Considering figure 13, we understand that scenarios 2 and 4 significantly show a better performance over scenarios 1 and 3.

As figure 14 shows, the performance of the fault prediction of the models based on the *training sampled data* (i.e. scenarios 2 and 4) is better than the *training original data* (i.e. scenario 1 and 3), regardless of selection of the features from the sampled or original data.

In addition, scenario 4 (i.e. training sampled data and selection of features from the sampled data) shows the *most* mean value of performance using all datasets. If we call the *impact* of a scenario as the mean value for the performance of all classifiers using all datasets, the deviation of scenario 2 (i.e. training the sampled data and selection of features from the original data) from the *impact mean* is the *best* (least).

Overall, scenario 2 achieves better than the others. Therefore, considering figure 14, we came into this conclusion that the *impact* of the scenarios on the performance of the classifiers is 3<1<2<4 if we consider the mean value, and 2<4<1<3 if we do the standard deviation value.

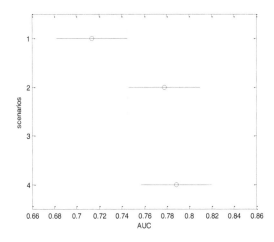

Figure 13. Multiple comparison for four scenarios.

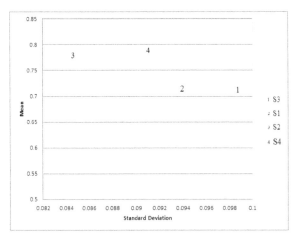

Figure 14. Mean value of performance of all classifiers (impact) for each scenario and deviation of scenarios from their impact using all datasets.

6. Conclusions and future work

This paper experimentally evaluated the ability of 17 classifiers in predicting fault-prone software modules with 4 scenarios in the context of 13 cleaned NASA datasets.

In a given classification problem, an important challenge is the choice of the convenient features when the underlying data is imbalanced. To deal with this problem, we discussed the different combinations of the feature selection and data sampling to create the training data for construction of a software fault prediction model. This study answered these research questions: (1) for which of the original or sampled data should feature selection be used? (2) given a set of picked features, based on which type of data (the original or sampled), we create the training data? (3) which of the classifiers have a better performance?

The results obtained showed that feature selection based on sampled or original data is not affected

in the performance of the fault prediction models. Furthermore, the performance of the fault prediction models is better when the training data is created using the sampled data over the original data. In addition, *Bagging*, *Random Forest*, and *K** have the best performance in the mean for all datasets with scenarios 2 and 4.

A future work may conduct the additional experimental studies on the other datasets, feature selection, and sampling methods, and may use additional in dependent variables (i.e. features) such as *coupling* and *cohesion* metrics.

Another new idea that may be considered as the future work is thinking of the fault prediction of the concurrent programs such as the multi-thread programs. For such programs, metrics such as the number of concurrent and sequential threads should be considered. Two significant classes for such programs are (1) execution sequences of a concurrent program leading to deadlock, and (2) those not leading to deadlock. We have an experience on fault prediction of concurrent programs using the NARX neural network, where executions are classified into deadlock-prone and non-deadlock-prone [66]. However, this classification was based on the runtime (dynamic) behavior of the concurrent programs, and not the use of software static metrics.

Another future work may apply sample reduction to training phase inspired by [67]. In [67], authors addressed an instance reduction method to discard irrelevant instances from the training set.

References

[1] Menzies, T., Greenwald, J., & Frank, A. (2007). Data mining static code attributes to learn defect predictors. IEEE transactions on software engineering, vol. 33, no. 1, pp. 2-13.

[2] Catal, C., & Diri, B. (2009). Investigating the effect of dataset size, metrics sets, and feature selection techniques on software fault prediction problem.Information Sciences, vol. 179, no. 8, pp. 1040-1058.

[3] Jiang, Y., Lin, J., Cukic, B., & Menzies, T. (2009). Variance analysis in software fault prediction models. In the 20th International Symposium on Software Reliability Engineering, pp. 99-108.

[4] Khoshgoftaar, T. M., Rebours, P., & Seliya, N. (2009). Software quality analysis by combining multiple projects and learners. Software quality journal, vol. 17, no. 1, pp. 25-49.

[5] Lessmann, S., Baesens, B., Mues, C., & Pietsch, S. (2008). Benchmarking classification models for software defect prediction: A proposed framework and

novel findings. IEEE Transactions on Software Engineering, vol. 34, no. 4, pp. 485-496.

[6] Shepperd, M., Song, Q., Sun, Z., & Mair, C. (2013). Data quality: Some comments on the NASA software defect datasets. IEEE Transactions on Software Engineering, vol. 39, no. 9, pp. 1208-1215.

[7] Khoshgoftaar, T. M., Seliya, N., & Sundaresh, N. (2006). An empirical study of predicting software faults with case-based reasoning. Software Quality Journal, vol. 14, no. 2, pp. 85-111.

[8] Hall, M. A. (1999). Correlation-based feature selection for machine learning (Doctoral dissertation, The University of Waikato), www.cs.waikato.ac.nz/~mhall/thesis.pdf, Access date: 11/21/2016.

[9] Chawla, N. V., et al. (2011). SMOTE: synthetic minority over-sampling technique. Journal of Artificial Intelligence Research, vol. 16, pp. 321-357.

[10] Kamei, Y., Monden, A., Matsumoto, S., Kakimoto, T., & Matsumoto, K. I. (2007). The effects of over and under sampling on fault-prone module detection. In the 1st International Symposium on Empirical Software Engineering and Measurement, pp. 196-204.

[11] Riquelme, J. C., Ruiz, R., Rodríguez, D., & Moreno, J. (2008). Finding defective modules from highly unbalanced datasets. In the Workshops of the Conference on Software Engineering and Databases, vol. 2, no. 1, pp. 67-74.

[12] Catal, C., & Diri, B. (2007). Software defect prediction using artificial immune recognition system. In the 25th conference on IASTED International Multi-Conference: Software Engineering, pp. 285-290.

[13] Shirabad, J. S., & Menzies, T. J. (2005). The PROMISE repository of software engineering databases. http://promise.site.uottawa.ca/SERepository, Access date: 11/21/2016.

[14] Catal, C., & Diri, B. (2008). A fault prediction model with limited fault data to improve test process. In International Conference on Product Focused Software Process Improvement, pp. 244-257.

[15] Catal, C., & Diri, B. (2007). Software fault prediction with object-oriented metrics based artificial immune recognition system. In International Conference on Product Focused Software Process Improvement, pp. 300-314.

[16] Elish, K. O., & Elish, M. O. (2008). Predicting defect-prone software modules using support vector machines. Journal of Systems and Software, vol. 81, no. 5, pp. 649-660.

[17] Kanmani, S., Uthariaraj, V. R., Sankaranarayanan, V., & Thambidurai, P. (2007). Object-oriented software fault prediction using neural networks. Information and software technology, vol. 49, no. 5, pp. 483-492.

[18] Gondra, I. (2008). Applying machine learning to software fault-proneness prediction. Journal of Systems and Software, vol. 81, no. 2, pp. 186-195.

[19] Malhotra, R., & Singh, Y. (2011). On the applicability of machine learning techniques for object oriented software fault prediction. Software Engineering: An International Journal, vol. 1, no. 1, pp. 24-37.

[20] Liu, H., & Yu, L. (2005). Toward integrating feature selection algorithms for classification and clustering. IEEE Transactions on knowledge and data engineering, vol. 17, no. 4, pp. 491-502.

[21] Hall, M. A., & Holmes, G. (2003). Benchmarking attribute selection techniques for discrete class data mining. IEEE transactions on knowledge and data engineering, vol. 15, no. 6, pp. 1437-1447.

[22] Saeys, Y., Abeel, T., & Van de Peer, Y. (2008). Robust feature selection using ensemble feature selection techniques. In Joint European Conference on Machine Learning and Knowledge Discovery in Databases, pp. 313-325.

[23] Khoshgoftaar, T. M., Gao, K., & Napolitano, A. (2014). Improving software quality estimation by combining feature selection strategies with sampled ensemble learning. In the 15th IEEE International Conference on Information Reuse and Integration, pp. 428-433.

[24] Gao, K., & Khoshgoftaar, T. M. (2011). Software Defect Prediction for High-Dimensional and Class-Imbalanced Data. In the 23rd International Conference on Software Engineering & Knowledge Engineering, pp. 89-94.

[25] Gao, K., Khoshgoftaar, T. M., & Napolitano, A. (2015). Combining feature subset selection and data sampling for coping with highly imbalanced software data. In the 27th International Conference on Software Engineering and Knowledge Engineering, pp. 439-444.

[26] Gao, K., Khoshgoftaar, T. M., & Wald, R. (2014). Combining Feature Selection and Ensemble Learning for Software Quality Estimation. In the 27th International Florida Artificial Intelligence Research Society Conference.

[27] Wang, H., Khoshgoftaar, T. M., Gao, K., & Seliya, N. (2009). Mining data from multiple software development projects. In IEEE International Conference on Data Mining Workshops, pp. 551-557.

[28] Engen, V., Vincent, J., & Phalp, K. (2008). Enhancing network based intrusion detection for imbalanced data. International Journal of Knowledge-Based and Intelligent Engineering Systems, vol. 12, no. 5- 6, pp. 357-367.

[29] Kamal, A. H., Zhu, X., Pandya, A. S., Hsu, S., & Shoaib, M. (2009). The impact of gene selection on

imbalanced microarray expression data. In the 1st International Conference on Bioinformatics and Computational Biology, pp. 259-269.

[30] Zhao, X. M., Li, X., Chen, L., & Aihara, K. (2008). Protein classification with imbalanced data. Proteins: Structure, function, and bioinformatics, vol. 70, no. 4, pp. 1125-1132.

[31] Chawla, N. V., Bowyer, K. W., Hall, L. O., & Kegelmeyer, W. P. (2002). SMOTE: synthetic minority over-sampling technique. Journal of Artificial Intelligence Research, vol. 16, pp. 321-357.

[32] Cieslak, D. A., Chawla, N. V., & Striegel, A. (2006). Combating imbalance in network intrusion datasets. In the IEEE International Conference on Granular Computing, pp. 732-737.

[33] Seiffert, C., Khoshgoftaar, T. M., & Van Hulse, J. (2009). Improving software-quality predictions with data sampling and boosting. IEEE Transactions on Systems, Man, and Cybernetics-Part A: Systems and Humans,vol. 39, no. 6, pp. 1283-1294.

[34] Chen, Z., Menzies, T., Port, D., & Boehm, D. (2005). Finding the right data for software cost modeling. IEEE software,vol. 22, no. 6, pp. 38-46.

[35] Liu, H., Motoda, H., & Yu, L. (2004). A selective sampling approach to active feature selection. Artificial Intelligence, vol. 159, no. 1, pp. 49-74.

[36] Khoshgoftaar, T. M., Gao, K., & Seliya, N. (2010). Attribute selection and imbalanced data: Problems in software defect prediction. In 22nd IEEE International Conference on Tools with Artificial Intelligence, vol. 1, pp. 137-144.

[37] Dietterich, T. G. (1998). Approximate statistical tests for comparing supervised classification learning algorithms. Neural Computation, vol. 10, no.7, pp. 1895-1923.

[38] Duda, R. O., Hart, P. E., & Stork, D. G. (2012). Pattern classification. John Wiley & Sons.

[39] Kothari, C. R. (2004). Research methodology: Methods and techniques. New Age International.

[40] Le Cessie, S., & Van Houwelingen, J. C. (1992). Ridge estimators in logistic regression. Applied statistics, pp.191-201.

[41] Breiman, L. (2001). Random forests. Machine learning, vol. 45, no. 1, pp. 5-32.

[42] Biau, G., Devroye, L., & Lugosi, G. (2008). Consistency of random forests and other averaging classifiers. Journal of Machine Learning Research, vol. 9, pp. 2015-2033.

[43] Fenton, N. E., & Ohlsson, N. (2000). Quantitative analysis of faults and failures in a complex software system. IEEE Transactions on Software engineering, vol. 26, no. 8, pp. 797-814.

[44] Livingston, F. (2005). Implementation of Breiman's random forest machine learning algorithm. Machine Learning : ECE519.

[45] Freund, Y., & Schapire, R. E. (1996). Experiments with a new boosting algorithm. In the 13th International Conference on Machine Learning, pp. 148-156. 1996.

[46] Friedman, J., Hastie, T., & Tibshirani, R. (2000). Additive logistic regression: a statistical view of boosting (with discussion and a rejoinder by the authors).The Annals of Statistics, vol. 28, no. 2, pp. 337-407.

[47] Witten, I. H., & Frank, E. (2005). Data Mining: Practical machine learning tools and techniques. Morgan Kaufmann.

[48] Haykin, S. S. (2001). Neural networks: a comprehensive foundation. Tsinghua University Press.
[49] Broomhead, D.S. & Lowe, D. (1988). Radial basis functions, multi-variable functional interpolation and adaptive networks. Royal Signals and Radar Establishment Publisher.

[50] Park, J., & Sandberg, I. W. (1991). Universal approximation using radial-basis-function networks. Neural Computation, vol. 3, no. 2, pp. 246-257.

[51] John, G. H., & Langley, P. (1995). Estimating continuous distributions in Bayesian classifiers. In the 11th Conference on Uncertainty in artificial intelligence, pp. 338-345.

[52] Heckerman, D. (1998). A tutorial on learning with Bayesian networks. Learning in graphical models, MIT Press Cambridge, pp. 301-354.

[53] Vapnik, V. (2000). The nature of statistical learning theory. 2nd Edition, Springer.

[54] Press, W. H., Teukolsky, S. A., Vetterling, W. T., & Flannery, B. P. (2007). Numerical Recipes: The Art of Scientific Computing, Section 16.5, Support Vector Machines, Cambridge University Press, The 3rd Edition,

[55] Cleary, J. G., & Trigg, L. E. (1995). K*: An instance-based learner using an entropic distance measure. In the 12th International Conference on Machine learning, vol. 5, pp. 108-114.

[56] Iba, W., & Langley, P. (1992). Induction of one-level decision trees. In the 9th International Conference on Machine Learning, pp. 233-240.

[57] Quinlan, J. R. (2014). C4.5: programs for machine learning, Morgan Kaufmann Publishers.
[58] Freund, Y., & Mason, L. (1999). The alternating decision tree learning algorithm. In the 16th International Conference on Machine Learning, vol. 99, pp. 124-133.

[59] Holmes, G., Pfahringer, B., Kirkby, R., Frank, E., & Hall, M. (2002). Multiclass alternating decision

trees. In the European Conference on Machine Learning, pp. 161-172.

[60] Frank, E., & Witten, I. H. (1998). Generating accurate rule sets without global optimization. In the 15th International Conference on Machine Learning, pp. 144-151.

[61] McCabe, T. J. (1976). A complexity measure. IEEE Transactions on Software Engineering, vol. 2, no. 4, pp. 308-320.

[62] McCabe, T. J., & Butler, C. W. (1989). Design complexity measurement and testing. Communications of the ACM, vol. 32, no.12, pp. 1415-1425.

[63] Kohavi, R. (1995). A study of cross-validation and bootstrap for accuracy estimation and model selection.

In the 14th International Joint Conference on Artificial Intelligence, vol. 2, pp. 1137-1143.

[64] Rutherford, A. (2011). ANOVA and ANCOVA: a GLM approach. John Wiley & Sons.

[65] One-way analysis of variance-MATLAB anova1-MathWorks (2016), http://www.mathworks .com/help/stats/anova1.html, Access date: 11/21/2016.

[66]. Babamir, S. M., Hassanzade, E., & Azimpour, M. (2015). Predicting potential deadlocks in multithreaded programs. Concurrency and Computation: Practice and Experience, vol. 27, no.17, pp. 5261-5287.

[67] Hamidzadeh, J. (2015). IRDDS: Instance reduction based on distance-based decision surface, Journal of IA and Data Mining, vol. 3, no. 2, pp. 121-130.

8

Competitive Intelligence Text Mining: Words Speak

A. Zarei*, M. Maleki, D. Feiz and M. - A. Siahsarani Kojouri

Faculty of Economic, Management and Administrative Sciences, Semnan University, Semnan, Iran.

Corresponding author: a_zarei@semnan.ac.ir (A. Zarei).

Abstract
Competitive intelligence (CI) has become one of the major subjects for researchers in the recent years. The present research work is aimed to achieve a part of CI by investigating the scientific articles on this field through text mining in three inter-related steps. In the first step, a total of 1143 articles released between 1987 and 2016 are selected by searching the phrase "competitive intelligence" in the valid databases and search engines; then through reviewing the topic, abstract, and main text of the articles as well as screening the articles in several steps, the authors eventually selected 135 relevant articles in order to perform the text mining process. In the second step, pre-processing of the data is carried out. In the third step, using non-hierarchical cluster analysis (k-means), 5 optimum clusters are obtained based on the Davies–Bouldin index, for each of which a word cloud is drawn; then the association rules of each cluster are extracted and analyzed using the indices of support, confidence, and lift. The results obtained indicate the increased interest in research works on CI in the recent years and tangibility of the strong and weak presence of the developed and developing countries in formation of the scientific products; further, the results show that information, marketing, and strategy are the main elements of CI that along with other prerequisites can lead to CI and, consequently, the economic development, competitive advantage, and sustainability in the market.

Keywords: *Competitive Intelligence, Text Mining, Association Rules Mining, Word Cloud.*

1. Introduction

Today, the organizations are increasingly paying attention to the competitive intelligence (CI) because it supports the needs of an organization for collecting, interpreting, and publishing the external information [1]. CI supports the strategic process in an organization and, like a sensor, shows the managers whether the organization is competitiveness [2]. It is a vital element of the company's planning and management process that puts together the data and information from a very broad and strategic perspective and allows the company to foretell what would happen in the competitive environment [3]. This indicates that the CI has become the latest weapon in the economic war so that many of the emerging economies view it as a way to overcome the larger and more industrialized countries in the economic war [4]. CI does not mean industrial espionage, and its key principle is that 90% of all the information that a company requires for making important decisions and understanding the market and competitors is available in the general environment of the industry or can be systematically developed from the data of the industry's general environment [5]. The reason for emergence of this new scientific field is the explosion of information due to the increased access to information as well as the rapid and widespread proliferation of information in the commercial databases; besides, the broad social and political changes, increased pace of business, increased global competition due to emergence of new competitors, and technological changes can be mentioned as other reasons [6]. Data mining has become one of the major tools of business intelligence for discovering knowledge so that several extensive research works [7-9] have focused on the potential tools of this technique. One of the major branches of data mining is text mining, which generally deals with extraction of the hidden knowledge from unstructured textual documents [10]. One of the main applications of text mining is to help CI that the activists of the business world are seeking to acquire. In the scientific-academic area, numerous articles have been written on CI by various authors in different countries in successive years; however, further exploration in this regard can result in valuable applicable knowledge, which seems uninvestigable without using the data mining techniques. For example, searching the term "competitive intelligence" in the Science Direct and Emerald databases results in 1248 and 15549 accessible articles, respectively, the investigation, study, and summation of which would be an exhausting, time-consuming, and, in some cases, impossible task for researchers, indicating the necessity of the use of data mining to achieve the initial exploratory vision of the research work. The present research work is seeking to achieve the following objectives:

-Choosing the most relevant articles in the field of CI through screening the articles by investigating the titles, abstracts, and texts.

-Clustering the articles in the field of CI, extracting the central words, and drawing the word cloud of each cluster.

-Discovering the association rules for each cluster and extracting the application rules in accordance with the support, confidence, and lift indices as well as the experts' opinions.

2. Literature review

The CI concept embraces the two main keywords intelligence and competitiveness. The concept of intelligence is a part of the marketing strategy, which causes the increase in the company's competitive power and processes of its strategic plans [11]. Today the concept of intelligence is considered as a process that improves the competitiveness and process of strategic planning [12]. For instance, according to the UNCTAD's definition, competitiveness in the field of export refers to diversifying the export baskets, maintaining higher values of the export growth over time, improving the content of export activity in terms of skill and technology, and expanding the base of the domestic companies in order to achieve competitiveness in the international arena so that the competitiveness becomes sustainable and continuous and, subsequently, the level of living standard in the country is promoted [13]. Regarding the above-mentioned definitions for intelligence and competitiveness, CI referring to the intelligence of a company or a business is the art of absorbing and transferring the knowledge from the extra-organizational elements and the environment through specific rules and certain

standards to the organization in order to protect the competitive threats, identify and utilize the potential opportunities, and build the future, and thus it can influence the competitive position of the company [14-16].

According to Rouach and Santi (2010), in the knowledge-based organizations, which emphasize on managing the organizational knowledge, rearing the learning organizational culture, and implementing the supportive organizational structures in order to achieve the organizational intelligence, five classes of intelligence play fundamental roles, and are considered as the antecedents of intelligence in the age of knowledge. The five classes include market intelligence, competitor intelligence, technology-based intelligence, human intelligence, and structural intelligence [16]. Some researchers believe that the first two types of intelligence, namely market intelligence and competitor intelligence, are sub-categories of the competitive intelligence, and the other three including human intelligence, structural intelligence, and technological intelligence are sub-categories of the organizational intelligence [17]. Champs and Nayak (1995) has presented CI in three classes [18], as what follow. 1) Market intelligence: this type of intelligence is responsible for providing and supplying the current and future trends of the requirements and preferences of the customers for the new markets; in this intelligence, the information of the customers, suppliers, buyers, and distributors is collected and analyzed. 2) Competitors' intelligence: this type of intelligence is responsible for evaluating the evolution of the competitors' competitive strategy through continuous and systematic investigation of the competitors' structure and providing new alternative products for the industry. Competitor intelligence is a continuous effort to evaluate the behaviors and capabilities of competitors to develop the competitive advantage [19]. Competitor intelligence is aimed to refine and analyze the actions and performance of the competitors in order to achieve their vision [20]. 3) Technological intelligence: this type of intelligence is responsible for the cost-benefit analysis of the new and current technologies, prediction of the technologies that will disappear in the future as well as the technologies that will dominate in the future.

Environmental changes have caused changes in the commercial companies' decision-making and competition methods. The leaders in modern companies are facing decisions that require merging, analysis, and summarization of the internal and external information from various resources. The information technologies such as extensive organizational systems, data mining, and text mining are responsible for collecting and merging the interactions from different perspectives in order to support the decisions [21, 22]. The data mining process is a process of knowledge discovery since it embraces the human knowledge [23]. One of the fields of data mining is text mining [24]. Text mining refers to the process of deriving or extracting high quality information from a text. Text mining is based, on the one hand, upon the computational linguistics and, on the other hand, upon the mathematical-statistical computations and data analysis. The technologies used in text mining include information retrieval, information extraction, subject tracking, summarization, categorization, conceptual relationship, information visualization, and question responding [24, 25]. The main advantage of using the text mining technologies for CI is the high capability of text mining for rapid processing, objectification, and exclusion of large amounts of text data [26].

3. Methodology

Approach of the present research work is close to the three-step model of the process of knowledge discovery in text (KDT) presented by Karanikas and Theodoulidis (2002) [27]. The KDT model is composed of three steps: 1) data collection, 2) text pre-processing, and 3) text mining. The present research work passed the above-mentioned three steps. In the first step, a total of 1143 articles published between 1987 and 2016 were selected by searching the phrase "*competitive intelligence*" in the databases such as Science Direct, IEEE, Springer, Wiley, Taylor & Francis, Sage, Emerald, and Jestor as well as the search engines such as Google and Google scholar. By reviewing the titles, abstracts, and original texts as well as various steps of screening, the authors finally selected 135 articles on CI in order to perform the text mining process. In the second step of this research work, pre-processing of the data was performed. The tasks such as segmentation, conversion of the uppercase letters to lowercase letters, and removal of the stop word were performed in this step. Tokenization refers to the process of breaking a sequence of strings into the pieces called segments. The purpose of tokenization is to discover the words in a sentence and identify the meaningful keywords [28]. The stop words are the non-verbal words with no information load. The prepositions, prefixes, and pronouns can be considered as stop words. Etymology is the process of converting words into their roots. Many words in the English language are indeed the different forms of the same words (Liau and Tan, 2014) [28]. In the third step, using the non-hierarchical cluster analysis (k-average), the number of optimum clusters was obtained based on the Davies–Bouldin index, the word cloud of each cluster was drawn, and, finally, the association rules of each cluster were extracted and analyzed. Figure (1) shows the steps covered in the present research work.

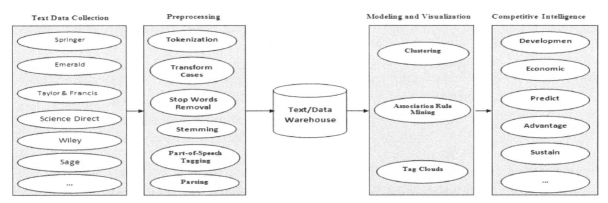

Figure 1. Steps covered in present research work.

4. Data analysis
4.1. Descriptive statistics

Investigating the selected articles in terms of the publication year and their producing continent can be notable from various aspects. Analysing the slope of production of the articles on CI indicated that taking this subject into consideration is increasing with a slight slope so that the importance of this field has reached its peak with publication of 26 articles in 2015. Diagram (1) shows the selected articles of the present research work based on their publication year.

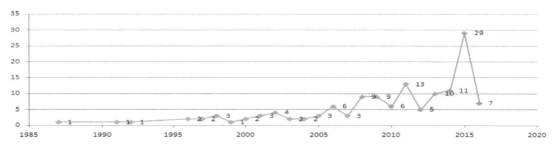

Diagram 1. Articles of present research work based on their publication year.

Investigating the published articles on CI based on the continent producing the articles indicates that this subject is of special position and importance among the Asian researchers, and Europe and South America rank the second and third, respectively. The interesting point is that among the Asian, European, and South American countries, China, Spain, and the United States have published the highest number of published articles on CI, respectively, indicating the research orientations in these countries. Reviewing the countries producing the articles on the field of CI obviously shows an outstanding gap between the developed and developing countries as well as tangibility of strong and weak presence of both groups in formation of the scientific products. Diagram (2) represents the article-producing countries based on their continent.

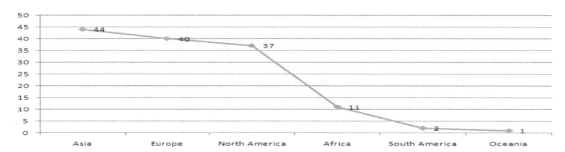

Diagram 2. Article-producing countries based on their continent.

4.2. Non-hierarchical cluster analysis (k-means)

Cluster analysis is aimed for decomposing a dataset into groups so that the data within a group has the highest similarity to each other and the highest differences with other groups [29]. The K-means cluster method was used to achieve the Euclidean distance between the clusters. During clustering, the number of groups (K) would be discovered, which is not clear at the beginning of the heuristic approach of clustering [30, 31]. K-means algorithm is a well-known clustering algorithm. In spite of its advantages such as high speed and ease of employment, this algorithm suffers from the problem of local optima [32]. In order to find the number of optimum k, the k-means algorithm with entry of k = 2 to k = 10 was performed, and then the Davies–Bouldin index was used to determine the number of optimum clusters. The Davies–Bouldin index calculates the average similarities between each cluster and the cluster that is most similar to it so that the lower the index value, the better the produced clusters. Table (1) shows the values for the Davies-Bouldin index based on the k (number) of different clusters.

Table 1. Values for Davies-Bouldin index based on number of clusters.

Number of clusters	2	3	4	5	6	7	8	9	10
Davies–Bouldin index	3.281	3.082	2.70	2.432	2.598	2.543	2.501	2.471	2.762

As shown in Table (1), the Davies–Bouldin index considers 5 clusters as appropriate for clustering. In case of 5 clusters, the Davies–Bouldin index has obtained the lowest value that is 2.432. The results of cluster analysis showed that the statistical population of the present research work could be clustered in five clusters, each of which is different from other clusters in terms of the studied dimensions. Afterwards, 10 words were presented in each cluster along with their final center; besides, the Knime software was used to draw the word cloud of each cluster. These word clods are unique to each cluster, demonstrating its specific conditions. The fact that the word "information" is centralized in all tag clods indicates its importance in the domain of competitive intelligence. Other words surrounding this one differ among the tag clods in terms of importance, distance, and size, and these word clods must not be considered equal. These figures show the details of the dispersion of words in each cluster on the one hand, and the distance of each word from cluster centers on the other. Moreover, they demonstrate the importance of each word in each cluster through the size of the word (more important words in each tag clod are larger).

Therefore, since these word clods offer good visual representations of each cluster, the readers can more easily understand each cluster through these word clods.

First cluster: This cluster accounted for 37% of the statistical sample's articles, and the pivotal subjects in this cluster included marketing, information, and corporation. Marketing, as the most important keyword, was located at the center of this cluster, and other words such as information, corporation, and competitors were at longer distances from this word. Analysis of the words in the first cluster shows the importance of taking into account the internal (companies, products, marketing) and external (competitors, customers) environments considering the strategy and applying the information to accomplish industrialization and development. The importance of marketing in CI is such that it is referred to as the marketing intelligence. Marketing intelligence has been defined as the capability to achieve and use the commercial resources and the processes that "the companies learn about their markets and use the market knowledge" [33]. Table (2) presents the words and final centers of the first cluster.

Table 2. Words and final centers of first cluster.

Words	Marketing	Information	Firm	Competitor	Strategy	Analysis	Development	Product	Industrial	Customer
Cluster Center	0.394	0.343	0.161	0.146	0.146	0.134	0.120	0.106	0.104	0.085

In this cluster, the word "information" ranked first in terms of frequency with 2795 times of repetition, and appropriated the center of the word cloud, indicating the importance of this word in

the cluster. The words "marketing" and "strategy" acquired the next ranks with 1456 and 1197 times of repetition, respectively. Figure (2) shows the first word cloud.

Figure 2. Word cloud of first cluster.

Second cluster: This cluster accounted for 30% of the statistical sample articles, and the pivotal subjects of the cluster included data, information, knowledge, and technology. This cluster embraced the various subjects from analysis and

path of data to knowledge, and it seemed that the secret of excellence (superiority) was rooted in being equipped and armed with knowledge, awareness of the competitors' status, awareness of the environment, and being updated in terms of technology. The information that is somewhere between data and knowledge would help the decision-makers to understand their competitors and make quick and intelligent strategic decisions [34, 35]. Table (3) represents the words and final centers of the second cluster.

Table 3. Words and final centers of first cluster.

Words	Information	Data	Analysis	Competitor	Marketing	Product	Knowledge	Environment	Development	Technology
Cluster Center	0.679	0.143	0.136	0.115	0.106	0.106	0.105	0.102	0.091	0.084

In this cluster, the word "information" ranked first in terms of the frequency with 2177 times of repetition, and appropriated the center of the word cloud, indicating the importance of this word in this cluster. The words "marketing" and "strategy" were in the next ranks with 1209 and 1179 times of repetition, respectively. Figure (3) shows the word cloud of the second cluster.

Figure 3. Word cloud of second cluster.

Third cluster: This cluster accounted for 18% of the statistical sample articles, and the pivotal subjects included knowledge, information, environment, and network. In this cluster, on one hand, special importance was put on knowledge and analysis and, on the other hand, the environmental factors were also taken into consideration. Knowledge is a flowing combination of the experiences, values, ground information, and expert vision, providing a framework for evaluation and application of the experiences and new information [36]. Acquisition of knowledge requires technology, environmental exploration, and strategy sharing it with the internal and external units. Table (4) represents the words and final centers of the third cluster.

Table 4. Words and final centers of third cluster.

Words	Knowledge	Information	Strategy	Development	Analysis	Environment	External	Network	Marketing	Share
Cluster Center	0.304	0.264	0.141	0.120	0.112	0.102	0.079	0.077	0.076	0.075

In this cluster, the word "information" ranked first in terms of the frequency with 1575 times of repetition, and appropriated the center of the word cloud, indicating the importance of this word in this cluster. The words "marketing" and "knowledge" were in the next ranks with 830 and 557 times of repetition, respectively. Figure (4) shows the word cloud of the third cluster

Figure 4. Word cloud of third cluster.

Fourth cluster: This cluster accounted for 8% of the statistical sample articles, and the pivotal subjects included technology, data, and analysis. In this cluster, the two words "technology" and "competitive advantage" attract the attention, and it seems that, in this cluster, in addition to other factors such as data, information, and strategy, the technology has been specially taken into consideration, and this word has been assumed as the main focus of the keywords of the cluster, which can pave the ground for achieving the competitive advantage. Technology is considered as the most important element in many industrialized companies, and means any kind of information that can affect development or production of the products [37]. The importance of technology in formation of CI is to the extent that Champs and Nayak (1995) have referred to it as the technological intelligence [18]. Table (5) represents the words and final centers of the fourth cluster.

Table 5. Words and final centers of fourth cluster.

Words	Technology	Data	Analysis	Information	Development	Industry	Marketing	Strategy	Technique	Advantage
Cluster Center	0.435	0.263	0.257	0.252	0.145	0.103	0.083	0.077	0.075	0.075

In this cluster, the word "information" ranked first in terms of frequency with 406 times of repetition, and appropriated the center of the word cloud, indicating the importance of this word in this cluster. The words "marketing" and "knowledge" were in the next ranks with 318 and 275 times of repetition, respectively. Figure (5) shows the word cloud of the fourth cluster.

Figure 5. Word cloud of fourth cluster.

Fifth cluster: This cluster accounted for 7% of the statistical sample articles, and the central subjects included competitors, information, market, and industry. In this cluster, the subject of "competitors" has been specially taken into consideration, representing the great importance of this subject in CI. Legally and ethically, CI uses the public resources to achieve the strengths and weaknesses of the competitors. CI would enable the companies to develop the corporation in order to achieve a larger share of the market and have a successful competition against the international competitors [38]. The companies competing at the global level face numerous challenges since the consumers use the internet to compare products and prices, and thus these companies need to be ahead of their competitors [39]. Table (6) represents the words and final centers of the fifth cluster.

Table 6. Words and final centers of fifth cluster.

Words	Competitor	Information	Market	Industry	Strategy	Product	Develop	Data	Plan	Technology
Cluster Center	0.454	0.316	0.290	0.172	0.167	0.146	0.138	0.131	0.128	0.090

In this cluster, the word "information" ranked first in terms of frequency with 783 times of repetition, and appropriated the center of the word cloud, indicating the importance of this word in this cluster. The words "market" and "strategy" were in the next ranks with 454 and 381 times of repetition, respectively. Figure (6) shows the word cloud of the fifth cluster.

Figure 6. Word cloud of fifth cluster.

4.3. Association rules mining

Data mining is the implicit, valid, and potential extraction of the useful knowledge from a raw dataset [40], and is widely used for discovering the hidden rules from the data with the aim of extracting the knowledge for making decisions such as predicting the costumers' behaviors [41, 42]. The "association rules" is a data mining technique, which helps discovering the interesting relationships between the variables in massive data [43, 44]. The "association rules" is a sign of the cooperation of occurrence of two variables, meaning that if two variables frequently concur, there will be a strong relationship between them [40]. Since the association rules have the potential to produce many patterns and rules, the three indices of support, confidence, and lift as well as the researchers' opinions were used to evaluate and extract the rules. The support index has a numerical value between zero and one so that the greater values indicate that two objects are more inter-related. By determining a threshold for this criterion, the user can obtain only the rules, the support of which is greater than the threshold value; accordingly, by reducing the search space, the time required to find the association rules can be minimized. The confidence criterion has also a numerical value between zero and one so that the greater the number, the higher the quality of the rules. The use of this criterion along with the support index would be an appropriate complement for assessment of the association rules but there still remains the problem that there might be a rule with high confidence that is not valuable from our viewpoint. The lift criterion represents the rate of independence between the objects A and B, which can be a numerical value between zero and infinity. In fact, the lift criterion considers the value of the concurrence between the features and imports the value of individual occurrence of the consequent section of the rule, namely the object B, in its calculations. The values close to 1 imply that A and B are independent from each other and, accordingly, do not represent the lift rule. For this criterion, the values lower than 1 indicate a negative relationship between A and B, while the values higher than 1 indicate that A provides more information about B, and thus the rule of A => B is evaluated to be of higher lift. Table (7) presents a summary of the definitions along with the formula of the three above-mentioned indices [45].

Table 7. Summary of definitions along with formula of three measures [45].

Measure	Description	Formula
Support	Usefulness of discovered rule A → B	$P(A \cap B)$
Confidence	Certainty of discovered rule A → B	$P(B\|A)$
Lift	Correlation between the occurrence of items in discovered rule A → B	$\dfrac{P(B\|A)}{P(B)}$

In the present work, the three above-mentioned indices along with the experts' opinions were used to extract the practical and interesting rules, the results of which are presented for each cluster in Table (8).

Table 8. Practical and interesting rules for each cluster.

Rule	Premises (If)	Conclusion (Then)	Confidence	Support	Lift
		Cluster 1			
C1-1	data, develop, technology	specify, advantage	0.769231	0.2	3.496503
C1-2	strategy, marketing, data	develop, specify, advantage	0.769231	0.2	3.496503
C1-3	strategy, public, develop, critic	challenge, advantage	0.833333	0.2	3.472222
C1-4	strategy, marketing, technology, critic	product, develop	1	0.22	3.333333
C1-5	strategy, market, data, specify	develop, advantage	1	0.22	3.333333
C1-6	strategy, data, critic	marketing, advantage	0.833333	0.2	3.205128
C1-7	strategy, product, plan	economic, generate	0.666667	0.2	3.030303
C1-8	market, technology	develop, critic, future	0.666667	0.2	3.030303
C1-9	strategy, market, data, critic	develop, advantage	0.909091	0.2	3.030303
C1-10	strategy, technology	market, develop, advantage	0.714286	0.2	2.97619
C1-11	plan, relationship	develop, knowledge	0.769231	0.2	2.95858
C1-12	technology, critic, relationship	market, develop	1	0.2	2.941176
C1-13	marketing, knowledge	develop, relationship	0.909091	0.2	2.840909
C1-14	data, analysis	technology	0.75	0.3	1.63043478
C1-15	information	product	0.68	0.34	1.36
C1-16	analysis	information	0.64	0.32	1.28
C1-17	environment	information	0.625	0.3	1.25
C1-18	information	place	0.6	0.3	1.30434783
C1-19	strategy, information	product, economic	0.714286	0.2	2.55102
C1-20	data, analysis	information, technology	0.6	0.24	2.142857
		Cluster 2			
C2-1	scan, demand	economic	1	0.325	2
C2-2	competitor, strategy	marketing	1	0.325	2
C2-3	scan, information	strategy	0.928571	0.325	1.954887
C2-4	Scan	knowledge, economic	0.65	0.325	1.857143
C2-5	Data	pattern, inform	0.65	0.325	1.857143
C2-6	import	inform, competitor	0.65	0.325	1.857143
C2-7	scan, knowledge	economic	0.928571	0.325	1.857143
C2-8	information, data	pattern	0.928571	0.325	1.857143
C2-9	information, import	competitor	0.928571	0.325	1.857143
C2-10	aware	knowledge	0.8125	0.325	1.625
C2-11	marketing, competitor	public	0.722222	0.325	1.520468
C2-12	information	knowledge	0.75	0.375	1.5
C2-13	demand	knowledge	0.736842	0.35	1.473684
C2-14	Data	custom	0.65	0.325	1.444444
C2-15	Scan	knowledge	0.7	0.35	1.4
C2-16	Scan	information	0.7	0.35	1.4
C2-17	knowledge	economic	0.7	0.35	1.4
C2-18	Scan	demand	0.65	0.325	1.368421
C2-19	environment	information	0.65	0.325	1.3
C2-20	environment	knowledge	0.65	0.325	1.3
		Cluster 3			
C3-1	people, communication	aware, culture	0.888889	0.333333	2.666667
C3-2	communication, know	aware, knowledge	0.8	0.333333	2.4
C3-3	intellectual	sustain, industry	0.727273	0.333333	2.181818
C3-4	secondary, communication	know	1	0.333333	2.181818
C3-5	secondary, knowledge	world	1	0.333333	2.181818
C3-6	human, employee	intellectual	1	0.333333	2.181818
C3-7	communication, knowledge	know	1	0.333333	2.181818
C3-8	culture, train	intellectual	1	0.333333	2.181818
C3-9	secondary, aware, primary	know	1	0.333333	2.181818
C3-10	social, promotion, commit, environment	consumer	1	0.333333	2.181818
C3-11	employee	sustain, intellectual	0.8	0.333333	2.133333
C3-12	employee	sustain, advantage	0.8	0.333333	2.133333
C3-13	purchase, market	profit	0.888889	0.333333	2.133333
C3-14	secondary	inform, anticipate	0.666667	0.333333	2
C3-15	relationship	experience, collaboration	0.666667	0.333333	2
C3-16	advantage, employee	sustain	1	0.333333	2

Continued Table 8. Practical and interesting rules for each cluster.

C3-17	marketplace, finance	promotion	1	0.333333	2
C3-18	relationship, quality	consumer	0.888889	0.333333	1.939394
C3-19	human, intellectual	industry	0.888889	0.333333	1.939394
C3-20	market, employee	profit	1	0.333333	2.4
Cluster 4					
C4-1	social, network	relationship	1	0.454545	2.2
C4-2	communication	knowledge, customer	1	0.454545	2.2
C4-3	knowledge	communication	1	0.454545	1.833333
C4-4	opportunity, network, economic, develop, competitor	future	1	0.454545	2.2
C4-5	network	global	0.833333	0.454545	1.833333
C4-6	strategy	opportunity, capable	0.833333	0.454545	1.833333
C4-7	strategy, data	capable	1	0.454545	1.833333
C4-8	extern, capable	opportunity	1	0.454545	1.833333
C4-9	market, data	capable	1	0.454545	1.833333
C4-10	custom, communication	knowledge	1	0.454545	1.833333
C4-11	strategy, opportunity, extern	capable	1	0.454545	1.833333
C4-12	opportunity, economic, competitor	development	1	0.454545	1.833333
C4-13	network, economic, competitor	development	1	0.454545	1.833333
C4-14	knowledge, economic, competitor	development	1	0.454545	1.833333
C4-15	firm, environ, economic	development	1	0.454545	1.833333
C4-16	opportunity, network, economic, competitor	development	1	0.454545	1.833333
C4-17	environment	knowledge	0.833333	0.454545	1.527778
C4-18	customer	knowledge	0.833333	0.454545	1.527778
C4-19	competitor	knowledge	0.833333	0.454545	1.527778
C4-20	information	competitor	0.833333	0.454545	1.527778
Cluster 5					
C4-1	network, efficiency, distribution, data	customer	1	0.4	2.5
C4-2	Strategy	way, sustain, product	1	0.4	2.5
C4-3	strategy, marketing, external	industry	1	0.4	2.5
C4-4	systematic, strategy, external	world, expert	1	0.4	2.5
C4-5	vision, plan, future, experience	share	1	0.4	2.5
C4-6	systematic, strategy, extern	expert, development	1	0.4	2.5
C4-7	strategy, market, force, external	industry	1	0.4	2.5
C4-8	systematic, strategy, external, development	world, expert	1	0.4	2.5
C4-9	vision, strategy, plan, external	sustain, practitioner	1	0.4	2.5
C4-10	strategy, logic, extern, employee	product, culture	1	0.4	2.5
C4-11	Skill	world	1	0.4	2
C4-12	Relationship	experience	1	0.4	2
C4-13	technology, marketing	global	1	0.4	2
C4-14	strategy, logic, external, employee, culture	product	1	0.4	2
C4-15	people, skill, world	develop	1	0.4	2
C4-16	world, strategy, external	expert	1	0.4	2
C4-17	vision, strategy, practitioner, plan, external	sustain	1	0.4	2
C4-18	way, vision, transfer, plan, employee	culture	1	0.4	2
C4-19	network, efficiency, data, custom	distribution	1	0.4	2
C4-20	practitioner, information	expert	1	0.4	2

In the first cluster, the notable point is that on one hand, the competitive advantage is achieved through development and knowledge so that the above-mentioned keywords have been obtained in many subsequent rules, which can show us appropriate prerequisites in this regard. For example, the rule C1-5 has assumed that development and acquisition of the competitive advantage are achieved through taking into consideration the strategy, marketing, data, and specialization; thus the support number of this rule (that is 0.22) indicates that the probability of occurrence and relationship is antecedent and consequent, and the number 1 in the confidence index implies the high quality of this rule and its 100% repetition in all the articles in this cluster. On the other hand, in this cluster, the methods of information acquisition (C1-16 and C1-17) as well as its applications (C1-15 and C1-18) have been discovered. In fact, two methods of information

acquisition, and analysis as well as paying attention to the surrounding environment have been considered in this cluster and application of the information obtained in the production and distribution of the products have been shown.

In the second cluster, the methods of knowledge acquisition, knowledge application, necessity of intelligence in monitoring, and economization method have been shown. Analysis of the rules in this cluster shows that acquiring the knowledge requires awareness, information, considering the demands, monitoring, and considering the surrounding environment since the acquired knowledge can lead to economization. For instance, the C2-12 rule shows the pre-requisiteness of information for knowledge as well as the difference between knowledge and information so this rule with support of 0.375 indicates the appropriate relationship of these two variables; on the other hand, the value of 0.75 for confidence of this rule indicates the repetition of this rule in the articles and the importance of this subject. In this cluster, it is worth taking into consideration the C2-6 rule since it shows us two applications of import, namely acquisition of information and awareness about the competitors. In other words, according to this rule, import is also the origin of CI for successful companies.

In the third cluster, the emphasis has been put on the importance of the staff and human capital. Education and culture, which can lead to the intellectual capital; furthermore, the necessity of paying attention to the primary and secondary data for acquisition of knowledge has been taken into account. For example, the rules C3-6 and C3-8 show that the staff, human capital, education, and culture are considered as the appropriate and essential tools for obtaining the intellectual capital, which can result in favorable outcomes such as sustainability and durability in the market and industrialization (C3-3 rule). In the C3-9 rule, the results of using the primary and secondary data have been shown, which should be particularly considered in acquisition of the CI. Further analysis of the rules of this cluster reveals the special importance of the staff in acquisition of the competitive advantage and the intellectual capital (rules C3-11 and C3-12).

In the fourth cluster, the methods of communicative development, development, and foresight have been presented. In this cluster, the emphasis is put on the social intelligence and communicational networks for expanding the relationships, and the costumer, environment, and competitor have been referred to as the resources and prerequisites, and their relevant rules have been presented. In the field of business, success and superiority belong to the pioneer and futuristic companies, and there are various ways to achieve this goal. In the C4-4 rule, some of the prerequisites for reaching a successful future have been discovered including opportunity seeking, network relations, paying attention to the competitors, and developed and dynamic economy. This rule with support of 0.45, confidence of 1 and lift of 2.2 can provide the appropriate factors for the futuristic companies.

In the fifth cluster, some of the prerequisites of industrialization, export, sustainability in market, globalization, culture, and production have been presented. For instance, the C4-7 rule shows that industrialization requires strategy, marketing, force, and paying attention to the environment. Further, the C4-10 rule reminds us that our products and culture reflect our strategy, laws, environment, and staff; besides, the rules C4-12 and C4-13 show the methods of gaining experience and globalization, respectively. It should be noted that the value for the confidence index in this cluster is 1 for all the rules, indicating their 100% repetition in all the articles.

5. Discussion and conclusion

Changes in the structure of global economic system resulting from application of the modern technologies, response to the changes in the global demand patterns, strict competition at the global level, etc. have caused many alterations in the competition patterns and factors affecting the competitiveness among the countries around the world. The prerequisite for success and excellence in the current highly competitive market is being equipped with CI, which has been specially taken into consideration in the current era. In the present research work, the patterns and rules hidden in the research articles were investigated using the text mining techniques. The present work offered a precise review and analysis in the domain of CI using text-mining techniques (clustering and association rules), neglected by previous works. The major findings of the current work can be categorized into descriptive and inferential statistics. In the former, a good visual representation was offered to the readers and researchers in the domain of CI using the clustering technique and tag clods. In the latter, the most important finding of the work led to association rules, which can be valuable and practical for researchers in the domain of CI. The results of the present research work are notable in four categories including descriptive statistics, clustering, word cloud, and association rules, which will be discussed now.

Analysis of the articles on CI in terms of descriptive statistics indicates the ascending slope and more interest in this field in the academic studies so that the use of it in the companies and various production-service organizations such as medicine [46, 47], stores [48], hotels, restaurants [49], e-commerce, schools and universities [50], shipping companies [47], multi-national corporations [51], libraries [52], small and medium enterprises [53, 54], knowledge-based companies, etc. has been investigated; on the other hand, it shows the gap between the countries in terms of production of knowledge in the field of CI so that the gap between the developed and developing countries is tangibly obvious.

Clustering and drawing the word cloud in the present research work led to discovering significant results. In the field of CI, the keywords (data, information, knowledge, strategy, marketing, technology, communications, network and knowledge sharing, competitors, product, customer) form its foundation and basis, without which CI would not be achieved; thus they should be regarded as a systematic view consistent with the organizational goals and strategies. Analysis of the words resulted in each cluster is also notable. The emphasis is put in the first cluster on the internal and external environments; in the second cluster, on data path, information, and knowledge; in the third cluster, on knowledge, information, network, and knowledge sharing; in the fourth cluster, on technology and competitive advantage; and in the fifth cluster, on competitors. Drawing the word cloud in each cluster showed that the word "information" should be specially taken into consideration as the heart of CI; furthermore, the words like marketing, strategy, and knowledge are of especial importance in the formation and effectiveness of CI. The use of the association rules in this research work led to two important results. First, it led to the discovery of the prerequisites of the CI dimensions such as knowledge, technology, products, distribution, etc., and showed us the abilities required for achieving these capabilities as well as the field on which the investment should be focused; second, putting together these dimensions would lead to more significant results, which can be referred to as the consequence of CI. Some of these results include development, acquisition of competitive advantage, sustainability, economization, future, and production at global level. In other words, the first result shows the business activists the path to achieve CI, and the second result draws the outcome of achieving CI.

Reference

[1] Strauss, A. C. and du Toit, A. S. A. (2010). Competitive intelligence skills needed to enhance South Africa's competitiveness, Aslib Proceedings: New Information Perspectives, vol. 62, no. 3, pp. 302-320.

[2] Havenga, J. and Botha, D. (2003). Developing competitive intelligence in the knowledge-based organization, available at: www.saoug.org.za/archive/2003/0312a.pdf (accessed 7 February 2008).

[3] Bose, R. (2008). Competitive intelligence process and tools for intelligence analysis. Industrial Management and Data Systems, vol. 108, no. 4, PP. 510-528.

[4] Kahaner, L. (1996), Competitive Intelligence: From Black Ops to Boardrooms – How Businesses Gather, Analyse, and Use Information to Succeed in the Global Marketplace, Simon and Schuster, New York, NY.

[5] Thompson, S. H., Choo, W. Y. (2001). Assessing the Impact of Using the Internet for Competitive Intelligence, Information & Management, Vol. 30 ,pp. 67-83.

[6] Combs, R. E., Moorhead, J. D. (1992). The Competitive Intelligence Handbook, Metuchen, MJ: Scarecrow Press.

[7] Wang, J., Hu, X. and Zu, D. (2007). Diminishing downsides of data mining, International Journal of Business Intelligence and Data Mining, vol. 2, no. 2, pp. 177-96.

[8] Pechenizkiy, M., Puuronen, S. and Tsymbal, A. (2005). Why data mining research does not contribute to business?, in Soares, C. et al. (Eds), Proc. of Data Mining for Business Workshop DMBiz (ECML/PKDD'05), Porto, Portugal, pp. 67-71.

[9] Seo, W., Yoon, J., Parkc, H., Coh, B. Y., Jae-Min Lee, J. M., and Kwond, O. J. (2016). Product opportunity identification based on internal capabilities using text mining and association rule mining, Technological Forecasting & Social Change, vol. 105, pp. 94–104.

[10] Yoon, B., Park, I., Coh, B.-Y. (2014). Exploring technological opportunities by linking technology and products: application of morphology analysis and text mining. Technol. Forecast. Soc. Chang, vol. 86, pp. 287–303.

[11] Juhari, M and Stephens, K. (2006). Tracing the Origins of Competitive Intelligence throughout History, Journal of Competitive Intelligence and Management, vol. 3, no. 4, pp. 61-82.

[12] Saayman, A. Pienaar, J. Pelsmacker, P. Viviers, W. Cuyvers, L. Muller, M. and Jegers, M. (2008). Competitive intelligence: construct exploration, validation and equivalence, Adlib Proceedings: New Information Perspectives, vol. 60, no. 4. pp. 383-411.

[13] UNCTAD (2002). Trade and Development Report, pp. 87-89.

[14] Fourie, L. H. (1999). World-Wide Web as an Instrument for Competitive Intelligence in a Tertiary Educational Environment, South African Journal of Information Management, vol. 1, no. 2, pp. 137-151.

[15] Fuld, L. (1985). Competitor Intelligence: How to Get it? How to Use it?, Wiley, New York.

[16] Rouach, D., and Santi, P. (2001). Competitive intelligence adds value, European management journal, vol. 19, no. 5, pp. 200-224.

[17] Alon, I. & Higgins, M. (2005). Global Leadeship Success Trough Emotional & Cultural intelligence, Bussiness Horizons, vol. 48, pp. 501-512.

[18] Des champs, J. P. & Nayak, P. R. (1995). Product Juggernauts: How Companies Mobilize to Generate A Stream of Market Winner. Harvard Business Press.

[19] Adidam, P. T., Gajre, S. & Kejriwal, S. (2009). Cross-cultural competitive Intelligence Strategies, Marketing Intelligence & Planning, vol. 27 no. 5, pp. 666-680.

[20] Johns, P., Van Doren, D. C. (2010). Competitive intelligence in service marketing A new approach with practical application, Marketing Intelligence & Planning, vol. 28, no. 5, pp. 551-570.

[21] Johnson, G., Scholes, K. & Whittington, R. (2008). Exploring Corporate Strategy: Text & Cases, FT Prentice Hall Financial Times, Harlow, U.K.

[22] Sauter, V. L. & Free, D. (2005). Competitive intelligence systems: qualitative DSS for strategic decision making, The DATA BASE for Advances in Information Systems, vol. 36, no. 2, pp. 43–57.

[23] Brachman, R. J., Khabaza, T., Kloesgen, W., Piatetsky-Shapiro, G. & Simoudis, E. (1996). Mining business databases, Communications of the ACM, vol. 39, no. 11, pp. 42-48.

[24] Oliveira, J. P. M. D., Loh, S. & Wives, L. K. (2004). Applying text mining on electronic messages for competitive intelligence, Proceedings of the 5th International Conference on Electronic Commerce and Web Technologies, Zaragoza, Spain.

[25] D. Sullivan (2004). The need for text mining in business intelligence, Information Management Special Reports, available at: http://www.informationmanagement.com/specialreports/20040210/8100-1.html.

[26] Dai, Y., Kakkonen, T. & Sutinen, E. (2010). Min EDec: a decision support model that combines text mining with competitive intelligence, 2010 International Conference on Computer Information Systems and Industrial Management Applications (CISIM), pp. 211-216.

[27] Karanikas, H. & Theodoulidis, B. (2002), Knowledge discovery in text and text mining software", technical report, Centre for Research in Information Management (CRIM), Department of Computation, UMIST, Manchester. key issues and future trends, Marketing Intelligence & Planning, vol. 19, no. 4, pp. 245-53.

[28] Liau, B., Y. & Tan, P., P. (2014). Gaining customer knowledge in low cost airlines through text mining, Industrial Management & Data Systems, vol. 114, no. 9, pp. 1344 – 1359.

[29] Hand, D., Mannila, H. & Smyth, P. (2001). Principles of Data Mining, MIT Press, Cambridge, MA.

[30] Bacher, J., Pöge, A. & Wenzig, K. (2010). Clusteranalyse: Anwendungsorientierte Einführung in Klassifikationsverfahren, 3. erg., vollst. überarb. und neu gestaltete Aufl, Oldenbourg, Munich.

[31] Izenman, A. (2008). Modern Multivariate Statistical Techniques: Regression Classification and Manifold Learning, Springer, New York, NY.

[32] Lashka, M. & Moattar, M. H. (2017). Improved COA with Chaotic Initialization and Intelligent Migration for Data Clustering, Journal of AI and Data Mining, vol. 5, no. 2, pp. 293-305.

[33] Vorhies, D. W. & Morgan, N. A. (2005). Benchmarking marketing capabilities for sustainable competitive advantage, Journal of Marketing, vol. 69 no. 1, pp. 80-94.

[34] Tan Tsu Wee, T. (2001). The use of marketing research and intelligence in strategic planning: key issues and future trends, Marketing Intelligence & Planning, vol. 19, no. 4, pp.245 – 253.

[35] Simkin, L. & Cheng, A. (1997). Understanding competitive strategies: the practitioners-academic gap, Marketing Intelligence & Planning, vol. 15, no. 3, pp. 124-34.

[36] Davenport, T. H., & Prusak, L. (2003). What's the Big Idea? Boston, Harvard Business School Press.

[37] Benczúr, D. (2006). Competitive Intelligence and IT, towards a Knowledge-based approach, 37-44, 3-7 April 2006, 1-4244-0176-3/06/$20.00 (C) 2006 IEEE.

[38] Pellissier, R. & Kruger, J. P. (2011). Understanding the use of strategic intelligence as a strategic management tool in the long-term insurance industry in South Africa. South African Journal of Information Management, vol. 13, no. 1, pp. 1-13.

[39] Sewdass, N. & Toit, A., D. (2014). Current state of competitive intelligence in South Africa, International Journal of Information Management, vol. 34, pp. 185–190.

[40] Han, J. & Kamber, M. (2001). Data Mining: Concepts and Techniques, Morgan Kaufmann Publishers Academic Press, San Francisco.

[41] Forcht, K. A. & Cochran, K. (1999). Using data mining and data warehousing techniques, Industrial Management & Data Systems, vol. 99, no. 5, pp. 189-196.

[42] Çiflikli, C. & Kahya-Özyirmidokuz, E. (2012). Enhancing product quality of a process, Industrial Management & Data Systems, vol. 112, no. 8, pp. 1181-1200.

[43] Kim, C., Lee, H., Seol, H. & Lee, C. (2011). Identifying core technologies based on technological cross-impacts: an association rule mining (arm) and analytic network process (anp) approach. Expert Syst. Appl. Vol. 38, no. 10, pp. 12559–12564.

[44] Shih, M.-J., Liu, D.-R. & Hsu, M.-L. (2010). Discovering competitive intelligence by mining changes in patent trends. Expert Syst. vol. 37, no, 4, pp. 2882–2890.

[45] Kim, C., Lee, H., Seol, H. & Lee, c. (2011). dentifying core technologies based on technological cross-impacts: An association rule mining (ARM) and analytic network process (ANP) approach, Expert

Systems with Applications, vol. 38, no, 10, pp. 12559-12564.

[46] Canongia, C. (2007). Synergy between Competitive Intelligence (CI), Knowledge Management (KM) and Technological Foresight (TF) as a strategic model of prospecting - The use of biotechnology in the development of drugs against breast cancer, Biotechnology Advances, vol. 25, pp. 57–74.

[47] Tuan, L. T. (2013). Knowledge sharing and competitive intelligence, Marketing Intelligence & Planning, vol. 32, no. 3, pp. 269-292.

[48] Rapp, A., Agnihotri, R. & Baker. T. L. (2011). Conceptualizing Salesperson Competitive Intelligence: An Individual-Level Perspective, Journal of Personal Selling & Sales Management, vol. 31, no. 2, pp. 141-155.

[49] Köseoglua, A., Rossc, G. & Okumus, F. (2016). Competitive intelligence practices in hotelsMehmet, International Journal of Hospitality Management, vol. 53, pp. 161–172.

[50] Garcia-Alsina, M., Cobarsí-Morales, J. & Ortoll, E. (2016). Competitive intelligence theoretical framework and practices, Aslib Journal of Information Management, vol. 68, no. 1, pp. 57 - 75.

[51] Tuan, L. T. (2015). Entrepreneurial orientation and competitive intelligence: cultural intelligence as a moderator, Journal of Research in Marketing and Entrepreneurship, vol. 17, no. 2, pp. 212–228.

[52] Nitse, P. S. & Parker, K. R. (2002). Library Science, Knowledge Management, Competitive Intelligence, The Reference Librarian, vol. 38, no.79-80, pp. 395-407.

[53] Wright, S., Bisson, C. & Duffy, A. P. (2012). Applying a behavioral and operational diagnostic typology of competitive intelligence practice: empirical evidence from the SME sector in Turkey, Journal of Strategic Marketing, vol. 20, no. 1, pp. 19-33.

[54] Smith, J., R., Wright, S. & Pickton, D. (2010). Competitive Intelligence programmes for SMEs in France: evidence of changing attitudes, Journal of Strategic Marketing, vol. 18, no. 7, pp. 523-536.

9

Fuzzy multi-criteria selection procedures in choosing data source

E. Azhir[1], N. Daneshpour[2]* and S. Ghanbari[3]

1. Department of Computer Engineering, Qazvin Azad University, Qazvin, Iran.
2. Department of Computer, Shahid Rajaee Teacher Training University, Tehran, Iran.
3. IRIB Technical Research Center, Tehran, Iran.

*Corresponding author: ndaneshpour@srttu.edu (N. Daneshpour).

Abstract

Technology assessment and selection has a substantial impact on the organization procedures in regard to technology transfer. Technological decisions are usually made by a group of experts, and whereby, integrity of these viewpoints to a single decision can be quite complex. Today, operational databases and data warehouses exist to manage and organize data with specific features, and henceforth, the need for a decision-aid approach is essential. The process of developing data warehouses involves time-consuming steps, complex queries, slow query response rates, and limited functions, which is also true for operational databases. In this regard, fuzzy multi-criteria procedures used to choose efficient data sources (data warehouse and traditional relational databases) based on organization requirements are addressed in this paper. In proposing an appropriate selection framework, the paper compares a triangular fuzzy number (TFN)-based framework and a fuzzy analytical hierarchy process (AHP) based on data source models, business logic, data access, storage, and security. The results obtained show that the two procedures rank data sources in a similar manner and due to an accurate decision-making.

Keywords: *Analytical Hierarchy Process, Data Warehouse, Fuzzy, Multi-Criteria Decision-Making, Operational Database.*

1. Introduction

Today's digital world has accounted for an exponential rise of data. However, data can only be useful if it is appropriately managed and accessed. This rise has caused organizations to reconsider their data management technologies. While some simply enhance their existing operational databases, others consider larger solutions, data warehouses. The evaluation and selection of a suitable solution is a typical decision-making problem.

Data warehouses store large amounts of data using a multi-layer architecture. Data can be integrated from a number of sources including operational databases and/or other distributed data sources of different organizations. Whereas operational database tables are analyzed and designed based on entities, the analysis and design of data warehouse tables are based on the subjects that the system has been designed to analyze. Therefore, the fact and dimension tables of a data warehouse are designed by the operational database tables that take into consideration the subjects and goals of analysis.

Although most data warehouse queries are writable through operational database commands, and also elements of data warehouse are provided by operational databases, some of these queries are not expressed easily using operational database queries, and when they are actually expressed, their performance is extremely low. Other disadvantages of operational databases include formulating complex queries, slow response rates to queries, limited support of a number of functions and operations, and insufficient memory in answering queries. Nonetheless, it should be considered that operational databases are quite adequate for some organizations [1]. When correctly implemented, a data warehouse system enables companies to enjoy its benefits and obtain timely information for decision-making.

In the recent decades, various decision-making methods and algorithms have been designed. More often multi-criteria decision-making methods are proposed, taking the advantages of multiple criteria. Multi-criteria decision-making problems can be classified into two types, one of which exactly measures the weights of the criteria [2], and the other type uses fuzzy multi-criteria decision-making (FMCDM) such that the weight is approximately measured and is expressed in linguistic terms and transformed into fuzzy numbers (first introduced by Zadeh [3]). Furthermore, various multi-criteria decision-making methods including value measurement models (such as Fuzzy AHP), goal, aspiration, and reference models (such as TOPSIS) and outranking methods (such as ELECTRE and PROMETHEE) are implemented [4].

AHP decomposes complicated problems from higher hierarchies into lower ones. Also the analytical network process (ANP) technique is a multi-attribute approach that allows feedback loops among decision elements in the hierarchical or non-hierarchical structures, and is used to determine data sources in a longer term. In both techniques, impreciseness of human judgments can be handled through the fuzzy set theory.

Moreover, a variety of methodologies and frameworks have already been developed for software selection and evaluation. A method used for selecting enterprise resource planning (ERP) systems has been proposed based on the fuzzy set theory and analytical hierarchy process in [5]. Mamghani [6] has applied the analytic hierarchy process, designed for the decisions that require integration of quantitative and qualitative data in order to evaluate and select the anti-virus and content-filtering software. Combination of the fuzzy set theory and hierarchal structure analysis has resulted in a robust selection algorithm, as proposed by Liang and Wang [7].

Furthermore, a comprehensive framework has been developed for evaluation of the software systems based on the multi-criteria decision-making methods using the fuzzy set theory [8]. A new decision-making approach has been proposed by Eldrandaly and Naguib for solving the geographic information system (GIS) software selection by integrating expert systems and multi-criteria decision-making techniques [9]. Blanc and Jelassi [10] have developed a multi-criteria decision methodology for the decision support system (DSS) selection. Philips Wren, Hahn, and Forgionne [11] have applied fuzzy technologies to choose an appropriate ERP. A new model of assessing enterprise implementation readiness of ERP based on the fuzzy multi-criteria decision-making has been proposed in [12]. Furthermore, a fuzzy multi-criteria decision-making procedure has been proposed in [13] to facilitate the data warehouse system selection with consideration given to both the technical and managerial criteria. A fuzzy set approach has been developed in [14] for the multi-criteria selection of the object-oriented simulation software for analysis of the production systems.

Selection of the most suitable data source system from a set of alternatives on the basis of many criteria is a multi-criteria decision-making problem. We found that using TFN made data collection and interpretation of results easier for the experts and decision makers. In this work, a fuzzy multi-criteria decision-making framework was developed using TFN.

Furthermore, fuzzy AHP, which is a multi-criteria evaluation method evolved from Saaty's AHP [15], has become one of the best known and most widely used multi-criteria decision-making methods. In this case, the criteria that have to be considered are quite a lot, and AHP that can take into consideration the relative priorities of the factors or alternatives and represent the best alternative, in turn, provides a simple and very flexible model for a given problem. In this situation, all levels of details about the main focus can be listed or structured in this method. Computer software can aid decision-makers to apply AHP quickly and precisely. AHP relies on the judgments of experts from different backgrounds, and thus the main focus can be evaluated easily from different aspects. Subsequently, the decision-maker can analyze the elasticity of the final decision by applying the sensitivity analysis.

However, the method has some disadvantages such as scoring the relative importance among related criteria that can be difficult about a certain amount. However, over-simplifying the hierarchy may lose important inter-dependencies among criteria, and over-extending the hierarchy may increase the time complexity for creating pairwise comparison matrices. There is not always a solution to the linear equations since the computational requirements are tremendous, even for a small problem. AHP allows only the triangular fuzzy numbers to be used, and the subjective nature of the modeling process is a constraint of AHP (that means that the methodology cannot guarantee the decisions as definitely true). When the number of levels in the hierarchy increases, the number of pair comparisons also increases, and hence, building the AHP model takes much more time and effort [16].

Considering the multi-criteria structure of the data source selection problem and the vagueness in real environment, fuzzy AHP is thought to be suitable and simple enough for selecting the best data source. Any level of details about the main focus can be listed or structured in this method. Through this way, the overview of the main problem can be represented very easily.

Based on a case study conducted in this paper and a comparison between the TFN-based fuzzy method and a Fuzzy AHP, the proposed selection framework is shown to reduce both cost and time of data source selection due to a proper decision-making based on organization requirements.

This paper is organized as follows. In the next section, a basic concept is discussed in relation to data warehouse generation. In the third section, the TFN and Fuzzy AHP procedures for data warehouse selection using a case study is described. In the fourth section, application of TFN and Fuzzy AHP is compared, and the results obtained are presented. Finally, conclusions based on this study are presented in the fifth section.

2. Basic concepts; data warehouse generation

The common steps involved in data warehouse generation comprises organizational requirements, physical environment set-up, data modeling, data preprocessing, extraction, transformation, data loading, and reporting. Each of these steps are fully-discussed in this section.

Collection and analysis of business requirements: In this step, based on the meetings held with different groups of data warehouse users, and other known approaches in gathering requirements [17] including interviews, standard templates, requirement prioritization, knowledge of subject areas, and through the review of the existing documents, the analytical requirements of end-users are documented.

Physical environment set-up: Once the business requirements have been collected and the analytical requirements of end-users have been clearly defined, it is necessary to set-up the physical servers and databases. At a minimum, it is necessary to set-up the development and production environments. For this, it is best for the different environments to use distinct applications and database servers. Having different environments is very important since all changes can be tested without affecting the production environment. Notably, development and production can occur during the user activity in the data warehouse.

Data modeling: A logical data model is built based upon the user requirements, and is subsequently translated into the physical data model. Deliverables of this step includes the definition and identification of the data sources as well as the logical and physical data models.

Data preprocessing: Once the fact and dimension tables of the data warehouse are designed based on the goals and subjects of the analysis, potential errors in the operational databases are identified and subsequently removed. Data errors include incorrect, incomplete, redundant, inconsistent or inappropriate structured data.

Extraction, transformation, and data loading (ETL): Kimball [18] has stated that the processes of extraction, transformation, and data loading in data warehouses is time-consuming, and he has even specified that it can take up to approximately 60% of the data warehouse implementation time. His reasoning is based upon the fact that it should extract data from operational databases, transform data into appropriate formats, and finally, load data into target tables. A relational data warehouse is the deliverable of this step.

Front end and report development: Data-source users use a variety of reporting tools to query the data warehouse such as excel and dashboard monitoring.

3. Fuzzy-based decision-making procedures

In this section, after a brief introduction to the basic concepts of fuzzy sets, algebraic operations, triangular fuzzy numbers, linguistic variables, and ranking fuzzy numbers, the proposed fuzzy-based decision-making framework is presented in section 3.1, followed by Fuzzy AHP in section 3.2.

The theory of fuzzy sets, introduced by Zadeh (1965), was developed to describe vagueness and ambiguity in real-world systems. Fuzzy set is a class of objects that defines membership degree through interval [0:1]. Zadeh has defined a fuzzy set A in X as a function $f_A(x)$, which associates each point in X a real number in the interval [0:1], with the value of $f_A(x)$ at x representing the "grade of membership" of x in A. If the degree of the membership of an object is "1", it means that the objects are completely bounded, and an object value of "0" means that the object is not absolutely bounded. Uncertain values are set between 0 and 1. This fuzzy set definition can be used to effectively express the vagueness of many real-world cases. In this paper, triangular fuzzy numbers are used as membership functions, since they are straightforward for decision-makers to use and calculate.

Calculation of the membership functions can also be achieved, considering Zadeh principle, after mapping fuzzy set via a function. For example, assume A_1 and A_2 as two triangular fuzzy numbers, where their addition and multiplication are respectively shown in (1) and (2) [2].

$$A_1 = (c_1, a_1, b_1), A_2 = (c_2, a_2, b_2)$$
$$A_1 \oplus A_2 : (c_1, a_1, b_1) \oplus (c_2, a_2, b_2) = \qquad (1)$$
$$(c_1 + c_2, a_1 + a_2, b_1 + b_2)$$

$$A_1 \otimes A_2 : (c_1, a_1, b_1) \otimes (c_2, a_2, b_2) = \qquad (2)$$
$$(c_1 * c_2, a_1 * a_2, b_1 * b_2) c_1 \geq 0, c_2 \geq 0$$

The importance weights of various criteria and the rating values of alternative data sources are considered as linguistic terms throughout this paper. In [14], professionals have used linguistic terms such as very low, low, medium, high, and very high for the importance weights of various criteria, which can be expressed via triangular fuzzy numbers (Table 1), and use linguistic terms such as very poor, poor, fair, good, and very good for rating values of alternative data sources (Table 2).

Table 1. Linguistic terms for importance weight of each criterion.

	Very low (VL)	Low (L)	Medium (M)	High (H)	Very high (VH)
Membership function	(0,0,0.3)	(0,0.3,0.5)	(0.2,0.5,0.8)	(0.5,0.7,1)	(0.7,1,1)

Table 2. Linguistic terms for rating.

	Very poor (VP)	Poor (P)	Fair (F)	Good (G)	Very good (VG)
Membership function	(0,0,0.2)	(0,0.2,0.4)	(0.3,0.5,0.7)	(0.6,0.8,1)	(0.8,1,1)

The aforementioned membership functions have been used in different areas such as robot selection [7] and selection of the object-oriented simulation software [14].

Selection of the most suitable data source from a set of alternatives (data warehouse and operational database) on the basis of many criteria creates a multi-criteria decision-making problem.

The alternative set provided to compare and choose is $A = (A_1, A_2, \ldots, A_n)$, in which, each alternative A_i has two possibilities: selected and unselected. There is a group of k decision makers $(D_1, D_2, \ldots, D_k)$ that evaluate the importance weights of m criteria $(C_1, C_2, \ldots, C_m)$, and the appropriateness of n alternatives $(A_1, A_2, \ldots, A_n)$ under each one of these m criteria. Let $A_{td}(t = 1,2,\ldots,m; d = 1,2,\ldots,k)$ be the weight given to C_t by decision-maker D_d, and let $R_{dti}(d = 1,2,\ldots,k; t = 1,2,\ldots,m; i = 1,2,\ldots,n)$ be the rating assigned to alternative A_i by decision-maker D_d under criterion C_t. A_{td} and R_{dti} are defined as follow ((3) and (4)):

$$R_{dti} = \left(\frac{1}{k}\right) * \begin{bmatrix} \sum_{d=1}^{k} r_{d11} & \cdots & \sum_{d=1}^{k} r_{dm1} \\ \vdots & \ddots & \vdots \\ \sum_{d=1}^{k} r_{d1n} & \cdots & \sum_{d=1}^{k} r_{dmn} \end{bmatrix} \qquad (3)$$

$$A_{td} = \left(\frac{1}{k}\right) * \left(\sum_{d=1}^{k} a_{1d}, \ldots\ldots, \sum_{d=1}^{k} a_{md}\right) \qquad (4)$$

Notably, the fuzzy set theory is applied to give values of matrices ((3) and (4)).

Choosing the most appropriate data source and considering the importance of weights of various criteria and the rating values of alternative data sources will be done by matrix F in (5). In these matrices, $F_1, F_2, \ldots, F_m$ show the weight of each data source for selection by the decision-makers to make a choice.

$$F = \left(\frac{1}{m}\right) * (R \otimes A^T) =$$

$$\left(\frac{1}{m}\right) \begin{bmatrix} \frac{\sum_{d=1}^{k} r_{d11}}{k} & \cdots & \frac{\sum_{d=1}^{k} r_{dm1}}{k} \\ \vdots & \ddots & \vdots \\ \frac{\sum_{d=1}^{k} r_{d1n}}{k} & \cdots & \frac{\sum_{d=1}^{k} r_{dmn}}{k} \end{bmatrix} \otimes \begin{pmatrix} \frac{\sum_{d=1}^{k} a_{1d}}{k} \\ \frac{\sum_{d=1}^{k} a_{2d}}{k} \\ \cdot \\ \cdot \\ \cdot \\ \frac{\sum_{d=1}^{k} a_{md}}{k} \end{pmatrix} \qquad (5)$$

$$= (F_1, F_2, \ldots, F_m)^T$$

The objective functions are written as a function of decision variables, and express the purpose of the problem and where the decision-maker attempts to maximize or minimize the objective function. In situations where the purpose is maximization, the most suitable option is when their objective function has the highest value. In considering (6) and according to calculations carried out by Chen [19], the maximizing set M is $M = \{(x, f_M(x)) | x \in R\}$:

$$f_M(x) = \begin{cases} \dfrac{(x - x_{min})}{(x_{max} - x_{min})}, & x_{min} \leq x \leq x_{max} \\ 0 & \text{otherwise} \end{cases} \qquad (6)$$

and the minimizing set $G = \{(x, f_G(x)) | x \in R\}$, considering (7), is defined as:

$$f_G(x) = \begin{cases} \dfrac{(x - x_{max})}{(x_{min} - x_{max})}, & x_{min} \leq x \leq x_{max} \\ 0 & \text{otherwise} \end{cases} \quad (7)$$

where:

$$x_{min} = \inf S, x_{max} = \sup S,$$
$$S = \bigcup_{i=1}^{n} F_i, F_i = \{x | f_{Fi}(x) > 0\}, i = 1,2, \dots, n$$

Furthermore, the right utility value $U_M(F_i)$, left utility value $U_G(F_i)$, and total utility value $U_T(F_i)$ for alternative i are denoted as follow ((8)-(10)).

$$U_M(F_i) = \sup\big(f_{Fi}(x) \cap f_M(x)\big), i = 1,2, \dots, n \quad (8)$$

$$U_G(F_i) = \sup\big(f_{Fi}(x) \cap f_G(x)\big), i = 1,2, \dots, n \quad (9)$$

$$U_T(F_i) = \frac{U_M(F_i) + 1 - U_G(F_i)}{2} \quad (10)$$

The alternative with a maximum $U_T(F_i)$ value is the optimal choice in the decision-making problem.

3.1. Fuzzy-based multi-criteria decision-making framework using TFN

A generalized fuzzy multi-criteria decision-making procedure is depicted in figure 1 as an activity diagram. Each level of this activity diagram is described as follows.

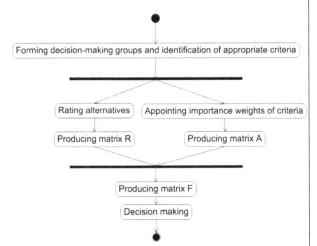

Figure 1. Activity diagram of a fuzzy-based decision-making procedure for selection of a data source.

Forming decision-making groups for analysis of data sources and identification of appropriate

criteria: Due to different advantages and disadvantages of the data sources, different organizations based on their requirements may decide to create data warehouse or use existing data sources (those that do not create data warehouse). Therefore, several groups are formed in the organization to investigate possible data storage alternatives, organization requirements, and influencing factors in order to determine appropriate selection criteria.

Delphi is a technique of committee research, developed by Dalkey and Helmer [20]. It is a widely used and accepted methodology for achieving convergence of opinion concerning real-world knowledge solicited from experts within certain topic areas. Assuming the skills of experts are more important than their quantity. Delphi is used in this paper to choose the committee experts. First of all, lists of the names of professionals of the organization have been grouped by their profession. Professionals of each group were rated by their level of competency, and subsequently, the organization research team chose six experts. The six data source experts have an average of 9/5 years of experience in business.

The main purpose of choosing criteria is to provide a vision for a better decision-making. At first, the initial list of objectives including major and minor objectives of the organization is drawn. These are the organization objectives that have been organized in a hierarchal structure. In this paper, the hierarchal structure of objectives was developed during a two-week period, whereby three questionnaires were sent to the chosen experts.

It is important to note that too many criteria may lead to conflict of evaluations and consequently unsuccessful decision-making. For this reason, in this study, at first 30 objectives were expressed in the committee. Subsequently, fuzzy Delphi was used to ensure the selection of appropriate criteria, and as a result, 15 criteria were chosen. The chosen criteria were discussed and approved by four data warehouse professionals of two reputable organizations. Figure 2 shows the proposed criteria that are derived by committee decisions and studies conducted in [19,20] and are suitable for decision-making to choose the most suitable data source in a hierarchical structure.

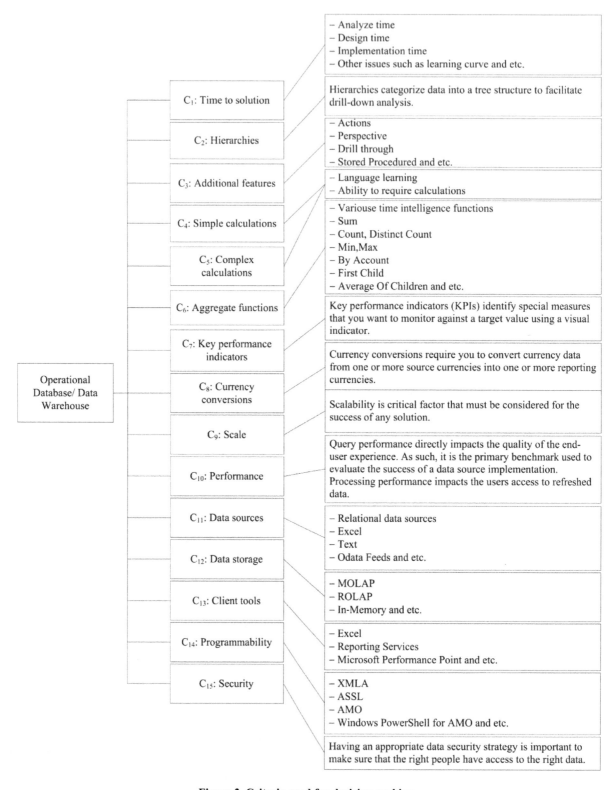

Figure 2. Criteria used for decision-making.

Rating alternatives and producing matrix R activities: In these activities, data sources are rated by the fuzzy method. This rating and assigning of importance weights of criteria and producing matrix A activities of figure 1 can be carried out simultaneously. The rating alternatives under the figure 2 criteria are defined according to the standard characteristics of the operational databases and data warehouses defined by their vendors, conducted studies, and selected expert experiments using the terms in table 2. The ratings acquired by the six experts are expressed as follows.

Rating according to criterion C_1 (solution time): Design and implementation of data warehouse is in the form of a multi-layer architecture, where the first layer is composed from data sources such as relational databases, flat files, and other sources.

After designing the tables of a relational data warehouse, the extracted and transformed data of the operational databases is loaded into this data warehouse. Henceforth, to design a data warehouse, in addition to analysing tables of data sources, it is necessary to create fact, dimension, and multidimensional cube in business intelligence (BI) environment.

Although comprehensive data modelling and sophisticated analytics are important benefits of data warehouse, they often come with the trade-off of longer development cycles. Based on the average comments of the six experts and the provided definitions, the quantitative values $(0.61, 0.81, 0.95)$ and $(0.1, 0.3, 1)$ are assigned to criterion C_1 for the operational databases and data warehouse accordingly.

Rating according to criterion C_2 (hierarchies): Creation of data warehouse hierarchies such as standard, parent-child, and ragged [22] is easily available by BI wizard features, while creation of these hierarchies in the operational databases is more difficult and requires complex queries. Henceforth, based on the average comments of the six experts and the provided definitions, the quantitative values $(0.73, 0.93, 1)$ and $(0.31, 0.51, 0.7)$ are assigned to criterion C_2 for the data warehouse and operational database.

Rating according to criterion C_3 (additional features): Data warehouse additional features, which are provided in table 3, are easily available by BI environment, although in operational databases, some of these features are much more complex. For example, a translation feature is not available in operational databases, and drill-through and write-back is more difficultly provided and requires writing complex queries. Linguistic terms of these six experts is transformed into fuzzy numbers and then assigned to the values $(0.4, 0.6, 0.8)$ and $(0.7, 0.9, 1)$ for criterion C_3 in operational database and data warehouse.

Rating according to criterion C_4 (simple calculations): Calculations in the data warehouses and operational databases depend on both the learning data source language and the ability of the language to handle the required queries. As multi-dimensional expressions language (MDX) is more complicated in the data warehouses in comparison with operational databases languages such as structured query language (SQL) and excel functions, it is not recommended for simple calculations. After comparing these two data sources by six experts and due to the ease of operational database calculation language learning and ability of operational database in processing simple queries, the fuzzy values $(0.4, 0.6, 0.8)$ and $(0.53, 0.73, 0.9)$ are assigned to criterion C_4.

Rating according to criterion C_5 (complex calculations): MDX calculation languages are more applicable to complex calculations than operational databases languages such as SQL, excel functions, oracle and so forth, as in the majority of cases they will fail in processing such complex calculations. Henceforth, based on the average comments of the six experts and the provided definitions, the quantitative values $(0.7, 0.9, 1)$ and $(0.05, 0.18, 0.35)$ are assigned to criterion C_5 for the data warehouse and operational database.

Rating according to criterion C_6 (aggregate functions): As shown in table 4, data warehouse, in addition to providing aggregate functions that is supported by operational databases, provides other aggregate functions. Due to the storage of pre-computed aggregate functions in data warehouse multi-dimensional cube cells that improves the efficiency of query retrieves, and based on the average comments of the six experts, the quantitative values $(0.6, 0.93, 1)$ and $(0.1, 0.3, 0.5)$ are assigned to criterion C_6 for the warehouse and operational database.

Table 2. Aggregate functions.

Aggregate functions	Data warehouse	Database
Sum	✓	✓
Count, Distinct Count	✓	✓
Min, Max	✓	✓
None	✓	✗
By account	✓	✗
Average of children	✓	✗
First child, Last child	✓	✗
First non-empty	✓	✗
Last non-empty	✓	✗
STDEV	✗	✓
VAR	✗	✓

Rating according to criterion C_7 (key performance indicators (KPIs)): KPIs that are provided by each data source and expressed in the third level of figure 2 are shown in table 5. KPIs of operational

Table 1. Additional features.

Additional features	Data warehouse	Database
Actions	✓	✓
Perspective	✓	✓
Drill through	✓	Complex solutions
Stored procedures	✓	✓
Write-back	✓	Complex solutions
Translations	✓	✗

database are provided by components such as SQL reporting services and performance point services. However, while these are not available as a wizard in an operational database environment, the KPIs are provided in the data warehouse BI environment. Due to the higher capability of the data warehouse in criterion C_7, difficulty of preparation of KPIs by operational database, and average comments of the six experts, the quantitative values (0.7,0.9,1) and (0.05,0.18,0.18) are assigned to criterion C_7 for the data warehouse and operational database.

Table 3. Key-performance indicators.

key performance indicators	Data warehouse	Database
Actual	✓	Complex solutions
Goal	✓	Complex solutions
Status	✓	Complex solutions
Trend	✓	Complex solutions
Graphical indicators	✓	Complex solutions

Rating according to criterion C_8 (currency conversions): In data warehouse, the BI Wizard can be used to create the MDX currency conversion calculations that are optimized to support multiple source and reporting currencies. In an operational database currency, conversions can be made by SQL queries. These currency conversions are easier to perform in data warehouses. Based on the average comments of the six experts and the capability of data warehouse in currency conversions, the quantitative values (0.6,0.93,0.1) and (0.05,0.21,0.41) are assigned to criterion C_8 for the data warehouse and operational database.

Rating according to criterion C_9 (large scale): Data warehouses have the ability of extending into large scales (multi-terabyte) without affecting query performances. Data warehouses provide extensive capabilities to manage the most complex and largest-scale BI challenges. Sophisticated models and complex business logic can be implemented in data warehouses. On-disk data storage, pre-calculated aggregates, and in-memory caching enable multi-dimensional models to grow to multi-terabyte scale and to provide fast query responses.

However, operational databases that only have one processor and are without suitable indexing, partitioning, and tables normalization are not able to extend into large scales. This feature of operational database and data warehouse is compared. In this comparison, the scaling ability of data warehouse based on average comments of six experts is represented by fuzzy numbers (the quantitative values (0.6,0.93,1) and

(0.15,0.35,0.41) are assigned to criterion C_9 for the warehouse and operational database).

Rating according to criterion C_{10} (performance): data warehouses provide a variety of mechanisms to accelerate query performance including aggregations, caching, indexed data retrieval, and data compression. In addition, one can improve query performance by optimizing the design of dimension attributes, cubes, and MDX queries. As a result of data compression and storing pre-calculated aggregate functions in multi-dimensional cube cells, I/O will reduce. A disadvantage of operational databases is that they cannot compress data, although in certain situations, through indexing, caching, and storing pre-calculated aggregate function response rates to queries can be reduced.

Performance of data warehouse and operational database based on C_{10} is compared. This comparison is achieved by taking the average comments of decision-makers and converting them to fuzzy numbers and then assigning them to the quantitative values (0.7,0.9,1) and (0.1,0.3,0.5) for the data warehouse and operational database, respectively.

Rating according to criterion C_{11} (data sources): A number of data sources supported by data warehouse and operational database are expressed in the third level of figure 2 and table 6. Henceforth, the data warehouse and operational databases are compared based on the linguistic terms of six decision-maker experts. (The linguistic terms of these six experts are transformed into fuzzy numbers, and then assigned to the average values (0.38,0.71,0.73) and (0.05,0.21,0.41) for criterion C_{11} in operational database and data warehouse.)

Rating according to criterion C_{12} (data storage): In a data warehouse, data can be stored in multi-dimensional online analytical processing (MOLAP), relational online analytical processing (ROLAP) and hybrid online analytical processing (HOLAP) data architectures. In MOLAP, the data is stored on disk in an optimized multi-dimensional format. In ROLAP, the data is stored in the source relational database. Due to optimized storage, multi-dimensional indexing, and caching, query response time is fast in MOLAP but in MOLAP, on-disk size of data compared to data stored in the relational database is smaller.

The ROLAP tools access the data in a relational database, and generate SQL queries to calculate information at the appropriate level as and when requested by end-users.

As ROLAP places no limitation on the quantity of data and since each ROLAP report is essentially a

SQL query (or multiple SQL queries) in the relational database, the query time can be long if the underlying data size is large. HOLAP combines features of the MOLAP and ROLAP data architectures.

Table 4. Supported data sources.

Database	Data warehouse
Microsoft SQL Server	SQL Server relational databases
Microsoft SQL Server Analysis Services for MDX, DMX, Microsoft PowerPivot, and tabular models	Teradata relational databases
	Informix relational databases
Microsoft Windows Azure SQL Database	IBM DB2 relational databases
SQL Server Parallel Data Warehouse	Sybase relational databases
Oracle	Other relational databases (OLE DB provider or
SAP Net Weaver BI	ODBC driver)
Hyperion Essbase	
Microsoft SharePoint List	
Teradata	
OLE DB	
ODBC and XML	

In operational databases, information storage and retrieval is achieved through SQL queries. Based on the average comments of the six experts and the capability of data warehouse in information storage and retrieval, the quantitative values (0.7,0.9,1) and (0.15,0.35,0.60) are assigned to criterion C_{12} for the data warehouse and operational database.

Rating alternatives according to criterion C_{13} (client tools): As shown in the third level of figure 2, Excel reporting services and Microsoft performance point are supported as data warehouse client tools. Furthermore, these tools are also supported in operational databases. After linguistic comparison of these two data sources by the six experts, the fuzzy values (0.66,0.88,1) and (0.61,0.81,0.95) are assigned to criterion C_{13} accordingly.

Rating according to criterion C_{14} (programmability): A variety of application programming interfaces (APIs) that can be used to develop and manage operational database objects such as tables, SQL scripts, and data warehouse objects such as cubes, dimensions, measures groups, and MDX scripts are tabulated in table 7. Considering the provided comparison given in table 7, data warehouses have more functionality than operational databases. After linguistic comparison of these two data sources by the six experts, the fuzzy values (0.7,0.9,1) and (0.4,0.6,0.8) are assigned to criterion C_{14} for the data warehouse and operational database.

Rating according to criterion C_{15} (security): Having an appropriate data security strategy is important to certify that the right people have access to the right data.

Table 5. Programmability.

Data warehouse	Database
XMLA	XML
ASSL	ADO.NET
ADOMD.NET	
MSOLAP	
AMO	
Windows PowerShell for AMO	

Both data warehouse and operational databases offer a set of robust capabilities that satisfy a broad range of security requirements. However, there are subtle differences in their capabilities, which are important to understand before choosing the data source experience that will best meet the security needs. In a data warehouse project, the concept of dimension data security can be used to manage row-level access. In operational database project, a row-level security can be implemented by granting access to rows in a table. In a multi-dimensional project, cell-level security can be implemented to restrict access to a particular cell or group of cells. Cell-level security is not provided in an operational database. Since security of access level in data warehouse is higher than operational database and based on the collected comments, the quantitative values (0.7,0.9,1) and (0.2,0.4,0.6) are assigned to criterion C_{15}.

Appointing importance weight of criteria and producing matrix A activities: In order to create a data warehouse in organization, six experts determine importance weights of figure 2 criteria based on their wide experience and knowledge about requirements of organization. First, the organization requirements in creating a data warehouse are collected, as shown in table 8.

Table 8. Organization requirements to create data warehouse.

Criterion	Organization requirements
C_1	Importance of solution time for organization
C_2	Massive creation of hierarchies and fast retrieval of them based on the nature of organization's analyzes
C_3	Stored Procedures , Actions, Drill through
C_4	60 percent of the organization's calculations need simple queries
C_5	40 percent of the organization's calculations need complex queries
C_6	Organization uses common aggregate functions in its process
C_7	As organization do not require monitoring then key performance indicators is not required either
C_8	Organization do not require currency conversions
C_9	in order to facilitate organization's process, data source must have the ability of extending into gigabyte scales
C_{10}	Organization need to reduce response time of quires and process
C_{11}	Organization need to create data sources based on Microsoft Sql Server relational data sources
C_{12}	Saving data in memory
C_{13}	Probability of using excel client tool
C_{14}	Organization should not need to use different programming environments
C_{15}	Row level security

3.2. Fuzzy AHP

Fuzzy AHP is one of the most commonly used methods for solving multi-criteria decision-making problems. After decomposing the complex problem into a hierarchical structure, the pair-wise comparison matrices are calculated as follow:

$$A = (aij) = \begin{bmatrix} 1 & \frac{w1}{w2} & \cdots & \frac{w1}{wn} \\ \frac{w2}{w1} & 1 & \cdots & \frac{w2}{wn} \\ \vdots & \vdots & \vdots & \vdots \\ \frac{wn}{w1} & \frac{wn}{w2} & \cdots & 1 \end{bmatrix}, \quad (11)$$

Weight calculation: $w_i = \frac{\sum_{j=1}^{n} aij}{n}$

for all $j = 1, 2, \ldots, n$

In this study, the extent fuzzy AHP is utilized, which was originally introduced by Chang (1996). The value of fuzzy synthetic extent with respect to the object is defined as:

$$S_i = \sum_{j=1}^{n} M_{gi}^j \otimes \left[\sum_{i=1}^{n} \sum_{j=1}^{m} M_{gi}^j \right]^{-1} \quad (12)$$

Where $M_{gi}^j (j = 1, \ldots, m)$ are TFNs and goal set G = $\{g_1, g_2, g_3, \ldots, g_n\}$

To obtain fuzzy summation of rows, the fuzzy addition operation of m extent analysis values for a particular matrix is performed such as:

$$\sum_{j=1}^{m} M_{gi}^j = \left(\sum_{j=1}^{m} l_j, \sum_{j=1}^{m} m_j, \sum_{j=1}^{m} u_j \right) \quad (13)$$

and to obtain S_j, the following multiplication is performed such as:

$$S_j = \sum_{j=1}^{m} M_{gi}^j \otimes \left[\sum_{j=1}^{m} \sum_{j=1}^{m} M_{gi}^j \right]^{-1} = \quad (14)$$
$$\left(\sum_{j=1}^{m} l_j \otimes \sum_{i=1}^{n} l_i, \sum_{j=1}^{m} m_j \otimes \sum_{i=1}^{n} m_i, \sum_{j=1}^{m} u_j \otimes \sum_{i=1}^{n} u_i \right)$$

As $M_1 = (l_1, m_1, u_1)$ and $M_2 = (l_2, m_2, u_2)$ are two triangular fuzzy numbers, the degree of possibility of M2 ≥ M1 is defined as:

$$V(M_2 \geq M_1) = \begin{cases} 1, & \text{if} M_2 \geq M_1 \\ 0, & \text{if} l_1 \geq l_2 \\ \frac{l_1 - u_2}{(m_2 - u_2) - (m_1 - l_2)}, & \text{otherwise} \end{cases} \quad (15)$$

The degree possibility for a convex fuzzy number to be greater than k convex fuzzy M_i (i = 1,2,3, …, k) numbers can be defined by:

$$V(M \geq M_1, M_2, \ldots, M_k) = \min V(M \geq M_i), \quad (16)$$
$$i = 1,2,3, \ldots, k$$

Finally, $W = (\min V(S_1 \geq S_k), \min V(S_2 \geq S_k), \ldots, \min V(S_n \geq S_k))^T$ is the weight vector for $k = 1,2, \ldots, n$.

The importance weights of various criteria and the rating values of alternative data sources are considered as linguistic terms, which can be expressed via triangular fuzzy numbers (Table 9).

Table 9. Membership function of linguistic scale.

Linguistic	Scale of fuzzy number
Perfect	(8,9,10)
Absolute	(7,8,9)
Very good	(6,7,8)
Fairly good	(5,6,7)
Good	(4,5,6)
Preferable	(3,4,5)
Not bad	(2,3,4)
Weak advantage	(1,2,3)
Equal	(1,1,1)

Importance weights of criteria based on organizations requirements are assigned by six groups and fuzzy summation of pair-wise comparison matrix is calculated, as shown in table 10.

Table 10. Fuzzy summation of rows (sum of l, m, and u values).

Criterion	Fuzzy summation of rows
C_1	(33,55,79)
C_2	(28.25,45.5,66)
C_3	(24.95,38.83,55)
C_4	(23.95,36.83,53)
C_5	(34,54,78)
C_6	(18.53,28.83,42)
C_7	(6.04,10.30,19.23)
C_8	(4.057,5.20,9.3)
C_9	(15.48,27.72,42.7)
C_{10}	(26.25,44.53,64.25)
C_{11}	(19.85,33.56,50)
C_{12}	(8.49,12.64,23.65)
C_{13}	(9.70,19.92,32.58)
C_{14}	(6.52,13.27,23.08)
C_{15}	(4.73,7.63,13.76)

The weight vector from table 10 is calculated and normalized, as shown in table 11.

Table 11. Normalized weight calculation.

Possibility Degree of Si vs. Sk														Degree of possibility	Normalized weight
1	1	1	1	1	1	1	1	1	1	1	1	1	1	1	**0.1164**
0.901	1	1	0.910	1	1	1	1	1	1	1	1	1	1	0.901	**0.1049**
0.809	0.915	1	0.817	1	1	1	1	1	1	1	1	1	1	0.809	**0.0942**
0.782	0.887	0.972	0.790	1	1	1	1	0.900	1	1	1	1	1	0.782	**0.0910**
0.991	1	1	1	1	1	1	1	1	1	1	1	1	1	0.991	**0.1153**
0.643	0.751	0.840	0.869	0.648	1	1	1	0.767	1	1	1	1	1	0.643	**0.0748**
0.178	0.267	0.345	0.371	0.171	0.510	1	0.550	0.292	0.442	1	1	1	1	0.171	**0.0199**
0	0	0	0	0	0.111	0.688	0.181	0	0.068	0.564	0.375	1	1	0	**0**
0.639	0.743	0.828	0.856	0.644	0.981	1	1	0.758	1	1	1	1	1	0.639	**0.0744**
0.889	0.989	1	1	0.898	1	1	1	1	1	1	1	1	1	0.889	**0.1035**
0.738	0.842	0.926	0.953	0.745	1	1	1	1	1	1	1	1	1	0.738	**0.0859**
0.285	0.379	0.460	0.487	0.282	0.621	1	1	0.655	0.551	1	1	1	1	0.282	**0.0328**
0.474	0.576	0.662	0.690	0.476	0.822	1	1	0.847	1	1	1	1	1	0.474	**0.0552**
0.014	0.092	0.162	0.186	0	0.327	0.874	1	0.380	0.267	1	1	1	1	0	**0**
0.277	0.373	0.455	0.483	0.273	0.622	1	1	0.657	1	1	1	1	1	0.273	**0.0318**

Similar procedures are carried out to calculate relative importance weight of alternatives with respect to each selection criterion.

4. Evaluation and comparison of data sources by two fuzzy procedures

4.1. Evaluate data sources by TFN based decision-making framework

The average of these six expert comments based on fuzzy values of table 2 that are used to create matrix R, and is denoted in rating alternatives and producing matrix R activities, is calculated and tabulated in table 12.

Table 12. Average comments of six experts.

Criterion	Database	Data warehouse
C_1	(0.61,0.81,0.95)	(0.1,0.3,1)
C_2	(0.31,0.51,0.7)	(0.73,0.93,1)
C_3	(0.4,0.6,0.8)	(0.7,0.9,1)
C_4	(0.53,0.73,0.9)	(0.4,0.6,0.8)
C_5	(0.05,0.18,0.35)	(0.7,0.9,1)
C_6	(0.1,0.3,0.5)	(0.6,0.93,1)
C_7	(0.05,0.18,0.18)	(0.7,0.9,1)
C_8	(0.05,0.21,0.41)	(0.6,0.93,1)
C_9	(0.15,0.35,0.41)	(0.6,0.93,1)
C_{10}	(0.1,0.3,0.5)	(0.7,0.9,1)
C_{11}	(0.38,0.71,0.73)	(0.05,0.21,0.41)
C_{12}	(0.15,0.35,0.6)	(0.7,0.9,1)
C_{13}	(0.61,0.81,0.95)	(0.66,0.88,1)
C_{14}	(0.4,0.6,0.8)	(0.7,0.9,1)
C_{15}	(0.2,0.4,0.6)	(0.7,0.9,1)

Importance weights of criteria of figure 2 based on organization requirements are assigned by six experts, as shown in table 12. A hierarchy approach is applied to determine the importance of the weights of criteria. Weights of second level criteria of figure 2 are calculated based on third-level criteria. For example, based on organization requirements of table 8, value of C_2 is determined, as shown in table 12. The organization needs to create more hierarchies such as standard and parent-child hierarchies, and then retrieves them fast based on the nature of organization analysis. Based on the organization requirements and the comment of one of the decision-makers (D_1), standards and parent child's hierarchies sub-criteria are assigned to a very high term and transformed to the fuzzy number (0.7, 1, 1). As ragged hierarchy is less required by organizations, it is assigned to a very low term and transformed to the fuzzy number (0, 0, 0.3). The average of aforementioned sub-criteria is (0.46, 0.66, 0.76) for C_2.

After determining the importance weights of criteria based on organization requirements in table 13 using Matrix (4), matrix A_1 is created and two columns of table 12 are inserted in matrix R.

Producing matrix F and final decision-making activities: Decision-making in regard to creating data warehouse and/or using the existing operational databases, based on the organization requirements, is achieved through matrix F in (17).

Table 6. Importance weight of each criterion based on requirements of organization.

	Decision-makers						Average of comments
Criterion	D_1	D_2	D_3	D_4	D_5	D_6	
C_1	(0.7,1,1)	(0.63,0.9,0.7)	(0.36,0.66,0.86)	(0.73,0.93,0.46)	(0.83,0.93,0.53)	(0.63,0.9,1)	(0.55,0.83,0.90)
C_2	(0.46,0.66,0.76)	(0.38,0.83,46)	(0.33,0.56,0.83)	(0.66,0.76,0.46)	(0.83,0.93,0.53)	(0.4,0.56,0.76)	(0.44,0.60,0.79)
C_3	(0.35,0.6,0.71)	(0.43,0.66,0.8)	(0.28,0.43,0.68)	(0.55,0.68,0.35)	(0.35,0.6,0.71)	(0.28,0.4,0.65)	(0.34,0.63,0.54)
C_4	(0,0,0.25,0.55)	(0.35,0.6,0.9)	(0.35,0.6,0.9)	(0.35,0.6,0.9)	(0.5,0.7,1)	(0.6,0.85,1)	(0.35,0.60,0.87)
C_5	(0.6,0.85,1)	(0.6,0.85,1)	(0.35,0.6,0.9)	(0.6,0.85,1)	(0.6,0.85,1)	(0.7,1,1)	(0.57,0.83,0.98)
C_6	(0.36,0.55,0.21)	(0.53,0.68,0.23)	(0.21,0.39,0.54)	(0.3,0.45,0.66)	(0.3,0.45,0.66)	(0.23,0.53,0.68)	(0.24,0.45,0.62)
C_7	(0,0.3,0.5)	(0,0,0.3)	(0,0.3,0.5)	(0.2,0.5,0.8)	(0.2,0.5,0.8)	(0,0.15,0.4)	(0.06,0.29,0.55)
C_8	(0,0,0.3)	(0,0,0.3)	(0.1,0.4,0.65)	(0.1,0.25,0.55)	(0.1,0.25,0.55)	(0,0,0.3)	(0.05,0.15,0.44)
C_9	(0.2,0.5,0.8)	(0.2,0.5,0.8)	(0.2,0.5,0.8)	(0.2,0.5,0.8)	(0.5,0.7,1)	(0.2,0.5,0.8)	(0.25,0.45,0.83)
C_{10}	(0.7,1,1)	(0.73,0.93,0.46)	(0.46,0.73,0.93)	(0.73,0.93,0.46)	(0.7,1,1)	(0.3,0.4,0.7)	(0.51,0.76,0.91)
C_{11}	(0.41,0.58,0.11)	(0.5,0.7,1)	(0.11,0.41,0.58)	(0.2,0.5,0.8)	(0.5,0.7,1)	(0.5,0.7,1)	(0.32,0.57,0.82)
C_{12}	(0.72,0.95,0.47)	(0.4,0.67,0.9)	(0.2,0.5,0.8)	(0.5,0.7,1)	(0.5,0.7,1)	(0.5,0.7,1)	(0.42,0.66,0.94)
C_{13}	(0.27,0.5,0.72)	(0.1,0.4,0.75)	(0.2,0.5,0.8)	(0.27,0.5,0.72)	(0.1,0.4,0.75)	(0.2,0.5,0.8)	(0.19,0.46,0.75)
C_{14}	(0,0,0.3)	(0,0,0.3)	(0.2,0.5,0.8)	(0.2,0.5,0.8)	(0,0.3,0.5)	(0,0,0.3)	(0.06,0.21,0.50)
C_{15}	(0.1,0.4,0.65)	(0.35,0.6,0.9)	(0,0,0.3)	(0.1,0.25,0.55)	(0.1,0.4,0.65)	(0.1,0.25,0.55)	(0.12,0.31,0.60)

As expressed, objective functions are written by the decision variables and express the problem statement. Here, decision-makers try to maximize or minimize the objective functions.

In problems where the goal is maximization, a suitable alternative is the one whose objective functions have a maximum measure. The membership functions of fuzzy numbers F_1 (operational database) and F_2 (data warehouse) are calculated in (17).

$$F = \left(\frac{1}{15}\right).(R \otimes A_1) =$$

$$\left(\frac{1}{15}\right).\begin{bmatrix} (0.61,0.81,0.95)(0.31,0.51,0.7)(0.4,0.6,0.8) & \cdots & (0.61,0.81,0.95) \; (0.4,0.6,0.8) \; (0.2,0.4,0.6) \\ \vdots & \ddots & \vdots \\ (0.1,0.3,1) \quad (0.73,0.93,1)(0.7,0.9,1) & \cdots & (0.66,0.86,1) \; (0.7,0.9,1)(0.7,0.9,1) \end{bmatrix} \otimes \begin{bmatrix} (0.55,0.83,0.90) \\ (0.44,0.60,0.79) \\ (0.34,0.63,0.54) \\ (0.35,0.60,0.87) \\ (0.57,0.83,0.98) \\ (0.24,0.45,0.62) \\ (0.06,0.29,0.55) \\ (0.05,0.15,0.44) \\ (0.25,0.45,0.83) \\ (0.51,0.76,0.91) \\ (0.32,0.57,0.82) \\ (0.42,0.66,0.94) \\ (0.19,0.46,0.75) \\ (0.06,0.21,0.5) \\ (0.12,0.31,0.6) \end{bmatrix} = \qquad (17)$$

$$((0.07,0.24,0.46) \quad , \quad (0.15,0.38,0.69))$$

Figure 3 is derived from calculation of F_1 and F_2.

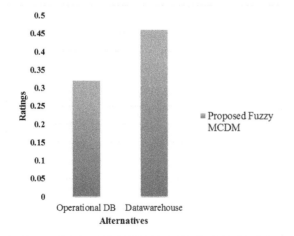

Figure 2. Rating with TFN-based decision-making framework.

Hence, it is clear that the most appropriate data source is F_2. Thus the committee can be comfortable in recommending alternative F_2 as the most suitable data source based on the organization requirements.

4.2. Comparison between TFN-based decision-making approach and fuzzy AHP

Amongst the multi-criteria decision-making methodologies, fuzzy AHP, due to its compatibility and paired comparisons, provides efficient results. In fuzzy AHP, information is decomposed into a hierarchy of alternatives and criteria for decision-making. In this section, the proposed framework is implemented using fuzzy AHP, and is such to determine its significance, it is compared with the results obtained from the fuzzy-based decision-making approach.

As figure 4 shows, similar to the developed FMCDM method, the highest weights are for the complex calculations, running time, and performance criteria. As figure 5 shows, rankings of models by the developed FMCDM method and the fuzzy AHP method present the same results.

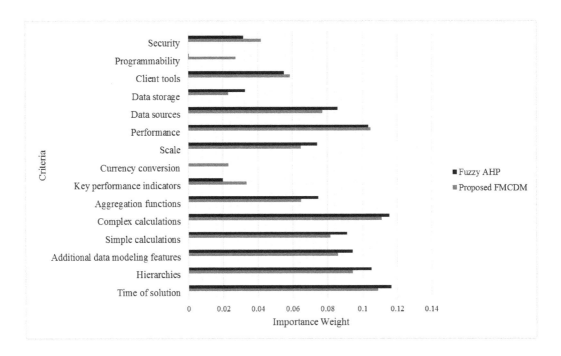

Figure 4. Importance weights of criteria for selected data source.

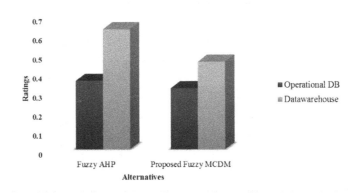

Figure 3. Rating alternatives with FMCDM (TFN-based) and Fuzzy AHP methods.

Furthermore, sensitivity analysis graphs allow for ranking the alternatives to be examined, whilst changing the criteria's importance. For example, the need of the organization to perform complex calculations (C_5) is 11%; as a result data warehouse has more capability rather than operational database for this criterion.

Data warehouse and relational database functionalities differ in a number of situations. For example, due to the weakness of the data warehouse in data sources criterion, if the organization reduces this criterion's importance from 78% to 23%, then instead of data warehouse, operational database will be selected.

5. Results and discussion

The use of data warehouses and operational databases in different situations was shown, Operational databases possess a number of disadvantages including the requirement of writing complex queries, slow response rates to queries, limitations in supporting functions and operations, and insufficient memory for answering queries. However, data warehouses with multi-dimensional structures have distinctive functionalities compared to the operational databases. As shown in this study, in data sources, query optimization plays a key role in performance, where each one of these data sources, for each criterion possesses different abilities. One of the reasons for the organizations failing to create suitable data sources without extra cost and time is the lack of suitable or optimal decision-making. In this study, an effective framework was proposed based on the organization requirements and comparison of the characteristics of data sources such as their models, business logic, data access and storage and security for suitable decision-making for deciding either the generation of a data warehouse or for the use of the existing operational databases. Fuzzy Delphi is used to ensure the selection of appropriate criteria, and as a result, 15 criteria were chosen.

In this paper, the authors proposed an alternative fuzzy-based multi-criteria decision-making model and compared it with Fuzzy AHP. The efficiency of this method was proved through a case study. The results obtained showed that complex calculations (0.116) and solution time (0.116) have higher weightings. Finally, the results obtained show that the decisions made through this framework are the same when implemented using the fuzzy-based decision-making and fuzzy AHP methods. The results of ranking by means of FAHP and the proposed MCDM method show that operational databases perform best, followed by data warehouses.

References

[1] Daneshpour, N. & Abdollahzadeh Barforoush, A. (2007). AUT-QPM: the framework to justify data warehouse systems. 3th International Computer Engineering Conference on Smart Applications for the Information Society, Cairo, Egypt, 2007.

[2] Hwang, C. L. & Yoon, K. (1981). Multiple Attribute Decision Making: Methods and Application. Berlin, Heidelberg. New York: Springer-Verlag.

[3] Zadeh, L. A. (1965). Fuzzy sets. Information and Control. vol. 8, no. 8, pp. 338-353.

[4] Wang, J. W., Cheng, C. H., & Cheng, H. K., (2009). Fuzzy Hierarchical TOPSIS for Supplier Selection. Applied Soft Computing, vol. 9, no. 1, pp. 377-386.

[5] Lan, H. E. & Congbo, L. I. (2009). Method for selecting ERP system based on fuzzy set theory and analytical hierarchy process. Global Congress on Intelligent Systems, Xiamen, China, 2009.

[6] Mamaghani, F. (2002). Evaluation and selection of antivirus and content filtering software. Information Managment and Computer Security, vol. 10, no 1, pp. 28-32.

[7] Liang, G. S. & Wang, M. J. J. (1993). A fuzzy multi-criteria decision making approach for robot selection. Robotics and Computer-Integrated Manufacturing, vol. 10, no 4, pp. 267-274.

[8] Vijayalakshmi, S., Zayaraz, G. & Vijayalakshmi, V. (2010). Multicriteria decision analysis method for evaluation of software architectures. International Journal of Computer Applications, vol. 1, no 25, pp. 33-38.

[9] Eldrandaly, K. & Naguib, S. (2013). A knowledge-based system for GIS software selection. International Arab Journal of Information Technology, vol. 10, no. 2, pp. 152-159.

[10] LeBlance, L. A. & Jelassi, M. (1989). DSS software selection: a multiple criteria decision methodology. Information and Management, vol. 17, no. 1, pp. 49-65.

[11] Phillips, G. E., & Hahnb, E. D. & Forgionne, G. A. (2004). A multiple-criteria framework for evaluation of decision support systems. Omega International Journal of Managment Science, vol. 32, no. 4, pp. 323-332.

[12] Huang, H., Cheng, H., Wang, Q. I. & Shao, Y. (2007). A research of the implementation readiness model for ERP. 6th Wuhan International Conference on E-Business, Wuhan, China, 2007.

[13] Lin, H. Y., Hsu, P. Y. & Sheen, G. J. (2007). A fuzzy-based decision-making procedure for data warehouse system selection. Expert systems with Applications, vol. 32, no. 3, pp. 939-953.

[14] Cochran, J. K. & Chen, H. N. (2005). Fuzzy multi-criteria selection of object-oriented simulation software for production system analysis. Computers & Operations Research, vol. 32, no. 1, pp. 153-168.

[15] Saaty, T. L. (1980). The analytic hierarchy process. McGraw-Hill, New York.

[16] Oğuztimur, S. (2011) Why Fuzzy Analytic Hierarchy Process Approach for transport problems? Available:http://wwwsre.wu.ac.at/ersa/ersaconfs/ersa11/e110830aFinal00438.pdf

[17] Pressman, R. (2009). Software Engineering: A Practitioner's Approach. McGraw-Hill, Science/ Engineering/ Math.

[18] Kimball, R. (1996). The Data Warehouse Toolkit: Practical Techniques for Building Dimensional Data Warehouses. Wiley.

[19] Chen, S. H. (1985). Ranking fuzzy numbers with maximizing set and minimizing set. Fuzzy Sets and Systems, vol. 17, no. 2, pp. 113-129.

[20] Dalkey, N. C. & Helmer, O. (1963). An experimental application of the Delphi method to the use of experts. Managment Science, vol. 9, no. 3, pp. 458-467.

[21] Russo, M., Ferrari, A. & Webb, C. (2012). Microsoft SQL Server 2012 Analysis Services: The BISM Tabular Model. Microsoft Press.

[22] LeBlance, P. (2013). Microsoft SQL Server 2012 Step by Step. Microsoft Press.

10

Employing data mining to explore association rules in drug addicts

F. Zahedi[1*] and M. R. Zare-Mirakabad[2]

1. Department of Engineering, College of Computer Engineering, Yazd Science and Research Branch, Islamic Azad University, Yazd, Iran.
2. School of Electrical and Computer Engineering, Department of Computer Engineering, Yazd University, Yazd, Iran.

*Corresponding author: f.zahedi@tvu.ac.ir (F. Zahedi).

Abstract
Drug addiction is a major social, economic and hygienic challenge that impacts on all the community and needs serious threat. Available treatments are only successful in short-term unless underlying reasons making individuals prone to the phenomenon are not investigated. Nowadays, there are some treatment centers which have comprehensive information about addicted people. Therefore, given the huge data sources, data mining can be used to explore knowledge implicit in them; their results can be employed as knowledge-based support systems to make decisions regarding addiction prevention and treatment. We studied 471 participants in such clinics, where 86.2% were male and 13.8% were female. The study aimed to extract rules from the collected data by using association models. Results can be used by rehab clinics to give more knowledge regarding relationships between various parameters and help them for better and more effective treatments. The finding shows that there is a significant relationship between individual characteristics and LSD abuse, individual characteristics, the kind of narcotics taken, and committing crimes, family history of drug addiction and family member drug addiction.

Keywords: *Drug Addiction, Data Mining, Association Rules, Rules Discovery.*

1. Introduction

Nowadays, most societies face the serious challenge of drug addiction, which is often associated with social problems. Yet, no sure method has been proposed to treat it though much research has been conducted in this regard. Drug addiction is closely related to cultural, religious, economic, social, and historical aspects of a community and is affected by different factors such as biological, psychological, and social ones[1].

It affects individuals' physical, social, and mental performance and increases the number of hepatitis and AIDS victims. In particular, the youth has been heavily influenced by this phenomenon, which can lead to mental and behavioral deviations [2]. Considering that in many cases addiction-related treatments are not successful, identifying factors influencing drug addiction is of paramount importance for preventive purposes. That is, preventive steps and appropriate treatments reduce risk behaviors and consequently, mental and physical impacts of the behaviors and treatment costs are lessened [3].

On the other hand, using data mining to explore health-related issues proposes a lot of potentials and advantages and it has been shown that data mining algorithms dramatically diminish diagnosis costs and health-related risks. It should be noted that the success of data mining in health systems is a function of employing and having access to valid and comprehensive data. Then, efficient procedures for collecting, storing, and processing the data are vital [4].

In addition, using machine learning techniques in medicine and psychiatry offers a totally new research avenue for monitoring, diagnosing, and categorizing psychiatric disorders such as schizophrenia, psychosis, depression, anxiety, and alcohol abuse [5]. According to [6], qualitative questionnaires and statistical procedures are dominantly used in social studies. The authors suggest that data mining can be introduced into social sciences such as psychology and cognitive sciences as well.

A large number of research projects have been carried out on the factors influencing drug addiction in many fields of study such as medicine, psychology, and psychiatry.

In most of these research projects, specific statistical procedures have been used to analyze data and the usual way of hypothesis testing has come to be statistical procedures.

This is where data mining comes in since numerous variables can be investigated, through which meaningful, recurrent, and implicit patterns can be extracted without the need for formulating a hypothesis. The results of data mining studies can be applied as the knowledge source of backup systems to prevent addiction or make decision treatment.

2. Literature review

Evidence coming from the available literature suggests that data mining has different applications in different fields of study such as medical diagnosis and treatment options. Authors of [7] applied associative rules to youth drug addiction databases and indicated that there is a relationship between parents' behaviors, abnormal behaviors of the youth, peer group addiction, and taking illegal drugs.

Also, [8] aimed to analyze data and quantify the extent to which personal, environmental, and familial factors could predict cannabis use among the youth by using the ZINB model, decision tree, and association rules techniques. Also, [9] used a combination of k-medoids and hierarchical clustering procedures and launched genetic analyses in order to identify genes responsible for triggering addiction-related risks.

The present study aimed to use available data on drug addicts in order to reveal meaningful relationships beneficial to decision making regarding prevention, addiction diagnosis and treatment, and educating families. The ultimate goal was to use the data to ameliorate the current situation.

Results of the study can help educational system authorities and be included in preventive programs so as to raise the consciousness of the youth and promote well-being.

Moreover, findings of the study are useful for other domestic centers such as the Welfare Organization, Ministry of Health and Medical Education, and other affiliated organizations.

3. Data mining

Data mining is simply defined as extracting knowledge implicitly exists in a given database [10]. That is, data mining refers to the process of studying and analyzing a huge amount of data in order to extract underlying, meaningful patterns, relationships, and laws. In recent years, increasing importance has been given to data mining since databases are inoperable unless turned into knowledge. New patterns can be investigated for descriptive and predictive purposes. The former aims to unveil patterns in a way that is understandable and interpretable. On the other hand, the latter focuses on identifying variables or characteristics of a database and is used to predict the amount or future behavior of some variables [11].

Exploring and generating knowledge is a multi-staged process; its quality is affected by the accurate implementation of every single stage, which is as follows: 1) understanding a given problem and data, 2) collecting, analyzing and preprocessing relevant data, 3) selecting a method from data mining functionalities, 4) interpreting and evaluating the results in order to validate them and calculate accuracy of the model, and 5) utilizing the unveiled knowledge. Following some data mining techniques exploited in this study are surveyed.

3.1. Data mining techniques: Association rules

Different data mining techniques are employed to examine databases and result in various kinds of discovered knowledge. One of the important data mining techniques is the association rule techniques, which are used to extract correlations, recurrent patterns, causal relationships, and associations among a colossal number of items in a database, and then, the results form the basis of decision-making [12].

Association rules are simple, clear, intuitive, intelligible, and practical tools which expose the relationships among various variables in a descriptive way and aim to mine data so as to identify patterns without having background information on a given reality [7]. Perhaps, the main weakness of association rules is the number of produced rules, which require operators to do a lot of filtering. Also, it should be noted that extracting an association rule does not necessarily mean that it is efficient [7].

Finding attractive association rules helps decision-making process [13]. The attractiveness of a rule can be determined objectively or subjectively. Support and confidence coefficients are the criteria based on which attractiveness of a rule can be assessed. The coefficients show efficiency and determination of the generated rules, respectively [14]. Applying the coefficiency may result in a large number of rules from which some operators may find uninteresting. Therefore, support-confidence framework can be complemented by the lift correlation so as to reduce the number of produced rules and find more meaningful ones. In the case of A=>B, if the lift is lower than 1, then the occurrence of A is negatively correlated with the occurrence of B. That is, occurrence of one result in the absence of another, from which it can be concluded that a negative correlation renders the association rule meaningless though it may have a high support coefficient. If the outcome of the association rule lift is higher than 1, then A and B are positively correlated, meaning that the occurrence of one proceeds the other one. If the outcome of the association rule is 1, then, A and B are independent meaning that there is no correlation between them [14].

Producing association rules is usually divided into two steps [12]:

- Applying the minimum support in order to find all frequent items in a database.

- Applying the minimum confidence to the frequent item sets to generate rules.

4. Introducing the proposed system

A successful treatment of drug addicts is very difficult and challenging. Hence, in order to save costs and time, it is preferably required to identify factors affecting drug addiction in an attempt to prevent addiction, something which can be fulfilled through data mining. Thus, the present study focused on discovering the patterns existing in the data related to people referring to rehabilitation clinics to undergo treatment.

4.1. Participants of the study (Dataset)

Target population of the study was all the individuals referring to rehab centers in Yazd, Iran, which included 471 patients. Of the participants, 86.2% were male and 13.8% were female. The participants were selected from an exclusively female rehab center, a prison clinic, Yazd Narcotics Anonymous Society, and other clinics across Yazd, Iran. Table 1 shows the dataset schema collected in this study.

Table 1. Conceptual schema of dataset.

No.	Items	Data category
1	sex, birth year, address, number of children, income, education, residence, marriage status, current job	Personal Information
2	number of family members, parents job, parents education, family history of drug addiction	Family Information
3	first substance, starting age of use and addiction, job, Marital Status , bidder, location, feeling, Risk factors, Parental reactions	First Use Information
4	Treatment count, Treatment type, Treatment Reason, Recurrence reason	Treatment Information
5	crime, number of arrests, arrest time	Crime Information
6	Physical Disease ، Mental Disease	Disease Information
7	used substance, time of consumption	Drug Use Information

4.2. Understanding and preparing the data

In order to get familiar with the subjects studied, an interview was conducted with experts in the rehab center. Then, histograms and distribution diagrams were used to display the distribution of variables.

After the initial data understanding, the data was rounded up and the number of variables, their amounts, and columns, as the case may be, were reduced. Not only is the quality of results not damaged by this, but it also improves the results of data mining. Columns reduction is performed by human analysts or a number of automated processes, based on an understanding of the domain of use and purposes of the exploration.

After the preparatory stage, the association rules model was used to expose relationship existing in the data.

4.3. Discovering relationships

In order to discover association rules hidden in the data, a priori model was employed. However, due to the multiplicity of features and to avoid generating meaningless rules, specific features were nominated. That is, before modeling, useful features were selected and used as the input and then, support and confidence coefficients were extracted. In order to make sure of the validity of the generated rules, the lift correlation was applied, too. Table 2 shows the most valid rules generated after applying rule pruning. Obviously, some of the generated rules can evidence the validity of the relationships that experts discover through experimental procedures. On the other hand, some are more speculative and can be employed to take preventive and rehabilitating measures against drug addiction.

Table 2. Some generated association rules with interestingness measures.

Number	Association rules	Support	Confidence	Lift
1	If the person is young and unmarried and has started substance use since he was a teenager, he consumes LSD.	5.52	57.69	3.19
2	If the person feels hatred when he uses substance for the first time, he gives up the addiction.	1.69	25	2.35
3	If one of the members of a family is addicted, the woman gets addicted at home if she is suggested to use substance.	7	84.68	4.41
4	If a depressed young person uses different kinds of drugs, he'll commit drug sale crime.	5.14	56.66	4.23
5	If a low-income depressed person uses different kinds of drugs, he'll commit the robbery.	5.52	57.69	5.54
6	If a low-income middle aged man , is not resident in Yazd, he'll commit drug traffic crime.	5.3	36	3.94
7	If a middle-aged woman is a housewife, her addiction will return due to physical, mental or family problems.	5.94	39.28	2.66

As an example, according to rule 1, 57.69% of single young people experiencing drug early in their adolescence are using LSD. In other words, the likelihood of LSD abuse is 18%. Being celibate, adolescent, and an early drug abuse raises the amount to 57.69% meaning that those who are single and abuse drug early in their adolescence are three times more likely to turn to LSD abuse. According to rule 2, a feeling of hatred following the first drug abuse raises the likelihood of rehabilitation up to 2.35 times. Rule3 indicates that for women a family history of drug abuse results in home drug abuse. Rule 4 suggests that young addicts who suffer from depression and simultaneously take different narcotics such as LSD and Heroine are approximately four times more likely to commit crimes.

5. Conclusion

The present work aimed at exploring drug addiction-related databases from different rehab centers in order to find underlying patterns using association rules mining. Some of the extracted rules provided insights into the following issues: the role of individuals' feelings after the first drug abuse in the success of following treatments, characteristics of LSD abusers, main reason of addiction among different age groups, and the influence of family history on individuals' addiction. Findings of the study can help different organizations in making decisions about addiction.

References

[1] Goreishizade, M. & Torabi, K. (2002). A study of co morbidity of substance abuse and psychiatric disorders in self-referred addicts to Tabriz welfare center. Medical journal of Tabriz University of medical sciences, vol. 55, pp. 49-53.

[2] Pourmovahed, Z., Yassini Ardakani, M., Ahmadieh, M., Dehghani, K., & Kalani, Z. (2010). Evaluation of the Knowledge of Rural High School Students in Yazd About Drugs. SSU_Journals, vol. 18, no. 3, pp. 179-183.

[3] Dastjerdi, G., Ebrahimi Dehshiri, V., Kholasezade, G. & Ehsani, F. (2010). Effectiveness of Methadone in Reduction of High Risk Behaviors in Clients of MMT Center. SSU_Journals, vol. 18, no. 3, pp. 215-219.

[4] Padhy, N., Mishra, P. & Panigrahi, R. (2012). The Survey of Data Mining Applications And Feature Scope. International Journal of Computer Science, Engineering and Information Technology (IJCSEIT), vol. 2, no. 3, pp. 43-58.

[5] Diederich, J., Al-Ajmi, A. & Yellowlees, P. (2007). E_x-ray: Data mining and mental health. Applied Soft Computing, vol. 7, no. 3, pp. 923-928.

[6] Liao, S. H., Chu, P. H. & Hsiao, P. Y. (2012). Data mining techniques and applications –A decade review from 2000 to 2011. Expert Systems with Applications, vol. 39, no. 12, pp. 11303-11311.

[7] Garcia, E. G., Blasco, B. C., López, R. J. & Pol, A. P. (2010). Study of the factors associated with substance use in adolescence using Association Rules. Adictiones, vol. 22, no. 4, pp. 293-299.

[8] Gervilla, E., Cajal, B. & Palmer, A. (2011). Quantification of the influence of friends and antisocial behaviour in adolescent consumption of cannabis using

the ZINB model and data mining. Addictive behaviors, vol. 36, no. 4, pp. 368-374.

[9] Sun, J., Bi, J., Chan, G., Oslin, D., Farrer, L., Gelernter, J. & Kranzler, H. R. (2012). Improved methods to identify stable, highly heritable subtypes of opioid use and related behaviors. Addictive Behaviors, vol. 37, no. 10, pp. 1138-1144.

[10] Yun, L. & Xiang-sheng, L. (2010). The data mining and knowledge discovery in biomedicine. 5th International Conference on Computer Science and Education (ICCSE), IEEE. China, pp. 1050-1052.

[11] Chhieng, D. C. (2007). Data Mining and Clinical Decision Support Systems. Clinical Decision Support Systems, Springer New York, pp. 44-63.

[12] Divya, R. & Vinodkumar, S. (2012). Survey on AIS, Apriori and FP-Tree algorithms. International Journal of Computer Science and Management Research, vol. 1, no. 2, pp. 194-200.

[13] Khare, N., Adlakha, N. & Pardasani, K. R. (2010). An Algorithm for Mining Multidimensional Association Rules using Boolean Matrix. 2010 International Conference on Recent Trends in Information, Telecommunication and Computing (ITC), Kochi, Kerala, India, pp. 95-99.

[14] Han, J., Kamber, M. & Pei, J. (2006). Data mining: concepts and techniques. Morgan Kaufmann Publishers.

11

A case study for application of fuzzy inference and data mining in structural health monitoring

S. Shoorabi Sani[*]

Faculty of Electrical and Computer Engineering, Hakim Sabzevari University, Iran.

Corresponding author: s1sani91@gmail.com (S. Shoorabi).

Abstract

In this work, a system is designed for monitoring the structural health of bridge deck and predicting various possible damages to this section based on measuring the temperature and humidity using wireless sensor networks, and then it is implemented and investigated. A scaled model of a conventional medium-sized bridge (of 50 m length and 10 m height, and with 2 piers) is examined for the purpose of this work. This method includes installing two sensor nodes with the ability of measuring temperature and humidity on both side of the bridge deck. The data collected by the system including the temperature and humidity values is received using a LABVIEW-based software to be analyzed and stored in a database. The proposed structural health monitoring (SHM) system is equipped with a novel method using data mining techniques on the database of climatic conditions of past few years related to the location of the bridge to predict the occurrence and severity of future damages. In addition, this system has several alarm levels, which are based on the analysis of bridge conditions by the fuzzy inference method, so it can issue proactive and precise warnings and alarms in terms of place of occurrence and severity of possible damages in the bridge deck to ensure the total proactive maintenance (TPM). Very low costs, increased efficiency of the bridge service, and reduced maintenance costs make the SHM system a practical and applicable one. The data and results related to all mentioned subjects are thoroughly discussed, and the accuracy and reliability of the SHM systems are evaluated. The results obtained show that this system is qualified to be used as a SHM system in a sample *hypothetical* bridge.

Keywords: *Structural Health Monitoring, Wireless Sensor Networks, Proactive Maintenance of Bridges, Data Mining and Fuzzy Inference Techniques.*

1. Introduction

Maintaining the safety and a reliable service of a large bridge over its relatively long life requires obtaining continuous and reliable data regarding its structure including the damage caused by the temperature gradient, cracking, fatigue, corrosion, and decrease in the load capacity of the bridge, all of which should be carefully evaluated. Common measurements such as periodic visual inspections and controlled loading test are typical in this respect, and their disadvantages have been thoroughly investigated. A new technology called structural health monitoring (SHM) that uses wireless sensor networks [1-8] has recently attracted a lot of attention in the field of measurement and analysis of those mentioned factors. There are various SHM systems that can detect the damages to the bridge structure through analyzing the dynamic characteristics of the bridge such as shifts in the pier frequencies and changes in the vibration modes and assessing the structural damping index or modal assurance criterion. The characteristics of low-frequency pier vibrations are not sensitive to small damages and changes in the structure, so the monitoring systems have to cover higher frequencies to detect such changes [9], and this necessarily requires a significant number of highly sensitive transducers and also a data acquisition system with a high rate of sampling [10]. It also requires a complex procedure of data processing for the detection of changes in the dynamic characteristics of the structure. In addition, changes in the natural frequencies caused by structural damage can be easily overlooked under the influence of environmental effects, especially changes in temperature and humidity [11-19]. The presence of these difficulties and limitations [20-26] is the main motivation for the investigation of other SHM methods for bridges. In this work, a SHM system that utilizes the wireless sensor networks (WSNs) and is based upon monitoring humidity and thermal environmental responses was designed, and it was then analyzed with the help of a hypothetical bridge. A researcher has claimed that this method has the ability to by-pass the mentioned problems and limitations. Exposure to sun and heat exchange with the environment leads to temperature differences in different parts of the bridge. Such changes occur continuously and slowly every day and affect the structure of the bridge [12,13,14]. The temperature difference between the different parts leads to the thermal response of the bridge including thermally-induced strains, stresses, and changes in the reactions of bridge piers [15]. The change in these responses is slow, so they can be easily distinguished from the thermal responses caused by temporary traffic. Furthermore, they have many measureable effects. In the case of pre-stressed concrete bridges, thermally-induced stresses are usually in the same range of live load stresses but are often greater than these stresses [16]. The slow and wide-range changes facilitate the use of thermal response methods such as measuring the temperature in different parts of the bridge that can be easily monitored. This monitoring can be easily performed through conventional and inexpensive transducers and data acquisition systems that have low sampling rates and can simultaneously monitor the environmental heat loads and the responses of the bridge. The condition of a bridge structure (especially the metal sections) can also be monitored for the effects of humidity, so timely measures can be taken based on these data to improve its condition. Such SHM system provides a large amount of valuable data than can be used to perform calculations in a comprehensive manner and on a daily basis. In addition, the thermal responses are semi-static, so the required analyses are less complex than the dynamic behavior. On a sunny day, the temperature of the surface of the bridge deck is much higher than that of the underside of the deck, and this causes the bridge flexure to be drawn upward. For a typical curved bridge, this phenomenon has a little effect on the reaction of the pier section or the internal forces such as stresses or strains. On the other hand, for a continuous bridge with several curves, this phenomenon changes the reaction of piers and causes thermally induced momentary stresses and strains along the bridge flexure. These thermally induced responses are a function of EL. Therefore, the cracks and damages in the curved sections of the bridge can substantially alter the effective EL of the bridge [15, 16]. In view of the above discussion, a SHM based on environmental thermal responses seems to be suitable for long bridges with several curves. The main focus of this research work is on the pre-stressed concrete bridges with medium to high curve lengths. This study also examines the evaluation and monitoring of the effect of humidity on different parts of the bridge and also the corrosion and damage caused by humidity or those damages for which humidity acts as an accelerating factor. The results obtained showed that a well-designed and well-implemented SHM system based on environmental thermal responses and humidity has the ability of detecting the structural damages and identifying their location and severity [17,18].

It seems necessary to state clearly why we use KNN instead of the other similarity measures at the data mining stage of this research work. Nearest neighbor search (NNS), also known as proximity search, similarity search or closest point search, is an optimization problem for finding the closest (or most similar) points. Closeness is typically expressed in terms of a dissimilarity function: the less similar the objects, the larger the function values. Formally, the nearest-neighbor (NN) search problem is defined as follows: given a set S of points in a space M and a query point $q \in M$, find the closest point in S to q. Donald Knuth in Vol. 3 of The Art of Computer Programming (1973) called it the post-office problem, referring to an application of assigning to a residence the nearest post-office. A direct generalization of this problem is a k-NN search, where we need to find the k closest points.

Most commonly, M is a metric space, and dissimilarity is expressed as a distance metric, which is symmetric and satisfies the triangle inequality. Even more common, M is taken to be the d-dimensional vector-space, where dissimilarity is measured using the Euclidean distance, Manhattan distance or other distance metric. However, the dissimilarity function can be arbitrary. One example is the asymmetric Bregman divergences, for which the triangle inequality does not hold.

The simplest solution to the NNS problem is to compute the distance from the query point to every other point in the database, keeping track of the "best so far". This algorithm, sometimes referred to as the naive approach, has a running time of O(dN),where N is
the cardinality of S and d is the dimensionality of M. There are no search data structures to maintain, so a linear search has no space complexity beyond the storage of the database. A naive search can, on average, outperform space partitioning approaches on higher dimensional spaces.

Since the 1970s, branch and bound methodology has been applied to the problem. In the case of the Euclidean space, this approach is known as the spatial index or spatial access method. Several space-partitioning methods have been developed for solving the NNS problem. Perhaps the simplest is the k-d tree, which iteratively bisects the search space into two regions containing half of the points of the parent region. Queries are performed via traversal of the tree from the root to a leaf by evaluating the query point at each split. Depending on the distance specified in the query, the neighboring branches that might contain hits may also need to be evaluated. For a constant dimension query time, an average complexity is O(log N). In the case of randomly distributed points, the worst case complexity is $o\left(kN^{\left(1-\frac{1}{k}\right)}\right)$. Alternatively, the R-tree data structure was designed to support the nearest neighbor search in dynamic context, as it has efficient algorithms for insertions and deletions such as the R* tree. R-trees can yield the nearest neighbors not only for the Euclidean distance but can also be used with other distances. Particular examples include VP-tree and BK-tree.

Using a set of points taken from a 3D space and putting into a BSP tree, and given a query point taken from the same space, a possible solution to the problem of finding the nearest point-cloud point to the query point is given in the following description of an algorithm. (Strictly speaking, no such point may exist because it may not be unique. However, in practice, usually we only care about finding any one of the subsets of all point-cloud points that exist at the shortest distance to a given query point.) The idea is, for each branching of the tree, to guess that the closest point in the cloud resides in the half-space containing the query point. This may not be the case but it is a good heuristic. After having recursively gone through all the troubles of solving the problem for the guessed half-space,

now compare the distance returned by this result with the shortest distance from the query point to the partitioning plane. This latter distance is that between the query point and the closest possible point that could exist in the half-space not searched. If this distance is greater than that returned in the earlier result, then clearly, there is no need to search for the other half-space. If there is such a need, then you must go through the trouble of solving the problem for the other half space and then compare its result with the former one, and then return the proper result. The performance of this algorithm is nearer to the logarithmic time than the linear time when the query point is near the cloud since as the distance between the query point and the closest point-cloud point nears zero, the algorithm needs only perform a look-up using the query point as a key to get the correct result.

On the other hand, due to the repeatability of weather periods in terms of the effective parameters in different weather conditions like temperature, humidity, and wind speed, their repeat pattern is so complicated and is beyond the scope of this research work. The nearest neighbor algorithm can search similar weather conditions which are dominant in the recent days in the location of bridge in different parts of its structure that they are measured and logged by the SHM system in this article, which will be saved -at the preset time interval - in a data bank which is involved in weather parameters' profile related to the recent years of the location of the bridge.

This system has the ability to provide alarms and warnings -for Total Proactive Maintenance (TPM) principles before damages and crisis situations occur-. All the above-mentioned methods will be introduced, investigated, and evaluated thoroughly in the second and third parts of this article. Also it should be noted that in this article we will assess measurement of pair parameters of temperature and humidity due to the easier measurements and cheaper equipment for logging data regarding to temperature and humidity parameters. .Their important effects on health of bridges' structure are studied in different recent researches [10-14].

The second section of this article introduces the details of the proposed SHM system and its implementation, the hardware and configuration of the sensor network, and designed monitoring program. Then discusses the manner of improving the proposed method to a proactive system with the ability to predict the temperature and humidity using the especial data mining techniques. The third section assesses and evaluates the results of the proposed SHM, average and maximum error, and mean squared error, whether in the measurement stage or in the process of predicting the temperature and humidity. This section also assesses the details of a warning system based on the fuzzy inference. The final part of the third section presents some examples of the practical applications of the proposed monitoring system in the maintenance procedures of conventional bridges. The fourth section summarizes the discussed issues and the advantages and disadvantages of the method.

2. Proposed SHM system and its hardware, software, and implementation

2.1. Description of proposed SHM system and its components and principles

In this work, a SHM system with the following characteristics was designed, implemented, and simulated for a hypothetical bridge. An overview of the proposed SHM system and its components and functions is shown in figure 1.

Figure 1. An overview of proposed SHM system and its components and function.

As shown in figure 2, the parameters temperature and humidity are monitored at two points of the bridge deck. This data will be used for the data mining process and prediction of the critical values for the following days, and a warning system based on the fuzzy inference techniques will assess the status of the mentioned points, and will announce timely pre-emptive alerts to the repair and maintenance team.

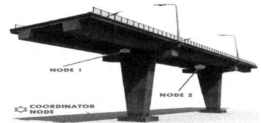

Figure 2. SHM systems of presumed bridge and layout of its components [7].

2.2. Description of hardware and wireless sensor nodes for monitoring temperature and humidity

The inexpensive and analog sensors LM35 and HIH4000 were used for sensing and measuring the temperature and humidity, respectively, for the design of the nodes of a wireless sensor network. To assess the reliability and accuracy of the system, the wired SHT11 sensor was used to obtain the temperature and humidity data in the desired nodes. This sensor calculates the humidity and temperature with high precision in digital form and does not need signal conditioning. A USB DAQ Digital Sensor was used to obtain its information. The sensor nodes were designed using the Protel (Altium Designer) software. Figure 3 shows the layout of PCB used.. This design includes a board for the LM35 and HIH4000 analog sensors and a separate board for the SHT11 sensor, which is considered as a reference for the measurement. Figure 4 shows the final view of the above-mentioned designs.

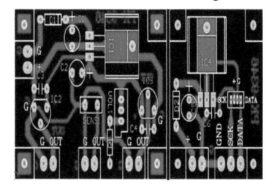

Figure 3. layout of PCB of board and bias circuits of temperature and humidity sensors.

Figure 4. Final image of sensor nodes (analog nodes including LM35 and HIH4000 sensors on the right, and SHT node on the left).

In the next step, the ProBee-ZE10 ZigBee module was used as the wireless module. The default development board of this device was used to ensure an easier application and also for an easier installation of the connectors. The image of this module and its development board can be seen in the figures 5 and 6, respectively.

Figure 5. Image of ZE10 module [2].

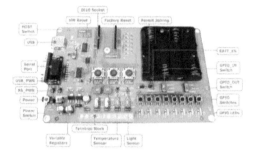

Figure 6. Image of ZE10 development board [2].

2.3. Description of application software used for monitoring temperature and humidity

In the coordinator node connected to a computer through a USB port, the values related to the analog channels 3 and 4 (the temperature and humidity) in each node can be read and received through the especial commands [1].

After sending the above data string in the Labview software program, a series of 32-bit hexadecimal values sampled from 4 analog channels of node 1 and node 2 will be sent to the coordinator node (with about 2 to 3 seconds delay), and then will enter in the software through a serial port. The Labview software will perform the processes of retrieving and separating data strings and converting hexadecimal data to decimal, then applies calibration coefficients to obtain correct values for temperature and humidity, and subsequently, displays these values while also saving them in Excel format in separate files with the date and time of data recording. These files include "hum1" and "temp1" for node 1 and "hum2" and "temp2" for node 2. Figure 7 shows further details of the front panel of this software.

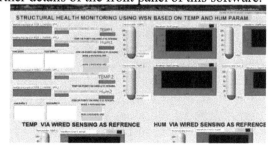

Figure 7. Front panel of software.

In this panel, all the received values and data strings and all the operations performed on them at each step can be easily reviewed by the user through String indicators. It also plots a graph for temperature and humidity at each node, and a graphical barometer separately shows the accuracy of the system performance. The values that are stored in the Excel files are also displayed in this application. Actually, in the front panel of the software, we can see the values (strings or digits) for all steps of the sending and receiving data including the first start string that is sent via the coordinator to the two end notes for initializing the A/D channel and making the A/D conversion.

Also we can see the hexadecimal input of the global propose input and output of the wireless modules, decimal values of the raw data for temperature and humidity, and trend or waveform of the temperature and humidity parameters. Also we can see the temperature and humidity values and graphs from SHT11 as the reference data.

The main parts of the temperature and humidity monitoring application, which is based on the LABVIEW coding language (in node1, for example) and the SHT11 sensor data acquisition application are shown in figures 8a-d. In figure 8a, in rectangle 1, the serial port of the computer is configured and the parity, bit-rate, and other necessary parameters for the wireless channel are set. In rectangle 2, the received string is devised via an "un-concatenate" block, and in rectangle 3, the strings are converted to the decimal digits and form the raw temp data. Finally, in rectangle 4, the raw data is scaled and/or offset to provide the final temperature value. Similar explanations exist for the humidity at the 4 rectangles in figure 8b. In figure 8c, the configuration of the port and serial and wireless communication channel is done in rectangle 1, and converting the received string to the final temperature value is done in rectangle 2. Similar explanations exist for the humidity at 2 rectangles in the figure 8d.

2.4. Implementation of temperature and humidity monitoring system

In the next step, 3 selected wireless modules were configured. 2 modules were defined as the end device and one module was defined as the coordinator. Configuration of the end devices and coordinator was performed through the USB terminal of a laptop and by the use of the Hyper Terminal software. These settings are also available through the pro-Bee manager software. There are 4 analogs to the digital channels in the final module, and their configuration was performed through the software in a way that channels 0 and 1 were dedicated to potentiometers in the development board for the initial and required tests of the program, and channels 2 and 3 were dedicated to connecting the output of the temperature and humidity sensor in each node, respectively. After performing the initial configuration of all nodes and connecting the

sensors and feeds of all the three nodes, the sensor network will have the overall configuration as shown in figure 9. The final configuration of the two end nodes (node 2 & node 3) and one coordinator node (node 1) are shown in figures 10-12, respectively. On the other side, figure 13 shows the reference digital sensor and its Data Acquisition (DAQ) board.

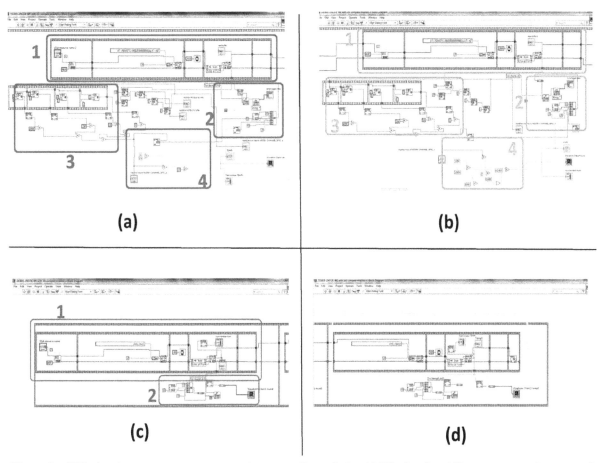

(a)   (b)

(c)   (d)

Figure 8. a)Wireless temperature measurement program for node 1,   b) Wireless humidity measurement program for node 1, c) SHT11 sensor data acquisition program for temperature, d) SHT11 sensor data acquisition program for humidity.

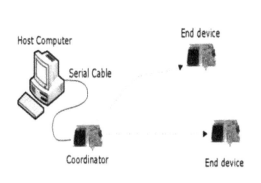

Figure 9. Overall configuration of wireless sensor network used in SHM system.

Figure 10. Node 2 (end node).

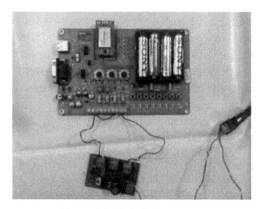

Figure 11. Node 3 (end node).

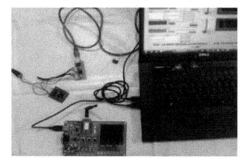

Figure 12. Mother node (COORDINATOR) + PC.

Figure 13. SHT11 digital sensor board + USB DAQ.

2.5. Upgrading proposed method to a proactive system capable of predicting temperature and humidity

After formation of the temperature and humidity monitoring system mentioned above, a novel method was used to predict the temperature and humidity in the nodes for the following days (according to the database of the weather condition in the past 3 years in the area where the bridge is located). The details of this method are as follow.

The basis of this method is to use the temperature and humidity data for the past 3 years (collected in a database and sorted based on different months) and the temperature and humidity data the last 3 days recorded on the "hum1" and "temp1" files for node 1 and "hum2" and "temp2" for node 2, and also utilize MATLAB software and a data mining technique called K-Nearest

Neighbour (K-NN) to predict the temperature and humidity for the desired date. If the values for this predicted data exceed the limits (alert level) determined by the fuzzy technique, the system will notify the maintenance personnel to perform proactive or predictive maintenance and repair procedures on the bridge. A graphical interface was designed for the user's convenience, the details of which will be discussed in the third section of the paper. This GUI provides the possibility of comparing and validating the predictions and values by numerical and graphical means. In fact, adding the ability of predicting the temperature and humidity conditions in the following days has upgraded the proposed SHM system from a simple monitoring system to an ideal system for bridge maintenance.

2.6. Dataset

The most important part while implementing any data related project is the collection of the proper data for the analysis using any technique (e.g. data mining). To test the algorithms in this research work, a huge amount temperature and humidity data was required for the large number of days or years. Hence, the dataset for a duration of three years was collected from the similar proposed SHM system [21]. The data regarding to the various parameters are obtained in excel format from the proposed SHM system in figure 14. The required parameters- i.e. temperature and humidity -can be extracted from these datasets and then can be exported in MATLAB files where they are available for more analysis. Figure 14 shows the schematic representation of the above-mentioned CSV file in the excel arrangement that includes temperature, dew point, humidity, sea level press, etc. In this research work we focused on the two parameters "temperature" and "humidity" because the equipment required for measuring them had a lower price with respect to those of the other parameters.

On the other hand, the average amount of humidity and temperature in the last 3 days was recorded by monitoring the system in the "hum1" and "temp1" files for node 1 and "hum2" and "temp2" for node 2; this dataset is called "query". The overall layout of the above technique used to predict the temperature and humidity is described in the following section.

March 2009	Temp(celsius degree)			Dew Point(celsius degree)			Humidity(%)			Sea Level Press(hPa)			Visibility (km)			Wind(km/h)		
	High	avg	Low	High	avg	Low	High	avg	Low	High	avg	Low	High	avg	Low	High	avg	Low
1	38	30	22	9	7	4	35	25	14	1014	1011	1009	6	6	6	42	5	2
2	40	29	19	10	7	4	52	27	11	1014	1011	1008	6	6	3	21	3	2
3	40	30	21	10	8	5	46	24	12	1013	1010	1008	6	6	5	11	2	2
4	40	32	24	12	7	3	44	24	11	1012	1010	1007	6	6	5	19	3	7
5	41	32	24	7	4	2	27	19	9	1013	1009	1006	6	6	5	27	8	2
6	39	31	23	10	5	2	33	21	10	1014	1010	1008	6	6	3	19	6	3
7	39	31	23	10	4	1	44	20	11	1012	1010	1007	8	5	2	14	5	2
8	40	30	21	14	6	3	40	24	11	1013	1009	1006	6	5	4	11	2	1
9	38	30	22	12	12	7	44	32	21	1014	1010	1008	6	5	0	19	3	2
10	38	31	25	12	9	7	41	28	18	1016	1013	1011	6	5	3	14	6	3

Figure 14. Database (sorted in Excel file).

2.7. Aggregation, converting raw data

The algorithm in this research work takes the monthly temperature and humidity data as the input. The data is available in the excel format, and for the analysis of the temperature and humidity variation throughout the year, the monthly data need to be aggregated in one file. After aggregations, three matrices were formed for the years 2012, 2013, and 2014. Each column of a matrix represents the date (day of month/year) whereas each row consists the values of the temperature and humidity on a particular day(date).

For the purpose of temperature and humidity prediction, only the data for these parameters from the raw dataset is required, and hence, they must be extracted. Thus the temperature and humidity data for each month was extracted and stored in Matrix format named by the particular month. Only the values for temperature or humidity in a particular month of a year will have a maximum resemblance to its values for that particular month for any other year, and hence twelve matrices are created for these data for each month of the year as Jan, Feb, Mar, Apr, May, Jun, Jul, Aug, Sept, Oct, Nov, and Dec, These consist of the temperature and humidity data for that respective month for the complete duration of the three years 2012, 2013, and 2014. The data for more years can be added to this. These dataset matrices are then used for the prediction of temperature and humidity.

2.8. Implementing K-nearest neighbor for temperature and humidity prediction input

```
    dataMatrix  //  Candidate  trace  data  matrix  for  a
particular month for duration of 4 years
    (2012, 2013, 2014)
    queryMatrix  //  Reference  trace  data  matrix  consists of
data for previous 3 days to the day of prediction
    K // Number of neighbors, K=4 in this research work.
    Output:
    mtP[4]  // Predicted Temperature values for 4 days
    mhP[4]  // Predicted Humidity values for 4 days
    dataMatrix  //  Candidate  trace  data  matrix  for  a
particular month for duration of 4 years
    (2012, 2013, 2014)
    queryMatrix  //  Reference  trace  data  matrix  consists of
data for previous 3 days to the day of prediction
    K // Number of neighbors, K=4 in this research work.
    Output:
    mtP[4]  // Predicted Temperature values for 4 days
    mhP[4]  // Predicted Humidity values for 4 days
    KNN Algorithm: // Algorithm to predict temperature
and humidity
    Step 1:  Initialize variables
        numDataVectors = size of dataMatrix
        numQueryVectors = size of queryMatrix
    Step 2:  Initialize For i = 1 to numQueryVectors
        Calculate Euclidian Distance.
    Sort Euclidian Distances and neighborIds in ascending
order.
        Calculate
    NeighborDistance(i) = sqrt(sortval(i to k))
        End for loop
    Step 3:  Initialize i = 1 to 3
        Initialize i = 1 to 4
        tP (i, j) = dataMatrix(2)
        hP (i, j) = dataMatrix(3)
        end loop
        end loop
    Step 4:   Calculate predicted temperature and
        humidity
        mtP = tP/3
        mhP = hP/3
        return predicted temperature and humidity.
    Step 5:   Exit
```

2.9. Working of KNN Algorithm

Figure 15 shows the working of KNN algorithm for the temperature and humidity prediction. Figure 15(a) shows two matrices, dataMatrix and queryMatrix. DataMatrix consists of the temperature and humidity data for three years for the months whose prediction is to be made. For example, if the prediction is to be made for 28-2-2015, then dataMatrix consists of the temperature and humidity data for the month February for the years 2013, 2014, and 2015; The size of the matrix so formed is 113 x 2. QueryMatrix consists of the temperature and humidity data for 25-2-2015, 26-2-2015, and 27-2-2015. The KNN algorithm calculates the four nearest neighbor (NN) for the temperature and humidity data for each day of queryMatrix. The index for all of these neighbors for each day is shown in neighbors matrix in figure 15(b), and the Euclidian distance is shown in Dist matrix in figure 15(c); the rows in Dist matrix indicates the ith day in queryMatrix, and the   ith column

indicates the ith NN for temperature and humidity for the ith day.

Figures 15(d) and 15(e) show the temperature and humidity values from dataMatrix for the index obtained in neighbors matrix. The average values of the ith column in tP and hP matrix give the predicted values for temperature and humidity for the ith day. Figure 15(f) shows the predicted values for temperature and humidity for four days, i.e. 28-2-2015 to 2-3-2015. The mean square error was calculated for the above prediction, and it was found to be 1.65 for the temperature prediction and 2.192 for the humidity prediction. A discussion is presented in more details in section 3.2. For the other similar data mining techniques refer to [23].

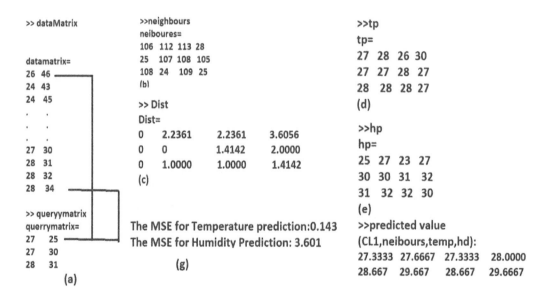

Figure 15. Overall layout of NN algorithm.

2.10. Clustering
In this research work, the datasets were divided into a number of clusters based on the type of analysis required. Regarding to the 'Clustering' method which is used here, figure 22 (which will be discussed later in section 3 in more details) shows an example of the procedure which is used to create the clusters for the month April. The clustering output forms a data matrix of size 90 X 3, which consists of the date temperature and humidity values for April for the years 2012, 2013, and 2014. The cluster formed is shown in figure 23. Twelve such clusters for each month from January to December are already created in the system based on the three years dataset. In the same way, 38 clusters for all months from January 2012 to February 2015 were created, and 6 clusters were already stored in the database for

temperature and humidity 2 for the years 2012, 2013, and 2014.

3. Evaluation of proposed SHM
3.1. Evaluation of real-time monitoring of temperature and humidity
The SHM-related parameters can be assessed based on the humidity and temperature values for the proposed monitoring system. As mentioned earlier in the introduction section, temperature and humidity can cause damage to the bridge structure including cracking caused by temperature gradient (itself caused by the different degrees of sunlight on the different parts of the bridge), corrosion caused by humidity and climatic factors (corrosive sea salts), and the corrosion and damage that have different origins but in which humidity and temperature act as the accelerating factors. In this section, the short-term measured data and graphs are presented for the proposed monitoring system

for two points. An example of the temperature values logged in the Excel files (TEMP1, TEMP2) and an example of humidity values logged in the Excel files (HUM1, HUM2) are shown in tables 1 and 2 , respectively.

Table 1. An example of temperature values logged in Excel files (TEMP1, TEMP2).

TEMP REFFRENCE SHT11	Temperature Celsius degree	TIME	DATE
27.7	29	5.19pm	04/14/2015
27.7	29	5.20pm	04/14/2015
27.5	29	5.21pm	04/14/2015
27.5	29	5.22pm	04/14/2015
27.5	29	5.23pm	04/14/2015
27.5	29	5.24pm	04/14/2015
27.5	29	5.25pm	04/14/2015

Table 2. An example of humidity values logged in Excel files (HUM1, HUM2).

HUM REFFRENCE SHT11	HUMIDITY RH%	TIME	DATE
35	38	5.18pm	04/14/2015
36	38	5.19pm	04/14/2015
36.3	37	5.20pm	04/14/2015
36.3	36	5.21pm	04/14/2015
36.3	39	5.22pm	04/14/2015
36.3	37	5.23pm	04/14/2015
36.3	38	5.24pm	04/14/2015

It is worthy to note that these two tables are just as examples for proving the accuracy and reliability of the proposed system results with respect to the reference data which is obtained from the sht11(digital sensor) reference input. Assessment of the temperature and humidity values and their comparison of with the critical threshold values at different points provide the possibility of detecting the present structural issues (or those that are going to happen). To assess the accuracy and reliability of the proposed system, it was deployed for 3361 minutes (approximately two and a half days) to store the temperature and humidity data, and then the results obtained were compared with those for the SHT 11 sensor, for which the digital temperature and humidity data was collected through a data acquisition card. Figure 16 shows the temperature data that was stored by wireless monitoring, and figure 17 shows the temperature data that was stored by the wired SHT11 sensor in the same period.

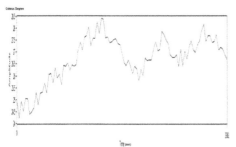

Figure 16. Temperature data stored by wireless sensor network monitoring system and LM35 analog sensor.

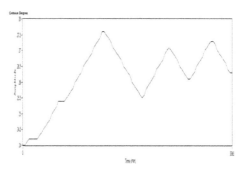

Figure 17. Temperature data stored by wired SHT11 digital sensor.

The humidity data logged by wireless sensor network monitoring system and HIH400 analog sensor is shown in figure 18 and the humidity data logged by the wired SHT11 digital sensor is shown in figure 19.

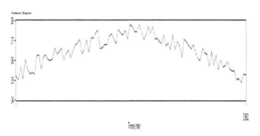

Figure 18. Humidity data logged by wireless sensor network monitoring system and HIH400 analog sensor.

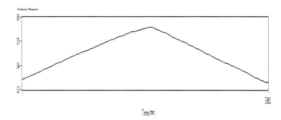

Figure 19. Humidity data logged by wired SHT11 digital sensor.

Relative error of proposed SHM system in the calculation of temperature and humidity is shown in figure 20.

According to the assessments and the results of similar studies, discussed in the introduction section, the thermal response of the bridge structure (measured by the proposed SHM system) can be used to assess and evaluate the health status and structural condition of the bridge and stresses, strains, and loads in the structure and the reaction of the structure to these elements. According to the studies mentioned in the the introduction section [19,20,21], the total longitudinal tensile strain (εT) at the height of (y) from under the arch of the bridge in one of its sections is:

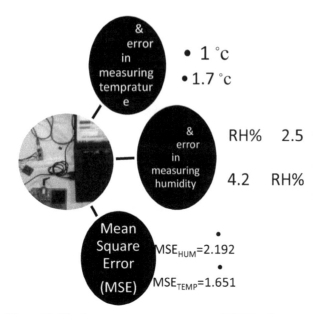

Figure 20. Maximum error, mean error, and MSE values for temperature and humidity parameters monitored by proposed system.

$$\varepsilon_T(Y) = \varepsilon_b - \psi_b y \tag{1}$$

where, ε_b is the total longitudinal tensile strain at the height of arch of the bridge; in other words, $\varepsilon_b = \varepsilon_T(0)$, and ψ_b is the amount of curvature in the section that we have chosen for calculation. The difference between ε_T and ε_f (thermal tensile strain) equals ε_m (mechanical strain), which means:

$$\varepsilon_m = \varepsilon_T - \varepsilon_f \tag{2}$$

In the end, the mechanical stress at point y that is shown by σ is equal to:

$$\sigma(y) = E\varepsilon_m = E(\varepsilon_T - \varepsilon_f) \tag{3}$$

where, E is the modulus of elasticity of the material (concrete in this case). On the other hand, according to the results of the model proposed and proved in [19,20,21], we have:

$$\sigma(y) = \beta E\varepsilon_m = \beta E(\varepsilon_b - \psi_b y - \varepsilon_f) \tag{4}$$

In the above equation, β is a dimensionless function of X. The β values are in the range between zero (full damage and total loss of EL) and one (without damage and one hundred percent intact). When the value for the β function is known, the thermal response of a damaged bridge can be estimated and calculated by equation (3). However, in this study, our aim was to determine β (refer to Figure 21 [20]). Determination of β through matching and assessing the predicted values [19,20,21] and the thermal response of the damaged bridge (obtained from the proposed monitoring system) will enable

us to identify and map the distribution and severity of the damages (fractures and wave-form cracks) in the bridge.

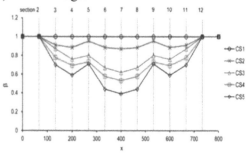

Figure 21. β function as an indicator of severity and location of damage in model structure [20].

The mentioned idea is the basis of the proposed method in order to detect the structural damages using the thermal response of the structures [19, 20, 21]. As it can be seen, the β function shows that the extent of damage to the wave-form fractures in the model bridge mentioned in [19, 20, 21] is proportional to the levels of damage of CS1, CS2, CS3, CS4, and CS5, which increase in that order. On the other hand, the structural thermal response and profile will be determined through the proposed WSN-based SHM system. More comprehensive information regarding the operations and calculations related to the preparation and use of the thermal response of the structure is available in [19,20]. Overall, the $\varepsilon_T, \varepsilon_f$ parameters in (3) will be determined by the thermal response monitored by the system, and then $\sigma(y)$ (mechanical stress) will be calculated at each y, and in the end, once all the parameters are determined, β will be obtained. For more details for the SHM system details and the procedure for the damage identification, refer to our previously published work [22].For other similar data mining techniques refer to [23].

3.2. Evaluation of prediction of temperature and humidity values based on data mining and fuzzy inference

A graphical user interface (GUI) was designed to facilitate the data entry and display the outputs for the application section that predicts the temperature and humidity to prevent the spread of the damage and to guarantee the predictive and proactive maintenance and repair.

This GUI was designed by the C# software, and about 700 lines of code were added to link the tags to the main program of the KNN algorithm. An overview of the designed GUI and description of different parts, GUI is presented in figure 22.

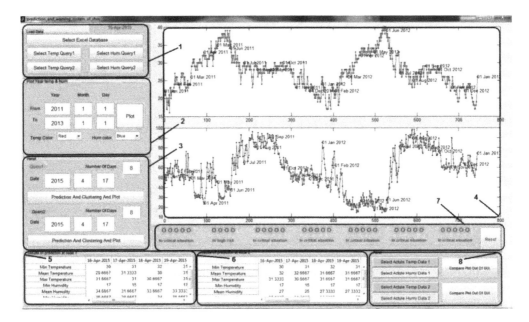

Figure 22. An overview of GUI for temperature and humidity prediction section.

Section 1: in this section, the files containing the database information and queries 1 and 2 each of which containing one file for temperature and one file for humidity (five Excel files in total) will be uploaded as input.

Section 2: this section provides the ability to display and select any date or range of data in the database (for the times when we want to take a closer look at the historical profile of the bridges and climatic conditions of its location in a specific period).

Section 3: this section provides the user to enter his/her desired date for prediction based on the data for the first or second node and also enables the user to choose the number of days after that date for prediction.

Section 4: this section displays the prediction charts and the historical profile for the user's desired time period.

Section 5: this section displays the average, maximum, and minimum values for humidity and temperature in node 1.

Section 6: this section displays the average, maximum, and minimum values for humidity and temperature in node 2.

Section 7: this section displays the alarm level and the possibility of resetting it.

Section 8: this section provides the possibility of making a visual comparison between the predicted values for temperature and humidity in nodes 1 and 2 and actual values measured by the proposed SHM systems.

It should be mentioned that this simulation system has the ability of issuing an alarm and warning the maintenance personnel of the bridge. The mechanism of this warning system includes

deriving 5 levels of alert (which will be thoroughly discussed in the upcoming sections) though conducting a fuzzy analysis on the humidity and temperature values and through a fuzzy instruction set and designing a fuzzy inference system (FIS). These alert levels will be displayed in GUI below the predicted values for temperature and humidity for each given day. In addition, the ability of resetting these levels for the next predictions is also embedded in GUI.

The specifications of the designed Mamdani FIS for the alarm system are as follows:

- **1-First input: temperature (refer to Figure 23)**
- **Three membership functions: low, medium, high**
- **Input range: between 0 and 50 degrees**

2- Second input: humidity (refer to Figure 24)
- **Three membership functions: low, medium, high**
- **Input range: between 0% to 100% (%RH)**

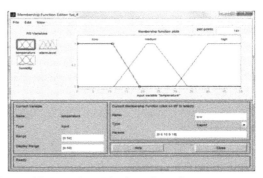

Figure 23. Membership functions for temperature (input) and its range.

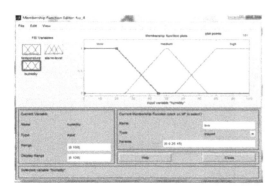

Figure 24. Membership functions for humidity (input) and its range.

3- Output: Alarm level (refer to Figure 25)

- **Five membership functions: one, two, three, four, five**
- **Output range: between 0 and 5**

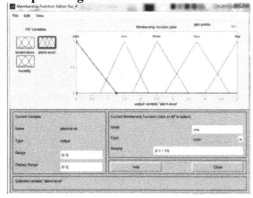

Figure 25. Membership functions for Alarm level (output) and its range

There are 9 rules for the above FIS system, as follow:

1. If (temperature is low) and (humidity is low), then (alarm-level is one)
2. If (temperature is low) and (humidity is medium), then (alarm-level is two)
3. If (temperature is low) and (humidity is high), then (alarm-level is four)
4. If (temperature is medium) and (humidity is low), then (alarm-level is one)
5. If (temperature is medium) and (humidity is medium), then (alarm-level is three)
6. If (temperature is medium) and (humidity is high), then (alarm-level is four)
7. If (temperature is high) and (humidity is low), then (alarm-level is two)
8. If (temperature is high) and (humidity is medium), then (alarm-level is four)
9. If (temperature is high) and (humidity is high), then (alarm-level is five)

The weighted average method is used for de-fuzzyfication. The details of the FIS performance in determining the alarm level are as figure 26.

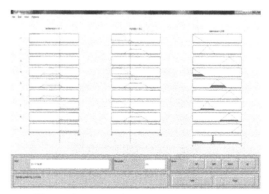

Figure 26. Rule-viewer of designed FIS.

In the end, representation of the above system as Surface will be like figure 27.

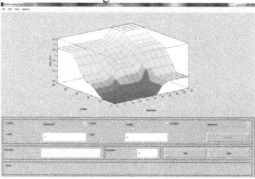

Figure 27. Surface view of FIS and summarization of effects of temperature and humidity (inputs) on alarm level (output).

The system with the above specifications determines an alarm level for the predicted values based on the details of the inputs and outputs and through using fuzzy inference techniques. They include:

1. *ideal*
2. *suspicious*
3. *at risky conditions*
4. *in high risk conditions*
5. *in critical situation*

With these alarms, the bridge maintenance personnel can perform the proactive maintenance operations with greater efficiency and before temperature and humidity values reach the critical conditions in order to prevent the growth and spread of the damage and to fix it with minimum cost when the damage is still in its initial stages. At the end of the third section of this article, we will mention some examples of the application of the above system in bridge maintenance. On the other hand, the possibility of comparing and validating the above predicted values with the actual data is provided in our SHM system. Figures 28 and 29 show the comparison of the predicted temperature and humidity values with the actual logged values in node 1 and node 2, respectively.

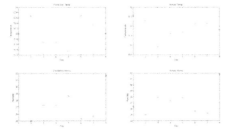

Figure 28. Comparison of predicted temperature and humidity values in node 1 with actual logged values.

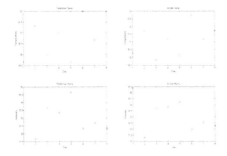

Figure 29. Comparison of predicted temperature and humidity values in node 2 with actual logged values.

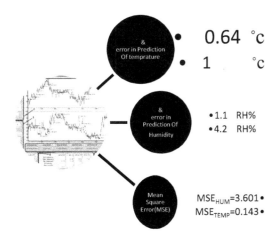

Figure 30. Maximum error, mean error, and MSE values for temperature and humidity predicted by proposed system.

The calculations showed that the mean squared error (MSE) of the prediction was about 0.143 for temperature and 3.601 for humidity. The results obtained are summarized in figure 30.

3.3. Examples of the application of proposed monitoring system

In this section, we present some examples of the applications of the multi-level alarm system discussed in the previous section. As mentioned

earlier, this system contains 5 levels of alarm for temperature, humidity, and displacement based on fuzzy definition of critical thresholds. (The exact details of the alarm levels were presented in the previous section).

- ALARM-LEVEL-2: removing garbage and debris from the road surface and drainage system in response to alarm level 2 regarding humidity of the nodes located on the surface and edge of drainage system (as an example, refer to Figure 31).

Figure 31. Removing garbage and debris from road surface and drainage system to address alarm [5].

- ALARM-LEVEL-3: Pressure washing the drainage system in response to level 3 regarding the increased humidity in the node located at the throat of drainage system, which indicate that it is clogged (as an example, refer to Figure 32).

Figure 32. Pressure washing the drainage system [5].

- ALARM-LEVEL-2: Filling the cracks in the initial stages of their formation in response to alarm level 2 regarding the temperature of the node located on the deck surface area (as an example, refer to Figure 33).

Figure 33. Filling cracks in initial stages of their formation [5].

4. Conclusion

In this study, a system with multiple functions was designed, implemented, and simulated for monitoring the structural health of a medium-sized assumed bridge (length of 50 m, height of 10 m, and with 6 piers) with the use of wireless sensor networks. The proposed SHM system monitors the temperature and humidity parameters in two points of the bridge deck.

To monitor the temperature and humidity, sensor nodes include two end nodes both of which have the LM35 sensor for temperature and HIH4000 sensor for humidity and a coordinator node in which the data is acquired, processed, and stored by the LABVIEW software. The mean errors in the calculation of temperature and humidity values were (1 degree) and (2.5 degrees), respectively; the maximum error in the calculation of temperature and humidity values were (1.7 degrees) and (4.2 degrees), respectively; the mean squared error in the calculation of temperature and humidity values were (1.651 degrees) and (2.192 degrees), respectively. The data for a wired SHT11 digital sensor was used as the reference and standard for measuring the errors.

In this study, the proposed SHM monitoring system was equipped with a novel method of using data mining techniques (KNN algorithm) on the temperature and humidity data for the past few years related to the location of the bridge to predict the temperature and humidity values in the nodes, and this ability has upgraded it from a simple monitoring system to a proactive system of maintenance. On the other hand, using a fuzzy inference system provided the possibly of issuing alerts and messages based on the fuzzy analysis on the predicted values for temperature and humidity to move toward the total productive maintenance (TPM) and proactive maintenance. The mean errors in the prediction of temperature and humidity values were (0.64 degree) and (1.1 degrees), respectively; the maximum error in the prediction of the temperature and humidity values were (1 degree) and (4.2 degrees), respectively; the mean squared error in the prediction of the temperature and humidity values were (0.143 degree) and (3.601 degrees), respectively. The data for the monitoring system was used as the reference and standard for measuring the errors of the prediction section of MATLAB program.

In the end, given the accuracy and reliability of the assessments, the analysis results, and the much lower costs of this system in terms of the initial equipment and maintenance (due to the simplicity of its structure), the proposed SHM system (which at this stage is still a combination of hardware and simulation) can be used for along-term and real-time monitoring of the medium-sized to the large-sized bridges.

5. Suggestions for future works

Measures that can be taken to improve this study are as follows:

- Providing all nodes with the ability of sensing all four parameters of temperature, humidity, displacement and stress-strain and integration of related programs and applications in the form of user friendly software for the bridge supervisor.
- Integration of proposed SHM systems with traffic control centers and smart energy networks.
- Equipping the proposed system with new ideas in the discussion of structural health monitoring, including the use of strain gauges, FBG, optic fibers, RFID.
- Designing the nodes with the ability of energy harvesting for this SHM system.
- Expanding the platform designed for this SHM for other structures and applications, especially for the structures, installations, and pipelines in oil and gas extraction and transportation industry and other related sectors.

References

[1] Sohraby, K., Minoli, D., & Znati, T. (2007). Wireless sensor networks: technology, protocols, and applications. New York, USA: John Wiley & Sons.

[2] Abdelzaher, T., Pereira, N., & Tovar, E. (2015). Wireless Sensor Networks: 12th European Conference, EWSN 2015. Porto, Portugal: Springer.

[3] Krishnamachari, B., Murphy, A. L., & Trigoni, N. (2014).Wireless Sensor Networks: 11th European Conference, EWSN 2014. Oxford, UK: Springer.

[4] Picco, G. P., & Heinzelman, W. (2012). Wireless Sensor Networks: 9th European Conference, EWSN 2012. Trento, Italy: Springer.

[5] Younis, M., Senturk, I. F., Akkaya, K., Lee, S., & Senel, F. (2014). Topology management techniques for tolerating node failures in wireless sensor networks: A survey. Computer Networks, vol. 58, no. 3, pp. 254-283.

[6] Ammari, H. M. (2013). The Art of Wireless Sensor Networks: Volume 2: Advanced Topics and Applications. Berlin, Heidelberg. New York: Springer-Verlag.

[7] Nadeem, A., Hussain, M. A., Owais, O., Salam, A., Iqbal, S., & Ahsan, K. (2015). Application specific study, analysis and classification of body area wireless

sensor network applications. Computer Networks, vol. 55, no. 2, pp248-258.

[8] Hammoudeh, M., & Newman, R. (2015). Adaptive routing in wireless sensor networks: QoS optimisation for enhanced application performance. Information Fusion, vol. 22, no. 3, pp. 3-15.

[9] Moyo, P., Brownjohn, J., Suresh, R., & Tjin, S. (2005). Development of fiber Bragg grating sensors for monitoring civil infrastructure. Engineering structures, vol. 27, no. 12, pp. 1828-1834.

[10] Trifunac, M., & Ebrahimian, M. (2014). Detection thresholds in structural health monitoring. Soil Dynamics and Earthquake Engineering, vol. 66, no. 2, pp. 319-338.

[11] Mokhtar, M., Owens, K., Kwasny, J., Taylor, S., Basheer, P., Cleland, D., Bai, Y., Sonebi, M., Davis, G., & Gupta, A.(2012).Fiber-optic strain sensor system with temperature compensation for arch bridge condition monitoring. Sensors Journal, IEEE, vol. 12, no. 5, pp. 1470-1476.

[12] Ko, J., & Ni, Y. (2005).Technology developments in structural health monitoring of large-scale bridges. Engineering structures, vol. 27, no.12, pp. 1715-1725.

[13] Sani, S. S. (2016).Overcome to Some Technical Limitations and Challenges in Structural Health Monitoring of Concrete Structures Using Wireless Sensor Networks. Journal of Active & Passive Electronic Devices, vol. 11, no. 1, pp-58-68.

[14] Farrar, C. R., & Doebling, S. W. (1999). Structural health monitoring at los alamos national laboratory. IEE Colloquium on Condition Monitoring, Machinery, External Structures and Health (Ref. No. 1999/034), Berlin, Germany, 1999.

[15] Sani, S. S., Nejad, M. B., & Arabi, M. K. (2016). Using a phase difference detection technique for monitoring the structural health of bridge piers. Structural Control and Health Monitoring, vol. 23, pp. 857-875.

[16] Sani, S. S., Nejad, M. B., & Arabi, M. K. (2014). Remote Detection of Earthquake Induced Damage on Bridge Piers Using WSN Based on Dual Receiver and Phase Difference Measurement Technique. Journal of Seismology and Earthquake Engineering, vol. 16, pp. 281-288.

[17] Rodrigues, C., Félix, C., Lage, A., & Figueiras, J. (2010). Development of a long-term monitoring system based on FBG sensors applied to concrete bridges. Engineering Structures, vol. 32, no. 8, pp. 1993-2002.

[18] Li, H.-N., Li, D.-S., and Song, G.-B. (2004). Recent applications of fiber optic sensors to health monitoring in civil engineering. Engineering structures, vol. 26, no. 11, pp. 1647-1657.

[19] Kulprapha, N., & Warnitchai, P. (2012). Structural health monitoring of continuous prestressed concrete bridges using ambient thermal responses. Engineering Structures, vol. 40, pp. 20-38.

[20] Priestley, M., & Buckle, I. (1979). Ambient thermal response of concrete bridges. Engineering Structures, vol. 41, pp. 40-58.

[21] Barroca, N., Borges, L. M., Velez, F. J., Monteiro, F., Górski, M., & Castro-Gomes, J. (2013). Wireless sensor networks for temperature and humidity monitoring within concrete structures. Construction and Building Materials, vol. 40, pp. 1156-1166.

[22] Rad, H. N., Sani, S. S., & Rad, M. N. (2015). A new inexpensive system for SHM of bridge decks using wireless sensor networks based on measurements of temperature and humidity. 2nd International Conference on Knowledge-Based Engineering and Innovation (KBEI), Tehran, Iran, 2015.

[23] Ghaffari, H., & Nobahary, S. (2015). FDMG: Fault detection method by using genetic algorithm in clustered wireless sensor networks. Journal of AI and Data Mining, vol. 3, pp. 47-57.

12

Introducing an algorithm for use to hide sensitive association rules through perturb technique

M. Sakenian Dehkordi[*] and M. Naderi Dehkordi

Department of Computer Engineering, Najafabad Branch, Islamic Azad University, Najafabad, Isfahan, Iran.

Corresponding author: sakenian91@gmail.com (M. Sakenian).

Abstract
Due to the rapid growth of the data mining technology, obtaining private data on users through this technology has become easier. Association rules mining is one of the data mining techniques that is used to extract useful patterns in the form of association rules. One of the main problems with the application of this technique to databases is the disclosure of sensitive data, and thus endangering the security and privacy of the owners of the data. Hiding the association rules is one of the methods available to preserve privacy, and it is a main subject in the field of data mining and database security, for which several algorithms with different approaches have been presented so far. An algorithm for use to hide sensitive association rules with a heuristic approach is presented in this article, where the perturb technique based on reducing confidence or support rules is applied with an attempt to remove the considered item from a transaction with the highest weight by allocating weight to the items and transactions. The efficiency of this technique is measured by means of the failure criteria of hiding, the number of lost rules and ghost rules, and the execution time. The results obtained from this work are assessed and compared with the two known FHSAR and RRLR algorithms, which are based on the two real databases dense and sparse. The results obtained indicated that the number of lost rules in all the experiments performed decreased by 47% in comparison with the RRLR algorithm, and decreased by 23% in comparison with the FHSAR algorithm. Moreover, the other undesirable side effects in the proposed algorithm in the worst case were equal to those for the basic algorithms.

Keywords: *Data Mining, Association Rule Hiding, Privacy Preserving Data Mining.*

1. Introduction
Due to competitions in the political, military, economic, and scientific fields, and the importance of access to information in a short period of time without human intervention, the science of data analysis or data mining has defined some techniques to analyze data with the objective of finding patterns in them [1,2].

Extracting association rules is one of the main aspects of data mining that deals with discovering the correlation among the items and finding a set of frequent items from big data resources [3,4]. However, the data obtained may include sensitive personal/business information whose publishing and sharing can endanger the security and privacy of the owner of the information. For example, although sharing information about diseases is useful but releasing personal information about patients is not. Another example relates to the customers' purchasing behavior. Studying the customers' purchasing behavior can be very important and profitable for manufacturers but there exist some sensitive data that should be protected against jobbers [5]. To protect data security and to prevent the discovery of private data, the concept of privacy preserving data mining has been presented. The objective of this concept is to examine the side effects of the data mining process, which leads to protect the personal and organizational privacy. There exist many different approaches in the algorithm form. After data mining and hidden private knowledge, only insensitive data is identified in these algorithms [6].

In this paper, the new HSARWI algorithm is presented to hide the set of sensitive association rules, and to reduce the undesirable side effects.

After implementation, this algorithm will be compared with the two algorithms FHSAR [7] and RRLR [8] based on the two real databases dense and sparse.

In this paper, after studying some existing algorithms, the HSARWI algorithm will be introduced. Finally, the conclusions and suggestions for future studies will be presented.

2. Literature review

Attallah et al. [9,10] were the first to present an experimental algorithm for hiding the sensitive association rules in 1999.

In 2001, Dasseni et al. [11] introduced three algorithms for hiding the sensitive association rules. These rules should not have anything in common, and their performance in the field of controlling lost rules and ghost rules is not sufficient.

Saygin et al. [12] were the first who, in 2001, presented the use of unknown values instead of changing zero to one and vice versa in hiding the sensitive association rules. The objective of applying the unknown values was to protect the users from learning wrong rules.

Oliveira et al. [13] were the first who, in 2002, presented some manners for hiding the sensitive rules simultaneously.

Oliveira et al. [14] introduced an algorithm named SWA in 2003 with no respect to the database size and the number of sensitive rules that should be hidden. In SWA, the database is scanned only once. This algorithm is not based on memory, and so it can be applied to big databases.

Verykios et al. [15] introduced five algorithms in 2004, which reduced the support of item sets, while producing sensitive rules as long as its support was less than the minimum support threshold. The main drawback of these algorithms is that the rules should not overlap one another.

In 2007, Wang et al. [16] suggested two algorithms, where if the items are proposed, then the sensitive association rules are hidden automatically. The drawback of these two algorithms is that the sanitized database is different with respect to the order of removing the rules.

In 2007, Wang et al. [17] introduced two algorithms for hiding the predictive sensitive association rules, i.e. the rules that have sensitive items in their antecedent. Both algorithms hide these rules automatically. There is no need for data mining and manual selection of sensitive rules before the hiding process.

In 2007, Verykios et al. [18] suggested two algorithms based on weight allocation to the transactions.

By allocating weight to the transactions, the WSDA algorithm seeks to select useful transactions to remove item by considering a safety margin (SF). It hides the rules with a reduced confidence of rules less than MCT + SF.

The BBA algorithm applies the blocking technique for hiding. It also considers SF.

In 2008, Weng et al. [7] presented the FHSAR algorithm for hiding sensitive rules. This algorithm scans the database once, and consequently, reduces the execution time. This algorithm is a week selecting victim item.

In 2009, Dehkordi et al. [19] suggested a new method for maintaining privacy of the data mining association rules based on genetic algorithm, where there are no lost and ghost rules.

In 2010, Modi et al. [20] introduced an algorithm named DSRRC, which seeks to hide rules with minimum changes in the database through clustering rules based on the common item at the consequence of the rules as much as possible in a simultaneous manner. The drawback of this rule is that it only hides those rules that have one item on their right side.

In 2012, Shah et al. [8] presented two algorithms for correcting the DSRRC algorithm. The ADSRRC algorithm was presented for overcoming the restriction of multiple ordering, and the RRLR algorithm was introduced for overcoming the restriction of being a single item at the consequence of the sensitive rules.

Jain et al. [21] and Gulwani et al. [22] implemented hiding the rules as a group by applying the concept of representative rules [23] since the support of sensitive items does not change towards the original database.

In 2013, Domadiya et al. [24] proposed the MDSRRC algorithm for overcoming the DSRRC algorithm restriction. This algorithm can hide the rules that have multiple items in both their antecedent and consequent.

3. Problem definition

Association rules determine the correlations of different items in a set of input data, where these rules are selected according to the support and confidence criteria [5].

If $I = \{i_1, i_2, \ldots, i_m\}$ is a set of items, and $D = \{t_1, t_2, \ldots, t_n\}$ is a set of transactions or a database, every transaction includes a subset of I, and $t_i \subseteq I$. The common framework of the association rules is $X \rightarrow Y$, where $X \subset I$, $Y \subset I$, $X \cap Y = \Phi$, X is the left hand side named antecedent, and Y is the right hand side consequent of rule [25].

To calculate the support of rule X→Y and confidence, (1) and (2) are used, respectively [26].

$$\text{Support}(X \rightarrow Y) = (|X \cup Y|)/(|D|) \qquad (1)$$
$$\text{Confidence}(X \rightarrow Y) = (|X \cup Y|)/(|X|) \qquad (2)$$

where, $|X|$ is the number of occurrences of the item set of X in the set of transactions D, and $|D|$ is the number of transactions in D.

Association rule mining algorithms scan the database of transactions, and calculate the support and confidence of the candidate rules in order to determine whether they are significant or not. A rule is significant if its support and confidence are higher than the user specified criteria (MST and MCT), and to justify this, conditions (3) and (4) should be met at the same time [27].

$$\text{Support}(X \rightarrow Y) \geq \text{MST} \qquad (3)$$
$$\text{Confidence}(X \rightarrow Y) \geq \text{MCT} \qquad (4)$$

The sensitive association rule X→Y is hidden, whenever one of the following two conditions, (5) or (6), is met [27].

$$\text{Support}(X \rightarrow Y) < \text{MST} \qquad (5)$$
$$\text{Confidence}(X \rightarrow Y) < \text{MCT} \qquad (6)$$

Among the extracted association rules (ARs) from the original database (D), some of them are introduced as the sensitive rules from the database owner (SAR), SAR⊆AR.

The objective of the privacy preserving association rules mining algorithms is that in addition to having the basic database, MCT and MST and the set of sensitive rules or set of frequent sensitive patterns should make some changes in D. The changes prevent the extraction of sensitive rules or frequent patterns from the sanitized database (D'). The following side effects should be minimized in this process [5]:

- Execution time
- Number of hiding failure
- Number of lost rules
- Number of ghost rules

4. Proposed algorithm

The function of this algorithm is to hide the sensitive association rules through the heuristic approach, based on distorting values. The victim item and victim transaction are determined through this newly-introduced method, while it seeks to reduce the amount of support or confidence by removing the victim item. After removing any victim item, some rules whose amount of support or confidence are below the determined threshold values are added to the set of the hidden sensitive association rules.

Input: Original Database (D), SAR, MST, MCT. Output: Sanitized Database (D'). While it goes through the association rule mining once more, the unfavorable side effects become minimized. The notations applied in this study are presented in table 1.

4.1. Calculating transaction and item weight

To calculate the transaction weight, the presented concepts are adopted as follow [7]:

$$R_{ik} = \{j \mid sar_j \subseteq t_i \text{ and } k \in t_i\} \qquad (7)$$
$$MIC_i = \max(|R_{ik}|) \qquad (8)$$
$$WT_i = MIC_i/2^{(|t_i|-1)} \qquad (9)$$

where k is an item in t_i, and R_{ik} contains the number of sensitive association rules from SAR that is completely supported by transaction t_i. Full support means that transaction t_i should include at least all the available items in the antecedent and consequent of the sensitive association rules.

For each one of the available items in transaction t_i, the A and B sets are obtained through (10) and (11). The weight of each one of the items is calculated through (12).

$$A_{ik} = \{j \mid sar_j \subseteq t_i \text{ and } k \in RHS_j\} \qquad (10)$$
$$B_{ik} = \{j \mid sar_j \subseteq t_i \text{ and } k \in LHS_j\} \qquad (11)$$
$$WI_{ik} = |R_{ik}| + |A_{ik}| - |B_{ik}| \qquad (12)$$

Table 1. Notations and definitions.

Notation	Definition
t_i	Transaction i of database
$|S|$	Number of members of set S
AR	Association rules extracted from D
AR'	Association rules extracted from D'
SAR	Set of sensitive association rules, SAR = {sar_1, sar_2, ..., sar_m}
SAR'	Set of sensitive association rules has been hidden
Supp(sar_j)	Support(sar_j)
Conf(sar_j)	Confidence(sar_j)
WT_i	Weight of t_i
WI_{ik}	Weight of item k for transaction i
VT	Victim transaction
VI	Victim item
LHS_j	An item set on the left hand side of a rule (antecedent)
RHS_j	An item set on the right hand side of a rule (consequent)
k	Determines an item in t_i

4.2. CalculateTransactionWeight(t_i) function

This function receives the number of transactions as an input parameter, and obtains the number of association rules that are completely supported by it. It obtains MIC and calculates the weight of each transaction. Its pseudo-code is shown in figure 1.

4.3. CalculateVictimItem(t_i) function

This function receives the number of victim transactions as an input parameter, and the weight of each one of the items that are repeated at least in a sensitive rule and are supported by this transaction are calculated. This is followed by the selection of an item with the highest weight as the victim item for removal from the victim transaction. The pseudo-code for this function is shown in figure 1.

4.4. CheckingNotFailure(VT, VI) Function
This function receives the victim transaction and the victim item as the input parameters, and studies whether removing this item can lead to the violation of the previous hidings, and the True or False result is returned to the main program. If only the output of this function is true, the victim item will be removed from the victim transaction, otherwise, another item will be considered for removal. The pseudo-code for this function is demonstrated in figure 1.

HSARWI Algorithm Input: D, SAR, MST, MCT Output: D'		Functions
1.	For each $t_i \in D$	**CalculateTransactionWeight(t_i)**
2.	{	{
3.	For each $sar_j \in SAR$	For each $sar_j \in SAR$
4.	{	If t_i fully support sar_j
5.	Calculate supp(sar_j);	For each item $k \in sar_j$
6.	Calculate conf(sar_j);	$\|R_{ik}\|++$;
7.	}	$WT_i = max(\|R_{ik}\|)/2^{\wedge}(\|t_i\|-1)$;
8.	**CalculateTransactionWeight(t_i);**	}
9.	}	
10.	while(SAR $\neq \Phi$)	**CalculateVictimItem(ti)**
11.	{	{
12.	VT = Transaction with maximal weight;	For each $sar_j \in SAR$
13.	VI = **CalculateVictimItem(VT);**	{
14.	If (**CheckingNotFailure(VT,VI) = True**)	If t_i fully support sar_j
15.	{	For each item $k \in sar_j$
16.	Remove VI from VT;	{
17.	For each $sar_j \in SAR$	$\|R_{ik}\|++$;
18.	{	If ($k \in RHS_j$)
19.	Update supp(sar_j);	$\|A_{ik}\|++$;
20.	Update conf(sar_j);	If ($k \in RHS_j$)
21.	}	$\|B_{ik}\|++$;
22.	If (Supp(sar_j) < MST || Conf(sar_j) < MCT)	}
23.	{	$WI_{ik} = \|R_{ik}\| + \|A_{ik}\| - \|B_{ik}\|$;
24.	Remove sar_j from SAR;	}//end of for
25.	Add sar_j To SAR';	Return Item with maximal
26.	}	WI_{ik}
27.	CalculateTransactionWeight(t_i); //*Update Weight*	}
28.	} // If (**CheckingNotFailure(VT,VI) = True**)	**CheckingNotFailure(VT,VI)**
29.	Else	{
30.	{	For each $sar'_j \in SAR'$
31.	CalculateVictimItem(VT); // *Select another Item*	If (Supp(sar'_j) $\geq$ MST
32.	Go to 14;	&& VI $\in$ LHS$_j$ &&
33.	}	sar'_j don't Support with t_i)
34.	} //*end of while*	Return false;
		Else
		Return True;
		}

Figure 1. pseudo-code of this HSARWI algorithm.

4.5. Different levels of algorithm
In figure 1, lines 1-9 do the scanning database once, and the following cases are calculated:
- Support of each $sar_j \in SAR$
- Confidence of each $sar_j \in SAR$
- Weight of each transaction

The hiding operation begins from line 10, and a transaction with the highest weight will be selected as the victim transaction in line 12. The weight of items is calculated by calling the CalculateVictimItem(t_i) function, and an item with the highest weight, as the victim item, will be returned to the main program in line 13.
The CheckingNotFailure(VT, VI) function is called in line 14. If the value of this function is true, the victim item will be removed from the victim transaction, and in lines 17-26, the amounts of the support and confidence of all the sensitive association rules are updated, and if at least one of the amounts of the support or confidence of the rule is less than MST or MCT, the rule is hidden, removed from the set of sensitive association rules, and added to the set of hidden association rules. In line 27, the weight of transaction will be updated by calling CalculateTransactionWeight (ti).

If the CheckingNotFailure(VT, VI) function returns False, in line 31, with calling CalculateVictimItem(t_i) again, another item will be selected for removal from the transaction.

The above processes are continued until hiding all the sensitive association rules.

4.5. Example

To express the HSARWI algorithm well, an example is presented in this section with the database tabulated in table 2.

The sensitive association rules, minimum support threshold, and minimum confidence threshold are determined by the owner of the database as follow:

SAR = {(1→3),(1,3→4)}
MST = 40%, MCT = 75%

Scanning the existing transactions in the database begins from 1 in table 2.

Table 2. Sample database.

Transaction ID	Items	Transaction ID	Items
1	1,3,4	9	2,3,5,6,7
2	1,3,4,8	10	1,3,4,7
3	1,2,3,4,5,6,8	11	2,6,7
4	1,2,4,6,7	12	1,2,3,4,5
5	2,3,4,5	13	1,3,4,5,6,8
6	1,2,3	14	2,7
7	3,4,5,6,8	15	1,2,3,4,8
8	1,2,3,7		

First transaction (t_1) completely supports the first sensitive rule (1→3); therefore, Count (1→3) and Count (1) increase one. Next, the second sensitive association rule is studied; this rule is completely supported by t_1, Count (1, 3→4), and Count (1, 3) increase one. By calling the CalculateTransactionWeight (1) function, weight of t_1 is calculated. Lines 1-9 in figure 1 run to calculate the weight of all transactions. Table 3 includes the obtained data on the support and confidence of the sensitive association rules.

Table 3. Support and confidence of sensitive rules.

sar_j	Count(sar_j)	Count(LHS_j)	supp(sar_j)	conf(sar_j)
1→3	9	10	0.6	0.9
1,3→4	7	9	0.47	0.78

Table 4 shows the calculated weight for each one of the transactions in table 2.

Table 4. Calculated weights for transactions.

Transaction ID	WT(ti)	Transaction ID	WT(ti)
1	50	9	0
2	25	10	25
3	3.125	11	0
4	0	12	12.25
5	0	13	6.25
6	25	14	0
7	0	15	12.5
8	12.5		

According to table 4, t_1 has the highest weight, and it is selected as the victim transaction (VT = 1). By calling the CalculateVictimItem (1) function in line 13 of figure 1, the weight of each

one of the items in t_1 is calculated according to table 5.

Table 5. Weight of each item in t_1.

Item	$|R_{1k}|$	$|A_{1k}|$	$|B_{1k}|$	WI_k
1	2	0	2	0
3	2	1	1	2
4	1	1	0	2

Item number 3 has the highest weight, and is selected as the victim item (VI = 3). As the set of hidden sensitive association rules has no member, the CheckingNotFailure(1, 3) function returns True to the main program, lines 15-21 in figure 1 are executed, and the new support and confidence of the sensitive association rules are calculated according to table 6. None of the sensitive association rules are hidden in lines 22-26. The new weight for t_1 is calculated in line 27 of figure 1.

Table 6. Modified support and confidence after removing item 3 from t_1.

sar_j	Count(sar_j)	Count(LHS_j)	supp(sar_j)	conf(sar_j)
1→3	8	10	0.54	0.8
1,3→4	6	8	0.4	0.75

The algorithm steps are repeated, transaction 2 with the highest weight is selected as the victim transaction (VT = t_2) according to table 4, and the calculated weight for each one of its items is shown in table 7. Item 3 has the highest weight, and so it is selected for removal. The CheckingNotFailure(2,3) function returns True, so item 3 is removed from t_2. Table 8 represents the updated support and confidence of all the sensitive rules. By reducing the confidence of the sensitive rule 1→3 with less than MCT and reducing the support of the sensitive rule 1,3→4 with less than MST, both rules are hidden.

Table 7. Weight of each item in t_2.

Item	$|R_{1k}|$	$|A_{1k}|$	$|B_{1k}|$	WI_k
1	2	0	2	0
3	2	1	1	2
4	1	1	0	2
8	None of the sensitive association rules is repeated, so no weight is calculated for it.			

Table 8. Modified support and confidence after removing item 3 from t_2.

sar_j	Count(sar_j)	Count(LHS_j)	supp(sar_j)	conf(sar_j)
1→3	7	10	0.46	0.7
1,3→4	5	7	0.33	0.71

6. Comparison and evaluation

To evaluate the performance and efficiency of the HSARWI algorithm, the two well-known FHSAR and RRLR algorithms are implemented on a system including Windows 8 operating system, Intel Core i7 processor, and 8 GB of main memory in visual studio environment 2012 with coding language C#.

The two real databases Mushroom and Chess are applied for the experiments; their detailed characteristics and the amounts of MST and MCT are shown in tables 9 and 10, respectively.

Table 9. Characteristics of databases.

Database Name	Number of Transactions	Number of Items	Transaction Length	Density
Mushroom	8124	119	23	19%
Chess	3194	75	37	49%

The number of sensitive association rules of both databases is considered as 2, 4, 6, and 8. Then the evaluating criteria are studied.

Table 10. Amount of applied MCT and MST.

Database Name	MST	MCT	Number of AR
Chess	0.95	0.98	303
Chess	0.88	0.92	22085
Mushroom	0.5	0.75	664
mushroom	0.4	0.6	4570

Failure: This refers to the number of sensitive rules extracted from the sanitized database with data mining after the hiding operation [28].

Due to the existence of a function to evaluate and predict failure, the HSARWI and FHSAR algorithms have no failure in any experiment. The RRLR algorithm has a failure rate of 8% in all the experiments since it makes the hiding process with inserting and removing the items. Item insertion may cause an increase in the amount of confidence, leading to a failure in hiding the rules, whose support is higher than MST.

Lost rules: This refers to the number of insensitive association rules that are extracted from the original database but are not extracted from the sanitized database after the hiding process [28]. In the HSARWI algorithm, the victim item selection manner is effective in reducing the number of lost rules. An item is selected for removal that is repeated in the sensitive rules more than the other items with respect to repetition at the consequent of the sensitive rules, and therefore, this item has the highest effect on reducing the amount of support and confidence of rules. Due to the above-mentioned reasons, the HSARWI algorithm reduces the number of removed items from the database more, in comparison with the FHSAR and RRLR algorithms, and makes the sanitized database similar to the original database. Therefore, the number of lost rules is reduced with the HSARWI algorithm. In the RRLR algorithm, due to the selection of a transaction with more sensitivity and length, more insensitive rules are being missed. Diagrams related to figures 2, 3, 4, and 5 show that the HSARWI

algorithm has been more successful than the basic algorithms in reducing the number of lost rules.

Ghost rules: This refers to the number of insensitive association rules that are not extracted from the original database but are extracted from the sanitized database after the hiding process [28]. In the experiments conducted on the Chess database, no ghost rules were generated because the higher the database density, the less the generated ghost rules are, and since such databases generate many association rules, their removed element usually has a less effect on the generating ghost rules. The inserting and removing items generate the ghost rules, whose amounts of support and confidence are close to those for MST and MCT. The removing item does not always lead to the generation of ghost rules, while the inserting item is more effective in generating the ghost rules. Since the removing item always causes a decrement in the amount of support of the rules, and sometimes may cause an increment in the amount of confidence of rules, the inserting item may cause an increment in both the amounts of the support and confidence of rules. Since the hiding process is run through removing and inserting items in the RRLR algorithm, the number of ghost rules generated by this algorithm is more than those generated by the HSARWI and FHSAR algorithms. The diagrams shown in figures 6 and 7 show the number of ghost rules generated on the Mushroom database.

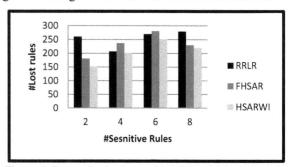

Figure 1. Lost rules in chess with MST = 0.95 and MCT = 0.98.

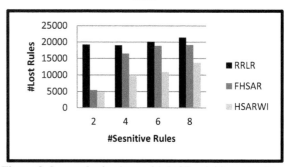

Figure 2. Lost rules in chess with MST = 0.88 and MCT = 0.92.

Execution time: This refers to the duration of executing algorithm to hide all the sensitive association rules [28]. In the FHSAR and HSARWI algorithms, scanning the database is run only once, so these two algorithms consume less time. As it is evident in figures 8, 9, 10, and 11, the execution time in HSARWI is equal to or less than the FHSAR and RRLR algorithms. Reduction in the execution time in HSARWI is directly related to the reduction in number of items removed from the database since after removal of every item, the amount of support and confidence of the rules are updated. Therefore, there is a direct relation between reduction in the number of removed items and reduction in the updating process time, and hence, a saving in time. To hide every one of the sensitive rules, the RRLR algorithm firstly removes the left hand side item and then inserts it, i.e. scanning twice for each removal and insertion. Therefore, the more the sensitive rules, the more the execution time is in the RRLR algorithm

7. Conclusion and future studies

By allocating weight to the transactions and items, the proposed algorithm has a more effective item in hiding the sensitive association rules, and removes it from a transaction with the highest weight that causes to reduce the number of removed items, the number of lost rules, and the number of ghost rules in the HSARWI algorithm. By reducing the number of removed items, the number of updates in calculating the support and confidence of rules are reduced, and this leads to a reduction in the execution time. Since the HSARWI and FHSAR algorithms have a function to predict failure, hiding failure is equal to 0 for them but the RRLR algorithm may undergo failure due to inserting item. It is possible to prevent the frequent calculation of support and confidence of rules after changing each transaction through adding the ability of calculating the number of required changes to hide the rule at the beginning of the implementation operation.

Figure 3. Lost rules in Mushroom with MST = 0.5 and MCT = 0.75.

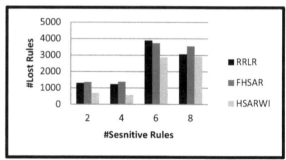

Figure 4. Lost rules in Mushroom with MST = 0.4 and MCT = 0.6.

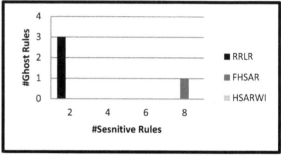

Figure 5. Ghost rules in Mushroom with MST = 0.5 and MCT = 0.75.

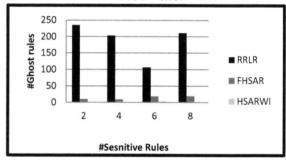

Figure 6. Ghost rule in Mushroom with MST = 0.4 and MCT = 0.6.

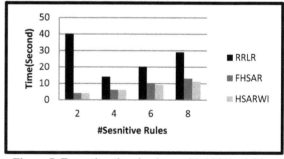

Figure 7. Execution time in chess with MST = 0.95 and MCT = 0.98.

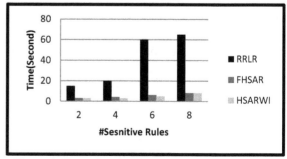

Figure 8. Execution time in chess with MST = 0.88 and MCT = 0.92.

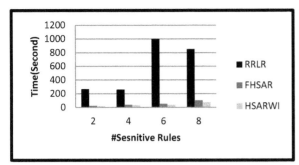

Figure 9. Execution time in Mushroom with MST = 0.5 and MCT = 0.75

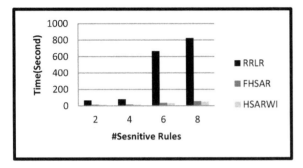

Figure 10. Execution time in Mushroom with MST = 0.4 and MCT = 0.6.

References

[1] Sathiyapriya, K. & Sadasivam, G. S. (2013). A survey on privacy preserving association rule mining. International Journal of Data Mining & Knowledge Management Process, vol. 3, no. 2, pp. 119-131.

[2] Han, J., Kamber, M. & Pei, J. (2011). Data mining: concepts and techniques: concepts and techniques. Elsevier.

[3] Gkoulalas-Divanis, A. & Verykios, V. S. (2010). Association rule hiding for data mining. Springer Science & Business Media.

[4] Gkoulalas-Divanis, A., Haritsa, J., & Kantarcioglu, M. (2014). Privacy issues in association rule mining. In Frequent Pattern Mining. Springer International Publishing.

[5] Lee, G. & Chen, Y. C. (2012). Protecting sensitive knowledge in association patterns mining. Wiley Interdisciplinary Reviews: Data Mining and Knowledge Discovery, vol. 2, no. 1, pp. 60-68.

[6] Shah, K., Thakkar, A. & Ganatra, A. (2012). A study on association rule hiding approaches. IJEAT International Journal of Engineering and Advanced Technology, vol. 1, no. 3, pp. 72-76.

[7] Weng, C. C., Chen, S. T. & Lo, H. C. (2008). A novel algorithm for completely hiding sensitive association rules. In Intelligent Systems Design and Applications, ISDA'08. Eighth International Conference. IEEE, 2008.

[8] Shah, K., Thakkar, A. & Ganatra, A. (2012). Association Rule Hiding by Heuristic Approach to Reduce Side Effects and Hide Multiple R. H. S. Items.

International Journal of Computer Applications, vol. 45, no. 1.

[9] Atallah, M., Bertino, E., Elmagarmid, A., Ibrahim, M. & Verykios, V. (1999). Disclosure limitation of sensitive rules. In Knowledge and Data Engineering Exchange, (KDEX'99) Proceedings. Workshop on. IEEE, pp. 45-52.

[10] Verykios, V. S. (2013). Association rule hiding methods. Wiley Interdisciplinary Reviews: Data Mining and Knowledge Discovery, vol. 3, no. 1, pp. 28-36.

[11] Dasseni, E., Verykios, V. S., Elmagarmid, A. K. & Bertino, E. (2001). Hiding association rules by using confidence and support. In Information Hiding. Springer Berlin Heidelberg. pp. 369-383.

[12] Saygin, Y., Verykios, V. S. & Clifton, C. (2001). Using unknowns to prevent discovery of association rules. ACM SIGMOD Record, vol. 30, no. 4, pp. 45-54.

[13] Oliveira, S. R. & Zaiane, O. R. (2002). Privacy preserving frequent itemset mining. In Proceedings of the IEEE international conference on Privacy, security and data mining. Australian Computer Society, 2002.

[14] Oliveira, S. R. & Zaiane, O. R. (2003). Protecting sensitive knowledge by data sanitization. IEEE 13th International Conference on Data Mining, 2003.

[15] Verykios, V. S., Elmagarmid, A. K., Bertino, E., Saygin, Y. & Dasseni, E. (2004). Association rule hiding. Knowledge and Data Engineering, IEEE Transactions on, vol. 16, no. 4, pp. 434-447.

[16] Wang, S. L., Patel, D., Jafari, A. & Hong, T. P. (2007). Hiding collaborative recommendation association rules. Applied Intelligence, vol. 27, no. 1, pp. 67-77.

[17] Wang, S. L., Parikh, B. & Jafari, A. (2007). Hiding informative association rule sets. Elsevier Expert Systems with Applications, vol. 33, no. 2, pp. 316-323.

[18] Verykios, V. S., Pontikakis, E. D., Theodoridis, Y. & Chang, L. (2007). Efficient algorithms for distortion and blocking techniques in association rule hiding. Springer Distributed and Parallel Databases, vol. 22, no. 1, pp. 85-104.

[19] Dehkordi, M. N., Badie, K. & Zadeh, A. K. (2009). A novel method for privacy preserving in association rule mining based on genetic algorithms. Journal of software, vol. 4, no. 6, pp. 555-562.

[20] Modi, C. N., Rao, U. P. & Patel, D. R. (2010). Maintaining privacy and data quality in privacy preserving association rule mining. In Computing Communication and Networking Technologies (ICCCNT), International Conference. IEEE, 2010.

[21] Jain, D., Khatri, P., Soni, R. & Chaurasia, B. K. (2012). Hiding sensitive association rules without altering the support of sensitive item (s). In Advances

in Computer Science and Information Technology. Networks and Communications. Springer Berlin Heidelberg, vol. 84, pp. 500-509.

[22] Gulwani, P. & Aloney, M. R. (2013). Securing Sensitive Rule by Changing the SC Values. Journal of Engineering, Computers & Applied Science, vol. 2, no. 7, pp. 12-17.

[23] Kryszkiewicz, M. (1998). Representative association rules. Research and Development in Knowledge Discovery and Data Mining. Springer Berlin Heidelberg, pp. 198-209.

[24] Domadiya, N. H., & Rao, U. P. (2013). Hiding sensitive association rules to maintain privacy and data quality in database. In Advance Computing Conference (IACC), IEEE 3rd International, 2013.

[25] Le, H. Q., Arch-Int, S., Nguyen, H. X. & Arch-Int, N. (2013). Association rule hiding in risk management for retail supply chain collaboration. Computers in Industry, vol. 64, no. 7, pp. 776-784.

[26] Shah, R. A. & Asghar, S. (2014). Privacy preserving in association rules using a genetic algorithm. Turkish Journal of Electrical Engineering & Computer Sciences, vol. 22, no. 2, pp. 434-450.

[27] Saygin, Y., Verykios, V. S. & Elmagarmid, A. K. (2002). Privacy preserving association rule mining. In Research Issues in Data Engineering: Engineering E-Commerce/E-Business Systems, RIDE-2EC Proceedings. Twelfth International Workshop, IEEE, pp. 151-158.

[28] Wang, H. (2013). Quality Measurements for Association Rules Hiding. AASRI Procedia, vol. 5, pp. 228-234.

13

Data sanitization in association rule mining based on impact factor

A. Telikani[1*], A. Shahbahrami[2] and R. Tavoli[3]

[1]*Department of Electronic & Computer Engineering, Institute for Higher Education Pouyandegan Danesh, Chalous, Iran.*
[2]*Department of Computer Engineering, University of Guilan, Rasht, Iran.*
[3]*Department of Mathematics, Chalous Branch, Islamic Azad University, Chalous, Iran.*

Corresponding author: akbar.telikani@gmail.com (A. Telikani).

Abstract

Data sanitization process is used to promote the sharing of transactional databases among organizations and businesses, and alleviates concerns for individuals and organizations regarding the disclosure of sensitive patterns. It transforms the source database into a released database so that counterparts cannot discover the sensitive patterns and so data confidentiality is preserved against association rule mining method. This process strongly relies on the minimizing the impact of data sanitization on the data utility by minimizing the number of lost patterns in the form of non-sensitive patterns which are not mined from sanitized database. This study proposes a data sanitization algorithm to hide sensitive patterns in the form of frequent itemsets from the database while controlling the impact of sanitization on the data utility using estimation of impact factor of each modification on non-sensitive itemsets. The proposed algorithm has been compared with Sliding Window size Algorithm (SWA) and Max-Min1 in terms of execution time, data utility and data accuracy. The data accuracy is defined as the ratio of deleted items to the total support values of sensitive itemsets in the source dataset. Experimental results demonstrate that the proposed algorithm outperforms SWA and Max-Min1 in terms of maximizing the data utility and data accuracy and it provides better execution time over SWA and Max-Min1 in high scalability for sensitive itemsets and transactions.

Keywords: *Data Sanitization, Association Rule Hiding, Frequent Itemsets, Association Rule Mining, Privacy Preserving Data Mining.*

1. Introduction

The Knowledge Discovery from Databases (KDD) [1] is an interactive, iterative and interdisciplinary process and it discovers the knowledge from the data using different methodologies, and these discoveries are useful, novel, relevant, and actionable [2-3]. The KDD process comprises five major steps (1) data selection, (2) preprocessing, (3) transformation, (4) data mining and (5) evaluation; data mining is key step in this process, where intelligent methods are applied to extract unknown data patterns [4-5]. In a data sharing environment, where businesses decide to share their data to other in a collaborative project to achieve some certain gain, sometimes an adversary may be able to violate the sensitive knowledge related with individual privacy or competitive advantage in businesses through abusing KDD process [6]. Privacy Preserving in Data Mining (PPDM) is a process that prevents privacy breach against data mining algorithms, it produces a modified version from database in order to alleviate concerns for individuals and businesses regarding the revelation of sensitive patterns [7]. In some applications such as market basket analysis, Association Rule Mining (ARM) [8] has recently gained more attention in businesses [9] where the regularities in the customer purchasing behavior are found. On the other hand, these discovered patterns may pose a threat to the privacy of data owner [10]; therefore, these patterns should be hidden before data sharing in such a way that the adversaries cannot discover the regularities in customer purchasing behavior. There are two general viewpoints in the privacy preserving in ARM, (1) *input privacy*, the data values are perturbed randomly or the identifiers are anonymized before delivering to data mining algorithms [11-13], (2) *output privacy*, some given transactions that generate the sensitive patterns are sanitized , and is known as Association Rule Hiding (ARH) [14-18].

There are two types of patterns in ARH, sensitive patterns and non-sensitive patterns. The sensitive patterns contain sensitive knowledge that show strategic patterns and trends, but the non-sensitive patterns are patterns that are general and do not disclosure the privacy of individuals. The ARH aims to achieve a solution for transforming a source database into a released database using data sanitization so that all sensitive patterns are hidden and all non-sensitive patterns are mined from released database after data sanitization; this problem is known as optimal solution. The optimal solution for data sanitization is NP-hard problem [19] and sanitization algorithms try to find this solution by minimizing undesirable effects in sanitization process. These side-effects include lost rule (misses cost), ghost rule (artifactual pattern) and hiding failure (false rule). The lost rules are non-sensitive patterns that cannot be discovered from sanitized database; this problem occurs when some corresponding transactions/ items for sensitive patterns that correspond with non-sensitive patterns are modified, and subsequently, the frequency of non-sensitive patterns are reduced and cannot be extracted from sanitized database. If number of lost patterns is reduced, the data utility is maximized. The artifactual patterns are non-sensitive patterns that are not discovered from the source database but can be mined from the released database. The hiding failure is measured in terms of the percentage of sensitive patterns that are not hidden by sanitization process and are discovered from sanitized database. For minimizing these side-effects, different approaches such as *border*, *exact* and *heuristic* have been presented, the *border approach* focuses on the maintaining the non-sensitive patterns and controls the impact of sanitization on the non-sensitive patterns and then performs the modifications with minimum impact [20-21]. The *exact approach* contains very complex algorithms, which conceive the hiding process as a constraint satisfaction problem and these algorithms solve the problem by using integer and linear programming or binary integer programming [4, 22]. Both the border and exact approaches have achieved good results when hiding a set of itemsets. These approaches hide a rule by hiding its productive itemset so that all rules generated from this itemset are hidden; therefore, they are

efficient in minimizing the side-effects. The *heuristic approach* includes efficient, fast and scalable algorithms, but involves between two conflicting requirements: data privacy and data utility [10, 14-18, 23-28]. This approach does not guarantee the optimal solution; but it usually finds a solution near the best one in a faster response time. Main difference between data sanitization approaches is in the selection of victim items and transactions for modification in order to minimize the side-effects.

This study proposes an algorithm, namely Hiding based on Impact Factor (HIF), which tries to maximize data utility, data accuracy and execution time by combining optimal sub-solutions in the heuristic and border approaches. This algorithm like other data sanitization algorithms includes two main phases: *victim item selection* and *transaction selection*, first phase formulates a heuristic solution to select the appropriate victim item and second phase uses the combination of border approach and Impact Factor (IF), so that appropriate transactions are selected for modification (removing victim item from transaction). We defined and formulated "IF" as a criterion for selecting transactions with minimum impact on the non-sensitive patterns so that data sanitization causes the least impact on data utility. Also, this algorithm introduces the indexing technique that reduces sanitization ratio and execution time. An experiment performed on a real dataset to show the performance of the proposed algorithm in real application terms, as well as comparisons with the previous studies. The experimental results show that our algorithm hides all sensitive itemsets in sanitized database (no hiding failure) and there is no extra pattern in the sanitized dataset (new rule) but some non-sensitive patterns are lost in released database (misses cost) that these patterns are less than other algorithms. This study provides evidence that combining optimal sub-solutions in border and heuristic approaches with indexing and IF have a harmonic combination that introduces less side-effect on the sanitized database.

The paper is organized as follows: In section 2, problem formulations and data sanitization problem have been defined. Section 3 presents a brief review of previous works. The proposed algorithm is presented in section 4 that trade-offs between knowledge hiding and data sharing using a combinational solution. Section 5 discusses the data used in conducting experimental results, and analyzes the results of these experiments and eventually, the main contents presented in this study are concluded in section 6.

2. Problem definitions and notations

The process of mining the association rules from transactional data was first introduced by Agrawal et al. [29]. Let in a transactional database (D), there are n-items:

$$I= \{i_1, i_2, \ldots, i_n\} \tag{1}$$

D is sequence of m-transaction, $D= (t_1, t_2, \ldots, t_m)$, where each transaction t_i is a set of items in I such that $t_i \subseteq I$. Each association rule is defined as an implication of the form $X \Rightarrow Y$, where X, Y are frequent itemsets in D, such that $X \subseteq I$, $Y \subseteq I$ and $X \cap Y = \emptyset$. Frequency of itemset X in D is defined as *support* of X, denoted by $\alpha(X)$, if $\alpha(X) > \alpha_{min}$, then itemset X is called *frequent itemset,* where α_{min} is the minimum support threshold given by user [30]. The *support* of an itemset, for example itemset X that contains {A, B}, is defined as fraction of transactions in the database that contain both items A and B, which are as follows:

$$\alpha (\{A, B\}) = |A \cup B| / m \tag{2}$$

where, m is the number of transactions in database. Association rule is other type of pattern in ARM that is derived from frequent itemsets using *confidence*, denoted by β. The *confidence* of the rule, denoted by $\beta(X \Rightarrow Y)$, is defined as the fraction of itemsets that support the rule among those that support the antecedent. If confidence of a rule exceeds β_{min}, $(\beta (X \Rightarrow Y) \geq \beta_{min})$, then the rule is known as a strong association rule, where β_{min} is the minimum confidence threshold given by a user. All association rules can directly be derived from the set of frequent itemsets [31]. The confidence is calculated as follows:

$$\beta (X \Rightarrow Y) = \alpha (X \Rightarrow Y) / \alpha (X) \tag{3}$$

The ARM algorithms include levelwise algorithms [32] such as apriori, and pattern-growth methods [33] such as FP-Tree and FP-Growth. The process of ARM contains two phases. In the first phase, the frequent itemsets that satisfy α_{min} are generated and then in second phase, the association rules that satisfy β_{min} are derived from the frequent itemsets, the process of ARM has been shown in figure 1.

The goal of data sanitization is to transform the source transaction database (D) to a sanitized database (D') in order that either the support of sensitive itemset is reduced below α_{min} or the confidence of sensitive association rule is reduced below β_{min} by modifying some transactions in D, while the number of non-sensitive itemsets/ association rules with support/ confidence lower than minimum thresholds in the sanitized database is minimized. The mentioned key notations have been summarized in table 1.

Table 1. Key notations.

Notation	Description
D	Source database
m	Number of transactions
n	Number of items in database
D'	Sanitized database
α	Support count of an itemset
α_{min}	Minimum support threshold
β	Confidence of an association rule
β_{min}	Minimum confidence threshold

Now, we clearly demonstrate the defined concepts using an illustrative example. Consider the sample transaction database as shown in table 2(a), which has set of items I= {a, b, c, d}. Let minimum thresholds are $\alpha_{min}=50\%$ and $\beta_{min} = 75\%$, frequent itemsets with support higher than 50% have been listed in table 2(b) and strong association rules, confidence higher than 75%, that have been derived from the frequent itemsets presented in table 2(c). Let us the itemset {b, c} be sensitive for data owner and should be hidden, and therefore the support of this itemset should be decreased in D' to lower than α_{min} by modifying items {b} or {c} in transactions #1 or #2.

Table 2. (a) Transaction data, (b) Frequent itemsets, (c) Association rules.

(a)

ID	Items
1	{a,b,c,d}
2	{a,b,c}
3	{a,b}
4	{a,c,d}

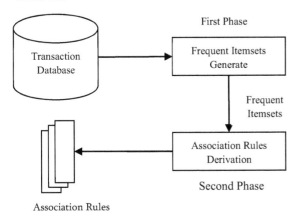

Figure 1. Association rule mining.

First Phase

Transaction Database

Frequent Itemsets Generate

Frequent Itemsets

Association Rules Derivation

Second Phase

Association Rules

(b)

Frequent itemset	Support
a	4(100%)
b	3(75%)
c	3(75%)
d	2(50%)
{a,b}	3(75%)
{a,c}	3(75%)
{a,d}	2(50%)
{b,c}	2(50%)
{c,d}	2(50%)
{a,b,c}	2(50%)
{a,c,d}	2(50%)

(c)

Association Rules	Confidence
a→b	75%
b→a	100%
a→c	75%
c→a	100%
d→a	100%
d→c	100%
b,c→a	100%
b→a,c	100%
d→a,c	100%
a,d→c	100%
c,d→a	100%

3. Related work

For minimizing side-effects in the sanitization process different approaches have been presented, including heuristic, border and exact. The algorithms that outperform these approaches are applied within the framework of decreasing support/confidence of itemsets/association rules and they modify the corresponding transactions using *distortion* or *blocking* techniques. In distortion, the transactions are modified via inserting or deleting items from transactions to decrease support [4, 20-23] or confidence [14, 18, 25 and 28] of patterns under given thresholds. Unlike distortion, the blocking technique modifies transactions by replacing the existing values of victim items with an unknown value [26-27].

The idea behind data sanitization has been introduced by Atallah et al. [19] to hide some frequent itemsets selectively by modifying transactions using distortion technique so that the support of a given set of sensitive itemsets is decreased below the minimum support threshold. This work has been extended to hide both sensitive itemsets and sensitive rules [23]. Most of sanitization algorithms try to find a right balance between protection of sensitive knowledge and pattern discovery. Following this purpose, *Sliding Window size Algorithm* (SWA) [17], is an efficient algorithm which outperforms sanitization process as compared to other heuristic-based algorithms in terms of speedup and it maintains data utility of the released database. Also, it hides the sensitive itemsets in only one pass through the dataset, regardless of its size or the number of sensitive itemsets that need to be protected.

The border-based approach focuses on the weight of the non-sensitive itemsets to reduce support of the sensitive itemsets while protecting the support of non-sensitive itemsets [21]. An extended approach of initial border-based approach, called Max-Min, has been proposed to decrease the side-effects, then two algorithms namely Max-Min1 and Max-Min2 have been proposed based on new extended approach. These algorithms select an itemset from non-sensitive itemsets as Max-Min itemset and modify the victim item indicated by the Max-Min itemset in such a way that the support of Max-Min itemset, if possible, is not to be changed [20].

The intersection lattice approach for hiding a specific set of association rules was first introduced by Hai and Somjit [34]. The algorithms based on intersection lattice, *Intersection Lattice-based Association Rule Hiding* (ILARH) [35], *Heuristic for Confidence and Support Reduction based on Intersection Lattice* (HCSRIL) [35] and *Algorithm of Association Rule Hiding based on Intersection Lattice* (AARHIL) [31] hide sensitive rules in three steps. The first step specifies a set of itemsets satisfying three conditions that (i) contain right-hand side of the sensitive rule, (ii) are maximal sub-itemset of a maximal itemset, and (iii) have minimal support among those sub-itemsets specified in (ii). An item in the right-hand side of the sensitive rule that is related to the specified maximal support itemset is identified as victim item. In the second step, a set of transactions supporting sensitive rule are specified. The third step removes the victim items from specified transactions until confidence of the rule is below minimum confidence threshold. In order to reduce side effects, HCSRIL sorts the set of transactions supporting the sensitive rules in ascending order of their size before sanitizing them. The AARHIL specifies the victim items based on the characteristics of the intersection lattice of frequent itemsets and identifies the transactions for data sanitization based on the weight of transactions.

4. Proposed algorithm

As discussed previously, the goal of sanitization process is to protect sensitive patterns against ARM techniques. The sanitization process which decreases the support count of sensitive itemsets

by removing items from transactions essentially includes four sub-problems:
(1) Identifying an item for each sensitive itemset to be deleted (called the victim item).
(2) Selecting the corresponding sensitive transactions to sanitize.
(3) Removing the victim item from selected transactions.
(4) Rewriting the modified database to disk.
In the next section, an efficient sanitization algorithm is proposed and outperforms these four sub-problems for hiding sensitive itemsets.

4.1. Sanitization algorithm

In order to hide an itemset, {A, B}, its support, (|A∪B|m), is decreased to below minimum support threshold. To decrease support count of an itemset, HIF modifies corresponding transactions by removing one item at a time in selected transactions. The HIF applies a heuristic to select an item as *victim item* in order to reduce the side-effects due to modification and then using border approach and an IF criterion, it controls the impact of each modification on the non-sensitive itemsets with low support. For reducing the side-effects using IF, the proposed algorithm is performed in two iterations, in first iteration, the modifications with IF=0 are done by removing victim item from transaction, if in first iteration, the support of sensitive itemsets do not decrease to below α_{min}, then HIF algorithm employs second iteration that modifications with IF=1 are done, while the support of itemset is above α_{min}, this iteration is continued. In each iteration, the HIF calculates IF for a non-sensitive itemset with minimum support that is related to victim item, instead of calculating IF for all related non-sensitive itemsets, we refer to this itemset as Minimum Support Itemset (MSI). For calculating IF, the proposed algorithm assesses the impact of each modification on the MSI, If modification affects the MSI, then IF=0, otherwise IF=1.

For selecting MSI, first the HIF selects one item from current sensitive itemset with the highest frequency as the victim item and then lists set of non-sensitive itemsets that depend on victim item, called *victim item-list* (vi-list), then from among all the listed itemsets, the itemset with minimum support is selected as MSI. Since the support of this itemset is closer to α_{min}, it takes more effect than other related non-sensitive itemsets from modification. Therefore, the impact of data sanitization on these itemsets should be controlled. To decrease execution time and also to increase data accuracy, the HIF uses indexing

technique so that the sensitive itemsets with shorter length and higher support are selected for hiding. Therefore, the number of itemsets for hiding is reduced by decreasing the support of superset itemsets and so data accuracy is improved because the HIF creates less modification and so the ratio of deleted items is reduced.

The use of optimal sub-solutions and IF minimizes the lost patterns. However, the use of indexing technique minimizes sanitization ratio and execution time. Our data sanitization algorithm has essentially five steps that are applied iteratively so that all sensitive itemsets are hidden. These steps are as follows:

Step 1: *Indexing*, firstly, the sensitive itemsets are sorted in ascending order of size (number of items in itemset) and then sorted itemsets are indexed based on subset itemsets. This follows from the fact that based on apriori property, similar to all level-wise search algorithms, if an itemset is infrequent then any superset of this itemset is also infrequent, this property is the basis for indexing. For example if the itemset {a, b} is hidden, then the itemset {a, b, c} is hidden subsequently.

Step 2: *Selecting victim item*, for each itemset in root of index table, the algorithm identifies an item with maximum support as *victim item* and then creates vi-list for this item, in vi-list the algorithm lists the non-sensitive itemsets that correspond with *victim item.*

Step 3: *Selecting MSI*, from among all listed itemsets in vi-list, the algorithm selects an itemset with minimum support as MSI. If there is several MSI for a victim item, the algorithm selects first itemset as final MSI.

Step 4: *Sorting corresponding transactions*, the algorithm finds the transactions that support the sensitive itemset and then sort those in ascending order of length. This is due to the fact that if the length of transaction is the shortest, the number of itemsets that occurs in transaction is less. For example in table 2(a) transaction {a, b} has shortest length and it supports an itemset only while transaction {a, b, c, d} is longest and it supports all itemsets.

Step 5: *Calculating impact factor*, the HIF starts from first transaction and calculates the impact of removing victim item in corresponding transactions on support of the MSI. If this modification affects the support of MSI, impact factor for modification is 1, otherwise impact factor is zero. This step performs in two iterations, in first iteration, the HIF performs modifications with impact factor equal to zero, and this operation is iterated while the support of sensitive itemset is reduced to below α_{min}. If in first iteration the support of sensitive itemset is not decreased to below α_{min} then HIF algorithm employs second iteration that modifications with IF=1 are done, while the support of itemset is above α_{min} this iteration is continued.

The pseudo-code of the HIF algorithm is shown in figure 2.

```
Input: Original database (D), minimum support threshold (αmin),
Sensitive Itemsets (SI), non-sensitive itemsets.
Output: Sanitized database (D') that sensitive itemsets are hidden.
    Step 1. Indexing sensitive itemsets
        1.1. Sort SI based on their length
        1.2. Index the sorted SI based on subset itemsets
    While SI are not hidden Do{
    Step 2. Create vi-list for current SI
    Step 3. Find minimum non-sensitive itemset
        3.1. Select victim item
    Step 4. Find corresponding transactions for current SI
        4.1. Sort corresponding transactions based-on length
    While current SI is not hidden Do{
    Step 5. Calculate impact factor
        5.1. Find corresponding transactions for MSI
        5.2. Select transactions without impact on MSI
        }

    }
```

Figure 2. The pseudo-code of the HIF.

4.2. Illustrative example

The application of the proposed data sanitization algorithm is demonstrated via an example step by step. Let us consider the sample transactional database in table 2(a) and extracted frequent itemsets with α_{min}=2 (50%) which have been shown in table 2(b). The itemsets {a, b},{a, b, c}, {a, d} are identified as sensitive itemsets, the sensitive and non-sensitive itemsets have been shown in table 3.

Table 3. Sensitive and non-sensitive itemsets.

Sensitive Itemsets	Non-Sensitive Itemsets
{a,b}	{a,c}
{a,b,c}	{b,c}
{a,d}	{c,d}
	{a,c,d}

In first step, the algorithm sorts sensitive itemsets in ascending order based on the length of itemsets and then indexes them by subset itemsets table 4(a). The HIF in second step, for itemset {a, b}, identifies the item {a} as victim item that has higher support and then non-sensitive itemsets are listed for it on table 4(b). In third step, from among listed itemsets on table 4(b) the {a, c, d} itemset has least support and it is identified as MSI. In fourth step, the algorithm finds

transactions that support the sensitive itemset. The set of transactions for sensitive itemset are #1, #2 and #3. So, the support itemset {a, b} is 3(75%) and for hiding it, we need two modifications in corresponding transactions. Eventually, HIF calculates the IF for each modification, IF for transactions #1, #2 and #3 are 1, 0 and 0, respectively. Accordingly, if we modify transaction #1, this modification has undesirable effects, because transaction #1 is corresponding for MSI too. Therefore, transactions #2 and #3 are modified that introduce no-undesirable effects on the MSI.

Table 4(a). Indexed sensitive itemsets, (b) Victim items list (vi-list), (c) Sanitized data.

(a)

Root	Subset
{a,b}	{a,b,c}
{a,d}	-

(b)

Item	Non-Sensitive Itemsets
{a}	{a,c},{a,c,d}
{a}	{a,c},{a,c,d}

(c)

ID	Items
1	{b,c,d}
2	{b,c}
3	{b}
4	{a,c,d}

For itemset {a, d}, the item {a} is selected as victim item (Table 4(a)) and the itemset {a, c, d} is identified as MSI (Table 4(b)). The transactions #1 and #4 are corresponding transactions for itemset {a, d} and so we need one modification for hiding itemset, but IF for both transactions #1 and #4 is 1. therefore, HIF is performed in second iteration and transaction #1 with IF=1 is modified. After sanitizing the original data, the sanitized data have been shown on table 4(c). The algorithm hides all sensitive itemsets, but introduces itemset {a, c} as lost pattern, that cannot be extracted with α_{min}=2 (50%).

5. Experimental results

In order to evaluate the performance of the proposed algorithm, we selected two algorithms based on several parameters. Since the HIF hides sensitive patterns in the form of frequent itemsets in the framework of decreasing support in the corresponding transactions, we selected the algorithms that are performed in this framework and since HIF tries to minimize side-effects using combining optimal sub-solutions in the heuristic and border approaches, we selected SWA from heuristic that has less computational time than other data sanitization algorithms and also Max-Min1 from border that is efficient in minimizing the side effects. The HIF, SWA and Max-Min1 were coded in Microsoft C#.net and ran on an Intel Pentium 4 with 4 GB of RAM running Windows 7 operating system at 2.53 GHz. Extensive computational tests conducted on real dataset Mushroom. In this section, we describe this dataset and analyze the results of comparisons.

5.1. Description of the dataset

Different datasets (real or synthetic) are used to evaluate the data sanitization algorithms. One of the outcomes of the first workshop on Frequent Itemset Mining Implementations (FIMI) was the creation of the FIMI repository (http://fimi.cs. helsinki.fi) that contains real datasets made available by participants; all these datasets are described in detail in [4]. Out of these, we selected Mushroom dataset from the Irvine Machine Learning Database Repository [36] that was made available by Roberto Bayardo from the University of California. It has varying characteristics in terms of the number of transactions and items contained, and in terms of the average transaction length that this information is shown in the first four columns of table 5. By applying the apriori algorithm with $\alpha_{min} = 3161$ (30%), the algorithm discovered 34154 frequent itemset. The minimum support threshold and the number of generated itemsets have been shown in the last two columns of table 5. The execution time of the apriori algorithm for this discovery was approximately 56 minutes.

5.2. Results and analysis

We compared the HIF algorithm with the SWA and Max-Min1 to evaluate the computational complexity and side effects such as data accuracy, data utility. The computational complexity criteria were considered to evaluate the applicability of the data sanitization algorithms in the real working context. The computational complexity is the number of operations required to transform the original database into the released database. We evaluated the complexity of these algorithms by comparing the execution time required by each algorithm vis-a-vis the number of sensitive itemsets to hide as well as the size of the dataset.

In the first case, we varied the number of sensitive itemsets to hide as 100, 500, 1000 and 1500. Figure 3(a) shows that our algorithm scales well with the number of itemsets to hide, this scalability is mainly due to the index table that is used to index the sensitive itemsets per subset itemsets. Thus, there is no need to iteration for each sensitive itemset and algorithm modifies database for itemsets in the root of index table only. Generally, the execution time for SWA and Max-Min1 is more expensive due to the number of iterations for sensitive itemsets.

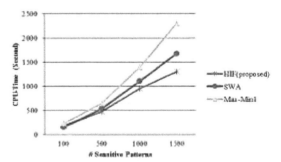

(a) Execution time in proportion to number of sensitive itemset.

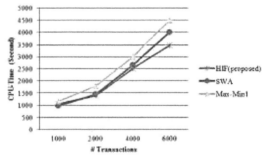

(b) Execution time in proportion to number of transaction.

Figure 3. Execution time used by HIF, Max-Min1 and SWA.

In the second case, we varied the size of the database follow as 1000, 2000, 4000 and 6000 transactions, while fixed α_{min}=30%, and then 2% of extracted itemsets specified as sensitive itemsets. The classes of transactions are shown in table 6. Figure 3(b) shows that HIF decreases computational complexity in terms of execution time as compared to SWA and Max-Min1. As can be seen, the HIF is approximately 0.25 times rather than Max-Min1, while for low transaction sizes the execution time for HIF is near to SWA, but there is an improvement increasingly in execution time with increasing transaction sizes.

Table 5. Characteristics of the Mushroom dataset.

Dataset	# items	# Transaction	Avg. Trans. Length	Minimum Support	# Itemsets
Mushroom	119	6807	23.0	1361	34154

Therefore, the HIF is more efficient generally in proportion to number of transactions. Figure 4 shows that HIF produces the lowest lost patterns. In other words, HIF achieves the best results in minimizing the lost patterns compared with SWA and Max-Min1 algorithms. The HIF selects appropriate victim item based on maximum frequency; this selection ensures that modifying the victim item causes least impact on the set of non-sensitive patterns. Moreover, HIF applies IF to compute impact of modification on the MSI. Recall that the data utility represents the percentage of the non-sensitive itemsets that are concealed and therefore cannot be mined from the sanitized database. The data utility of released database is shown in figure 5, which directly corresponds to the lost patterns.

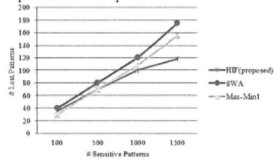

Figure 4. Number of lost patterns produced by HIF, Max-Min1 and SWA.

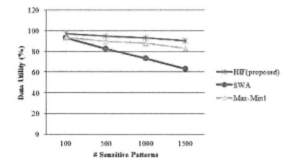

Figure 5. Data utility of dataset produced by HIF, Max-Min1 and SWA.

Figure 6 shows the comparison of HIF, SWA and Max-Min1 algorithms on the aspect of data accuracy of released dataset. With 100 sensitive itemsets for hiding, the accuracy of released dataset is high for three algorithms. This means that the hiding process causes few changes in the released dataset compared with the original dataset. Moreover, for the large-scale sensitive itemsets, the HIF algorithm achieves better accuracy compared to other algorithms and generates the most accurate sanitized database. Experimental results show that three sanitization algorithms produced no hiding failure and conceal all sensitive itemsets in the sanitized database; in

the other words, these three algorithms achieved the same performance in minimizing hiding failure. Therefore, the HIF algorithm introduces 0% artifactual itemsets similar to SWA and Max-Min1. The artifactual itemsets is provable by *Theorem1*.

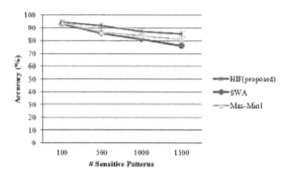

Figure 6. Accuracy of dataset produced by HIF, Max-Min1 and SWA.

Theorem1. A sanitization process, which conceals sensitive itemsets by deleting items from the source database does not generate any artifactual pattern. In summary, the results show that the HIF algorithm outperforms the SWA and Max-Min1 in terms of minimizing the side effects and execution time.

6. Conclusions

Data sanitization in association rule mining is guided by the need to minimize the impact on the data utility of the released database. In this paper we introduced a data sanitization algorithm namely HIF that incorporates optimal sub-solutions in heuristic and border approaches with indexing techniques and IF creation to balance between optimal sanitization and speedup. The experimental results show that HIF outperforms previous works, SWA and Max-Min1, in terms of maximizing data utility, data accuracy and minimizing execution time. The HIF uses heuristic approach and indexing technique for achieving to better execution time; also, it uses a border approach and IF criterion for maximizing data utility by controlling the impact of modification on the database and then selects the modifications with less IF for sanitization. Also, the indexing technique maximizes data accuracy in the released database. This contribution creates more suitable situations for businesses to share their data with other for mutual benefit and provides leverage to develop their businesses.

References
[1] Piatetsky-Shapiro, G. (1991). Report on the AAAI-91 Workshop on Knowledge Discovery in Databases. Technical Report 6.

[2] Mariscal, G., Marban, O. & Fernandez, C. (2010). A survey of data mining and knowledge discovery process models and methodologies. The Knowledge Engineering Review, vol. 5, no. 2, pp. 137-166.

[3] Vignani, B. & Satapathy, S. C. (2014). D-pattern evolving and inner pattern evolving for high performance text mining. Advances in Intelligent Systems and Computing, vol. 247, pp. 501-507.

[4] Menon, S., Sarkar, S. & Mukherjee, S. (2005). Maximizing accuracy of shared databases when concealing sensitive patterns. Information Systems Research, vol. 16, no. 3, pp. 256-270.

[5] Truta, T. M. & Campan, A. (2010). Avoiding Attribute Disclosure with the (Extended) p-Sensitive k-Anonymity Model, In: Stahlbock, R., and Crone, S. F. and Lessmann, S. (Eds.), Data Mining: Special Issue in Annals of Information Systems, pp. 353-373.

[6] Jena, L. K., Kamila, N. & Mishra, S. (2014). Privacy preserving distributed data mining with evolutionary computing. Advances in Intelligent Systems and Computing, vol. 247, pp. 259-267.

[7] Bertino, E., Fovino, I. N. & Provenza, L. A. (2005). A framework for evaluating privacy preserving data mining algorithms. Data Mining and Knowledge Discovery, vol. 11, no. 2, pp. 121-154.

[8] Agrawal, R., Imielinski, T. & Swami, A. (1993). Mining association rules between sets of items in large databases. ACM SIGMOD Conference on Management of Data, pp. 207-216.

[9] Lijffijt, J., Papapetrou, P. & Puolamäki, K. (2014). A statistical significance testing approach to mining the most informative set of patterns. Data Mining and Knowledge Discovery, vol. 28, pp. 238-263.

[10] Amiri, A. (2007). Dare to share: Protecting sensitive knowledge with data sanitization. Decision Support Systems, vol. 43, no. 1, pp. 181-191.

[11] Rizvi, S. & Haritsa, R. (2002). Maintaining data privacy in association rule mining. 28th International Conference on Very Large Databases, pp. 682-693.

[12] Evfimievski, A., Srikant, R., Agrawal, R. & Gehrke, J. (2004). Privacy preserving mining of association rules. Information Systems, vol. 29, pp. 343-364.

[13] Lin, J, & Cheng, Y. (2009). Privacy preserving itemset mining through noisy items. Expert Systems with Applications 36, pp. 5711-5717.

[14] Wang, S. L., Maskey, R., Jafari, A. & Hong, T. P. (2007a). Efficient sanitization of informative association rules. Expert Systems with Applications 35(1), doi:10.1016/j.eswa.2007.07.039.

[15] Saygin, Y., Verykios, V. S. & Elmagarmid, A. K. (2002). Privacy preserving association rule mining. 12th Workshop on Research Issues in Data Engineering.

[16] Oliveira, S. R. M. & Zaiane, O. R. (2002). Privacy preserving frequent itemset mining. IEEE ICDM Workshop on Privacy, Security and Data Mining, vol. 14, pp. 43- 54, Maebashi City, Japan.

[17] Oliveira, S. R. M. & Zaiane, O. R. (2003). Protecting sensitive knowledge by data sanitization. 3rd IEEE International Conference on Data Mining, pp. 613–616, Florida, USA.

[18] Oliveira, S. R. M. & Zaiane, O. R. (2003). Algorithms for balancing privacy and knowledge discovery in association rule mining. 7th International Database Engineering and Applications Symposium, pp. 54-63, Hong Kong, China.

[19] Atallah, M., Bertino, E., Elmagarmid, A. K., Ibrahim, M. & Verykios, V. S. (1999). Disclosure limitation of sensitive rules. IEEE Knowledge and Data Engineering Exchange Workshop, Chicago, USA.

[20] Moustakides, G. V. & Verykios, V. S. (2006). A max-min approach for hiding frequent itemsets. 6th IEEE International Conference on Data Mining Workshop, pp. 502–506.

[21] Sun, X. & Yu, P. S. (2005). A border-based approach for hiding sensitive frequent itemsets. 5th IEEE International Conference on Data Mining, pp. 426-433.

[22] Divanis, A. G. & Verykios, V. (2006). An integer programming approach for frequent itemset hiding. 15th ACM Conference on Information and Knowledge Management.

[23] Dasseni, E., Verykios, V. S., Elmagarmid, A. K. & Bertino, E. (2001). Hiding association rules by using confidence and support. 4th Information Hiding Workshop.

[24] Pontikakis, E. D., Tsitsonis, A. A. & Verykios, V. S. (2004). An experimental study of distortion-based techniques for association rule hiding. 18th Conference on Database Security, pp. 325-339.

[25] Wang, S. L., Patel, D., Jafari, A. & Hong, T. P. (2007). Hiding collaborative recommendation association rules. Applied Intelligence, vol. 26, no. 1, pp. 66-77.

[26] Saygin, Y., Verykios, V. S. & Clifton, C. (2001).Using unknowns to prevent discovery of association rules. ACM SIGMOD Record, vol. 30, no. 4, pp. 45-54.

[27] Wang, S. L. & Jafari, A. (2005). Using unknowns for hiding sensitive predictive association rules. IEEE International Conference on Information Reuse and Integration, pp. 223-228.

[28] Wang, S. L., Parikh, B. & Jafari, A. (2007). Hiding informative association rule sets. Expert Systems with Applications, vol. 33, no. 2, pp. 316-323.

[29] Agrawal, R., Imielinski, T. & Swami, A. (2013). Mining association rules between sets of items in large

databases. ACM SIGMOD Conference on Management of Data, pp. 207–216.

[30] Zeng, Y., Yin, S., Liu, J. & Zhang, M. (2015). Research of Improved FP-Growth Algorithm in Association Rules Mining. Scientific Programming, http://dx.doi.org/10.1155/2015/910281.

[31] Hai, L. Q., Somjit, A. & Ngamnij, A. (2013). Association rule hiding based on intersection lattice. Mathematical Problems in Engineering, http://dx.doi.org/10.1155/2013/210405.

[32] Park, J. S., Chen, M. S. & Yu, P. S. (1995). An effective hash-based algorithm for mining association rules. ACM-SIGMOD International Conference on Management of Data, pp. 175–186.

[33] Han, J., Pei, J., Yin, Y. & Mao, R. (2004). Mining frequent pattern without candidate generation: a frequent pattern tree approach. Data Mining and Knowledge Discovery, vol. 8, no. 1, pp. 53–87.

[34] Hai, L. Q. & Somjit, A. (2012). A conceptual framework for privacy preserving of association rule mining in e-commerce. 7th IEEE Conference on Industrial Electronics and Applications, pp. 1999–2003.

[35] Hai, L. Q., Somjit, A., Huy, X. N. & Ngamnij, A. (2013). Association rule hiding in risk management for retail supply chain collaboration. Computers in Industry, vol. 64, pp. 776–784.

[36] Bayardo, R. (1998). Efficiently mining long patterns from databases. ACM-SIGMOD International Conference on Management of Data, Seattle, WA.

14

Improved COA with Chaotic Initialization and Intelligent Migration for Data Clustering

M. Lashkari[1] and M.- H. Moattar[2*]

1. Department of Computer Engineering, Ferdows Branch, Islamic Azad University, Ferdows, Iran.
2. Department of Computer Engineering, Mashhad Branch, Islamic Azad University, Mashhad, Iran.

*Corresponding author: moattar@mshdiau.ac.ir (M. H. Moattar).

Abstract

K-means algorithm is a well-known clustering algorithm. In spite of its advantages such as high speed and ease of employment, this algorithm suffers from the problem of local optima. In order to overcome this problem, a lot of works have been carried out on clustering. This paper presents a hybrid extended cuckoo optimization algorithm (ECOA) and K-means (K) algorithm called ECOA-K. The COA algorithm has advantages such as fast convergence rate, intelligent operators, and a simultaneous local and global search work, which are the motivations behind choosing this algorithm. In ECOA, we have enhanced the operators in the classical version of the cuckoo algorithm. The proposed operator for production of the initial population is based upon a chaos sequence, whereas in the classical version, it is based upon a randomized series. Moreover, allocating the number of eggs to each cuckoo in the revised algorithm is done based on its fitness. Another improvement is in the cuckoos' migration, which is performed with different deviation degrees. The proposed method is evaluated on several standard datasets at the UCI database, and its performance is compared with those of black hole (BH), big bang big crunch (BBBC), cuckoo search algorithm (CSA), traditional cuckoo optimization algorithm (COA), and K-means algorithm. The results obtained are compared in terms of the purity degree, coefficient of variance, convergence rate, and time complexity. The simulation results show that the proposed algorithm is capable of yielding the optimized solution with a higher purity degree, faster convergence rate, and stability, in comparison with the other algorithms.

Keywords: *Clustering, K-means Algorithm, Cuckoo Optimization Algorithm (COA), Chaotic Function, Migration*

1. Introduction

Data clustering is one of the most important and popular data analysis techniques that refers to the process of grouping a set of data objects into clusters, in which within cluster similarity and between cluster divergence will be satisfied [1, 2, 3, 4, 5, 6]. Clustering is intrinsically a multi-dimensional high-complexity optimization problem with a deterministic objective that is to group related patterns to the same cluster. Since clustering is an unsupervised learning method, it has been used in many areas such as engineering, medical, and social sciences.

One of the widely-used clustering algorithms is the K-means algorithm [6, 7, 8, 9, 10, 11, 12, 13, 14, 15, 16, 17, and 18], which has been proposed by Macqueen in 1967 [3]. After four decades, this algorithm has remained a popular clustering technique. In spite of its advantages such as ease of implementation, high speed, and scalability for huge databases, it suffers from some weaknesses such as dependency on the initial centers. Improper selection of initial centroids may result in local optima. There have been different strategies suggested in the recent decades to improve the K-means algorithm. Most of them have been inspired by evolutionary algorithms that conduct a global and randomized search work around the problem space so that they achieve an optimal solution. For example, Nanda and Panda (2014) [19] have reviewed a number of major nature-inspired metaheuristic algorithms in order to solve this problem.

2. Related works

The literature includes numerous works proposing metaheuristic algorithms for improving clustering outputs. For example, Alam et al. (2014) [20] have reviewed different combinations of the PSO algorithm for clustering improvement. Ultimately, in all of these strategies, attempts have been made to use evolutionary algorithms independently or in combination with K-means algorithm and benefits from the advantages of the two algorithms, and have, therefore, moved the results outside the locally optimal trap to a great extent [4, 6, 8, 9, 10, 11, 12, 13, 14, 15, 16, 17, 18, and 21]. Mualik and Bandyopadhyay (2000) [6] have proposed a genetic algorithm-based method. They have proposed a mutation operator specific to clustering called distance-based mutation. Sung and Jin (2000) have proposed an approach based on the tabu search (TS) for cluster analysis [7]. Shelokar et al. (2004) [8] have proposed an approach based on ant colony optimization (ACO). Fathian and Amiri (2007) [9] have proposed the honey bees mating optimization (HBMO) algorithm to solve the clustering problem. Laszlo and Mukherjee (2007) have proposed a genetic algorithm that exchanges neighboring centers for K-means clustering [10]. Niknam et al. (2008) [11] have presented a hybrid evolutionary optimization algorithm based on a combination of ACO and simulated annealing (SA) to solve the clustering problem. Niknam et al. (2009) [12] have presented a hybrid evolutionary algorithm based on particle swarm optimization (PSO) and SA to find the optimal cluster centers. Rana and Jasola (2010) [13] have presented a hybrid evolutionary optimization algorithm based on a combination of PSO and K-means to solve the clustering problem. Firouzi et al. (2010) [14] have introduced a hybrid evolutionary algorithm based on combining PSO, SA, and K-means to find an optimal solution. Niknam and Amiri (2010) have proposed a hybrid algorithm based on a fuzzy adaptive PSO, ACO, and K-means for cluster analysis [15]. Niknam et al. (2011) [4] have proposed a hybrid algorithm based on imperialist competitive algorithm (ICA) and K-means for cluster analysis. Hatamlou et al. (2011) [16] have proposed a new optimization method that is based upon one of the theories of the evolution of the universe, namely the big bang and big crunch theory (BBBC) for cluster analysis. Hatamlou (2013) [17] has proposed a new heuristic optimization approach for data clustering that is inspired by the black hole (BH) phenomenon. Manikandan and Selvarajan (2014) [18] have presented a new algorithm based on the cuckoo search algorithm (CSA) to solve the clustering problem. Hatamlou et al. (2012) [21] have presented a hybrid data clustering algorithm based on the gravitational search algorithm (GSA) and K-means algorithm (GSA-KM), which uses the advantages of both algorithms and helps the k-means algorithm to escape from local optima and also increases the convergence speed of the GSA algorithm.

Some other applications of optimization algorithms include [29], which has proposed a new hybrid optimization algorithm based on the gravitational search algorithm and Nelder-Mead algorithm to improve crash performance of vehicles during frontal impact. Ref. [30] has proposed a new hybrid optimization approach based on the PSO algorithm and the receptor editing property of immune system. The aim of this work was to develop an approach in the design and manufacturing areas. Differential evolution algorithm is proposed to solve optimization problems in the manufacturing industry [32]. Ref. [34] has presented a comparison on the evolutionary optimization techniques for the structural design problems, and proposes a hybrid optimization technique based on the differential evolution algorithm to solve these problems. Also [35] has proposed a hybrid technique based on differential evolution for solving manufacturing optimization problems.

In [36], a particle swarm-based optimization approach has been presented for multi-objective optimization of vehicle crash worthiness, so the optimized structure can absorb the crash energy by controlled vehicle deformations, while maintaining enough space of the passenger compartment. The approach proposed in [37] is based upon an improved genetic algorithm, used to solve the multi-objective shape design optimization problems. The purpose of [38] has been to develop a novel hybrid optimization method (HRABC) based on the artificial bee colony algorithm and the Taguchi method. This approach is applied to a structural design optimization of a vehicle component and a multi-tool milling optimization problem. Also [39] has presented an optimization approach based on the artificial bee colony algorithm for optimal selection of cutting parameters in multi-pass turning operations.

Overall, the evolutionary algorithms introduced so far can be divided into two groups. The first is being those capable of global search such as GA,

ACO, and PSO versus those with a local search capability such as TS and SA. In the first group, the probability of the results getting trapped in the local optimum is lower than in the second group. However, due to no local search works, the final solutions in this group are less precise. In the second group, due to the lack of a global search around the problem, the probability of the results getting trapped in the local optimum is higher. However, due to the local search works, more attempts should be made to enhance the precision of the final solutions. Usually, in order to resolve the above-mentioned weaknesses, researchers hybridize these two approaches, which would enhance the precision of the final solutions but the complexity of the computational processes emerges.

Cuckoo optimization algorithm (COA) is a novel approach introduced, for the first time, in 2011 by Rajabioun (2011) [31] in order to solve a vast majority of optimization problems. In this algorithm, which is inspired by a cuckoo's life, there are certain operations that are capable of both local and global search works around the problem simultaneously. There are also certain operations contrived in case of emergence of the local optimum. Therefore, this algorithm is capable of achieving highly precise solutions with high rates of convergence. This algorithm, however, has its own weaknesses that we tried to overcome in an enhanced version, namely extended cuckoo optimization algorithm (ECOA). To do this, we optimized some of the traditional operators in a systematic way. The remainder of this paper is organized as what follows. In Section 3, the classical COA is introduced. In Section 4, the cluster analysis problem is discussed. Sections 5 and 6 introduce the proposed extended COA and hybrid ECOA-K algorithms, respectively. Sections 7 and 8 introduce the experimental setup and evaluations of the proposed approach, and comparisons are made with the BH, BB-BC, CSA, COA, and K-means approaches for different datasets. Finally, Section 9 includes the conclusion.

3. COA
COA is inspired by the life of a bird family, called cuckoo. The special lifestyle of these birds and their characteristics in egg-laying and breeding has been the basic motivation for development of this new optimization algorithm. Similar to the other evolutionary methods, COA starts with an initial population. The cuckoo population is of two types: mature cuckoos and eggs. The effort to survive among cuckoos constitutes the basis of

COA. During the survival competition, some of cuckoos or their eggs demise. The survived cuckoo societies immigrate to a better environment and start reproducing and egg laying. Cuckoos' survival effort hopefully converges to a state that there is only one cuckoo society, all with the same fitness values. The COA algorithm is composed of the following steps [31]:

1- Initialize cuckoo habitats using some random points.
2- Dedicate some eggs to each cuckoo.
3- Define egg-laying radius (ELR) for each cuckoo based on the following formula:

$$ELR = \beta * \frac{No.\,of\,current\,eggs}{Total\,No.\,of\,eggs} * (var_{hi} - var_{low}) \quad (1)$$

In this equation, var_{hi} and var_{low} are the higher and lower limits of the search space, respectively, and β is an integer supposed to handle the maximum value for ELR.
4- Let cuckoos lay eggs inside their corresponding ELR.
5- Kill those eggs that are recognized by host birds. After that, all cuckoos' eggs are laid in host birds' nests, and some of them that are less similar to the host birds' eggs are detected by the host birds and thrown out of the nest. Thus after the egg-laying process, $P\%$ of all eggs (usually 10%) with less fitness values will be killed.
6- Let eggs hatch and chicks grow.
7- Evaluate the habitat of each newly-grown cuckoo.
8- Limit the cuckoos' maximum number in the environment and kill those in the worst habitats.
9- Cuckoos are clustered, and select a goal habitat.
10- New cuckoo population immigrates toward the goal habitat.
11- If the termination condition is not satisfied, go to 2.

In what follows, we explain the advantages of COA and the reasons behind selecting it as the fundamental clustering algorithm:
1- Fast convergence rate: The convergence rate of this algorithm is faster compared to the other optimization algorithms, and it is able to reach the optimum solution in less iterations [31, 32].
2- Simultaneous local and global search: In this algorithm, unlike the other optimization algorithms, both local and global searches are inherited in the algorithm nature. This improves the precision of the algorithm [33].
3- Intelligent operators: In this algorithm, there are intelligent operators as compared with the other

algorithms. For instance, the egg-laying procedure is a local search operator that helps exiting the local optimum [34].

4- Variable population size: This helps to destruct the population in poor areas and provide less fitness calculations [31].

There are numerous works in the literature that use COA and its variants for different optimization problems. For example, in [35], the cuckoo search (CS) algorithm has been introduced for solving the manufacturing optimization problems. This research work is the first application of the CS algorithm to the optimization of machining parameters. In [36], the CS algorithm has been proposed for solving structural design optimization problems. Also [37] shows the effectiveness of gravitational search algorithm (GSA) and charged system search algorithm (CSS) for the optimum design of a vehicle component.

4. Cluster analysis problem

K-means algorithm is one of the simplest unsupervised learning algorithms. The procedure follows a simple and easy way to classify a given dataset through a certain number of clusters (assume K clusters) fixed as a priori [4]. The resulting clusters will have high intra-similarity and inter-variability. Basically, to evaluate the similarity between the data objects, the distance measure is used. Particularly, the problem is specified as follows: given N objects, assign each object to one of the K clusters and minimize the sum of the squared Euclidean distances between each object and the center of the clusters:

$$F(O,Z) = \sum_{i=1}^{N} \sum_{j=1}^{K} W_{ij} \left\| (O_i - Z_j) \right\|^2 \qquad (2)$$

where, $\|O_i\text{-}Z_j\|$ is the Euclidean distance between a data object O_i and the cluster center Z_j. N and K are the number of data objects and the number of clusters, respectively. w_{ij} is the association weight of data object O_i with cluster j, which will be either 1 or 0 (if object i is assigned to cluster j; w_{ij} is 1, otherwise 0) [17].

ence, the fitness function for measuring the goodness of a clustering solution is based on the following formula:

$$Fitness(h) = \sum_{m=1}^{K} \sum_{z=1}^{N} \left\| x_z - h_m \right\| \qquad (3)$$

where, $hi = \{h_1, h_2... h_k\}$ denotes the cluster centers, and the ith solution has k cluster centers. h_m indicates the center of the mth cluster in the ith

solution. Furthermore, $x_z = \{x_1, x_2, ...,x_N\}$ and N are the data points and the total number of data points in the mth cluster, respectively. The desired solution is reached when the above fitness function becomes minimal.

5. Extended COA

COA, in its primary version, suffers from certain deficiencies. In our proposed extended algorithm, we have improved and systematized a number of them. In the extended cuckoo algorithm, we intend to enhance the convergence rate, stability, and purity degree in comparison with the classical version. In what follows, we will discuss further the steps involved in the ECOA algorithm.

5.1. Producing initial population based on chaotic sequence

The traditional version of the cuckoo algorithm uses random sequences to produce an initial population. The randomized parameters of COA might influence the algorithm efficiency. It might not be able to cover a global search, and therefore, the convergence rate may be reduced. In the suggested extended cuckoo algorithm, the chaotic numbers are used instead of the random sequences in order to improve the searching of the cuckoos. As a result, the population produced would be semi-randomized. A search supported by chaotic mappings has the possibility of access to most states in a certain zone and without any iteration. Through an extended population positioning via this process, most of the searching space would be explored. Then the results obtained would have the required distribution within the searching domain, which, in turn, would contribute to find a more efficient optimum. Then a number of members are found in the population that are either optimal by themselves or are distributed within a short distance of the optimal solution and would be selected as the best in the next round. It would also provide a possibility of escaping the locally-optimal points in which the algorithm might get entangled. This way, the convergence rate of the algorithm is raised. The chaotic mapping that was selected to produce chaos sequences in this work was a logistic map. This mapping is defined in (4).

$$Cr_{n+1} = \delta * Cr_n * (1 - Cr_n) \ for \ 0 < \delta \le 4 \qquad (4)$$

Here, δ is the initial value of the function. Equation 5 indicates the formula for producing the initial population based on a randomized sequence in classic COA algorithm:

$$(VAR_{hi} - VAR_{low}) * \text{rand} + VAR_{low} \qquad (5)$$

On the other hand, (6) indicates the production of the initial population based on the proposed chaotic approach in ECOA:

$$(VAR_{hi} - VAR_{low}) * Cr + VAR_{low} \qquad (6)$$

In this equation, Cr represents a function based on the behavior of the logistic map varying between 0 and 1. Therefore, using the chaos sequence in the production of the initial population, we expect diversity of that population. An increase in the algorithm's convergence rate would lead to the final optimized solution. The primary formula for producing the initial population as in (5) causes the population to densely concentrate on some regions and have less distribution and diversity in the initial population. However, using the proposed approach as in (6), due to the ability of chaotic sequences to generate longer random sequences, the diversity of the solutions and their coverage is improved.

5.2. Systematic egg laying
In the primary version of the cuckoo algorithm, the number of eggs and the egg-laying radius for each bird are decided through randomization. Using a randomized sequence for estimating the number of eggs would decrease the convergence rate of the algorithm. That is due to the fact that some cuckoos in a better state in the problem space might be given fewer eggs, and vice versa. Therefore, an inappropriate state in the problem space will be analyzed more than an appropriate state in the space. This would, in turn, degrade the convergence rate of the primary cuckoo algorithm. In the suggested method, the number of eggs allocated to each bird depends on the bird's fitness. This variable can be estimated using (7).

$$Egg_i = min_{egg} + round(fitness_i - min_{fit})$$
$$+ \frac{max_{egg} - min_{egg}}{max_{fit} - min_{fit}} \qquad (7)$$

In which Egg_i is the number of allocated eggs to the ith cuckoo, min_{egg} represents the minimum number of eggs, $fitness_i$ is the ith cuckoo fitness, and min_{fit} is the minimal value of the cuckoo fitness function, whereas max_{egg} is the maximum number of eggs, and max_{fit} represents the maximal value for the fitness function. This would help to allocate an appropriate number of eggs systematically to each cuckoo. This formula assigns the number of eggs to each cuckoo based on a definite approach in spite of a random assignment. In this formula, when the fitness of the ith solution ($fitness_i$) is higher, more eggs are assigned to the cuckoo in that region. To control

the number of eggs, the fitness is normalized, considering the minimum and maximum fitness of the solutions in the current population.

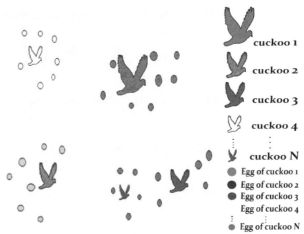

Figure 1. Results of egg-laying based on randomized policy in classical version of cuckoo algorithm.

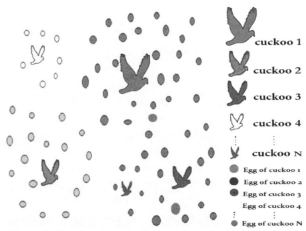

Figure 2. Results of estimating number of eggs for each cuckoo based on its fitness in extended cuckoo algorithm.

Figure 1 indicates the result of estimating the number of eggs for each cuckoo randomly as in the traditional version of the cuckoo algorithm, while figure 2 represents the result of allocating eggs to each cuckoo based on an intelligent policy in the proposed version of the cuckoo algorithm. In these figures, the cuckoos of bigger sizes are those in better positions in the problem space, while those of a smaller size belong to less proper positions.

As it can be observed in figure 1, due to the randomized policy of egg allocation to cuckoos, fewer eggs might be allocated to birds at a better position, and vice versa. This would slow down the convergence rate and purity degree of the algorithm in achieving the final optimal solution. This problem has been met in the extended algorithm with the help of an intelligent egg allocation.

5.3. Systematic migration

In the original version of the cuckoo algorithm, after the birds' egg-laying in the space and the destruction of eggs with less fitness, the remaining cuckoos are clustered. Then the fitness of each cluster is estimated and the one with the highest fitness is selected as the superior region in which the most fitted cuckoo is identified and then the global optimal cuckoo is updated. The problem with this method is that once clustered, the number of cuckoos would differ across the clusters. Therefore, comparing the fitness in clusters with different numbers of cuckoos is a misleading attempt, and might lead to an improper optimal cuckoo in a cluster and a wrong updating of the global optimal cuckoo. This would be followed by a wrong migration and deviation of cuckoos in space as well as a decreased convergence rate of the algorithm.

For the same reason, in the extended cuckoo algorithm, to make up for this deficiency, before the clustering step, the best cuckoo in the present generation would be specified, and then the globally optimal cuckoo is updated. Once the clustering is done, diverse groups of cuckoos are produced that are ready for migration. In order to provide a wider global coverage in this problem, we would let different groups of cuckoos migrate towards the globally optimal cuckoo in the space with a different degree of deviation. In other words, only one group migrates towards the optimal point with a low deviation. They are to search for more optimal points of higher fitness in that region. The other groups follow different degrees of deviation in searching the space. In fact, the migration of all groups of cuckoos in the primary algorithm towards a certain point would create a high density of cuckoos in a particular region. This would provide a lower coverage of the problem space. In case the globally optimal cuckoo is better than the currently existing solutions, it is not identified. Therefore, it would have less chance of achieving the real globally optimal point through the classical cuckoo algorithm. Figure 3 illustrates migration in the primary version of the cuckoo algorithm; the manner of migration in the extended algorithm is indicated in figure 4.

As it can be seen in part (a) of figure 3, all the birds would follow the same degree of deviation towards the globally optimal cuckoo, which is indicated in part (b) of figure 3. If there exists a better globally optimal cuckoo than the current one in the problem at hand, the chance of finding it is reduced since all the cuckoos would be searching the same domain. Equation 8 indicates

the migration function in the original COA algorithm.

a) Before migration.

b) After migration.
Figure 3. Migration in classical cuckoo algorithm.

$$X_{Nextij}(t+1) = X_{Currentij}(t) + F * (X_{Goal} - X_{Currentij(t)}) \ for \ \forall i, j \quad (8)$$

In (8), F is the degree of deviation during migration that is constant for all clusters and different iterations, and $X_{Nextij}(t)$ and $X_{Nextij}(t+1)$ are the locations of the jth cuckoos in the ith cluster at iterations t and $t+1$, respectively. X_{Goal} is the location of the globally optimal cuckoo in the search space, and N represents the total number of cuckoo in the ith cluster. As it can be seen in figure 4 part (a), in the extended algorithm, each group of cuckoos follows a different degree of deviation towards the globally optimal cuckoo. This would disperse them in the space. Even if there exists a globally optimal cuckoo better than the current optimal position, the chance for finding it increases. Equation 9 indicates the migration in the proposed extended COA algorithm.

$$X_{Nextij}(t+1) = X_{Currentij}(t) + F_h * (X_{Goal} - X_{Currentij(t)}) \ for \ \forall i, j, h \quad (9)$$

In (9), F_h serves as the degree of deviation during their migration, and is different for any clusters. Yet in another improvement, we considered β of egg-laying radius and F adaptive to the iteration. In other words, when the algorithm approaches its end, these variables start reducing. A step-by-step reduction in the egg-laying radius and cuckoos' degree of deviation during migration improves the searching process. In other words, it increases the exploration rate in the initial iterations of our algorithm, and would decrease the exploitation rate. The closer we get to the final iterations, due to approaching the optimal solution, the exploration rate is reduced, and the exploitation rate is increased.

6. Hybrid ECOA-K algorithms
The randomized selection of the initial cluster centers in the K-means algorithm occasionally causes the clustering results to be located within the local optimum. In order to solve this deficiency, we use a hybrid of ECOA and K-means algorithms for clustering. In this hybrid algorithm, first, all the initial optimal centers are produced by ECOA, and the data points are clustered through the K-means algorithm. This algorithm is named ECOA-K in the paper, and is described in figure 5. Figure 6 shows the pseudo-code for the hybrid ECOA-K algorithm.

7. Experimental setup
To validate our method, three datasets, named iris, contraceptive method choice (CMC), and wine are used, which are available in the repository of the machine-learning databases (UCI) [38]. These datasets are used in evaluations to have the best correspondence with the previous works. On the other hand, these datasets have different dimensions (different number of records and different number of features). Thus we can study the generalizability and scalability of the approach for small-scale to large-scale problems. Table 1 summarizes the main characteristics of these datasets.

• **Iris:** This dataset has been collected by Anderson (1935). It contains three classes of 50 objects each, where each class refers to a type of iris flower. There are 150 random samples of iris flowers with four numeric attributes in this dataset. These attributes are sepal length and width in cm, and petal length and width in cm. There is no missing value for attributes.

• **CMC:** Contraceptive method choice is denoted as CMC. This dataset is a subset of the 1987 National Indonesia Contraceptive Prevalence Survey. The samples are married women who either were not pregnant or did not know if they were at the time of interview. The problem is to predict the choice of the current contraceptive method (no use has 629 objects, long-term methods have 334 objects, and short-term methods have 510 objects) of a woman based on

her demographic and socioeconomic characteristics [39].

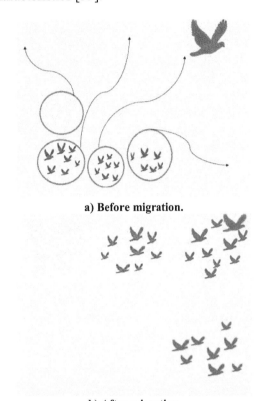

a) **Before migration.**

b) **After migration.**
Figure 4. Migration in extended cuckoo algorithm.

• **Wine:** The wine dataset consists of 178 objects characterized by 13 features: alcohol, malic acid, ash content, alcalinity of ash, concentration of magnesium, total phenols, flavonoids, non-flavanoid phenols, proanthocyanins, color intensity, hue, and OD280/OD315 of diluted wines and pralines. The results were obtained by the chemical analysis of wines produced in the same region of Italy but derived from three different cultivars [40].

Table 1. Main characteristics of validation datasets.

Dataset	Number of clusters	Number of features	Number of data objects
Iris	3	4	150
Wine	3	13	178
CMC	3	9	14783

The performance of the ECOA-K algorithm was compared against the well-known and most recent algorithms reported in the literature including K-means [3], big bang-big crunch (BB-BC) [16], Black hole (BH) [17], cuckoo search algorithm (CSA) [18], and cuckoo optimization algorithm (COA) [31].

As mentioned in the literature, the BB-BC algorithm has advantages such as a simple structure and an easy implementation [16], although this algorithm has disadvantages such as a relatively low accuracy rate, low stability, and low convergence rate in some cases. The BH algorithm has similar Cons and Pros [17]. The CSA algorithm has a simple structure but a low accuracy rate, a low stability, and a low convergence rate [41]. Finally, the COA algorithm has a fast convergence rate and a high accuracy but a high computation cost and a low stability. The performance of the algorithms is evaluated and compared using the following criteria.

▪ **Purity index:** This index examines the purity degree of the clustering algorithm, and can be estimated using (10).

$$Purity = \sum_{r=1}^{k} \frac{n_r}{n} p(S_r)$$ (10)

In this equation, k indicates the number of clusters, and $p(S_r)$ represents the purity degree of cluster r, which can be estimated through (11). This equation would take into account the highest distribution of the samples for a given cluster.

$$p(S_r) = \frac{1}{n_r} \max_i (n_r^i)$$ (11)

In this equation, n_r refers to the number of samples in cluster r; r is the number of clusters, and n represents the total number of samples. The output would vary between 0 and 1. The closer it is to 1, the higher the purity index of data clustering [42].

▪ **Coefficient of variance (CV):** In the probability theory and statistics, CV is a normal criterion used to measure the distribution of statistical data. It is obtained by driving the standard deviation by the mean as in (12).

$$C_v = \frac{\lambda}{\mu}$$ (12)

An algorithm whose CV measure is lower after several iterations would yield more stable and reliable results. In other words, it can help to provide the stability of responses to a great extent.

▪ **Convergence rate:** An algorithm that manages to gain the optimal solution with a higher purity degree in comparison with the other algorithms and with less iteration, and the estimation is said to be the most efficient one.

▪ **Time complexity:** It is defined as the time it takes for an algorithm to be conducted to gain an optimal solution. Since the actual time (in seconds) highly depends on the encoding and programming language, we considered the

number of fitness function evaluations as the time complexity measure.

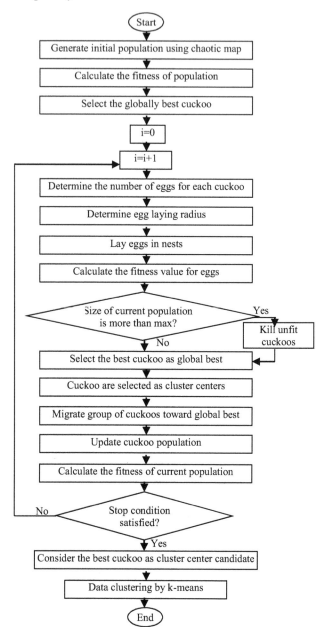

Figure 5. Flowchart of ECOA-K algorithm.

8. Experimental results

In this section, the proposed algorithm is evaluated for 3 different scenarios with purity index, CV index, convergence rate, and time complexity. Almost all control parameters are adaptive with the convergence of the algorithm, and they do not need specific tuning prior to running the algorithm. These performances are the results of 20 independent runs, and show the stability of the approach.

The values for the variables such as Var_{hi} and Var_{low} are selected based on the dimension scales of the datasets. Similar values for parameters for different datasets are not appropriate because using smaller or bigger values for the parameters may lead to slower or faster movements in the search space that leads to a slower convergence and a more search time. These parameter values are determined experimentally, and the only weakness of the proposed approach is selecting the appropriate values form these parameters. However, this weakness is general for all the optimization algorithms. Other algorithms such as those evaluated in this work are also highly parameter-dependent.

Initialize:
Numcuckoos: The initialize of population cuckoos.
Maxcuckoos: The maximum number of cuckoo in the environment.
Minegg; Maxegg: The minimum and maximum number of eggs.
Maxiteration: The maximum number of iteration;
Cr (1, 1) =0. 80; a=4; the initial values for the chaos sequence.
K; the number of cluster;
Varlow; Varhigh; Fi;
Generate an initial population based on logistic chaotic map using (6).
Calculate the fitness function for the initial population using (3).
Select cuckoo with the best fitness as global best cuckoo.
Begin
While (number of Maxiteration, or the stop criterion is not met)
   For j=1: Numcuckoos
      Dedicate some egg to jth cuckoo based on its fitness using (7).
   End
   For h=1: Numcuckoos
      Define ELR for hth cuckoo using (1).
   End
   Let cuckoos to lay eggs inside their corresponding ELR
   Check eggs and delete duplicate eggs in a nest.
   For z=1: sumeggs
      Calculate the fitness function for zth egg.
   End
   Sort the population based on their fitness (cuckoos and eggs).
   Check the size of population.
   If size of current population is more than Maxcuckoos
      limit cuckoos number and kill those who live in worst habitats
      Numcuckoos=Maxcuckoos;
   End if
   Find best cuckoo in population and update global best cuckoo.
   Cuckoos are clustered to k clusters.
   Let new population immigrate toward global best using (9).
   Update population of cuckoos.
   Calculate the fitness function for the current population.
End while
Select global best cuckoo as initial cluster center for k-means.
Assign objects to the group that has the closest centroid (run k-means).

Figure 6. Pseudo-code for hybrid ECOA-K algorithm.

8.1. Evaluations on iris dataset

The first experiment concerns the evaluations of the proposed algorithm on the iris dataset, which are depicted in table 2.

The simulation results given in table 2 show that our proposed algorithm is capable of achieving solutions of a higher purity degree in comparison with those of the other methods. The results obtained on the iris dataset show that the ECOA-K algorithm converges the global optimum by a purity degree equal to 0.8933, while purity in the K-means, CS, BH, BBBC, and COA algorithms are 0.8299, 0.8486, 0.8896, 0.8810, and 0.8733, respectively.

Table 2. Experimental results on iris data.

Algorithm	Purity degree	CV Index	Convergence	
			Number of iterations	Fitness function calculations
K-means	0.8299	0.4924	9.3	9.3
CSA	0.8486	0.1681	8.9	340
BH	0.8896	0.055	6.2	255
BBBC	0.8810	0.1446	14.65	832
COA	0.8733	0.2720	7.45	2134
ECOA-K	0.8933	0	4.6	1685

Therefore, due to the application of intelligent operators such as chaotic sequences, systematic egg-laying and intelligent migration, the proposed approach is more precise than the other compared approaches, which makes it appropriate for sensitive problems such as medical applications. Also CV for the proposed algorithm is zero, which is significantly less than the other methods. Therefore, this algorithm is capable of providing more stable results, as compared to the other algorithms. Its solutions are similar across iterations, and its fluctuation is minimal. The results obtained on the iris dataset show that the ECOA-K algorithm converges the global optimum by a CV index equal to 0, while this index in the K-means, CS, BH, BBBC and COA algorithms are 0.4924, 0.1681, 0.055, 0.1446, and 0.2720, respectively. Due to a better distribution of cuckoos in the problem space and its better convergence, the proposed approach results are more robust and trustable solutions, which means that the results are less different in different runs of the proposed approach.

The proposed algorithm is capable of converging the global optimum in 4.6 iterations, which is significantly less than other methods but the number of fitness function calculations is more than K-means, BH, BBBC, CS, and lower than COA. The results obtained on the iris dataset show that ECOA-K converges the global optimum by 1685 fitness function calculation, while the average number of calculations in K-means, CS, BH, BBBC, and COA are 9.3, 340, 255, 832, and 2134, respectively. As seen from the results obtained, the ECOA-K algorithm is far superior to the other algorithms and leads to a faster convergence than the other approaches including the original versions of COA.

In order to find the degree of significance of the results obtained by the clustering algorithms, the statistical analysis was carried. We employed the non-parametric Wilcoxon test to determine whether there were significant differences in the results of the clustering algorithms. The purpose behind each statistical test was to see whether the research results had been induced as a result of the independent hypothesis or the mere effect of random factors. The test has two hypothesis called H0 and H1, which are defined as follow:

$H0 = method\ X_1\ is\ better\ than\ X_2$

$$E(X_1) \geq E(X_2)$$

$H0 = method\ X_2\ is\ better\ than\ X_1$ $\qquad$ (13)

$$E(X_2) \geq E(X_1)$$

If case H0 is rejected, we can conclude that the result obtained has not been due to random factors but due to the independent variable. In this method, we do always consider our claim or method as H1 and other methods as H0. Then with the help of a significance test, the hypotheses will be either accepted or rejected. In the following tests, we used α = 0.05 as the confidence level. A wider description of these tests has been presented in [43,44].

Table 3. Results obtained by statistical analysis of algorithms based on purity criteria on iris dataset.

	K-means vs. ECOA-K	CS vs. ECOA-K	BH vs. ECOA-K	BBBC vs. ECOA-K	COA vs. ECOA-K
z	−2.850	−2.090	−2.000	−2.096	−2.431
Sig.	0.004	0.037	0.04	0.036	0.01

Tables 3 and 4 show the results obtained by statistical analysis of the proposed algorithm and the other compared algorithms based on purity criteria and CV index on the iris dataset.

According to table 3 and the significance level (below 0.05), H0 was rejected. Therefore, at the confidence level of 95%, the suggested method was superior to the other algorithms in terms of the purity index.

Table 4. Statistical analysis of algorithms based on CV criteria on iris dataset.

	K-means vs. ECOA-K	CS vs. ECOA-K	BH vs. ECOA-K	BBBC vs. ECOA-K	COA vs. ECOA-K
z	−2.848	−2.803	−2.823	−2.8112	−2.805
. Sig.	0.004	0.005	0.005	0.005	0.005

According to table 4 and the significance level (below 0.05), H0 was rejected. Therefore, at the confidence level of 95%, the suggested method was superior to the other algorithms in terms of the CV index. The statistical tests demonstrated that the experimental results were stable and trustable, and we could expect that the proposed

approach performed the same in different executions.

8.2. Evaluations on CMC dataset

The second experiment concerns the evaluations of the proposed algorithm on the CMC dataset, which are depicted in table 5.

As seen in the results tabulated in table 5, the ECOA-K algorithm achieved the best results among all the algorithms. The results obtained on the CMC dataset showed that the proposed algorithm was capable of achieving solutions of higher purity degree as compared to the other algorithms. The purity index in ECOA-K equaled 0.4427, while this index in K-means, CS, BH, BBBC, and COA were 0.4320, 0.4349, 0.4388, 0.4337, and 0.4354, respectively.

Table 5. Experimental results on CMC dataset.

Algorithm	Purity degree	CV index	Convergence	
			Number of iterations	Fitness function calculations
K-means	0.4320	0.041	14.5	14.5
CSA	0.4349	0.050	3.1	260
BH	0.4388	0.055	-	-
BBBC	0.4337	0.011	-	-
COA	0.4354	0.07	12.2	4838.7
ECOA-K	0.4427	0.004	1.2	1697

Also the proposed algorithm was able to converge in 1.2 iterations, in average, while BH and BBBC were unable to reach the convergence condition in some executions. Other algorithms suffered from a low convergence rate in low iterations (a dash is used to imply no convergence rate) for huge datasets, the suggested algorithm can achieve the optimal result with a higher purity degree in a less iteration. Achieving the optimum solution is always guaranteed in the proposed approach, which is due to better initialization and migration of the cuckoos that leads to better coverage of the algorithm throughout the iterations.

Moreover, the CVindex in the suggested algorithm was lower than all the other algorithms. Therefore, this algorithm was capable of providing more stable results as compared to the other algorithms. The CV index in ECOA-K equaled0.004, while this index in K-means, CS, BH, BBBC, and COA was0.041, 0.050, 0.055, 0.011, and 0.07, respectively.

As seen in the results obtained for the CMC dataset, the ECOA-K algorithm was far superior to the other algorithms. Again, statistical analysis was carried for these experiments. Tables 6 and 7 show the results obtained by the statistical analysis of the proposed algorithm and the other algorithms based on the purity criteria and the CV index in the CMC dataset.

Table 6. Results obtained by statistical analysis of algorithms based on purity criteria on CMC dataset.

	K-means vs. ECOA-K	CS vs. ECOA-K	BH vs. ECOA-K	BBBC vs. ECOA-K	COA vs. ECOA-K
z	−2.913	−2.608	−2.429	−2.987	−2.193
Sig.	0.004	0.009	0.015	0.003	0.028

Table 7. Results obtained by statistical analysis of algorithms based on CV criteria on CMC dataset.

	K-means vs. ECOA-K	CS vs. ECOA-K	BH vs. ECOA-K	BBBC vs. ECOA-K	COA vs. ECOA-K
Z	−2.848	−2.608	−2.805	−2.807	−2.805
Sig.	0.004	0.009	0.005	0.005	0.005

According to table 7, at the confidence level of 95%, the suggested method was superior to the other algorithms in terms of the CV index.

8.3. Evaluations on wine dataset

The third experiment concerns the evaluation of the proposed algorithm on the wine dataset (Table 8). The simulation results given in table 8 show that again our proposed algorithm was capable of achieving solutions of a higher purity degree in comparison with the other methods. For the wine dataset, the purity index for k-means, CS, BH, BBBC, and COA were 0.6980, 0.7089, 0.7132, 0.7106, and 0.7185, respectively, while it was 0.7196 for ECOA-K. As it can be seen in table 8, the CV index values for the suggested algorithm were significantly less compared with the other algorithms.

Table 8. Experimental results on wine dataset.

Algorithm	Purity degree	CV Index	Convergence	
			Number of iterations	Fitness function calculations
K-means	0.6980	0.046	8.4	8.4
CSA	0.7089	0.040	3.4	4.6
BH	0.7132	0.033	16.5	1142
BBBC	0.7106	0.08	13.3	1067.5
COA	0.7185	0.01	4.7	468.1
ECOA-K	0.7196	0.01	4.4	511.3

Tables 9 and 10 show the results obtained by the statistical test of the proposed algorithm and the

other algorithms based on the purity criteria and CV index in the wine dataset. According to table 9, at the confidence level of 95%, the suggested method was superior to the other algorithms in terms of the purity index.

Table 9. Results obtained by statistical analysis of algorithms based on purity criteria on wine dataset.

	K-means vs. ECOA-K	CS vs. ECOA-K	BH vs. ECOA-K	BBBC vs. ECOA-K	COA vs. ECOA-K
z	−2.859	−2.328	−2.070	−2.312	−1.34
. Sig.	0.004	0.02	0.038	0.021	0.18

Table 10. Statistical analysis of algorithms based on CV criterion on wine dataset.

	K-means vs. ECOA-K	CS vs. ECOA-K	BH vs. ECOA-K	BBBC vs. ECOA-K	COA vs. ECOA-K
z	−2.772	−2.814	−2.744	−2.603	−2.224
Sig.	0.006	0.005	0.006	0.009	0.026

Again, according to table 10 and the significance level (below 0.05), H0 was rejected. Therefore, at the confidence level of 95%, the suggested method was superior to the other algorithms in terms of the CV index.

9. Conclusion

In this paper, a novel hybrid methodology called ECOA-K was introduced and debated in detail. The hybrid ECOA-K algorithm is a combination of a modified COA and the K-means algorithm. In the hybrid new algorithm, we used the ECOA algorithm to select the initial centers for the K-means algorithm. The proposed algorithm is an extension of the classic COA algorithm with more intelligent and enhanced operations. These modifications include chaotic initial population generation, a systematic egg-laying procedure, and a modified migration function, all with the purpose of increasing the global search and convergence rate of the algorithm.

The experimental results using three benchmark datasets showed that the proposed optimization algorithm was capable of achieving solutions of higher purity degree in comparison with some recent methods, and the algorithm was capable of providing more stable results. The proposed ECOA-K algorithm is more efficient in finding the global optimum solution than the other compared algorithms. It can find high-quality solutions and provides a small coefficient of variance. Also the convergence rate of the proposed algorithm was faster than the other algorithms.

Regardless of the robustness and efficiency of the hybrid ECOA-K algorithm, it is applicable when the number of clusters is known a priori. In the future research works, the proposed algorithm can also be utilized for many different application areas, for example, clustering of unbalanced data. In addition, its performance can be improved via combining with some other evolutionary algorithms properly. Developing a method for selecting the algorithm parameters can be another good direction for future works.

References

[1] Chuang, L., Hsiao, C. & Yang, C. (2011). Chaotic particle swarm optimization for data clustering. Expert Systems with Applications, vol. 38, no. 12, pp. 14555–14563.

[2] Duda, R., Hart, P.E. & Stork, D.G. (1973). Pattern classification and scene analysis. Wiley-Interscience Publication, New York.

[3] Mac Queen, J. (1967). Some methods for classification and analysis of multivariate observations. Proceedings of 5th Berkeley Symposium on Mathematical Statistics and Probability, pp. 281–297.

[4] Niknam, T., TaherianFard, E., Pourjafarian, N. & Rousta, A. (2011). An efficient hybrid algorithm based on modified imperialist competitive algorithm and K-means for data clustering. Engineering Applications of Artificial Intelligence, vol. 24, no. 2, pp. 306-317.

[5] Singh, S. & Chauhan, N. (2011). K-means v/s K-medoids: A comparative study. National Conference on Recent Trends in Engineering & Technology.

[6] Khazaei, A. & Ghasemzadeh, M. (2015) Comparing k-means clusters on parallel Persian-English corpus. Journal of AI and Data Mining, vol. 3, no. 2, pp. 203-208.

[7] Sung, C. & Jin, H. (2000). A tabu-search-based heuristic for clustering. Pattern Recognition, vol. 3, no. 33, pp. 849–858.

[8] Shelokar, P., Jayaraman, V. & Kulkarni, B. (2004). An ant colony approach for clustering. AnalyticaChimicaActa, vol. 509, no. 2, pp. 187–195.

[9] Fathian, M. & Amiri, B. (2007). A honey-bee mating approach on clustering. International Journal of Advanced Manufacturing Technology, vol. 38, no. 7-8, pp. 809–821.

[10] Laszlo, M. & Mukherjee, S. (2007). A genetic algorithm that exchanges neighboring centers for k-means clustering. Pattern Recognition Letters, vol. 28, no. 16, pp. 2359–2366.

[11] Niknam, T., Olamaie, J. & Amiri, B. (2008). A hybrid evolutionary algorithm based on ACO and SA for cluster analysis. Journal of Applied Science, vol. 8, no. 15, pp. 2695–2702.

[12] Niknam, T., Amiri, B., Olamaie, J. & Arefi, A. (2009). An efficient hybrid evolutionary Optimization algorithm based on PSO and SA for clustering. Journal of Zhejiang University Science, vol. 10, no. 4, pp. 512–519.

[13] Rana, S. & Jasola, S. (2010). A hybrid sequential approach for data clustering using K-Means and particle swarm optimization algorithm. International Journal of Engineering, Science and Technology, pp. 167-176.

[14] Bahmani Firouzi, B., Shasadeghi, M. & Niknam, T. (2010). A new hybrid algorithm based on PSO, SA and K-means for cluster analysis. International Journal of Innovative Computing Information and Control, vol. 6, no. 4, pp. 1–10.

[15] Niknam, T. & Amiri, B. (2010). An efficient hybrid approach based on PSO, ACO and k-means for cluster analysis. Applied Soft Computing, vol. 10, no. 1, pp. 183–197.

[16] Hatamlou, A., Abdullah, S. & Hatamlou, M. (2011). Data Clustering Using Big Bang–Big Crunch Algorithm. Innovative Computing Technology, Communications in Computer and Information Science, pp. 383-388.

[17] Hatamlou, A. (2013). Black hole: A new heuristic optimization approach for data clustering. Information Sciences, pp. 175-184.

[18] Manikandan, P. & Selvarajan, S. (2014). Data clustering using cuckoo search algorithm (CSA). Advances in Intelligent Systems and Computing, vol. 236, pp. 1275-1283.

[19] Nanda, S. J. & Panda, G. (2014). A survey on nature inspired metaheuristic algorithms for partitional clustering. Swarm and Evolutionary Computation, vol. 16, pp. 1–18.

[20] Alam, S., Dobbie, G., Koh, Y., Riddle, P. & Rehman, S. (2014). Research on particle swarm optimization based clustering: A systematic review of literature and techniques. Swarm and Evolutionary Computation, vol. 17, pp. 1–13.

[21] Hatamlou, A., Abdullah, S. & Nezamabadi-pour, H. (2012). A combined approach for clustering based on K-means and gravitational search algorithms. Swarm and Evolutionary Computation, vol. 17, pp. 47–52.

[22] Yildiz, A. R., Kurtuluş, E., Demirci, E., Sultan Yildiz, B. & Karagöz, S. (2016). Optimization of thin-wall structures using hybrid gravitational search and Nelder-Mead algorithm. Materials Testing, vol. 58, no. 1, pp. 75-78.

[23] Yildiz, A. R. (2009). A novel particle swarm optimization approach for product design and manufacturing. International Journal of Advanced Manufacturing Technology, vol. 40, no. 5-6, pp. 617-628.

[24] Yildiz, A. R. (2013). A new hybrid differential evolution algorithm for the selection of optimal machining parameters in milling operations. Applied Soft Computing, vol. 13, no. 3, pp. 1561–1566.

[25] Yildiz, A. R. (2013). Comparison of evolutionary based optimization algorithms for structural design optimization. Engineering Applications of Artificial Intelligence, vol. 26, no. 1, pp. 327–333.

[26] Yildiz, A. R. (2012). A comparative study of population-based optimization algorithms for turning operations. Information Sciences, vol. 210, pp. 81-88.

[27] Yildiz, A. R. & Solanki, K. N. (2012). Multi-objective optimization of vehicle crashworthiness using a new particle swarm based approach. International Journal of Advanced Manufacturing Technology, vol. 59, no. 1-4, pp. 367-376.

[28] Yildiz, A. R., Öztürk, N., Kaya, N. & Öztürk, F. (2006). Hybrid multi-objective shape design optimization using Taguchi's method and genetic algorithm. Structural and Multidisciplinary Optimization, vol. 34, no. 4, pp. 317-332.

[29] Yildiz, A. R. (2013). A new hybrid bee colony optimization approach for robust optimal design and manufacturing. Applied Soft Computing, vol. 13, no. 5, pp. 2906-2912.

[30] Yildiz, A. R. (2013). Optimization of cutting parameters in multi-pass turning using artificial bee colony-based approach. Information Sciences, vol. 220, pp. 399–407.

[31] Rajabioun, R. (2011). Cuckoo Optimization Algorithm. Applied Soft Computing, pp. 5508-5518.

[32] Shadkam, E. & Bijari, M. (2014). Evaluating the Efficiency of Cuckoo Optimization Algorithm. International Journal on Computational Sciences & Applications (IJCSA), vol. 4, no. 2, pp.39-47.

[33] Yang, X. & Deb, S. (2014). Cuckoo search: recent advances and applications. Neural Computing and Applications, vol. 24, no. 1, pp. 169-174.

[34] Ameryan, M., Akbarzadeh Totonchi, M. R. & Seyyed Mahdavi, S.J. (2014). Clustering Based on Cuckoo Optimization Algorithm, 2014 Iranian Conference on Intelligent Systems (ICIS), pp. 1-6.

[35] Merz, C. & Blake, C. L. UCI Repository of Machine Learning Databases. <http://www.ics. uci. edu/-mlearn/MLRepository. html>.

[36] Loh, W. & Shih, Y. (2000). A comparison of prediction accuracy, complexity and training time of thirty-three old and new classification algorithms. Kluwer Academic Publishers, Manufactured in the Netherlands Machine Learning, pp. 203-228.

[37] Cortez, P., Cerdeira, A., Almeida, F., Matos, T. & Reis, J. (2009). Modeling wine preferences by data mining from physicochemical properties. Decision Support Systems, vol. 47, no. 4, pp. 533-547.

[38] Yildiz, A. R. (2013). Cuckoo search algorithm for the selection of optimal machining parameters in milling operations. International Journal of Advanced Manufacturing Technology, vol. 64, no. 1-4, pp. 55-61.

[39] Durgun, I. & Yildiz, A. R. (2012). Structural design optimization of vehicle components using Cuckoo search algorithm. Materials Testing, vol. 54, no. 3, pp. 185-188.

[40] Yildiz, B. S., Lekesiz, H. & Yildiz., A. R. (2016). Structural design of vehicle components using gravitational search and charged system search algorithms, Materials Testing, vol. 58, no. 1, pp. 79-81.

[41] Zhao, J., Lei, X., Wu, Z. & Tan, Y. (2014). Clustering using improved cuckoo search algorithm. Springer International Publishing Switzerland, pp. 479–488.

[42] Zhao, Y. & Karypis, G. Evaluation of hierarchical clustering algorithms for document datasets. Proceedings of the International Conference on Information and Knowledge Management, pp. 515-524.

[43] Derrac, J., Garcia, S., Molina, D. & Herrera, F. (2011). A practical tutorial on the use of nonparametric statistical tests as a methodology for comparing evolutionary and swarm intelligence algorithms. Swarm and Evolutionary Computation, vol. 1, no. 1, pp. 3-18.

[44] Mendenhall, W., Beaver, R. J. & Beaver, B. M. (2010). Introduction to Probability and Statistics, Thomson publications, 12th edition.

15

Comparing k-means clusters on parallel Persian-English corpus

A. Khazaei and M. Ghasemzadeh*

Electrical & Computer Engineering Department, Yazd University, Yazd, Iran.

*Corresponding author: m.ghasemzadeh@yazd.ac.ir (M. Ghasemzadeh).

Abstract
This paper compares clusters of aligned Persian and English texts obtained from k-means method. Text clustering has many applications in various fields of natural language processing. So far, much English documents clustering research has been accomplished. Now this question arises, are the results of them extendable to other languages? Since the goal of document clustering is grouping of documents based on their content, it is expected that the answer to this question is yes. On the other hand, many differences between various languages can cause the answer to this question to be no. This research has focused on k-means that is one of the basic and popular document clustering methods. We want to know whether the clusters of aligned Persian and English texts obtained by the k-means are similar. To find an answer to this question, Mizan English-Persian Parallel Corpus was considered as benchmark. After features extraction using text mining techniques and applying the PCA dimension reduction method, the k-means clustering was performed. The morphological difference between English and Persian languages caused the larger feature vector length for Persian. So almost in all experiments, the English results were slightly richer than those in Persian. Aside from these differences, the overall behavior of Persian and English clusters was similar. These similar behaviors showed that results of k-means research on English can be expanded to Persian. Finally, there is hope that despite many differences between various languages, clustering methods may be extendable to other languages.

Keywords: *Clustering, Mizan English-Persian Parallel Corpus, K-means, Principal Component Analysis (PCA).*

1. Introduction
Document clustering is the application of cluster analysis to textual documents and is widely used in the natural language processing (NLP) fields such as information retrieval and automatic text summarization. For example, document clustering has a significant impact on improving the information retrieval precision in search engines [1]. Document clustering automatically assigns each of the documents in a smaller group called clusters. Each cluster should contain documents with similar content. Document clustering input is a document collection while its output is documents grouped based on their similarity. So far, much text clustering research has been done and many clustering methods have been proposed. Is an efficient text clustering method for one language extensible to other languages? In other words, whether the parallel documents clusters obtained by the same clustering method will be similar. Based on document clustering goal, each cluster should contain documents with similar contents. Therefore, it is expected that a document clustering method should earn similar clusters for parallel documents in different languages. On the other hands, different languages usually have many differences in vocabulary, morphology, grammar, syntactic structures, and so on. Thus, clustering quality and its steps can be influenced by documents linguistic characteristics [1].

In this research, we want to know whether the clusters of aligned Persian and English texts obtained by the k-means method are similar. Persian and English languages have many differences that can affect the quality of clusters. In section 3.3, k-means method will be introduced in more details.

English is spoken as a first language by the majority populations in several countries, including the United Kingdom, the United States, Canada, Australia, Ireland, and New Zealand. Modern English is the international language of communication, science, information technology, business, entertainment, diplomacy, etc. Persian is spoken in Iran, and with a different dialect in Afghanistan, Tajikistan, and some other regions which historically came under Persian linguistic influence [2].

The rest of this research paper is organized as follows: related works in this area are dealt with in section 2. Section 3 describes the method. In this section, data selection and feature extraction methods are discussed. Then the PCA dimension reduction and the k-means clustering methods that used in this research are introduced. The experiments and their results are discussed in section 4. Finally, section 5 discusses and concludes the paper.

2. Related research works
Clustering is unsupervised learning techniques for grouping samples into clusters. Samples in the same cluster should be as similar as possible and samples in different clusters should be as dissimilar as possible. There are two types of Clustering techniques: hierarchical and partition [3]. Hierarchical techniques can create clusters with better quality but these techniques are relatively slow. The most widely used partition techniques are k-means and its variants [3]. Time complexity hierarchical techniques are higher than partition techniques. For this reason, k-means is still used by researchers. For example, Krishnasamy et al. proposed a hybrid approach for data clustering based on modified cohort intelligence and k-means [4]. In another research, Hang Wu et al. used k-means algorithm in the storm platform [5].

Many studies have focused on English documents clustering. Some researchers have also focused on the Persian documents clustering. For example, Parvin, et al. proposed an innovative approach to improve the performance of Persian text classification and clustering. Their proposed method used a thesaurus as a helpful knowledge to obtain the real frequencies of words in the corpus [6]. In other research, using Brown algorithm, Ghayoomi proposed a word-clustering approach to overcome Persian parsing problems [7].

The number of research on English texts clustering is much more than Persian. Therefore, the proposed English texts clustering methods are more efficient than those are in Persian. Although Persian and English have many differences that may affect the quality of clusters, this paper is to investigate whether an efficient text clustering method for English is extensible to Persian.

3. Method description
In the first step of comparing Persian and English clusters, the suitable data should be aggregated. Then, the appropriate features should be extracted. Data selection and feature extraction are discussed in section 3-1. The extracted features are high-dimensional. To increase clustering speed and the quality of clusters, dimension reduction methods were used. In section 3-2, the used dimension reduction methods are explained. The researchers make use of k-means as a clustering method. This method is described in section 3-3.

3.1. Data and feature extraction
A parallel English-Persian corpus is required to find out whether the aligned Persian and English texts clusters are similar. A parallel corpus in the simplest case is a collection of texts. They are texts placed alongside their exact translation or translations into one or more other languages. In this study, Mizan English-Persian parallel corpus was used [8].

Mizan parallel corpus has one million aligned Persian and English sentences. Using Mizan parallel corpus, Supreme Council of Information and Communication Technology developed a basic statistical translation system called "Online Translator" in collaboration with Iran University of Science and Technology [8].

In this research 100,000 sentences were selected from Mizan corpus. After selecting suitable data, the appropriate features should be extracted. The feature vectors were created using text mining techniques.

To create feature vectors, in the first step, the researchers extracted the words from Persian and English texts, separately. Then, extracted words were stemmed. Stemming is a process of reducing words to their stems. Stemming reduces different forms of words as well as the length of the feature vectors. Due to Persian and English differences, it is necessary to use different stemming algorithms and tools. The WVT tool was used for stemming English texts [9]. The WVT is a flexible Java library for statistical language modeling. For Persian stemming, Ferdowsi University Natural Language Processing Tool Version 1.1 was used [10].

After word extraction and stemming steps, stop-words are usually removed. Stop-words are words that almost never have any capability to distinguish documents, such as articles *a* and *the* and pronouns such as *it* and *them*. These common words can be discarded before completing the feature generation process. There are various lists for stop-words. There is no standard stop-words list for Persian or English languages. For example Ranks NL listed different stop-words lists for some languages [11].

Therefore, instead of using predefined stop-words lists, they are built automatically. The most frequent words are often stop-words [1]. The choice of the threshold value for frequent words is very important. There is no precise method to select this threshold. If many words are considered as stop-words, then there is a possibility that relatively informative words have been omitted from the feature vectors. The words that have more than 99,900 frequencies were removed in the present research. It reminds that our data are 100,000 aligned Persian and English sentences. This threshold was chosen empirically and with caution to avoid missing informative words.

On the other hand, the words that have less than 100 frequencies were also removed. The very rare words are often typos and can also be dismissed [1].

After words extraction, stemming, and removing more frequent and very rare words, TF-IDF (Term Frequency – Inverse Document Frequency) values were calculated for remaining words. TF-IDF is a weight often used in information retrieval and text mining. This weight is a statistical measure used to evaluate how important a word is to a document in a collection of documents. TF-IDF formula is

$$f_{ij} \log \frac{\text{number of documents}}{\text{number of documents that include word } i}$$

In this formula f_{ij}, is frequencies for word *i* in document *j*. In TF-IDF, the term frequency is modulated by a factor that depends on how the word is used in other documents [3]. If the word is in the document, the value of TF-IDF is not equal to zero. Otherwise, its value in the vector is zero.

Figure 1 shows feature extraction steps. The same method was used for the feature vectors construction from Persian and English texts. Length of obtained feature vector for each Persian sentence is 1415 and for each English sentence is 1095 using this feature extraction method. The length of feature vectors is the first difference of the clustering process in Persian and English texts. English is a morphologically poor language, while Persian is morphologically rich [12]. Morphological difference between English and Persian languages caused the larger feature vector length for Persian.

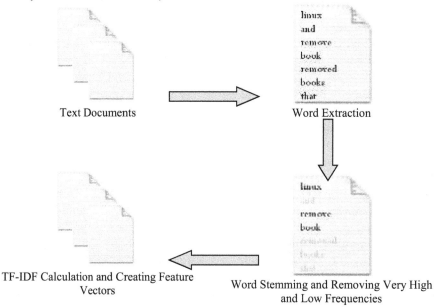

Figure 1. Feature extraction steps.

3.2. Principal component analysis

To improve feature vectors and reduce their dimensions, Principal Component Analysis (PCA) dimension reduction method was used before clustering. The PCA is a mathematical procedure to convert a set of possibly correlated features into a set of uncorrelated feature values. The number of principal components is less than or equal to the number of original features with minimal loss of information [3]. In many cases, the number of

PCA features may be more than expected number. For example, in this study, the length of feature vectors didn't change after using PCA, and there were no zero coefficients in eigenvector. In these cases, a threshold for more dimension reduction can be considered. This threshold can be the number of features or the maximum information that can be lost. In both cases, the best features are selected with minimal loss of information. Here, both methods have been used to determine threshold values and reduce dimensions of feature vectors (in section 4). Furthermore, MATLAB PCA function was used.

3.3. K-means clustering method

K-means method is one of the basic and popular clustering methods in data mining. This clustering method is also used in text clustering. K-means aims at partitioning n samples into k clusters. Each sample belongs to the cluster with the nearest mean. Final k-clusters should minimize the within-cluster sum of squares. Mean sum of squares is usually a metric for clusters comparison. Mean sum of squares formula is:

$$SS = \sum_{i=1}^{k} \sum_{x \in c_i} \sum_{j=1}^{n} (m_j^i - x_j)^2$$

$$meanSS = \frac{SS}{N}$$

In these formulas, x is one sample in C_i cluster and x_j is j-th feature for x sample. The m_j^i is j-th feature for C_i cluster center, k is the number of clusters, and n is the sample numbers.

Here, k-means method has been done several times for each experiment and those with minimum mean sum of squares was selected as the best [13].

The k-means clustering method has two challenges: Computational complexity problem and the appropriate number of clusters (that is k). For the computational complexity problem, there are efficient heuristic algorithms that are coverage quickly to local minimum and this problem is almost solved. The user has to provide the k value and he does not usually have any clue about it. Until now, many methods have been proposed to find the appropriate number of clusters. Some of them are simple and others are complicated and time consuming [13].

In this research, the optimal value for the number of clusters was not found. The experiments have been done for a few k values because in the current research:

1- The dimensions of feature vectors and the number of samples are high and k-means running with large k values would be very slow.

2- The number of categories in text categorization is not usually large. Thus, a few k values are enough for comparing the Persian and English clusters.

4. Evaluation and results

In section 3-1, feature vectors construction was described. The large numbers of samples and dimensions have a negative impact on k-means speed, and the dimension reduction methods can have a significant impact on running speed improvement. Thus, two types of experiments were designed for evaluation and comparison of Persian and English clusters.

In the first type, the same number of features for Persian and English were selected using PCA method. In these experiments, vector dimensions of both languages are equal. Thus, their results are not affected by differences in the length of vectors, but the amount of information loss for these vectors is different.

Table 1 shows these experiments results for several Ks. As mentioned in section 3-3, the mean-SS is our evaluation metric for clusters comparison. As expected, increasing the k values decreased the Mean-SS of clusters. Moreover, for each k value, increasing the length of the vectors increased the Mean-SS of clusters. Considering table 1, the difference between peer to peer Persian and English Mean-SS values is not significant in most cases. In most of table 1 experiments, English is a bit richer than Persian. Whenever the difference between Persian and English feature vectors information was less than 7%, English clusters were richer than Persian. However, for 800 features (with 7.17% difference in information loss) and 1000 features (with 8.17% difference in information loss), Persian results are a bit richer than English.

In the second type of experiments, the same amount of information loss for Persian and English vectors was considered. These results are not affected by differences in the amount of information loss, but the length of feature vectors for Persian and English are different. Table 2 shows these experiments results.

As table 2 indicates, the difference between peer to peer Persian and English Mean-SS values are more than table 1 results. In all of table 2 experiments, English is richer than Persian. These results were affected by differences of Persian and English vector dimensions.

Table 1. Comparing Persian and English clusters with equal vectors dimensions for several Ks.

Number of features	Persian					English				
	Sum of percentage of features variance	K=10	K=20	K=30	K=40	Sum of percentage of features variance	K=10	K=20	K=30	K=40
10	5.2823	0.0241	0.0168	0.0145	0.0136	6.2098	0.0206	0.0083	0.0060	0.0052
50	17.5365	0.1455	0.1252	0.1108	0.1011	18.4894	0.1390	0.1181	0.0925	0.0719
100	27.2206	0.2385	0.2198	0.2038	0.1918	28.8974	0.2378	0.2173	0.1907	0.1711
150	34.7899	0.3162	0.2965	0.2802	0.2724	37.0705	0.3117	0.2876	0.2739	0.2532
200	41.1538	0.3799	0.3613	0.3456	0.3291	43.8643	0.3788	0.3530	0.3338	0.3184
500	65.7843	0.6195	0.6108	0.5996	0.5884	71.0035	0.6112	0.6038	0.5971	0.5865
800	81.0270	0.7677	0.7578	0.7327	0.7265	88.1936	0.7858	0.7685	0.7653	0.7498
1000	88.6143	0.8418	0.8254	0.8126	0.7970	96.7822	0.8689	0.8477	0.8415	0.8107

Table 2. Comparing Persian and English clusters with equal amount of information loss for several Ks.

Sum of percentage of features variance	Persian					English				
	Number of features	K=10	K=20	K=30	K=40	Number of features	K=10	K=20	K=30	K=40
70%	572	0.6652	0.6489	0.6373	0.6238	486	0.6275	0.6106	0.5884	0.5783
80%	776	0.7571	0.7417	0.7286	0.7167	644	0.7189	0.6989	0.6843	0.6681
90%	1042	0.8510	0.8376	0.8248	0.8101	839	0.8092	0.7894	0.7776	0.7700
100%	1415	0.9511	0.9306	0.9190	0.9006	1095	0.9066	0.8903	0.8614	0.8503

5. Discussion and conclusions

Document clustering has many applications and it has been a matter of interest for many years. The goal of document clustering is grouping documents based on their content similarity. If similar documents are grouped in the same cluster, the language of documents should have little impact on the quality of clusters. In other words, an efficient document clustering method, regardless of its documents language, should be extensible to other languages. On the other hand, different languages usually have many differences and they may affect the documents clustering.

This study's purpose was to compare clustering of aligned Persian and English texts using k-means method. Persian and English languages have many differences. The k-means is one of the basic clustering methods and it is of interest documents clustering field researchers. In this paper, the feature extraction method for both languages was the same. The morphological difference between English and Persian languages caused the larger feature vector length for Persian. After feature extraction and using the PCA for dimensions reduction, the clustering was done with k-means method.

The results demonstrated that English clusters are a bit richer than Persian. Despite the slight superiority of English clusters, similar behaviors were observed for two languages in various experiments. These similar behaviors showed that the results of k-means research on English language can be expanded to Persian. Thus, there is a hope that despite the many differences between various languages, clustering methods may be extendable to other languages. Future research could examine whether the other clustering algorithms are extendable.

References

[1] Sholom, M. W., Nitin, I. & Tong, Z. (2010). Fundamentals of Predictive Text Mining. London: Springer Publishing Company.

[2] Windfuhr, G. (2009). The Iranian Languages. London, UK: Routledge Curzon.

[3] Han, J., Kamber, M. & Pei, J. (2011). Data Mining: Concepts and Techniques, Third Edition. Morgan Kaufmann Publishers.

[4] Krishnasamy, G., Kulkarni, A. J. & Paramesran, R. (2014). A hybrid approach for data clustering based on modified cohort intelligence and K-means. Expert Systems with Applications, vol. 41, no. 13, pp. 6009–6016.

[5] Wu, Sh., Wang, Zh., He, M. & Dong, H. (2014). Large-Scale Text Clustering Based on Improved K-Means Algorithm in the Storm Platform. Applied Mechanics and Materials, vol. 543-547, pp. 1913-1916.

[6] Parvin, H., Dahbashi, A., Parvin, S. & Minaei-Bidgoli, B. (2012). Improving Persian Text Classification and Clustering Using Persian Thesaurus. Advances in Intelligent and Soft Computing, vol. 151, pp 493-500.

[7] Ghayoomi, M. (2012). Word clustering for Persian statistical parsing. Advances in Natural Language Processing, vol. 7614, pp. 126-137, Springer.

[8] Supreme Council of Information and Communication Technology, Mizan English-Persian Parallel Corpus, (2013). Available: http://dadegan.ir/catalog/mizan [2014-01-01].

[9] The Word Vector Tool, Available: http://wvtool.sf.net [2014-01-01].

[10] Natural Language Processing Tool ver 1.1, Ferdowsi University, Available: https://wtlab.um.ac.ir/index.php?option=com_content& view=article&id=320&Itemid=200&lang=fa [2015-08-08].

[11] Ranks NL website, Available: http://www.ranks.nl/stopwords [2015-15-01].

[12] Mahmoudi, A., Faili, H. & Arabsorkhi, M. (2013). Modeling Persian Verb Morphology to Improve English-Persian Machine Translation. Advances in Artificial Intelligence and Its Applications, vol. 8265, pp. 406-418, Springer.

[13] Duda, R. O., Hart, P. E. & Stork, D. G. (2000). Pattern Classification, Second Edition. Wiley-Interscience Publication.

16

Extracting Predictor Variables to Construct Breast Cancer Survivability Model with Class Imbalance Problem

S. Miri Rostami[*] and M. Ahmadzadeh

Faculty of computer and IT Engineering, Shiraz University of Technology, Shiraz, Iran.

Corresponding author: S.Miri@sutech.ac.ir (S. Miri Rostami).

Abstract

Application of data mining methods as a decision support system has a great benefit to predict survival of new patients. It also has a great potential for health researchers to investigate the relationship between risk factors and cancer survival. However, due to the imbalanced nature of the datasets associated with breast cancer survival, the accuracy of survival prognosis models is a challenging issue for researchers. This work aimed to develop a predictive model for 5-year survivability of breast cancer patients and discover the relationships between certain predictive variables and survival. The dataset was obtained from the SEER database. First, the effectiveness of two synthetic over-sampling methods Borderline-Synthetic Minority Over-sampling Technique (Borderline-SMOTE) and Density-based Synthetic Oversampling (DSO) method is investigated to solve the class imbalance problem. Then a combination of Particle Swarm Optimization (PSO) and Correlation-based Feature Selection (CFS) is used to identify the most important predictive variables. Finally, in order to build a predictive model, the three classifiers decision tree (C4.5), Bayesian Network (BN), and Logistic Regression (LR) are applied to the datasets. Some assessment metrics such as accuracy, sensitivity, specificity, and G-mean are used to evaluate the performance of the proposed hybrid approach. Also the area under ROC curve (AUC) is used to evaluate the performance of the feature selection method. The results obtained show that among all combinations, DSO + PSO_CFS + C4.5 presents the best efficiency in terms of accuracy, sensitivity, G-mean, and AUC with the values of 94.33%, 0.930, 0.939, and 0.939, respectively.

Keywords: *Breast Cancer, Survival, Class Imbalance Problem, Over-Sampling Technique, Feature Selection.*

1. Introduction

Breast cancer is the most common cancer in women worldwide. In 2011, about 230,480 US women were diagnosed with breast cancer, and approximately 39,520 of them died due to this disease [1]. According to Iran's National Cancer Registry center, breast cancer incidence has increased dramatically from 2001; based on its report in 2011, 23% of all cancers diagnosed in women were breast cancer cases [2]. Knowledge about cancer prognosis helps physicians to estimate outcome of disease and determine chance of survival. Survival analysis is a part of medical prognosis, which predicts a patient survival in a specific time period [3]. Prognostic factors are important for detecting patients who may, or may not, benefit from treatment [4]. Data mining methods, as a decision support system, have a great benefit to predict survival of new patients. Recently, advances in diagnosis and treatment of breast cancer have caused decrease in the death rate, i.e. the number of patients who survive is more than the number of patients who die. Thus this issue leads to imbalanced datasets that are a special case for classification problems [5]. In such datasets, the class distribution is not uniform among the classes. Typically, they are composed of two classes: the majority (negative) class and the minority (positive) class. In supervised learning, particularly in classification, the goal is to accurately predict the target class from the attribute values for each sample in the dataset, where the dataset consists of many samples in the form of (attribute values, class Label). Classification of imbalanced dataset is a challenging issue for researchers. Thus in order to have a more accurate prognostic model for breast cancer survival, the class imbalance problem should be solved. Most of the standard data mining techniques assume the balanced dataset, and when they work with the imbalanced one, the results obtained are biased toward numerous majority class samples. Therefore, in spite of the high accuracy, the detection rate of the minority samples is very low [6]. In some fields such as medical, detecting minority samples are more important than overall accuracy. A large number of predictor variables is another issue in the field of constructing breast cancer survival models. Predictor variables are a set of attributes which their values are used to predict class label. Additionally, the presence of a correlation between the predictor variables can decrease the performance of models, so applying feature selection methods to the dataset by considering correlation between variables can improve the performance of models and provide a faster and more cost-effective prognosis model [7].

This work proposes a hybrid approach to predict a 5-year survivability of breast cancer patients. First, the two different methods Borderline-SMOTE (Borderline-Synthetic Minority Over-sampling Technique) and DSO (Density-based Synthetic Oversampling) are used to solve the class imbalance problem. Then a combination of PSO (Particle Swarm Optimization) and CFS (Coloration based Feature Selection) is used to extract the most important and relevant predictor variables. Finally, by applying the three classifiers decision tree (C4.5) [8], Bayesian Network (BN), and Logistic Regression (LR) to the datasets, the predictive model is built.

The rest of the paper is organized as what follows. In Section 2, the related works are reviewed. The methods used in the proposed approach are presented in Section 3. Section 4 describes the proposed approach. Section 5 provides the experiments, and results obtained are analyzed in this section. Finally, Section 6 concludes the paper.

2. Related works

Sampling methods, cost-sensitive learning methods, and techniques in algorithm level are solutions to handle the class imbalance problem [9]. Initial studies in the field of breast cancer survival prediction did not consider the class imbalance problem [4,10,11]. However, recently, researchers have investigated the effectiveness of

some techniques to handle this problem. In [12], Liu, Wang, and Zhang have used the under-sampling method to deal with the class imbalance problem. Under-sampling refers to the process of decreasing the number of records in the majority class. Afshar, Ahmadi, Roudbari, and Sadoughi in [13] have used the data mining techniques to build a predictive model for breast cancer. In this work, the class imbalance problem was solved using an over-sampling method which refers to the process of increasing the number of records in the minority class. However, random under-sampling might eliminate valuable information. On the other hand, random over-sampling by generating too many repeated samples for minority class increases the likelihood of over-fitting. When over-fitting occurs, a model loses its generalization power, which leads to poor performance on new data [14]. Wang, Makond, Chen, and Wang [15] have used the SMOTE method to balance a dataset. After data balancing, a combination of PSO and classifiers were used to extract the most relevant features for classification. A survey on predicting breast cancer survivability and its challenges can be found in [16].

SMOTE method [17] is a well-known over-sampling method, which has been employed in several data preprocessing studies [18,19]. It gives equal weight to each minority sample to generate new synthetic samples. It does not matter if the data sample is noise data or centroid data. A centroid is a data point (imaginary or real) at the center of a cluster; in fact, it is a vector containing a value for each variable, where each value is the mean of a variable for the observations in that cluster. Therefore, SMOTE is sensitive to the noise data. Wang and Liang [20] have proposed DSO to solve drawbacks of SMOTE. This method assigns different weight to each minority samples. Based upon the idea behind DSO, the samples that are positioned on the boundary of positive and negative classes are not as useful as samples located around centroid data. On the other hand, the authors in [21] believe that increasing border samples can be useful for predicting the minority samples because these boundary samples have more potential for mis-classification.

Ren et al. [22] have proposed a new ensemble-based adaptive over-sampling method for imbalanced data learning to improve microaneurysm detection. Their approach is integration of adaptive SMOTE and ensembles. They utilized an adaptive scheme to assign weights to the minority class instead of uniform sampling weight. It can automatically decide the number of synthetic samples that need to be generated for each minority instance. They used the three ensemble learning methods Boosting, Bagging, and Random sunspace to build a model. Lim et al. [23] have introduced a novel evolutionary cluster-based over-sampling ensemble framework named ECO-Ensemble. In order to deal with the class imbalance problem, i.e. to generate new synthetic samples, they tried to find oversampling regions using clusters. Thus the three methods mini-batch k-means [24], hierarchical agglomerative clustering, and Balanced Iterative Reducing and Clustering using Hierarchies (BIRCH) are applied for clustering. Then an evolutionary algorithm (genetic algorithm [25]) is used to optimize the parameters of cluster-based synthetic oversampling (CSO). Their proposed method was evaluated on a set of 40 imbalance datasets, and the results obtained showed that it could tackle the class imbalance problems very well. Douzas and Bacao [26] have proposed a new method named Self-Organizing Map Over-sampling (SOMO) for imbalanced dataset learning. The self-organizing map algorithm allows an effective generation of artificial data points by producing a 2D representation of the input space. In this method, SOM is used to map closed data points in the input space into nearby map units to create a neighborhood structure that connects the map units to the adjacent ones. In fact, this topology helps for a better data clustering by identifying adjacent clusters. Then based on the instances of minority class belonging to the same cluster and adjacent clusters in the 2D space, the intra-cluster and inter-cluster synthetic samples are produced, respectively. For the evaluation of the proposed method, two algorithms Logistic Regression (LR) and Gradient Boosting Machine (GBM) were used. The results of this work indicate that using artificial data generated by SOMO improves the performance of these algorithms.

Moreover, the previous studies in the field of breast cancer survival prediction used similar predictor variables to build prognostic model [4,10,13]. However, [15] has proposed a feature selection method based on PSO that used classifiers accuracy rate as its fitness function. But feature selection based on learning algorithms has a large computational cost in terms of time and resource [27-29]. Furthermore, the correlation between predictor variables must be analyzed because it decreases the performance of models. This work aimed to consider these issues and used hybrid PSO_CFS method for feature selection, PSO for feature subset generation and CFS as a

fitness function.

3. Preliminaries
3.1. Borderline-SMOTE

Han, Wang, and Mao have proposed a new over-sampling method named Borderline-SMOTE. They suggested that samples far from the borderline of minority class may contribute little to classification. Thus this method only over-samples or strengthens the borderline minority samples. It operates as follows [21]:

First, the borderline minority samples are found out; then the synthetic samples are generated from them and added to the original training set. Suppose that the original training set is T, the minority class is P, and the majority class is N,

$$P = \{p_1, p_2, ..., p_{num}\}, \quad N = \{n_1, n_2, ..., n_{num}\}$$

where, $pnum$ and $nnum$ are the number of minority and majority samples, respectively.

Step 1. For each p_i, $m = 5$ nearest neighbors from T are calculated. The number of majority samples existing among the m nearest neighbors is denoted by m'. Based on the relationship between m and m', three subsets are created as NOISE, DANGER, and SAFE.

Step 2. If $m = m'$, i.e. all the m nearest neighbors of p_i are majority samples, this sample is considered as NOISE. If $m/2 \le m' \le m$, p_i is a border sample of P and easily mis-classified, so it stays in DANGER. Finally, if $0 \le m' \le m/2$, it means that p_i is SAFE, and there is no need to generate new samples for this set.

Step 3. Samples in the DANGER set are the borderline data of minority class P,

$$DANGER = \{p_1', p_2', ..., p_{num}'\},$$
$$0 \le dnum \le pnum$$

where, dnum indicates the number of DANGER members. For each p_i', its k nearest neighbors from P are calculated.

Step 4. In this step, $s \times dnum$ synthetic positive samples for members of DANGER set are generated, where s is an integer between 1 and k. For each p_i', s nearest neighbors from its k nearest neighbors in P are selected randomly. The new synthetic samples are created as follow:

$$Synthetic_j = p_i' + r_j \times diff_{j'}, \qquad (1)$$
$$i = 1, 2, ..., dnum; \ j = 1, 2, ..., s$$

where, r_j is a random number between 0 and 1 and $diff_j$ is a distance between p_i and its s nearest neighbors from P. In this work, the parameters k and s are both set at 5 (based on the SMOTE method).

3.2. Density-based synthetic over-sampling

The DSO method is a kind of minority over-sampling technique that operates based on the density distribution of samples. This method assigns different weights to each minority sample. In order to generate new synthetic samples, it is needed to calculate the two parameters w_i and g_i, where the former is the sampling weight of instance i and the latter is the number of samples that must be generated from instance i. The DSO method works as follows [20]:

First, for each sample in the minority class P, the average distance (Dist) of it to all the other samples in minority class is calculated. Then the two parameters N_P and N_N should be calculated, where N_P is the number of positive neighbors (minority samples) in the specified area Dist and N_N is the number of negative neighbors (majority samples) in the same area Dist. w_i and g_i are calculated according to (2) and (3), respectively:

$$w_i = (\frac{N_P}{N_P + N_N})^P \tag{2}$$

where, P is a parameter representing how much punishment will be put on the impure of instance i.

$$g_i = (\frac{w_i}{\sum_{i=1}^{m_p} w_i}) \times N_{syn} \tag{3}$$

where, $N_{syn} = k_s \times m_p$ is the number of synthetic minority samples required to be generated and k_s is the parameter used to control the number of the generated samples. Finally, for each sample i, in the minority class ($1 \leq i \leq m_p$) k new synthetic samples are generated according to their g_i value. New synthetic samples X_k from sample X_i are generated as follow:

$$X_k = X_i + \delta(X_{point} - X_i) \tag{4}$$

where, X_{point} is one of the nearest neighbors of X_i, which is selected randomly, and δ is a random number between 0 and 1.

3.3. Particle swarm optimization (PSO)

PSO is a meta-heuristic algorithm that has been modeled based on the movement of organisms in a bird flock or fish school. In this algorithm, each candidate solution is considered as a particle that has a position and a fitness value. PSO finds the best solution based on a population in an iterative manner. Each population consists of many particles. Candidate solutions move in search space to find optimum position, so they have a velocity. In each iteration, each particle records its best position. The movement of particles depends on three factors: particle's current position (X_i), best position of the particle in the current iteration (P_{best}), and the best position among all particles in the neighborhood so far (G_{best}). The iterations are repeated until either the fitness value of the given particle equals the defined value or the number of iterations is achieved by the default value [30].

The velocity and position of the ith particle for a problem that has a search space with D dimensions are updated according (5) and (6), respectively, as follow:

$$V_{i,d}^{new} = \omega \times V_{i,d}^{old} + c_1 r_1 (P_{best\ i,d}^{old} - X_{i,d}^{old}).. \tag{5}$$
$$+ c_2 r_2 (G_{best\ d}^{old} - X_{i,d}^{old}), d = 1,2,...,D.$$

$$X_{i,d}^{new} = X_{i,d}^{old} + V_{i,d}^{new}), d = 1,2,...,D; i = 1,2,...,N. \tag{6}$$

where, $V_i = [v_{11}, v_{12}, ..., v_{1n}]$ is the velocity vector of the ith particle, ω is inertia weight between 0.4 and 0.9, c_1 and c_2 are positive constant values between 0 and 4, indicating the cognitive learning factor and the social learning factor, respectively, r_1 and r_2 are random numbers between 0 and 1, and N is the size of the swarms.

In order to apply PSO to a feature selection problem, the method proposed by Chen et al [31] is used. This method uses a binary digit to represent a feature; "0" indicates a feature that is non-selected and "1" indicates a feature that is selected. For this case, the position of dimension d of the ith particle was updated as follows:

$$X_{i,d}^{new} = \begin{cases} 1, & if\ sigmoid(V_{i,d}^{new}) > rand() \\ 0, & otherwise \end{cases} \tag{7}$$

where, $sigmoid(V_{i,d}^{new})$ is $\frac{1}{1 + e^{-V_{i,d}^{new}}}$ and $rand()$ is a random number drawn from $U(0,1)$.

The local best position of a particle (P_{best}) and global best position (G_{best}) in each iteration are updated according to (8) and (9), respectively.

$$P_{best\ i,d}^{new} = \begin{cases} X_{i,d}^{new}, & if: f(X_{i,d}^{new}) \leq f(P_{best\ i,d}^{old}) \\ else, & P_{best\ i,d}^{old} \end{cases} \tag{8}$$

$$G_{best}^{\ new} = \{P_{best\ d}^{\ new} \mid f(P_{best\ i}^{\ new}) \le f(G_{best}^{\ old})\} \qquad (9)$$

In this work, the fitness value (f: fitness function) of a particle is calculated based on the CFS method.

3.4. Coloration-based feature selection

CFS is a feature selection method that uses a correlation-based heuristic to evaluate the merit of features [32]. Based on CFS, the high merit is given to a subset whose features are highly correlated to the class attribute but have a low correlation to each other. CFS calculates the heuristic merit of a feature subset S that consists of k features, as follow:

$$Merit_s(k) = \frac{k\overline{r_{cf}}}{\sqrt{k + k(k-1)\overline{r_{ff}}}} \qquad (10)$$

where, $\overline{r_{cf}}$ is the average of the correlations between the subset features and the class variable and $\overline{r_{ff}}$ is the average inter-correlation between the subset features. Symmetrical Uncertainty is used to calculate the correlation between features according to (11).

$$SU(X,Y) = 2 \times \frac{IG(X \mid Y)}{H(X) + H(Y)} \qquad (11)$$

where, $IG(X \mid Y)$ is information gain that is calculated based on Equation (12), $H(X)$ is the entropy of a variable X and $H(Y)$ is the entropy of a class variable.

$$IG(X \mid Y) = H(X) - H(X \mid Y) \qquad (12)$$

where, $H(X \mid Y)$ is the entropy of a variable X conditioned on a variable Y.

4. Proposed approach

This work aimed to develop a predictive model for 5-year survivability of breast cancer patients and discovers the relationships between certain predictive variables and survival. Three challenges of the previous studies are the class imbalance problem, the large number of variables in original dataset and the lack of attention to the correlation between predictor variables. The proposed method is a hybrid approach that tries to overcome these limitations. Figure 1 shows the flowchart of the proposed method. As shown in this figure, the main contribution of this work is related to two parts: first dealing with the class imbalance problem and then using a

combinational feature selection method (PSO_CFS) to extract the important predictor variables; in fact, this combination of methods is new hybrid approach for building predictive model for breast cancer survival. In the pre-processing step, the original dataset was cleaned. After studying the data dictionary of dataset, the unrelated variables to breast cancer were removed and the records containing the missing values were removed from the dataset as well. Additionally, data transformation including feature normalization was provided to scale attribute values. Then the effectiveness of the two over-sampling methods Borderline-SMOTE and DSO was investigated. As mentioned in Section 2, these two methods generate new synthetic samples based on minority samples in two different regions; therefore, they were selected to deal with the class imbalance problem. After applying them to the original dataset, two new datasets, dataset_1 and dataset_2, were generated for Borderline-SMOTE and DSO, respectively.

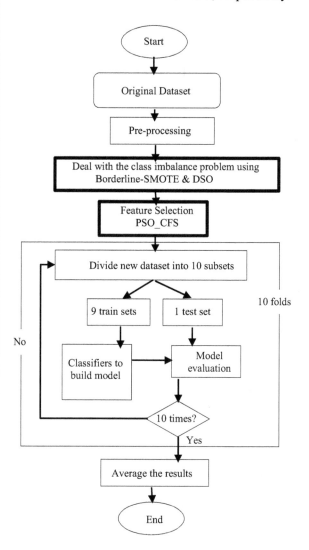

Figure 1. Flowchart of proposed approach.

Then a combination of the PSO method and the CFS algorithm is used as a feature selection approach. Since the correlation between predictor variables decreases the performance of a model, this measure is used as a fitness function in the feature selection method, and PSO is used as a feature subset generation. In this work, 10-fold cross-validation is used in order to evaluate predictive models to reduce the bias and variance of classification results. In this method, a full dataset is divided into 10 independent folds (subsets); each fold is approximately one-tenth of the full dataset (with approximately one-tenth of survival and one-tenth of non-survival). Nine out of the ten subsets are combined and used as the training set, and the remaining subset is used as the testing set. Each of the 10 subsets is used once as a testing set to evaluate the performance of a classifier, which is built from the combination of the other remaining subsets. The three classifiers decision tree (C4.5), BN, and LR are applied to the training set to build a predictive model.

5. Experiment and results
5.1. Data source
In this work, information of breast cancer patients was obtained from SEER (Surveillance, Epidemiology, and End Results) [33] with the SEERStat software. The data was recorded in 2004–2007 with 270,989 records and 151 variables, as shown in Appendix A. In the pre-processing step, the original dataset was cleaned. In fact, after studying the data dictionary of dataset, the unrelated variables to breast cancer and the records containing the missing values were removed from the dataset. Additionally, data transformation including feature normalization was provided to scale attribute values. One important thing that should be considered in the process of removing records with missing values is that data distributions should not be changed significantly. Here the records containing the missing values were removed from the dataset. Statistical analysis confirms that after removing missing values, there are not considerable changes in the distribution of variables. For instance, in terms of mean and standard deviation, there is no significant change in the normal distribution of age variable before (μ=59.18, σ=13.1) and after (μ=59.08, σ=12.92) the deletion of these records. After data pre-processing, the final dataset contains 117,561 records and 58 variables that are selected based on studying data dictionary attentively. The final variables are shown with

symbol "*" in Appendix A as well. The dependent variable is classified into two categories based on the method introduced in [10]: "Survival" class with a distribution of 91.76% and "Non Survival" class with 8.24%. After applying Borderline-SMOTE and DSO to original dataset to deal with the class imbalanced problem, the two different datasets dataset_1 and dataset_2 were generated, respectively. The distribution of the dependent variables for each dataset is shown in table 1. Then PSO_CFS method was applied to these two datasets to extract the most important predictor variables. Summaries of selected predictor variables from each dataset are shown in tables 2 and 3.

This work uses 20% of the dataset with random sampling. Sampling was performed 10 times by changing the seed of the random number generator. Since samples are random, the accuracy of one execution of the algorithm on one set cannot be an indicator of its accuracy on the entire data. Therefore, sampling was repeated 10 times, and 10-fold cross-validation is used to evaluate each execution of the algorithm. As seen in tables 2 and 3, two different sets of features are selected for each dataset that have some common variables such as Grade, Tumor Size, and Num_ positive _nodes. Two types of variables categorical and numerical exist in the selected variables. For categorical variables, distinct values of each variable is presented, and for numerical variables, some statistical metrics such as Mean, Standard Deviation (S.D.), Maximum number (Max), and Minimum number (Min) are measured. Brief descriptions of predictor variables are presented in Appendix B.

Table 1. Distribution of class variable. Dataset_1 and Dataset_2 are new generated datasets by applying Borderline-SMOTE and DSO to original dataset, respectively.

Dataset	Class	Number of records	Percentage
Original Dataset	Survival=1	107,880	91.76%
	Non Survival=0	9,681	8.24%
	Total	117,561	100%
Dataset_1	Survival=1	107,880	83.23%
	Non Survival=0	21,733	16.77%
	Total	129,613	100%
Dataset_2	Survival=1	107,880	69.03%
	Non Survival=0	48,405	30.97%
	Total	156,285	100%

Table 2. Summaries of predictor variables selected by applying PSO_CFS to dataset_1.

Feature number	Categorical variable	Distinct value			
A1_V3	Marital status at DX	5			
A2_V20	Grade	4			
A3_V37	Extension	26			
A4_V38	Lymph Nodes Involvement	32			
A5_V39	Met at Dx	7			
A6_V100	Stage of cancer	4			
A7_V121	ER Status Recode Breast Cancer	3			
Feature number	Numerical Variable	Mean	S.D.	Min	Max
A8_V36	Tumor Size	38.67	128.38	0	998
A9_V27	Num_positive_nodes	1.33	3.79	0	97

Table 3. Summaries of predictor variables selected by applying PSO_CFS to dataset_2.

Feature number	Categorical variable	Distinct value			
A1_V4	Race/ ethnicity	29			
A2_V15	Laterality	5			
A3_V18	Histology	86			
A4_V20	Grade	4			
A5_V65	Radiation	8			
Feature number	Numerical Variable	Mean	S.D.	Min	Max
A6_V8	Age at diagnosis	58.74	13.79	18	100
A7_V28	Num_Nodes	9.37	7.81	1	90
A8_V27	Num_positive_nodes	2.88	5.62	0	97
A9_V36	Tumor Size	50.94	144.54	0	998
A10_V105	Number of primaries	1.11	0.32	1	6

5.2. Assessment metrics

Accuracy is the most common measure for classification task. However, it can be a misleading metric in the presence of the class imbalance problem. Thus other metrics such as G-mean and sensitivity must be calculated in this case because these metrics specify the performance of classification for minority class. Also specificity indicates the proportion of majority samples that are correctly identified. In this work, these four metrics (Equations 13-16) were used to evaluate the performance of models [34,35]. Also the area under a ROC curve (AUC) (17) was used to evaluate the performance of the feature selection method. These metrics were calculated based on the confusion matrix shown in table 4.

Table 4. Confusion matrix.

Predicted class→ ↓Actual class	Non-Survival	Survival
Non-Survival	TP	FN
Survival	FP	TN

$$Accuracy = \frac{TP + TN}{TP + FP + FN + TN} \quad (13)$$

$$Sensitivity = \frac{TP}{TP + FN} \quad (14)$$

$$Specificity = \frac{TN}{TN + FP} \quad (15)$$

$$G - mean = \sqrt{Sensitivity \times Specificity} \quad (16)$$

$$AUC = \frac{1 + TP_{rate} - FP_{rate}}{2} \quad (17)$$

where, TP_{rate} refers to the proportion of positive samples that are correctly considered as positive, with respect to all positive samples, and FP_{rate} refers to the proportion of negative samples that are mistakenly considered as positive, with respect to all negative samples. In facts, TP_{rate} is equal to sensitivity and FP_{rate} is calculated as follows:

$$FP_{rate} = \frac{FP}{FP + TN} \quad (18)$$

Table 5. Average performance of models.

Model	Accuracy	Sensitivity	Specificity	G-mean
A 1: C4.5	92.50	0.215	0.989	0.460
B 1: [15] + C4.5	85.87	0.856	0.865	0.860
C 1: [23] + C4.5	80.88	0.780	0.813	0.634
D 1: Borderline-SMOTE + PSO_CFS + C4.5	90.14	0.867	0.911	0.888
E 1: DSO + PSO_CFS + C4.5	94.33	0.930	0.948	0.939
A 2: BN	87.05	0.611	0.883	0.734
B 2: [15] + BN	85.87	0.856	0.865	0.860
C 2: [23] + BN	78.88	0.800	0.787	0.630
D 2: Borderline-SMOTE + PSO_CFS + BN	92.29	0.839	0.946	0.891
E 2: DSO + PSO_CFS + BN	91.64	0.876	0.948	0.911
A 3: LR	92.50	0.200	0.989	0.433
B 3: [15] + LR	74.52	0.752	0.782	0.766
C 3: [23] + LR	85.66	0.880	0.853	0.751
D 3: Borderline-SMOTE + PSO_CFS + LR	90.19	0.829	0.922	0.874
E 3: DSO + PSO_CFS + LR	89.75	0.917	0.888	0.902

5.3. Results

Table 5 provides the performance of the proposed approach compared to the conventional classifiers, methods in [15] and [23]. In this table, each combinational method is represented by an alphabetic (A: conventional classifier, B: [15] +conventional classifier, C: [23] + conventional classifier, D and E: proposed method) and numbers (numbers 1 to 3 refer to three classifiers C4.5, BN, and LR, respectively). For example, C2 means [23] + BN. The comparison between the methods is based on the averaged results of accuracy, sensitivity, specificity, and G-mean. Also, the evaluation result of PSO_CFS method in terms of AUC is presented in table 6, in which DSO + classifiers are applied to four various datasets with different features including original 58 features, 16 features in [10], 20 features in [15] and 10 selected features by PSO_CFS (proposed method).

According to table 6, the feature set 4 (selected features using proposed approach) outperforms among others using all three classifiers. Further analysis about whether these differences are statistically significant or not will be discussed later.

The differences in the performances of the algorithms are detected by statistical tests using SPSS. This work used analysis of variance (ANOVA) test, in which the model is treated as a factor. ANOVA test is used to determine whether there are any statistically significant differences between the means of three or more independent groups. However, it cannot tell you which specific groups were significantly different from each other. To determine it, a post hoc test was used. In this work, Tukey's HSD post hoc test are used to identify the distinctive models. In this test, first the differences between the means of all groups are found. Then this difference score is compared to

HSD (honestly significant difference), which is calculated as follows:

$$HSD = q\sqrt{\frac{MS_{within}}{n}} \qquad (19)$$

where, MS_{within} is Mean Square value from the ANOVA test that is already computed, q or the Studentized Range Statistic is a table value, and n is the number of values in each group. If the difference is larger than the HSD value, it means the difference is significant. In this work, the significant level (α) is defined at 0.05. The results of ANOVA test in table 7 detect a significant difference (p values <0.05) among these algorithms for all indices. Thus post hoc test is required to determine which specific groups were significantly different. Figures 2-6 are outputs of this test for all metrics. Tukey's HSD test identifies the differences between methods, it lists the different algorithms in different columns while the indifferent algorithms are listed in the same column. In our test, there are 15 different combinational methods, so there should be 15 columns if there are significant differences between all methods. As seen in figure 2, there are 13 columns because there are not significant differences between C1-C2 and B1-B2.

Table 6. AUC results of DSO + Classifiers with different set of features.

Features	C4.5	BN	LR
1- 58 original features	0.889	0.893	0.876
2- 16 features in [10]	0.921	0.901	0.891
3- 20 features in [15]	0.930	0.891	0.868
4- 10 features PSO_CFS (proposed approach)	0.939	0.905	0.903

Table 7. F Statistic and P value of ANOVA test for all indices.

Index	F statistic	P Value
G-mean	1.036×10^4	0.000
Sensitivity	2.137×10^4	0.000
Specificity	1.516×10^3	0.000
Accuracy	1.356×10^3	0.000
AUC	1.356×10^4	0.000

5.4. Discussion

As mentioned in the previous sections, predicting "Non-Survival' samples (minority samples) is a challenging issue for conventional classifiers. According to table 5, when these conventional classifiers are applied to the imbalanced dataset in spite of high accuracy, detection rate of "Non-Survival" samples is low in term of sensitivity and G-mean.

Sensitivity and G-mean are two important metrics for analysing problems with imbalanced nature. Experimental results indicate that the proposed method in both cases using Borderline-SMOTE (method D in the Table 5) and DSO (method E in Table 5) are effective and could detect "Non-survival' samples with all three classifiers.

Furthermore, the results in table 5 show that the combination of DSO + PSO_CFS + classifiers is more effective that Borderline-SMOTE + PSO_CFS + classifiers. Thus it can be concluded that for the SEER dataset, increasing samples around centroid data is more effective than boundary samples.

Tukey's HSD test results figure 2-5 also indicate that the results of these two methods are significantly different in all metrics except for specificity metric figure 4 (the difference between E1, E2, and D2 is not significant). Among three classifiers, C4.5 with DSO offers the best performance with sensitivity 0.930, and the second and the third ones are DSO + LR and method in [23] + LR with values of 0.917 and 0.880, respectively.

Furthermore, the performance of the proposed method in [15] is not effective enough and even results in two metrics accuracy and specificity are worse than conventional classifiers.

The evaluation result of feature selection method in table 6 shows that the proposed method provides the best performance compared to the others, and the result of Tukey's HSD test for AUC in figure 6 confirms it as well.

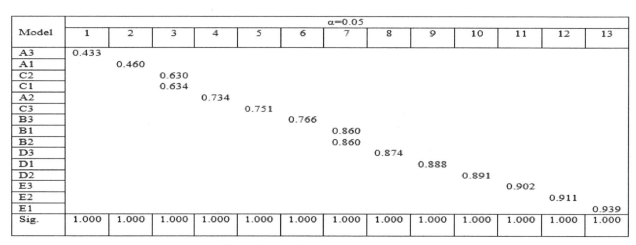

Model	$\alpha=0.05$												
	1	2	3	4	5	6	7	8	9	10	11	12	13
A3	0.433												
A1		0.460											
C2			0.630										
C1			0.634										
A2				0.734									
C3					0.751								
B3						0.766							
B1							0.860						
B2							0.860						
D3								0.874					
D1									0.888				
D2										0.891			
E3											0.902		
E2												0.911	
E1													0.939
Sig.	1.000	1.000	1.000	1.000	1.000	1.000	1.000	1.000	1.000	1.000	1.000	1.000	1.000

Figure 2. Tukey's HSD test for G-mean.

Model	$\alpha=0.05$													
	1	2	3	4	5	6	7	8	9	10	11	12	13	14
A3	0.200													
A1		0.215												
A2			0.611											
B3				0.752										
C1					0.780									
C2						0.800								
D3							0.829							
D2								0.839						
B1									0.856					
B2									0.856					
D1										0.867				
E2											0.876			
C3												0.880		
E3													0.917	
E1														0.930
Sig.	1.000	1.000	1.000	1.000	1.000	1.000	1.000	1.000	1.000	1.000	1.000	1.000	1.000	1.000

Figure 3. Tukey's HSD test for Sensitivity.

Model	$\alpha=0.05$								
	1	2	3	4	5	6	7	8	9
B3	0.782								
C2	0.787								
C1		0.813							
C3			0.853						
B1				0.865					
B2				0.865					
A2					0.883				
E3					0.888				
D1						0.911			
D3							0.922		
D2								0.946	
E1								0.948	
E2								0.948	
A1									0.989
A3									0.989
Sig.	1.000	1.000	1.000	1.000	1.000	1.000	1.000	1.000	1.000

Figure 4. Tukey's HSD test for Specificity.

Model	$\alpha=0.05$											
	1	2	3	4	5	6	7	8	9	10	11	12
B3	74.52											
C2		78.88										
C1			80.88									
C3				85.66								
B1					85.87							
B2					85.87							
A2						87.05						
E3							89.75					
D1								90.14				
D3								90.19				
E2									91.64			
D2										92.29		
A1											92.50	
A3											92.50	
E1												94.33
Sig.	1.000	1.000	1.000	1.000	1.000	1.000	1.000	1.000	1.000	1.000	1.000	1.000

Figure 5. Tukey's HSD test for Accuracy.

Model	$\alpha=0.05$							
	1	2	3	4	5	6	7	8
LR+3	0.868							
LR+1		0.876						
C4.5+1			0.889					
LR+2				0.891				
BN+3				0.891				
BN+1				0.893				
BN+2					0.901			
LR+4					0.902			
BN+4					0.905			
C4.5+2						0.921		
C4.5+3							0.930	
C4.5+4								0.939
Sig.	1.000	1.000	1.000	1.000	1.000	1.000	1.000	1.000

Figure 6. Tukey's HSD test for AUC.

6. Conclusion

Imbalanced problem is a challenging issue for predicting a 5-year survivability of breast cancer patients. This work investigated the effectiveness of the two methods Borderline-SMOTE and DSO on imbalanced breast cancer dataset obtained from SEER to build a more accurate survival predictive model. After balancing dataset, a combination of PSO and CFS was used for feature selection since the large number of predictor variables and also the presence of correlation between them decreased the performance of the model. Finally, the three classifiers C4.5, BN, and LR were used to evaluate the proposed hybrid approach. A combination of PSO and CFS selected 10 predictor variables that is fewer than two other studies [10,15] and AUC results showed that the feature selection approach (PSO_CFS) was effective for this dataset. Additionally, between the methods for solving the class imbalance problem, DSO was better than Borderline-SMOTE. In overall, DSO+ PSO_CFS + C4.5 presents best efficiency in criteria of accuracy, sensitivity, and G-mean with values 94.33%, 0.930 and 0.939, respectively.

References

[1] Khan, U., et al. (2008). WFDT - Weighted Fuzzy Decision Trees for Prognosis of Breast Cancer Survivability, presented at the AusDM.

[2] Ministry of Health and Medical Education, (2013). Center for Disease Management, Cancer Department. National Registration Cancer Cases Reported in 2010. Iran: Center for Disease Management, P.344-9.

[3] Gupta, D. K. S., & Sharma, A. (2001). Data mining classification techniques applied for breast cancer diagnosis and prognosis, Indian Journal of Computer Science and Engineering, 188-193.

[4] Delen, D., Walker, G., & Kadam, A. (2005). Predicting breast cancer survivability: a comparison of three data mining methods, Artif Intell Med, vol. 34, 113-27.

[5] Wang, K.-J. B., et al. (2014). A hybrid classifier combining SMOTE with PSO to estimate 5-year survivability of breast cancer patients, Applied Soft Computing, vol. 20, pp. 15-24.

[6] Chen, Y. (2009). Learning Classifiers from Imbalanced, Only Positive and Unlabeled Data Sets, Department of Computer Science Iowa State University, pp. 1-5.

[7] Wang, K-J., Makond, B., & Wang, K-M. (2013). An improved survivability prognosis of breast cancer by using sampling and feature selection technique to solve imbalanced patient classification data, BMC Medical Informatics and Decision Making, vol. 13.

[8] Ardakani, A., & Kohestani, V. R. (2015). Evaluation of liquefaction potential based on CPT results using C4. 5 decision tree. Journal of AI and Data Mining, vol. 3, no. 1, pp. 85-92.

[9] He, H., & Garcia, E., (2009). Learning from imbalanced data. IEEE Transactions on Knowledge and Data Engineering, vol. 21, pp. 1263-1284.

[10] Bellaachia, A., & Guven, E., (2006). Predicting Breast Cancer Survivability using Data Mining Techniques, presented at the Ninth Workshop on Mining Scientific and Engineering Datasets in conjunction with the Sixth SIAM International Conference on Data Mining, 2006.

[11] Endo, A., Takeo, S., & Tanaka, H., (2007). Predicting Breast Cancer Survivability: Comparison of Five Data Mining Techniques. Journal of Korean Society of Medical Informatics, vol. 13, pp. 177-180.

[12] Liu, Y-Q., Wang, Ch., & Zhang, L., (2009). Decision Tree Based Predictive Models for Breast Cancer Survivability on Imbalanced Data, 3rd International Conference on Bioinformatics and Biomedical Engineering, 2009.

[13] Lotfnezhad Afshar, H., et al. (2015). Prediction of breast cancer survival through knowledge discovery in databases, Glob J Health Sci, vol. 7, pp. 392-8.

[14] Holte, R.C., Acker, L., & Porter, B. (1989). Concept Learning and the Problem of Small Disjuncts, Proceedings of the Eleventh International Joint Conference on Artificial Intelligence (IJCAI-89), vol. 1, pp. 813-818.

[15] K.-J. Wang, et al. (2014). A hybrid classifier combining SMOTE with PSO to estimate 5-year survivability of breast cancer patients, Applied Soft Computing, vol. 20, pp. 15-24.

[16] Miri Rostami, S., Parsaei, M. R., & Ahmadzadeh, M. (2016). A survey on predicting breast cancer survivability and its challenges, UCT Journal of Research in Science, Engineering and Technology, vol. 4, no. 1, pp. 37-42.

[17] Chawla, N., et al. (2002). SMOTE: synthetic minority over-sampling technique, J. Artif. Intell. Res. Vol. 16, pp. 321-357.

[18] Zhao, X. M., Li, X., Chen, L., & Aihara, K., (2007). Protein classification with imbalanced data, Proteins vol. 70, no. 4, pp. 1125–1132.

[19] Parsaei, M. R., Miri Rostami, S., & Javidan, R. (2016). A Hybrid Data Mining Approach for Intrusion Detection on Imbalanced NSL-KDD Dataset. International Journal of Advanced Computer Science and Applications (IJACSA), vol. 7, no. 6, pp. 20-25. Doi: 10.14569/IJACSA.2016.070603.

[20] Chawla, N. V., et al. (2003). SMOTEBoost: improving prediction of the minority class in boosting, in: Proceedings of the 7th European Conference on Principles and Practice of Knowledge Discovery in Database, 2003, pp. 107-119.

[21] Han, H., Wang, W.-Y., & Mao, B.-H. (2005) Borderline-SMOTE: a new oversampling method in imbalanced data sets learning," Lect. Notes Comput. Sci, vol. 36, pp. 878-887.

[22] Ren, F., et al. (2016). Ensemble based adaptive over-sampling method for imbalanced data learning in computer aided detection of microaneurysm, Computerized Medical Imaging and Graphics, doi: http://dx.doi.org/10.1016/j.compmedimag.2016.07.011.

[23] Lim, P., Goh, C. K. & Tan, K. C. (2016). Evolutionary Cluster-Based Synthetic Oversampling Ensemble (ECO-Ensemble) for Imbalance Learning,

IEEE Transactions on Cybernetics, Doi: 10.1109/TCYB.2016.2579658.

[24] Parsaei, M.R., & Salehi, M. (2015). E-mail spam detection based on part of speech tagging. 2nd International Conference on Knowledge-Based Engineering and Innovation (KBEI), pp. 1010-1013. Doi: 10.1109/KBEI.2015.7436182.

[25] Parsaei, M. R., Javidan, R., & Sobouti, M. J. (2016). Optimization of Fuzzy Rules for Online Fraud Detection with the Use of Developed Genetic Algorithm and Fuzzy Operators. Asian Journal of Information Technology, vol. 15, no. 11, pp. 1856-1864. Doi: 10.3923/ajit.2016.1856.1864.

[26] Douzas, G. & Bacao, F. (2017). Self-Organizing Map Oversampling (SOMO) for imbalanced data set learning, Expert Systems with Applications, doi: 10.1016/j.eswa.2017.03.073.

[27] Parsa, S. S., Sourizaei, M., Dehshibi, M. M., Shateri, R. E., & Parsaei, M. R. (2017). Coarse-grained correspondence-based ancient Sasanian coin classification by fusion of local features and sparse representation-based classifier. Multimedia Tools and Applications, vol. 76, no. 14, pp. 15535-15560.

[28] Gao, W., Sarlak, V., Parsaei, M. R., & Ferdosi, M. (2017). Combination of fuzzy based on a meta-heuristic algorithm to predict electricity price in an electricity markets. Chemical Engineering Research and Design, pp. 1-13. Doi: 10.1016/j.cherd.2017.09.021.

[29] Komijani, H., Parsaei, M. R., Khajeh, E., Golkar, M. J., & Zarrabi, H. (2017). EEG classification using recurrent adaptive neuro-fuzzy network based on time-series prediction. Neural Computing and Applications, pp. 1-12. Doi: 10.1007/s00521-017-3213-3.

[30] Nabaei, A., Hamian, M., Parsaei, M. R., Safdari, R., Samad-Soltani, T., Zarrabi, H. & Ghassemi, A. (2016). Topologies and performance of intelligent algorithms: a comprehensive review. Artificial Intelligence Review, pp. 1-25. Doi: 10.1007/s10462-016-9517-3.

[31] Chen, L. F., et al. (2011). Particle swarm optimization for feature selection with application in obstructive sleep apnea diagnosis, Neural Computing and Applications, pp. 1–10.

[32] Hall, M. A. (2000). Correlation-based feature selection for discrete and numeric class machine learning. In Proceedings of the Seventeenth International Conference on Machine Learning, pages pp. 359–366.

[33] SEER (2015) Surveillance, Epidemiology, and End Results (SEER) Program (www.seer.cancer.gov) Research Data (1973-2012). National Cancer Institute, DCCPS, Surveillance Research Program, Surveillance Systems Branch, released April 2015, based on the November 2014 submission.

[34] Parsaei, M. R., Taheri, R. & Javidan, R. (2016). Perusing the effect of discretization of data on accuracy of predicting naive bayes algorithm. Journal of Current Research in Science, no. 1, pp. 457-462.

[35] Parsaei, M. R., Javidan, R., Kargar, N. S., & Nik, H. S. (2017). On the global stability of an epidemic model of computer viruses. Theory in Biosciences, pp. 1-10. Doi: 10.1007/s12064-017-0253-2.

Appendix

Appendix A. All variables from SEER database (151 variables).

Number	Feature	Number	Feature
1	Patient ID number	20	Grade *
2	Registry ID	21	Diagnostic confirmation
3	Marital status at DX*	22	Type of reporting source
4	Race/ethnicity*	23	EOD—Tumor size
5	Spanish/hispanic origin	24	EOD—Extension
6	NHIA derived hispanic origin	25	EOD—Extension prost path
7	Sex	26	EOD—Lymph node involv
8	Age at diagnosis*	27	Regional nodes positive*
9	Year of birth	28	Regional nodes examined*
10	Birth place	29	EOD—Old 13 digit
11	Sequence Number–Central *	30	EOD—Old 2 digit
12	Month of diagnosis*	31	EOD—Old 4 Digit
13	Year of diagnosis*	32	Coding System for EOD
14	Primary site*	33	Tumor Marker 1
15	Laterality*	34	Tumor Marker 2
16	Histology (92-00) ICD-O-2	35	Tumor Marker 3
17	Behavior (92-00) ICD-O-2	36	CS Tumor Size*
18	Histologic type ICD-O-3*	37	CS Extension*
19	Behavior code ICD-O-3*	38	CS Lymph Nodes*
Number	**Feature**	**Number**	**Feature**
39	CS Mets at Dx*	96	CS Schema v0204*

40	CS Site-Specific Factor 1*		97	Race recode (White, Black, Other)
41	CS Site-Specific Factor 2*		98	Race recode (W, B, AI, API)
42	CS Site-Specific Factor 3*		99	Origin recode NHIA (Hispanic, Non-Hisp)
43	CS Site-Specific Factor 4*		100	SEER historic stage A*
44	CS Site-Specific Factor 5*		101	AJCC stage 3rd edition (1988-2003)
45	CS Site-Specific Factor 6*		102	SEER modified AJCC Stage 3rd ed (1988–2003)
46	CS Site-Specific Factor 25*		103	SEER Summary Stage 1977 (1995–2000)
47	Derived AJCC T		104	SEER Summary Stage 2000 (2001–2003)
48	Derived AJCC N		105	Number of primaries*
49	Derived AJCC M		106	First malignant primary indicator*
50	Derived AJCC Stage Group		107	State-county recode
51	Derived SS1977		108	Cause of Death to SEER site recode
52	Derived SS2000		109	COD to site rec KM
53	Derived AJCC—Flag		110	Vital Status recode*
54	Derived SS1977—Flag		111	IHS Link
55	Derived SS2000—Flag		112	Summary stage 2000 (1998+)*
56	CS Version Input Original		113	AYA site recode
57	CS Version Derived		114	Lymphoma subtype recode
58	CS Version Input Current		115	SEER Cause-Specific Death Classification*
59	RX Summ—Surg Prim Site*		116	SEER Other Cause of Death Classification
60	RX Summ—Scope Reg LN Sur*		117	CS Tumor Size/Ext Eval*
61	RX Summ—Surg Oth Reg/Dis*		118	CS Lymph Nodes Eval*
62	RX Summ—Reg LN Examined		119	CS Mets Eval*
63	RX Summ—Reconstruct 1st		120	Primary by international rules
64	Reason for no surgery*		121	ER Status Recode Breast Cancer (1990+)*
65	RX Summ—Radiation*		122	PR Status Recode Breast Cancer (1990+)*
66	RX Summ—Rad to CNS		123	CS Schema -AJCC 6th ed (previously calledv1)
67	RX Summ—Surg/Rad Seq		124	S Site-Specific Factor 8*
68	RX Summ—Surgery type		125	CS Site-Specific Factor 10*
69	RX Summ—Surg site 98-02		126	CS Site-Specific Factor 11*
70	RX Summ—Scope Reg		127	CS Site-Specific Factor 13*
71	RX Summ—Surg Oth 98-02		128	CS Site-Specific Factor 15*
72	SEER record number		129	CS Site-Specific Factor 16*
73	Over-ride age/site/morph		130	Lymph vascular invasion*
74	Over-ride seqno/dxconf		131	Survival months*
75	Over-ride site/lat/seqno		132	Survival months flag
76	Over-ride surg/dxconf		133	Survival months – presumed alive
77	Over-ride site/type		134	Survival months flag – presumed alive
78	Over-ride histology		135	Insurance recode (2007+)
79	Over-ride report source		136	Derived AJCC-7 T
80	Over-ride ill-define site		137	Derived AJCC-7 N
81	Over-ride leuk, lymph		138	Derived AJCC-7 M
82	Over-ride site/behavior		139	Derived AJCC-7 Stage Grp
83	Over-ride site/eod/dx dt		140	Breast Adjusted AJCC 6th T (1988+)*
84	Over-ride site/lat/eod		141	Breast Adjusted AJCC 6th N (1988+)*
85	Over-ride site/lat/morph		142	Breast Adjusted AJCC 6th M (1988+)*
86	SEER type of follow-up		143	Breast Adjusted AJCC 6th Stage (1988+)*
87	Age recode <1 year olds*		144	CS Site-Specific Factor 7*
88	Site recode ICD-O-3/WHO 2008*		145	CS Site-Specific Factor 9*
89	Recode ICD-O-2 to 9		146	CS Site-Specific Factor 12*
90	Recode ICD-O-2 to 10		147	Derived HER2 Recode (2010+)
91	ICCC site recode ICD-O-3/WHO 2008		148	Breast Subtype (2010+)
92	ICCC site rec extended ICD-O-3/WHO 2008		149	Birthplace – country
93	Behavior Recode for Analysis		150	Birthplace – state
94	Histology Recode—Broad Groupings		151	Lymphomas: Ann Arbor Staging (1983+)
95	Histology Recode—Brain Groupings			

Appendix B. Description of selected variables using proposed method (Predictor variables)

Number	Predictor variables	Description
1	Race/ethnicity	It indicates ethnicity and race of patients.
2	Laterality	It describes the side of a paired organ or side of the body on which the reportable tumor originated.
3	Histology	It describes the microscopic composition of cells and/or tissue for a specific primary. The histology is a basis for staging and determination of treatment options.
4	Grade	It describes a tumor in terms of how abnormal the tumor cells are compared to normal cells.
5	Radiation	This variable indicates the method of radiation therapy performed as part of the first course of treatment.
6	Age at diagnosis	It represents the age of the patient at diagnosis for this cancer.
7	Num_Nodes	It records the total number of regional lymph nodes that were removed and examined by the pathologist.
8	Num_positive_nodes	It records the exact number of regional lymph nodes examined by the pathologist that were found to contain metastases.
9	Tumor Size	Information on tumor size. It records the largest dimension of the primary tumor in millimeters.
10	Number of primaries	It describes the number of all reportable malignant, in situ, benign, and borderline primary tumors, which occur over the lifetime of a patient.

17

Data Extraction using Content-Based Handles

A. Pouramini[*], S. Khaje Hassani and Sh. Nasiri

Department of Computer Engineering, University of Sirjan Technology, Sirjan, Iran.

Corresponding author: pouramini@sirjantehc.ac.ir (A. Pouramini).

Abstract
In this paper, we present an approach and a visual tool called Handle-based Wrapper (HWrap) for creating web wrappers to extract data records from web pages. In our approach, we rely mainly on the visible page content to identify the data regions on a web page. In our extraction algorithm, we were inspired by the way a human user scans the page content for a specific data. In particular, we use text features such as textual delimiters, keywords, constants or text patterns, which we call *handles*, to construct patterns for the target data regions and data records. We offer a polynomial algorithm, in which these patterns are checked against the page elements in a mixed bottom-up and top-down traverse of the DOM-tree. The extracted data is directly mapped onto a hierarchical XML structure, which forms the output of the wrapper. The wrappers that are generated by this method are robust and independent of the HTML structure. Therefore, they can be adapted to similar websites to gather and integrate information.

Keywords: *Web Data Record Extraction, Web Wrapper Generation, Web Information Extraction.*

1. Introduction

Extracting structured data from web pages has many applications in different areas including business and competitive intelligence, comparison shopping, customizable Web information gathering, and so on. [1]. Many research works have proposed methods to analyze web documents and extract their information in structured formats automatically; these proposals are commonly referred to as *information extractors* or *wrappers* [2-4]. These methods range from hard-coded wrappers to unsupervised wrapper induction methods. They vary mainly in the degree of automation they provide by reducing the human efforts. However, providing a higher automation can lead to a lower accuracy and a lesser flexibility [1].

Different approaches to wrapper generation model a web page in different ways. The most common approach is to work on the DOM-tree as the HTML structure of a document [2-4]. However, some other works claim that HTML is mainly used for the presentation layer. Therefore, it is not accurate enough to discriminate different semantic portions of a web document [8 ,10-12]. Moreover, as the complexity of typical web documents increases, information extractors have to analyze more and more irrelevant regions that have an impact on both efficiency and effectiveness [7, 10]. This has motivated a number of researchers to work on *region extractors* as a means to relieve information extractors from the burden of analyzing many regions of a web document that do not contain any relevant information [6-17].

From this viewpoint, a region is defined as an HTML fragment that shows information about an item or several related items when it is rendered on a web browser. Such items can be data records, e.g. information about products, goods, services or pieces of news, headers with navigation menus, footers with contact information or sidebars with advertisements, etc. The difference between region extractors and information extractors or wrappers is that the wrappers focus on extracting and structuring data records and their attributes, whereas region extractors focus on identifying the HTML fragments that contain this information.

In this paper, we present a supervised method to define patterns for the data regions on a webpage. Then we present an algorithm to apply the resulting patterns to a webpage.

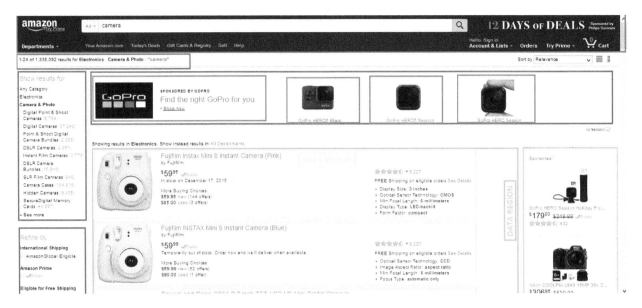

Figure 1. A sample results page of a website for "camera".

In our approach, we mainly rely on the page's visible content to locate the data regions and data records. As a result, the resulting wrappers are robust and easier to maintain. Moreover, they can be adapted to multiple websites with similar content structure to gather and integrate information from various sources. In the following sections, after reviewing the existing approaches, we present our data extraction method and an algorithm to implement it.

2. Related works

As mentioned before, a region extractor can be considered as a part of an information extractor or as a stand-alone application. Since in our method we focus on identifying data regions on a web page, we first review some proposals for extracting data regions from web documents.

Embley et al. [12] have proposed a method to extract the data records from the largest data region in a web document. It is an unsupervised method, which makes the following assumptions to identify data regions. There is a unique data region that is the largest region in the web document. This region contains multiple data records. Some tags are more likely to be data record separators based on their type and their occurrences. Finally, an ontology can help identify data records.

Some of the heuristics proposed by Embley et al. have been used in other region extractors [13]. For example, OMINI assumes that the main data region corresponds to the subtree with the largest number of children.

Mining Data Records [14] (or MDR for short) is another region extractor that aims to extract data records. It assumes that a data region contains

repetitive structures in a document. Each repetitive structure inside a data region is a data record, and they are usually rendered inside tables and forms. There are other methods such as TPC and U-REST that search for repetitive and similar structures in a document to identify data regions [16, 17, 21]. Some of the assumptions they make include a data region containing multiple contiguous or non-contiguous data records. The data records have similar HTML structures, have small separators and are rendered similarly, visually aligned.

One of the most-cited region extractors is VIPS [8]. It is a vision-based approach to build the content structure of a web page by exploring the visual characteristic of the page elements and not only relying on their HTML hierarchical structure. The algorithm divides a web page into a collection of contiguous regions based on their visual properties. For example, if the background color of a child node is different from the background color of its parent, that child is counted as a sub-region. Figure 1 shows the regions returned by VIPS on a sample web page of Amazon website. Note that VIPS only identifies and separates regions in a web document; it is the user's responsibility to select the regions of interest (e.g. the green boxes in Figure 1).

Subsequently, some approaches to information extraction used the regions returned by VIPS as the basis for detecting and extracting informative regions. VSDR, ViDRE, and RIPB are some examples of such methods [9, 10, 15]. For example, RIPB [15] is a supervised method that requires a few examples of data records. Then a DOM-tree is built for each example using a tree alignment method.

Figure 2. Identifying handles on a web page in our proposed system, HWrap.

These trees constitute tag patterns or the extraction rules. To extract data from an input document, the algorithm uses VIPS to segment the document into a collection of candidate regions. It then compares these regions with the tag patterns and returns the regions with the highest score. The similarity function is based on the tree-edit distance [18, 19]. In general, the proposed methods search for repetitive structures to identify data regions. As a result, they require the web page to contain at least two data records for the region extractor to work. Most of them are unsupervised and have assumptions about the structure of the data regions in a web document. Besides these assumptions about the layout of data regions, some may use an ontology [12, 13, 20]. While these unsupervised methods are scalable, they lack flexibility. Also, they may need many examples at the learning phrase. They often rely on the following algorithms to search a web document for data records: tree matching, string matching, and clustering [1, 18].

The majority of the proposed methods rely directly or indirectly on the DOM-tree or HTML tags. Some of them work on the region tree produced by VIPS [9, 10, 15]. This enables them to utilize visual information of the rendered page elements such as the position and the rendering box of each element to increase their accuracy. As a consequence, this makes it difficult to apply them to free-text documents whose contents do not rely heavily on HTML tags.

In the next section, we present our approach to identify data regions. We explain how our approach is different from the existing approaches.

3. Our approach

Figure 2 shows an example of a data-rich web page containing multiple instances of a data record. In such web pages, the HTML elements like table cells and divisions are frequently used to separate data records. Therefore, the DOM-tree is almost reliable to identify data regions. However, the main drawback of the approaches that mainly rely on the HTML structure is the lack of flexibility. They may use absolute HTML paths to locate an item. This approach is likely to fail when minor changes occur in the target HTML structure. Moreover, In the web of today, it is very common to use only DIV tags and describe the "semantics" of a particular division using style-sheet classes (CSS files). In this respect, the class name is perhaps the most notable semantic value among the element's attributes.

Our method basically relies on the DOM-Tree. However, we use the DOM-tree to make patterns based on delimiters and textual keywords in the content of a data record which is enclosed in one or more DOM-tree nodes. We assume that data regions are contiguous portions on a web page, comprised of one node or a range of nodes in the DOM-tree. To make the data region patterns independent of the DOM structure, we create them on the top of the page visible content. Our method is supervised, which means that we require the user to create the required patterns on a sample web page. However, as a future work, we aim to extract these patterns using some heuristics and an unsupervised learning.

In our method, we are inspired by the way people typically look for data on a web page. A human reader may scan a web page top-down or bottom-up, looking for signs to recognize the page structure. They rely on visual cues on the page (fonts, colors, text or link density) as well as semantic cues or text signals (titles, highlighted words, keywords, constants) to get a mental image of the content structure. We refer to such textual signals with the term *handle* throughout this paper. A handle can be a visible element that marks the start or end of a data region or it can be a textual element or a regular expression in the visible text of a data region so that it distinguishes the data region from the rest of the page. In data-rich web pages, which are the main target of this work, such handles are prevalent. For example, figure 2 shows a web page containing the search results for a product, that includes multiple instances of the product. In such pages, there is usually the phrase "Search Results" or the pattern "number + 'results'" somewhere above a list of items. Such a phrase or text pattern based on it (regular expression) can establish a handle for identifying the start of a data region. As another example, in each product item, fields such as the product name, the price or the shipping details can establish handles to distinguish the product region. Such elements are not tailored to the template of the website, and thus they are less affected by modifications and revisions to the layout. In the next section, we explain how a wrapper can be built using handles.

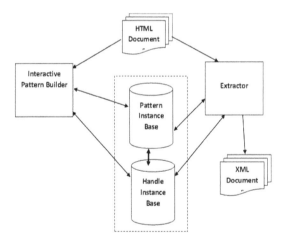

Figure 3. Architecture of HWrap.

3.1. Interactive wrapper generation

The overall architecture of HWrap wrapper generation toolkit is shown in figure 3. It consists of the following modules:

- The *Interactive Pattern Builder* provides the user interface that allows a user to visually specify the desired extraction patterns. The patterns are created by specifying one or more handles on a sample web page. The handles are saved

into *Handle Instance Base*, and are indexed using a unique key. The created patterns are separately saved into another file called *Pattern Instance Base*, where they have some external references to the handles. These instance bases can be also stored as separate tables in a relational database.

- The *extractor* is the extraction engine that is provided with one or more web documents and the instance bases of handles and patterns. It identifies and extracts data records from the input documents and save them into separate XML documents, one per each input document. It can be used for extracting data from the pages of one or more websites that share common patterns within their content. In that case, the output of different documents can be integrated into a single output XML document.

In what follows, we describe the steps required for creating a wrapper in our proposed system.

3.1.1. Creating handles

The user loads a sample page into an embedded web browser to specify handles (see Figure 2). To facilitate this task, the page elements get highlighted as the user hover the mouse pointer over each element. After selecting an element, a pop-up allows the user for creating a handle based on some of the element's properties. This window is shown in figure 4 (Left). As seen in this figure, in addition to the text or a text pattern within the content, the user can create a handle using the values of some more constant attributes such as *id* and *class name* (e.g. the "*main*" value for the identifier of the main division of the page). These values can also be specified using a regular expression.

3.1.2. Creating region patterns

After creating handles, the user must specify how target data regions are identified by using these handles. The user creates region patterns based on one or more handles. Through this paper, we refer to such region patterns with the term *pattern*. Figure 4 (Right) shows different ways to create a pattern using the given handles.

For a single handle, the possible patterns are:

- *Self*: The region enclosed by the node that matches the handle.

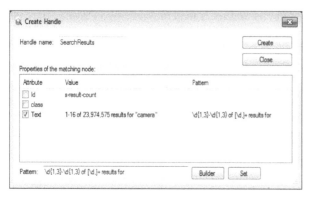 

Figure 4. Screenshot of dialog boxes for creating handles (left) and patterns (right).

- *Parent*: The region enclosed by the handle's parent node (container node of the handle).
- Following: The region following the handle.
- Preceding: The region preceding the handle.

For multiple handles, a region pattern can be specified using the following options:

- *Common ancestor*: The region enclosed by the container of two or more handles.
- *Between*: The region that lies between two handles.

Each pattern can be designated either for data extraction purpose or for restricting the location of the other patterns. To illustrate how these patterns are used in the data extraction process, let us return to our previous example of a web page containing the results of a search for a product. Suppose we want to identify the region that encloses the list of the product items. We create a handle using an element containing the text "Search Results" to mark the beginning of this region. We then create the target pattern named "Products" using this handle and the "Following" option. This pattern matches a region containing the elements that follow the handle in the document. In order to restrict the length of this region, we can find another handle to mark the end of it. For example, "page navigation bar", which usually appears under a search results, is a suitable candidate for this purpose. Finally, the pattern can be created using these two handles and the "Between" option. As another example, suppose we want to create a pattern for the region enclosing each product. We first identify two handles within a product item, such as the *price* and the *shipping details*. A

handle for the price can be created using a text pattern that matches a price value and currency (e.g. $NN.NN). Similarly, for the shipping information, the handle can be created using the "Ship" or "Get it by" keywords, and a text pattern for a calendar date (e.g. "Get it by Month Day" or "Ships within N days"). Alternatively, any constant keyword repeating in all the product items, such as "Add to Cart", can be a candidate for creating a handle. Having these handles, we create the pattern "Product" as the common ancestor or the immediate container of these handles. To restrict the occurrence of this pattern to a certain part of the page, we can assign it a parent pattern from the list of the previously defined patterns (e.g. "Products").

3.2. Data extraction algorithm

In this section the data extraction algorithm is described. The handles and the patterns created in the previous section are input to this algorithm (see Algorithm 1). It is mainly a recursive function that is initially called with the root of the DOM-tree (body element) and traverses its nodes in depth-first manner. However, the algorithm may backtrack and travers a node for several times.

First, the input node is checked against the list of handles. If no match found, the function is recursively called with the child nodes. Otherwise, the pattern associated with the matching handle is retrieved from the list of patterns. Let's name this pattern P. If P has a parent pattern that has not been matched, it is ignored and the algorithm continues with the rest of the nodes. Otherwise, the state of P is updated to "Open" or "Closed" depending on the handle that has been matched. If P has been defined as a region over a node (Self, Parent and Common Ancestor options), the corresponding node in the DOM-tree is retrieved. Let's name this node *PNode*.

Algorithm 1 Data Extraction Algorithm

```
function Extract(node)
        handle ← MatchHandle(node, handles)
        if (handle !=null) then
            pattern ← GetPattern(handle, patterns)
            if (pattern = null or pattern.Parent ≠ "Open") then
                return null
            end if
            UpdatePatternState(pattern, handle)
            patternNode ← FindNode(pattern)
            if (pattern.ExtractDataFlag) then
                ExtractData (pattern, patternNode)
            end if
            if (patternNode ≠ null and pattern.Node ≠ patternNode) then
                ▶ the data region hasn't been previously evaluated
                pattern.Node ← patternNode
                if (pattern.hasChild) then
                    return pattern
                end if
            end if
        else
            for (i ← 0; i ≤ node.children; i ← i + 1) do
                child ← node.children[i]
                prevPattern ← curPattern
                curPattern ← Extract(child)
                if (prevPattern ≠ null and prevPattern.State = "Open") then
                    prevPattern.State ← "Closed"
                end if
                if (curPattern ≠ null and curPattern.Node ≠ null) then
                ▶ then the children of the pattern node musb be reevaluated
                    if (curPattern.Node = child) then
                        curPattern.State = "Open"
                        i ← i -1 ▶ decrement the counter to reevaluate the child
                    else
                        return curPattern ▶ return the pattern up the stack
                    end if
                end if
            end for
        end if
        return null
end function
```

PNode encloses a portion of the page which corresponds to the region specified by P. After matching *P*, if it has been designated for data extraction, its content is added to the output XML structure as an XML node with the same name as the *P*'s name. If *P* has a parent pattern, this node is placed under a node that represents its parent. Finally, if *P* has one or more child patterns, the function must reevaluate the *PNode*'s children once again to match the child patterns. To do this, the *P* instance including a pointer to *PNode* is returned to the function calling point in the *"for"* loop (line 24 in Algorithm 1). At this point, the algorithm steps back (in the case of Self) or traverse up (in the cases of Parent and Common Ancestor) to find the *PNode* in order to reevaluate its child nodes (see Algorithm 1 (continued)).

3.2.1. Time complexity

The time complexity of this algorithm is polynomial and depends on the size of the DOM-tree and the number of handles and patterns. In the best case, if the algorithm does not traverse back to revisit a node (traversing a node twice), then the

time complexity is $O(N)$, where N is the number of the DOM-tree nodes. The explanation is as what follows. The algorithm is called N times, one call per each node of the DOM-tree. On each call, the input node is checked against the list of handles (*MatchHandle* at line 2), and if a match is found, a pattern is retrieved from the list of patterns (*GetPattern* at line 4). Searching through the list of handles and patterns depends on the number of handles, H, and the number of patterns, P. Therefore, $O(logH+logP)$ is the total time for these operations. The runtime of other functions in the algorithm is roughly $O(1)$. The *FindNode* function at line 9 returns either the current node (in the case of the Self option) or an ancestor of the input node (in the cases of the Parent and Common ancestor options). It is supposed that the immediate ancestor of any two handle nodes, from which one is the current node, is in the first few levels directly above the current node in the DOM-tree. Also the *ExtractData* at line 16 receives a reference to the pattern node, and therefore, extracting its content takes $O(1)$. Since, in the best case, the number of patterns and handles is not considerable, we can ignore the *(logH+logP)* term, and the time complexity is roughly *O(N)*.

In the worst case, when most of the patterns are defined using either "Parent" or "Common Ancestor" options, the algorithm's time complexity is $O(N^2 logN)$. The explanation is as what follows. In the worst case, for each node of the DOM-tree, at most one handle can be defined to match that node, and one pattern can be defined to match the region enclosed by this node. The algorithm, as before, is called *N* times. On each call, after matching a pattern, a sub-tree must be revisited, which in the worst case will be the entire DOM-tree; therefore, *N* is multiplied by *N* in the formula. *O(logH + logP)*, as before, is the time for searching through the lists of handles and patterns. By bounding *P* and *H* to *N*, the time complexity of these operations is *O(logN)*. The time complexity of the *FindNode* function is similarly *O(logN)* in the worst case because the algorithm must traverse the DOM-tree up to the root and it takes *O(logN)*. Therefore, the total time of the algorithm will be $O(N^2 logN)$, which is again polynomial. However, this is a very loose bound and in practice the time complexity is near to *O(N)*.

3.3. Data extraction and integration

Figure 5 displays the result of applying the extraction algorithm to the web page shown in fig. 2. In this structure, each pattern forms an XML node, which is nested in another node that corresponds to its parent. If the user desires to extract any specific data, he must first create an appropriate pattern for the region that encloses that data and mark it for data extraction ("Extract Data" checkbox in the form shown in Figure 4). As seen in fgure 5, the exact HTML source code of each product item is added to the "Product" node in the output XML tree. This code can be further processed to extract the subfields (e.g. price, bids, and supplier) or be directly rendered in a web browser to be displayed to the user for visual comparison.

If the user defines a pattern more generally by ignoring details, the resulting wrapper can be reused for gathering and integrating data from different websites that have this pattern in common. In some cases, minor changes are required to adapt an existing handle or pattern to a new website. Therefore, the user often needs to follow the same procedure to create wrappers for similar websites, and this makes creating them easier. To facilitate this process, the Pattern Builder automatically highlights the matching items on the page when the user loads a previously created pattern file.

On the other hand, the user can define a pattern in more details when he wants to extract some fields of a data record. To do so, he must create a pattern for each target filed inside the pattern that has been defined for the data record. For example, to extract the price field from each product and store it as a child node of the product's node in the XML tree, an appropriate pattern can be defined using the "price" handle, the "Self" option, and the "Products" pattern as its parent.

4. Experimental results

We tested the accuracy and expressiveness of our proposed method on a number of websites including Amazon, eBay, IMDB, world weather, and YouTube (see Table 1). We collected 30 pages from each website. Table 1 shows the number of handles and patterns required to identify the data records on each website.

In all cases, the website was wrapable and required a few number of handles to identify the data records. Similar to the example reviewed through this paper, the handles were easily identifiable on a sample web page. The "Common ancestor" option was very useful to specify a record by identifying two or more handles within it. The experiments show that by providing suitable handles and patterns, the system can achieve a high performance of 98.9% in F-Measure.

Table 1. Evaluation of generated wrappers.

Website	# Handles	# Patterns	Precision	Recall	F-Score
Amazon	5	3	98.5	100	99.2
eBay	5	3	98.7	100	99.3
IMDB Search	5	4	97.6	100	98.7
World Weather	4	2	98.4	99.5	98.9
Youtube	4	3	97.3	98.9	98.1
Average			98.1	99.7	98.9

The precision refers to the average fraction of regions that are identified by the system and correspond to the actual data regions. Recall refers to the average fraction of actual data regions that are identified by the system. The higher recall values in table 1 indicate that most of the actual data regions were identified by our method. However, the lower performance values indicate that some of the identified regions are not the actual data regions. For example, they can be some records on the advertisement area beside the main data region (see Figure 1).

The performance of our proposed system is close to the performances reported by the related works in this filed. Table 2 shows the performance measures reported by some of the proposals that were reviewed in the "Related Works" section.

Table 2. Performance of some related works.

Proposal	Precision	Recall
OMINI	100	94
MDR	100	99.8
RIPB	98.1	95.7
TPC	96.	97.0
VSDR	89	97.6

Note that they are not comparable side-by-side because they were calculated on different datasets. However, they can provide a rough reference for comparison. As is seen, the performance of our proposed method, especially in terms of recall, is higher than most of these proposals. One reason is that most of these methods are unsupervised and search for repetitive structures within the page. Therefore, when a data record has a slightly different structure than the rest, it can be ignored. Since our method relies on the content of the data records rather than their internal structures, it can better cover such structural dissimilarities in data records.

Table 3 shows the percentage of the handles that are common among the websites used in the experiment. Since our method relies on the visible content and textual identifiers, common handles can be found in the websites that offer a similar service. For example, in most shopping websites, the *price* and *shipping details* fields are among a product's information, and thus they can be used to identify a product item by selecting "Common Ancestors" Option. Note that this option finds the closest ancestor that encloses all the specified handles regardless of the specific structure of each website and the number of nesting elements.

Table 3. Shopping websites with similar handles.

Website	Common Handles
eBay	80%
DHGate	80%
AliExpress	80%
Etsy	50%

5. Conclusion and future works

In this paper, we presented an approach to the problem of extracting data records from web pages. We based our approach on the textual handles within the visible content of the web page. We were inspired by the way a human user scans a web page for the data of interest. Handles serve as identifiers for a data region so that a pattern can be constructed on the basis of one or more handles. Each pattern may be treated as the sub-pattern of another pattern. Given these patterns, we proposed a data extraction algorithm. This algorithm traverses the DOM-tree nodes in a mixed top-down and bottom-up manner to match the given handles and patterns. This algorithm is time-polynomial and in the worst case, has $O(N^2 logN)$ time complexity. However, in the average case, it grows linearly with the number of nodes $(O(N))$. As our proposed method relies mainly on the page visible content rather than the HTML structure, the generated wrappers are robust and maintainable. We showed that they could be adapted to gather data from similar web pages and integrate them into an XML document.

In this paper, we defined a pattern for a data region using one or several handles. In addition, we provided a means to restrict the location of a pattern inside another pattern. As a future work, we aim to provide an option to define a pattern based on handles and other patterns. For instance, a pattern can be defined as the common ancestor of two existing patterns or one handle and one existing pattern. For example, the data region enclosing several product records can be defined as the common ancestor of two product patterns.

As another work, we aim to find the required handles and patterns on a web page using an unsupervised method similar to the works reviewed in the "related works" section. Then we use these patterns in our proposed algorithm to extract the data records.

References

[1] Ferrara, E., De Meo, P., Fiumara, G., & Baumgartner, R. (2014, November). Web data extraction, applications and techniques: A survey. Knowledge-Based Systems, vol. 70, no. 1, pp. 301-323.

[2] Sahuguet, A., & Azavant, F. (1999, September). Building light-weight wrappers for legacy web data-sources using W4F. In Proceeding of VLDB, pp. 738-741.

[3] Liu, L., Pu, C., & Han, W. (2000). XWRAP: An XML-enabled wrapper construction system for web information sources. In Data Engineering Proceedings. 16th International Conference on (pp. 611-621). IEEE.

[4] Gottlob, G., Koch, C., Baumgartner, R., Herzog, M., & Flesca, S. (2004, June). The Lixto data extraction project: back and forth between theory and practice. In Proceedings of the twenty-third ACM SIGMOD-SIGACT-SIGART symposium on Principles of database systems (pp. 1-12). ACM.

[5] Wang, J., & Lochovsky, F. H. (2003, May). Data extraction and label assignment for web databases. In

Proceedings of the 12th international conference on World Wide Web (pp. 187-196). ACM.

[6] Bing, L., Lam, W., & Gu, Y. (2011, October). Towards a unified solution: data record region detection and segmentation. In Proceedings of the 20th ACM international conference on Information and knowledge management (pp. 1265-1274). ACM.

[7] Wang, J., & Lochovsky, F. H. (2002, December). Data-rich section extraction from html pages. In Web Information Systems Engineering, 2002. WISE 2002. Proceedings of the Third International Conference on (pp. 313-322). IEEE.

[8] Cai, D., Yu, S., Wen, J. R., & Ma, W. Y. (2003). VIPS: A vision-based page segmentation algorithm. Microsoft technical report, MSR-TR-2003-79

[9] Liu, W., Meng, X., & Meng, W. (2006, July). Vision-based web data records extraction. In Proc. 9th international workshop on the web and databases (pp. 20-25).

[10] Li, L., Liu, Y., Obregon, A., & Weatherston, M. (2007, August). Visual segmentation-based data record extraction from web documents. In Information Reuse and Integration, 2007. IRI 2007. IEEE International Conference on (pp. 502-507). IEEE.

[11] Li, L., Liu, Y., Obregon, A., & Weatherston, M. (2007, August). Visual segmentation-based data record extraction from web documents. In Information Reuse and Integration, 2007. IRI 2007. IEEE International Conference on (pp. 502-507). IEEE.

[12] Embley, D. W., Jiang, Y., & Ng, Y. K. (1999, June). Record-boundary discovery in Web documents. In ACM SIGMOD Record (vol. 28, no. 2, pp. 467-478). ACM.

[13] Buttler, D., Liu, L., & Pu, C. (2001, April). A fully automated object extraction system for the World Wide Web. In Distributed Computing Systems, 2001. 21st International Conference on. (pp. 361-370). IEEE.

[14] Liu, B., Grossman, R., & Zhai, Y. (2004). Mining web pages for data records. IEEE Intelligent Systems, vol. 19, no. 6, pp. 49-55.

[15] Kang, J., & Choi, J. (2008). Recognising Informative Web Page Blocks Using Visual Segmentation for Efficient Information Extraction. J. UCS, vol. 14, no. 11, pp. 1893-1910.

[16] Shen, Y. K., & Karger, D. R. (2007, May). U-REST: an unsupervised record extraction system. In Proceedings of the 16th international conference on World Wide Web (pp. 1347-1348). ACM.

[17] Miao, G., Tatemura, J., Hsiung, W. P., Sawires, A., & Moser, L. E. (2009, April). Extracting data records from the web using tag path clustering. In Proceedings of the 18th international conference on World wide web (pp. 981-990). ACM.

[18] Zhai, Y., & Liu, B. (2005, May). Web data extraction based on partial tree alignment. In Proceedings of the 14th international conference on World Wide Web (pp. 76-85). ACM.

[19] Bille, P. (2005). A survey on tree edit distance and related problems. Theoretical computer science, vol. 337, no. 1, pp. 217-239.

[20] Su, W., Wang, J., & Lochovsky, F. H. (2009). ODE: Ontology-assisted data extraction. ACM Transactions on Database Systems (TODS), vol. 34, no. 2, pp. 12-17.

[21] Naeem, M., Bilal Khan, M., & Tanvir Afzal, M. (2013). Expert Discovery: A web mining approach Journal of AI and Data Mining: Shahrood University of Technology, vol. 1, no. 1, pp. 35-47.

18

Extracting Prior Knowledge from Data Distribution to Migrate from Blind to Semi-Supervised Clustering

Z. Sedighi[*] and R. Boostani

Electrical & Computer Department, Shiraz University, Shiraz, Iran.

*Corresponding author: sedighi.63@gmail.com (Z. Sedighi).

Abstract
Although several works have been conducted to improve the clustering efficiency, most of the state-of-art schemes suffer from the lack of robustness and stability. This paper aims to propose an efficient approach to elicit a prior knowledge in terms of must-link and cannot-link from the estimated distribution of raw data to convert a blind clustering problem into a semi-supervised one. In order to estimate the density distribution of data, the Weibull Mixture Model is utilized due to its high flexibility. Another contribution of this work is to propose a new hill and valley seeking algorithm to find the constraints for a semi-supervised algorithm. The proposed valley-seeking algorithm does not require any user-defined parameter. It is assumed that each dominant density peak stands on a cluster center; therefore, the neighbor samples of each center are considered as the must-link samples, while the near-centroid samples belonging to different clusters are considered as the cannot-link ones. The proposed approach is applied to a standard image dataset (designed for clustering evaluation) of Berkeley University along with some UCI datasets. The results achieved on both databases demonstrate the superiority of the proposed method compared to the conventional clustering ones.

Keywords: *Semi-supervised, Clustering, Valley-seeking Scheme, Weibull Mixture Model.*

1. Introduction

Clustering techniques are used in a vast variety of data mining applications such as stream mining [15], image segmentation (clustering)[13], multi-objective systems [21], and spam filtering [9]. The conventional strategies of cluster forming are hierarchical [11], flat [17], graph-based [8], and density-based [14]. Each category of the mentioned methods has its own drawbacks. For instance, incorporating the tree structure into the clustering has led to the development of hierarchical clustering algorithms such as divisive and agglomerative (e.g. single and complete linkage) [5, 22], whereas hierarchical algorithms are faced with some challenges such as selecting an effective termination criterion, lack of back-tracking, and heavy computational burden. Despite the simplicity of the flat clustering methods such as *K*-means [10], they still suffer from the lack of learning stability due to high sensitivity of their performance to their initial cluster centers. Graph-based algorithms like

shared nearest neighbor (SNN) [6] prune a considerable number of instances as noisy samples, and do not assign them to any cluster. Density-based clustering methods try to form clusters in the directions of dense regions [20]. Nevertheless, among the mentioned cluster forming algorithms, density-based methods have attracted much attention since they try to make a relation among the samples in the dense regions and then consider each set of connected samples as a cluster. Although each density-based algorithm has its own shortcomings, this approach is more consistent with the nature of data.

In the case of having a prior knowledge about a part of our samples in terms of must-link and cannot-link connections, the problem of blind clustering is converted into semi-supervised clustering. Extracting such constraints require the confirmation of experts, which is an expensive and time-consuming process; consequently, it is a big deal to convert an unsupervised problem into a semi-supervised one, and the conventional methods fail to make this conversion for a wide range of problems. The main contribution of this work is to elicit a prior knowledge from the nature of data and then convert a blind clustering problem into a semi-supervised one.

1.1 Literature review

To the best of the authors' knowledge, there is no research work similar to the method proposed in this paper. Nevertheless, among different strategies of clustering (e.g. hierarchical, flat, graph-based, and density-based), it can be said that the family of density-based clustering algorithms has the highest degree of similarity to the proposed approach. Therefore, the density-based clustering techniques are introduced here and their pros and cons are analyzed.

Density-based Spatial Clustering of Applications with Noise (DBSCAN) [7] is the most famous algorithm among the density-based clustering methods. In fact, other density-based schemes are known as different derivations of DBSCAN. This method allows us to form clusters with arbitrary shapes in the directions of dense regions. The strongest property of DBSCAN is its low sensitivity to noisy and outlier samples. Also the complexity of this algorithm is quite low due to doing just one time scanning for each point; consequently, DBSCAN is suitable for handling large datasets (big data), and is vastly applied to the data mining applications. Nevertheless, the main flaw of DBSCAN is its high sensitivity of its user-defined parameters. Moreover, this method is not capable of detecting the gradient of density within a cluster. In order to overcome this deficiency, distributed DBSCAN (DDBSCAN) is proposed to detect clusters that are in hierarchy or clusters with different densities separately [1]. In contrast to DBSCAN, DDBSCAN still suffers from a high computational complexity and is sensitive to the user-defined parameters.

Ordering Points to Identify the Clustering Structure (OPTICS) is an efficient algorithm that can be considered as an extension of the DB-Scan method in which all instances are evaluated one by one, and the suitable radius along with the nearest core point of each instance is determined [2]. In this way, all user-defined parameters for each instance are adaptively determined, and finally, an extended DB-Scan is run over the processed data. Therefore, solving the problem of parameter dependency in DBSCAN is one of the advantages of the OPTICS algorithm. Nevertheless, OPTICS cannot guarantee to find the optimum radius for each point, and finds a suitable radius for all instances.

Density-based clustering (DenClue) is another density-based clustering method, which first tries to find the whole distribution of data by finding the local distribution of samples using an influence function [12]. The estimated distribution of DenClue is better than that of DBSCAN in terms of quality since it locally estimates a certain kernel for each sub-space, while DBSCAN starts with a certain radius that definitely is not optimal for all regions. After computing the gradient of the estimated kernel density functions to find the density attractors, a hill-climbing algorithm tries to group the samples that are located in the vicinity of each density attractor. The bottleneck of this method appears when the dimension of data increases.

The main contribution of this work is to extract a prior knowledge in terms of the must-link and cannot-link constraints by estimating the data distribution [24]. Here, Weibull Mixture Model (WMM) was chosen to estimate the data distribution due to its flexibility to model each arbitrary cluster with a low number of Weibull functions [19]. Next, the distribution is partitioned into primary clusters by proposing an efficient valley-seeking algorithm. Consequently, the constraints are extracted from the primary clusters by recognizing the must-link samples as the samples located around the distribution of each hill (center of each cluster) and the cannot-link samples as the must-link samples of different clusters. By this trick, the blind clustering problem is automatically converted into a semi-supervised one. Finally, the most proper number of clusters is found according to the best Silhouette score. Although a few similar works have been carried out for clustering using WMM [16, 18], their valley-seeking algorithms require a few user-defined parameters that cannot be automatically found from the data, whereas in the proposed method, the suggested valley-seeking scheme does not require any parameter, and it is fully automated.

The rest of this paper is structured as what follows. Section 2 explains the details of the compared clustering methods, and next, the proposed approach is presented. Section 3 introduces the evaluation methods and expresses the datasets. In Section 4, the experimental results produced by each one of the methods are separately presented, and the benefits and shortcomings of each scheme are discussed. Finally, in Section 5, the paper is concluded and, at the end, a new horizon to the future works is presented.

2. Methods

In this part, our objective is to introduce the implementation details of the following algorithms: K-Means, DB-SCAN, OPTICS, DenClue, Single-Linkage, Complete-Linkage, and SNN. As we see, in addition to the density-based clustering methods, flat, hierarchical, and graph-based clustering methods are explained in this work. Next, the proposed method is expressed using WMM as the distribution estimator and a new valley-seeking algorithm to determine the clusters.

2.1. *K*-Means

K-means is the most famous and effective flat clustering scheme that has been utilized in many applications. This method is randomly initialized by a certain number of cluster centers (K) defined by the user. Then the samples are assigned to the nearest cluster center. At each step, each cluster center is updated according to the cluster samples, and the points are again assigned to the new centers. This process continues until changes of the clusters' centers do not exceed a pre-defined threshold in two successive iterations.

2.2. DB-SCAN

The procedure of DBSCAN clustering algorithm can be explained as what follows. At first, it randomly selects a point (p) and considers this point as the center of a circle with radius *Eps*. The algorithm checks whether at least the *MinPts* number of samples are located in that circle or not. If the answer is yes, this point is considered as a core point; in contrast, the neighbor samples are checked. *Eps* and *MinPts* are user-defined parameters but in most papers, the value for *MinPts* has been set to 4. The neighbors that are placed within the circle of each core point are called direct reachable, and those indirectly connected to this point are called indirect reachable. Next, the algorithm evaluates a new point of data if there is no density-connected point from previous core points and repeats the above steps until all points are processed.

2.3. OPTICS

The OPTICs algorithm is known as an extension of the DBSCAN algorithm, which tries to automatically optimize its parameters [2]. The main components of this algorithm include the core distance and the reachable distance. OPTICS finds the neighbors of each sample with different radiuses and compares the number of neighbors for each radius to the *MinPts* parameter. Similar to DBSCAN, the samples that can construct a cluster regarding the *MinPts* parameter are selected as the core points.

If the graph of radius/samples is drawn, the core point samples and their corresponding radius are determined [2]. Each core point with its connected neighbors regarding the adjusted reachable distance is considered as a cluster. In other words, OPTICS adaptively finds the radius for different regions, and each cluster is grown from the densest region of that cluster. This algorithm ensures us to find clusters with different densities. Moreover, OPTICS is sensitive to the density gradient within each cluster and divides the cluster into clusters with uniform density.

2.4. DenClue

Among the density-based clustering algorithms, DenClue is the most similar approach to the proposed method in this paper. DenClue has two important phases. In the first phase, the density function is estimated in terms of summation of influence functions. In the second one, each cluster is characterized as the samples located around a local maximum point of the overall probability density function. In the case of using the continuous influence function, the overall density function is continuous at each point, and the density attractors (clusters) can be derived by a hill-climbing method taking a gradient from the overall density function. The influence function, summation of influence functions to construct the density, and the gradient of the whole density function are presented in (1), (2) and (3), respectively.

$$f_{Gaussian}(x, x_i) = e^{-\frac{d(x,x_i)^2}{2\delta^2}} \tag{1}$$

$$f_{Gaussian}^{D}(x) = \sum_{i=1}^{N} e^{-\frac{d(x,x_i)^2}{2\delta^2}} \tag{2}$$

$$\nabla f_{Gaussian}^{D}(x) = \sum_{i=1}^{N} \frac{d(x,x_i)}{\delta^2} e^{-\frac{d(x,x_i)^2}{2\delta^2}} \tag{3}$$

where, $d(x,x_i)$ is the Euclidian distance between x and x_i, δ is the variance of each Gaussian (influence) function, and N is the number of influence functions to construct the density. As far as the noisy and outlier points are located in low-dense regions, these samples have a very low effect on the whole performance.

2.5. Shared Nearest Neighbor (SNN)

Most challenges occur when the clustering methods are faced with groups of samples with different population, different densities, different shapes or dataset with noisy and outlier values. The SNN method tries to deal with all the mentioned problems. The algorithm first finds the nearest neighbors of each data point, and then redefines the similarity between two points using the number of nearest neighbor points that are common between the two points as the edge weight that connects these two points in the graph. Using this new definition of similarity, SNN prunes the noise and outlier samples because they do not connect to any point. In contrast, SNN identifies core points and then creates clusters around the cores. These clusters do not contain all points but finely represent different sets of connected points as clusters.

2.6. Standard semi-supervised clustering

In the case of having no prior knowledge, the clustering becomes an unsupervised process, while in some applications, there is little information available about a subset of samples. The problem of clustering a set of samples when prior knowledge (in terms of the must-link and cannot-link samples) is available about subsets of samples is called the semi-supervised clustering method. The must-link and cannot-link samples are normally determined by experts. Since the cost of labeling or finding the hidden constraints is very high, just the constraints among a small subset of samples are determined [24]. Recent studies have shown that when these limitations (must-link and cannot-link samples) are fed to the clustering process, the accuracy of clustering is significantly increased.

2.7. Proposed algorithm

In spite of using the summation of Gaussian functions to estimate the distribution of data (e.g. GMM), here, the Weibull functions are employed, which can incorporate a degree of skewness to the components. It is obvious that by incorporating the shape parameter to the Weibull functions, we can build a complex distribution with a lower number of Weibull functions compared to the Gaussian functions. In the following, first the Weibull function is introduced, and then the Weibull Mixture Model (WMM) is explained, and finally, the proposed algorithm is expressed.

2.7.1. Weibull distribution

Weibull distribution is one of the most flexible distributions in statistics, which can be adapted to the distribution of data with a few data points. This function is more flexible than the Gaussian function because its parameters allow the Weibull shape to become asymmetric. In other words, it has a shape parameter that regulates the skewness of the function toward the left or right direction. The Weibull distribution is defined as follows:

$$f(x) = \begin{cases} \dfrac{\beta}{\alpha}(\dfrac{x-L}{\alpha})^{\beta-1} e^{-(\frac{x-L}{\alpha})} & x \geq L \\ \\ 0 & otherwise \end{cases} \quad (4)$$

where, α, β, and L are the scale, shape, and location parameters, respectively. For this distribution, $the\ \alpha\ and\ \beta$ parameters should be positive. L is often assumed to be zero, and in this case, the three-parameter Weibull distribution becomes a two-variable function that is more common. In the case of $L = 0$ and $\beta = 1$, this distribution forms a shape similar to an exponential distribution. Similarly, when $\beta = 3.25$, the distribution is almost as glaring as the normal distribution.

2.7.2. Weibull mixture model (WMM)

Murthy et al. [18] have introduced the multivariate Weibull mixture model, in which several Weibull functions are linearly summed by different weights in order to model each complex arbitrary distribution. The WMM model is composed as follows:

$$y_i = \sum_{j=1}^{m} a_{ij} y_{ij} \quad (5)$$

where, y_{ij} is the jth Weibull distribution with parameters α_{ij}, β_{ij}, and a_{ij} determining the weight of the jth Weibull function in the mixture model. The multivariable p dimensional Weibull function is described in (6):

$$R(x) = \prod_{i=1}^{p} \sum_{j=1}^{m} a_{ij} \exp\left\{-(\beta_{ij} x_i^{a_{ij}} + \frac{\beta x_0}{p})\right\} \quad (6)$$

where, $x_0 = Max(x_1, ..., x_p) > 0$. One of the methods used to find the final distribution, similar to determining the kernel density estimation, is to convolve each sample like Dirac delta function form to the multivariate Weibull distribution function of the observed data, which is explained as follows:

$$p_{KDE}(x) = R_{s-1}(x) \times p_s(x) = \sum_{i=1}^{N} \alpha_i R_s(x - x_i) \quad (7)$$

where, $p_s(x)$ is the Weibull distribution of a new example, $R_{(s-1)}(x)$ is the Weibull kernel for the observed data, and $\hat{p}_{KDE}(x)$ is the approximate kernel density estimation of the whole distribution at point x.

2.7.3. Gap statistic

In order to find the correct number of Weibull functions in WMM, the gap statistic method [19], as a well-known manner of estimating the number of clusters, is employed. Consider a d-dimensional dataset with n independent observations. Let $d(x,y)$ be the Euclidean distance between two observations x and y. Assume that the data is categorized in k different clusters $C_1, ...,C_k$, and $n_r = |C_r|$ is the number of data belonging to the cluster r. The average distance of samples within the rth cluster is denoted as D_r, which is determined as follows:

$$D_r = \sum_{x,y \in C_r} \frac{d(x,y)}{2n_r} \qquad (8)$$

and, w_k is the summation of the within class average distances of all k clusters:

$$w_k = \sum_{r=1}^{k} D_r \qquad (9)$$

The main idea of the gap statistic method [19] is the standardization of graph $log(w_k)$ by comparing its expectation under a suitable null reference distribution of data. The optimal number of clusters is the k at which w_k is the farthest point under this reference curve:

$$Gap_n(K) = E\{\log w_k\} \qquad (10)$$

where, $E(.)$ is the expectation of examples with size n from a reference distribution. The estimated value of k is the value that maximizes (10).

2.7.4. Eliciting constraints from density function

After training WMM with the right number of Weibull functions determined by gap statistics, the clusters should be extracted from the estimated distribution. Local maxima of the density function can be easily obtained by taking a gradient of that density. The points placed below each local hill are considered as the must-link points. Since these points are located on the densest region of the distribution, we can consider these neighbor points belonging to a cluster, and consider them as the must-link samples.

One of the questions in the described algorithm is that how many samples around each density mean (below the density hill) should be selected as the must-link samples. In order to answer this question, some parameters are defined. Let n_0 and N_0 be the number of samples in the clusters with the lowest and highest population, respectively.

Accordingly, the following relation describes the worst portion of populations among the clusters:

$$I = \frac{n_0}{N_0} \qquad (11)$$

The number of selected samples as must-link samples around the center of each cluster is determined as follows:

$$k_{min} = \frac{n_c}{k} \times I \qquad (12)$$

where, n_c is the total number of samples in the dataset and k is the number of clusters.

2.7.5. Eliciting clusters from estimated density

Similar to the most clustering algorithms, here, small-size clusters are eliminated, and their samples are assigned to the other clusters; therefore, to avoid the density peak of clusters being close together, the distance between two hills should exceed a threshold. In other words, within a large cluster, the distribution function might fluctuate; consequently, each local peak should not be considered as a center for a new cluster. Therefore, just those density hills can be considered as the center of clusters that have a significant distance to each other; in addition, each cluster center should be the maximum hill in its vicinity.

In order to find the number of clusters, after calculating the approximate number of clusters (k) using the gap statistic, the real number of clusters is considered in the interval [k/2, 2k], similar to the Iso-Data clustering algorithm [3]. After determining the constraints (described in the former part), the semi-supervised clustering algorithm is executed, and the clustering index is determined to assess how well the clusters are formed.

The Silhouette method is one of the famous clustering validation methods that evaluates a cluster according to the score of its samples [4]. In other words, it gives a score to each sample, which measures the belongingness of that sample to the located cluster compared to that of the other clusters.

For each data sample i, let $a(i)$ be its average dissimilarity to the other samples in that cluster and $b(i)$ be the lowest average dissimilarity between this sample to the other clusters. The silhouette score of the ith sample, denoted as $s(i)$, is defined as follows:

$$s(i) = \begin{cases} 1 - a(i)/b(i) & \text{if } a(i) \langle b(i) \\ 0 & \text{if } a(i) = b(i) \\ \dfrac{b(i)}{a(i)} - 1 & \text{if } a(i) \rangle b(i) \end{cases} \qquad (13)$$

From the above equation, it is clear that s(i) is limited in the interval of [-1,1]. As *s(i)* gets close to one, the proper silhouette score is achieved. For each cluster, the average of all silhouette scores of its samples measures the validity of that cluster. We used the summation of silhouette scores of all clusters as the goodness of the number of achieved clusters. The number of clusters that provides the highest silhouette score is determined as the best number of clusters. In order to clarify different stages of the proposed method, the following pseudo-code is presented in figure 1.

Set the initial number of clusters to k/2
For c = k/2:1:2k

- *Hills are obtained by taking a gradient from the estimated density.*
- *These points are then sorted in an ascending order.*
- *The first c numbers of them are selected.*
- *Set the threshold distance as the average distances of hills.*
- *The must-link samples are chosen as the set of k_{min} samples around each cluster center.*
- *The semi-supervised clustering algorithm is executed, and the clustering index is determined.*

   End

The best number of clusters is the one that maximizes the average silhouette score.

Figure 1. Pseudo-code of proposed algorithm.

3. Datasets and evaluation methods

In this section, at first, the datasets employed are described, and then the evaluation methods are introduced to assess the proposed method in comparison with the other implemented methods. In this work, both the labeled and unlabeled data are used to assess the clustering methods.

One way to validate the clustering method is to execute it on a standard dataset, in which the clusters are known as a priori; therefore, we can measure the clustering error. Here, a standard image dataset prepared in Berkeley University is used to assess the methods.

Here, some of the datasets in the UCI machine learning database are used to evaluate the compared methods. The selected datasets cover all the possible cases in terms of high and low input dimensions including noise and clean instances and different numbers of classes (here clusters).

Important features associated with these datasets are shown in table 1.

Table 1. Description of selected UCI datasets in terms of number of instances, dimensions, and classes.

Data sets	#Instances	#dimensions	#clusters
Iris	150	4	3
Bupa	345	6	2
Vehicle	846	18	4
Breast-cancer	286	9	2
Glass	214	9	6

4. Experimental results and discussion

In this section, the results of applying the proposed methods (described in Section 2) to the data (described in Section 3) are presented. In order to show the suitability of WMM, the proposed method is executed over the data distribution estimated by both GMM and WMM. The results obtained are presented in two sub-sections; Case#1 demonstrates the results on the selected UCI datasets and Case#2 exhibits the results on the image dataset. It must be noted that there are two approaches for evaluating a clustering method. The first approach uses a labeled data that is blindly (without label) applied to a clustering method such as that through the clustering learning. It means that learning of the clustering method is carried out without the use of data labels. In the second approach, the input data does not contain any label, and when the clustering algorithm groups the samples into clusters, the goodness of the algorithm is assessed using some criteria like mean square error, discriminability among the clusters via distance.

In this work, the first approach is utilized, in which after blind clustering, we can precisely determine the purity of the clusters as the clustering accuracy.

4.1. Case #1

The results observed in table 2 illustrate the accuracy of the clustering methods on the five selected UCI datasets (described in Table 1). After applying the silhouette method to select the best number of clusters, the clustering accuracies for different schemes are demonstrated in table 2.

As we can see, the proposed method by GMM and WMM provides significantly a much higher clustering accuracy compared to the other state-of-the-art clustering methods. By employing the same number of core functions (Gaussian and Weibull) to estimate the density of each dataset, the proposed method using WMM produces slightly better results than those of GMM. This supremacy implies the significance of WMM compared to GMM.

The number of employed core functions for each dataset is chosen through the cross-validation phase such that the selected number of core functions provides the highest value for the expectation maximization (EM). The selected number of core functions for the Iris, Bupa, Vehicle, Breast-Cancer, and Glass are 3, 2, 3, 2, and 5, respectively. One can say that the number of core functions by GMM and WMM is not necessarily equal; it is right but the selected number of core functions for GMM and WMM for each dataset is considered the minimum number core function selected by GMM and WMM. The reason of supremacy of WMM to GMM rises from the high capability of the Weibull function in moto estimate each arbitrary shape. Although when the number of Gaussian functions increases, they are able to model arbitrary shapes but in the case of a limited number of core functions, the Weibull function performs better than the Gaussian function.

Table 2. Clustering accuracies (in %) of compared clustering methods on selected UCI datasets.

Data sets	K-means	DBSCAN	OPTICS	DenClue	SNN	Proposed method by GMM	Presented method by WMM
Iris	86.7	68.7	69.6	72.0	65.4	90.5	95.1
Bupa	40.1	50.6	53.3	65.1	46.8	69.1	77.0
Vehicle	23.8	52.9	54.6	63.1	35.2	63.2	75.6
Breast-Cancer	62.4	65.5	66.2	68.8	50.9	70.1	79.5
Glass	56.1	35.3	38.7	45.1	20.5	56.7	64.1

The bar chart shown in figure 2 graphically shows the drastic superiority of the proposed method compared to the other implemented methods. In addition, the T-test is executed on several runs of the clustering algorithms, and the results of the proposed method are significantly ($P < 0.05$) superior to the counterparts.

It should be mentioned that like the Gaussian distribution, the Weibull distribution is also able to fit on a symmetric shape; but when the data distribution is crooked to the left or right, the Weibull function can easily be adapted to this asymmetry, while one Gaussian cannot be lonely fitted on a skewed distribution with a high

accuracy; therefore, several Gaussian functions need to be added for modeling such data distribution.

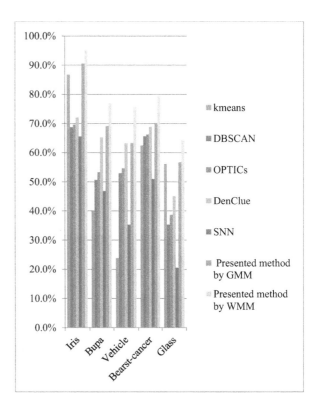

Figure 2. Clustering accuracy of compared clustering methods on UCI datasets.

Since the distribution of the input data is unknown in practice, using the Weibull functions enables us to deal better with the unknown data and finely arrange the samples in different clusters with arbitrary shapes. In addition, modeling each cluster with a very low number of Weibull functions provides good interpretability to describe the structure of data.

4.2. Case #2

In this part, the intensity values within each image are clustered (segmented) into uniform areas in which each area (cluster) contains the pixels with fairly similar intensity values. After applying each one of the clustering methods to the images, the segmented areas can be compared to the correct information in the dataset in order to determine the accuracy of each clustering method. The average clustering accuracies over the images for the mentioned clustering methods are represented in table 3. As we can see, the clustering accuracy of the proposed method is significantly higher than the other compared methods.

Table 3. Clustering accuracies (in %) of compared clustering methods on image clustering dataset.

Image number	K-means	DBSCAN	OPTICS	DenClue	SNN	Proposed method by GMM	Presented method by WMM
#8068	38.5	40.3	42.1	72.3	70.3	66	88.3
#3063	60.3	60.8	63.3	55.1	53.6	63	68.5
#6064	19.6	20.2	23.7	28.7	25.6	30	47.4

Figure 3 shows the segmented areas (clusters) for the image #8068 in the dataset by the implemented clustering methods.

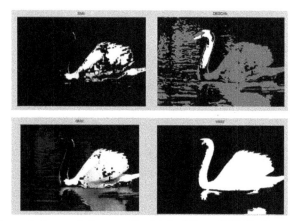

Figure 3. Segmentation results obtained from SNN (Left-top), DBSCAN (Right-top), GMM (Left-down), and WMM (Right-down).

As it can be observed, the SNN algorithm could not correctly segment the border points of the clusters. The reason comes back to this fact that the boarder points are considered as noisy samples, and are not assigned to any cluster. Incidentally, the DBSCAN results are not interesting; this deficiency comes back to this reality that different image segments are not very uniform, and the gradient of pixel intensities within each cluster is noticeable. Since DBSCAN considers a certain radius for all of the space, it cannot finely segment the areas that are in hierarchy. The proposed method using GMM and WMM provides better performance than the others but the segmented areas by WMM are obviously more accurate than those of GMM. This superiority was statistically proved (P < 0.05). Nevertheless, the proposed method using WMM could not cluster the beak and shadow of the swan.

As mentioned in sub-section 4.1., the number of employed core functions for each image is chosen through the cross-validation phase such that the selected number of core function resulted in a higher accuracy. The selected number core functions for images #8086, #3063, and #6064 were selected to be 3, 5, and 4, respectively.

4.3. Computational complexity

Since the computational complexity of WMM and Gaussian mixture model (GMM) is similar, expect one more learning parameter that WMM has compared to GMM, here, the computational complexity of GMM was determined. The complexity of GMM is O(kn), where n is the size of the dataset and k is the number of mixtures [23].

5. Conclusion

Clustering methods are encountered with some challenges such as validation of clusters, finding a proper number of clusters, measuring the accuracy of clusters (e.g. purity), limitation on the supremum and infimum number of samples within a cluster, and maximum variance of each cluster. In this work, we proposed a novel technique to automatically elicit the constraints from the estimated density of data in order to convert a blind clustering problem into the semi-supervised problem. Since performance of semi-supervised clustering techniques is higher than a blind one, the proposed scheme can drastically improve the clustering performance for real applications. The proposed technique is general and does not require any prior knowledge for its valley seeking part. The results achieved on two datasets demonstrated that the proposed model provided much higher results on two categories of datasets compared to the state-of-the-art methods in terms of clustering accuracy.

References

[1] Ali, T. & Asghar, S., et al. (2010). Critical analysis of dbscan variations, in Information and Emerging Technologies (ICIET), 2010 International Conference on, pp. 1-6.

[2] Ankerst, M. & Breunig, M. M., et al. (1999). OPTICS: ordering points to identify the clustering structure, in ACM Sigmod Record, pp. 49-60.

[3] Ball, G. H. & Hall, D. J. (1965). ISODATA, a novel method of data analysis and pattern classification, DTIC Document.

[4] de Amorim, R. C. & Hennig, C. (2015). Recovering the number of clusters in data sets with noise features using feature rescaling factors, Information Sciences, vol. 324, pp. 126-145.

[5] Defays, D. (1977). An efficient algorithm for a complete link method, The Computer Journal, vol. 20, pp. 364-366.

[6] Ertöz, L. & Steinbach, M., et al. (2004). Finding topics in collections of documents: A shared nearest neighbor approach, in Clustering and Information Retrieval, ed: Springer, pp. 83-103.

[7] Ester, M. & Kriegel, H.-P., et al. (1996). A density-based algorithm for discovering clusters in large spatial databases with noise, in Kdd, pp. 226-231.

[8] Flake, G. W. & Tarjan, R. E., et al. (2004). Graph clustering and minimum cut trees, Internet Mathematics, vol. 1, pp. 385-408.

[9] Halder, S. & Tiwari, R., et al. (2011). Information extraction from spam emails using stylistic and semantic features to identify spammers, in Information Reuse and Integration (IRI), 2011 IEEE International Conference on, pp. 104-107.

[10] Hartigan, J. A. & Wong, M. A. (1979). Algorithm AS 136: A k-means clustering algorithm, Journal of the Royal Statistical Society. Series C (Applied Statistics), vol. 28, pp. 100-108.

[11] Hastie, T. & Tibshirani, R., et al. (2009). Unsupervised learning, in the elements of statistical learning, ed: Springer, pp. 485-585.

[12] Hinneburg, A. & Keim, D. A. (1998). An efficient approach to clustering in large multimedia databases with noise, in KDD, pp. 58-65.

[13] Jain, A. K., Murty, M. N., et al. (1999). Data clustering: a review, ACM computing surveys (CSUR), vol. 31, pp. 264-323.

[14] Kriegel, H. P. & Kröger, P., et al. (2011). Density-based clustering, Wiley Interdisciplinary Reviews: Data Mining and Knowledge Discovery, vol. 1, pp. 231-240.

[15] Lu, Y.-H. & Huang, Y. (2005). Mining data streams using clustering, in 2005 International Conference on Machine Learning and Cybernetics, pp. 2079-2083.

[16] Mair, P. & Hudec, M. (2009). Multivariate Weibull mixtures with proportional hazard restrictions for dwell-time-based session clustering with incomplete data, Journal of the Royal Statistical Society: Series C (Applied Statistics), vol. 58, pp. 619-639.

[17] Manning, C. D. & Raghavan, P., et al. (2008). Scoring, term weighting and the vector space model, Introduction to Information Retrieval, vol. 100, pp. 2-4.

[18] McNicholas, P. D. (2011). On model-based clustering, classification, and discriminant analysis, Journal of the Iranian Statistical Society, vol. 10, pp. 181-190.

[19] Murthy, D. P. & Xie, M., et al. (2004). Weibull models vol. 505: John Wiley & Sons.

[20] Sclove, S. L. (1977). Population mixture models and clustering algorithms, Communications in Statistics-Theory and Methods, vol. 6, pp. 417-434.

[21] Shahsamandi Esfahani, P. & Saghaei, A. (2017). A Multi-Objective Approach to Fuzzy Clustering using ITLBO Algorithm, Journal of AI and Data Mining, vol. 5, pp. 307-317.

[22] Sibson, R. (1973). SLINK: an optimally efficient algorithm for the single-link cluster method, The computer journal, vol. 16, pp. 30-34.

[23] Verbeek, J. J. & Vlassis, N., et al. (2003). Efficient greedy learning of Gaussian mixture models, Neural computation, vol. 15, pp. 469-485.

[24] Wagstaff, K. & Cardie, C. (2000). Clustering with instance-level constraints, AAAI/IAAI, vol. 1097.

19

Ensemble Classification and Extended Feature Selection for Credit Card Fraud Detection

F. Fadaei Noghani and M.- H. Moattar*

Department of Computer Engineering, Mashhad Branch, Islamic Azad University, Mashhad, Iran.

Corresponding author: moattar@mshdiau.ac.ir (M. H. Moattar).

Abstract

Due to the rise of technology, the possibility of fraud in different areas such as banking has increased. Credit card fraud is a crucial problem in banking and its danger is ever increasing. This paper proposes an advanced data mining method, considering both the feature selection and the decision cost for accuracy enhancement of credit card fraud detection. After selecting the best and most effective features, using an extended wrapper method, an ensemble classification is performed. The extended feature selection approach includes a prior feature filtering and a wrapper approach using C4.5 decision tree. Ensemble classification is performed using cost sensitive decision trees in a decision forest framework. A locally gathered fraud detection dataset is used to estimate the proposed method. The method is assessed using accuracy, recall, and F-measure as the evaluation metrics and compared with the basic classification algorithms including ID3, J48, Naïve Bayes, Bayesian Network, and NB tree. The experiments carried out show that considering the F-measure as the evaluation metric, the proposed approach yields 1.8 to 2.4 percent performance improvement compared to the other classifiers.

Keywords: *Credit Card Fraud Detection, Feature Selection, Ensemble Classification, Cost Sensitive, Learning.*

1. Introduction

Generally, fraud "is the act of deceiving to gain unfair, undeserved and/or illegal financial profit" [1]. Fraud detection is an important issue in many areas including credit loans, credit cards, long distance communications, and insurance [2]. Any attempt to detect fraud in these areas is called a fraud detection process [3]. In banking, fraud happens in credit cards, online bank accounts, and call centres (telephone banking) [4]. The sooner the fraudulent transactions are detected, more damages can be prevented by stopping the transactions of counterfeit credit cards [5]. There are two main and important types of frauds related to credit cards. The first one is counterfeit fraud, which is done by organized crime gangs. The second type of credit card fraud is the illegal use of a missing or stolen credit card. Detecting fraud in a card with a larger balance is much more valuable than detecting fraud in a card with a smaller and limited balance. As a result, we have a classification problem with different costs [4].

Fraud detection is one of the best applications of data mining in the industry and the government [6]. Statistical methods of fraud detection are divided into two broad categories, supervised and unsupervised [7]. Traditional fraud detection is very costly due to expensive experts and broadness of the databases. Another deficiency is that not every human expert is able to detect the most recent patterns of fraud. Thus a data mining algorithm should analyze huge databases of transactions, and only then the expert will be able to do a further investigation about the diagnosed risky measures [3].

The purpose of this work is to propose an advanced method of data mining to detect credit card fraud. Feature selection is performed using an extension on the classical wrapper approach. This approach partitions the data prior to the wrapper algorithm. The goal is to select stable features that are independent from the size of the dataset and can be generalized on the other ones.

Also a cost-sensitive approach based on decision forest is proposed to tackle the unbalance data problem, which is an intrinsic property of fraud detection systems. The rest of this paper is organized as what follows. Section 2 introduces the previous works. In section 3, we investigate the feature selection methods and imbalanced datasets, and introduce approaches to overcome them, i.e. the cost-sensitive learning and ensemble methods. Section 4 introduces the proposed method. Section 5 deals with the results obtained and evaluations of the proposed approach.

2. Related works

Logistic models, Bayesian belief network, neural networks, and decision trees are the main data mining techniques for detecting financial frauds (credit card fraud, corporate fraud, and money laundry), and all of them provide original solutions to the problem of detection and classification of the counterfeit data. Generally speaking, approaches applied for detecting credit card fraud include neural network, data mining, meta-learning, and support vector machine [6].

Hilas and Mastorocostas (2008) [8] have proposed an approach based on the user model identification. In order to test the ability of each profile to discriminate between legitimate usage and fraud, feed-forward neural network (FF-NN) is used as classifier. Panigrahi et al. (2009) [9] have proposed a new method for detecting credit card fraud, which combines evidences of the past and present behavior. Their fraud detection system (FDS) consists of four components, which include law-based filter, Dempster-Shafer adder, transaction history database, and Bayesian learner. Duman and Ozcelik (2011) [4] have developed a method in which every transaction is marked and scored. Then based on the scores and ranks, transactions are categorized as legal or fraudulent. Their method has presented a combination of two metaheuristic techniques, namely genetic algorithms and scatter search. Bhattacharyya et al. (2011) [7] have investigated two advanced data mining techniques including support vector machines and random forests accompanied with logistic regression, for a better detection (as well as control and prosecution) of credit card fraud.

Jha et al. (2012) [5] have used the strategy of collecting transactions to foresee the purchase behavior of customers. They have used these sets to estimate a model for detecting fraudulent transactions. Dheepa and Dhanapa (2013) [10] have suggested a combination of supervised and unsupervised approaches to detect fraudulent transactions. Their model includes an approach of grouping basic behaviors benefited from patterns of animals' collective behavior to detect changes in the behavior of credit card users [10].

Sahin et al. (2013) [11] have proposed a cost-sensitive decision tree approach, which minimizes the total cost of incorrect classifications. The performance of this approach is compared with the traditional classification models in real datasets of credit cards. The cost of incorrect categorization is considered variable in this approach. Wei et al. (2013) [12] have suggested a model for an efficient online banking fraud detection, which combines several data mining techniques, cost-sensitive decision tree, and decision forest. Soltani Halvaiee and Akbari (2014) [13] have proposed a distributed model, considering a new method for credit card fraud detection using artificial immune system (AIS).

Santiago et al. (2015) [14] have proposed an approach to address the market fraud problem in on-line payment services. They have presented a model based on the history of entities involved in a transaction and extracted features to classify the transaction as fraud or legal. Kulkarni and Ade (2016) [15] have suggested a framework using logistic regression to tackle the problem of unbalanced data in credit card fraud detection. They have used an incremental learning approach for fraud modeling and detection. Bahnsen et al. (2016) [16] have expanded the transaction aggregation strategy, proposing a new feature based on the periodic behavior of a transaction. A valuable review on datamining approaches for credit card scoring can be found in [17].

Regarding the fact that datasets of credit cards include many features, there is an urgent need for selecting the best discriminating features. Also, datasets of credit cards for fraud detection include two classes that are not balanced. However, this has been overlooked in the previous works. Thus, it is necessary to pay special attention to the mentioned issues for proposing a practical framework for credit card fraud detection.

3. Material and methods
3.1. Feature selection methods

Feature is a unique and measurable characteristic of a process that is visible [18]. Any time a credit card is used, the transaction data including a number of features (such as credit card ID, amount of the transaction, etc.) are saved in the database of the service supplier [19]. Precise features strongly influence the performance of a fraud detection system [20]. Feature selection is the process of selecting a subset of features out of a larger set, and leads to a successful classification. The whole search space contains all possible subsets of features, meaning that its size is 2^N, in which N is the number of features. Thus feature selection is an NP-hard problem [21]. Figure 1 depicts the concept of feature selection [22].

In classification, a dataset usually includes a large number of features that may be relevant, irrelevant or redundant. Redundant and irrelevant features are not useful for classification, and they might even reduce the efficiency of the classifier regarding the large search space, which is the so-called curse of dimensionality [23].

$$\begin{bmatrix} X_1 \\ X_2 \\ \cdot \\ \cdot \\ \cdot \\ X_N \end{bmatrix} - - - -feature\ selection - --\rightarrow \begin{bmatrix} X_{i1} \\ X_{i2} \\ \cdot \\ \cdot \\ \cdot \\ X_{iM} \end{bmatrix}$$

Figure 1. Feature selection (here, N represents the number of original features, and M represents the number of reduced features, i.e. $M < N$).

The benefits of feature selection include reducing the computational costs, saving storage space, facilitating model selection procedures for accurate prediction, and interpreting complex dependencies between variables [24]. The features that are well selected not only optimize the classification accuracy but also reduce the number of required data for achieving an optimum level of performance of the learning process [25, 26]. Feature selection methods usually include search strategy, assessment measure, stopping criterion, and validation of the results. Search strategy is a search method used for producing a subset of candidate features for assessment. An assessment measure is applied for evaluating the quality of the subset of candidate features. The objective of the stopping criterion is to determine when a decision process should stop, and validation is the study of validity of the selected features with the real world datasets. It is obvious that search strategy and assessment measure are the two key factors in the feature selection process [27]. Filter and Wrapper methods are the most important methods of feature selection [25].

3.1.1. Filter methods
Filter approaches are independent from learning algorithm, and are cheaper and more general than the wrappers from the computational cost viewpoint [23]. Filter methods only evaluate the relation between features, and are independent from the classification and use measures such as distance, information, dependency, and compatibility. Filter methods are classified into

the feature subset selection (FSS) and feature ranking (FR) methods [25]. This classification is based on whether these methods evaluate the relation between the features separately or through feature subsets. In feature ranking methods, each feature is ranked separately, and then the features are ranked based on their relation with the objective variable. The subset selection methods explore all the subsets of features using a certain assessment measure [25].

3.1.2. Wrapper methods
Wrapper methods use the classifier as a black box and its performance as objective function for features subset assessment [18]. Wrapper approaches include a learning algorithm as assessment function [23]. Feature selection criterion in wrapper methods is a forecasting function that finds a subset with the highest performance [18]. Sequential backward selection (SBS) and sequential forward selection (SFS) are two common wrapper methods. SFS (SBS) starts without any features (or all features), and then the candidate features are, respectively, added to (or omitted from) until adding or omission does not increase the classification performance [23].

Comparing the two classes of feature selection approaches, we can say that the filter methods can be considered as preprocessing, which ranks features independent from the classifier. These approaches have a lower computational complexity, and are more generalizable (due to the classifier independence). When the number of initial features is high, the filter approaches are usually time-efficient, and can achieve an acceptable performance. However, their performance depends on the ranking measure and the factors that are taken under consideration (i.e. discrimination power, correlation, class relation, and so on). On the other side, the wrapper approaches span a large search space, and therefore, their time complexity is high, which is negligible in offline systems. Also since features are selected based on the classifier performance, the wrapper methods usually have a better performance on the evaluation datasets. However, the optimality of the wrapper approaches is classifier-dependent, and both their efficiency and generalizablity depend on the classifier. However, the frameworks such as the one proposed in this paper may lead to a better stability of the performance.

3.2. Unbalanced datasets
One of the main problems involved in data mining is the problem of classes being unbalanced. In

some classification problems, the number of samples of each class can be very different. The imbalance problem appears especially when facing a dataset with only two classes [2]. The problem of unbalanced datasets is very important in real world applications such as medical diagnoses, detecting software deficiencies, financial issues, finding drugs, and bioinformatics. In these issues, a class with fewer samples is more important from the learning viewpoint [27, 28], and when its detection is not done properly, the decision costs increase [28]. The methods dealing with the problem of unbalanced datasets can be grouped into three categories [28, 29]:

Data level methods work during pre-processing, and directly on the data and try to re-balance the class distributions. These methods are independent from the real classification stage, and can be used flexibly. The most famous approaches use the oversampling strategy. A popular approach is the synthetic minority oversampling technique (SMOTE), though, recently, better options have been suggested such as adaptive synthetic sampling (ADASYN), which investigates the most difficult objectives for learning or ranked minority sampling (RAMO), which uses the direct probabilistic method. However, the oversampling methods can cause other problems such as changes in class distribution in higher iterations.

The classifier level methods try to make the existing algorithms consistent with the problem of unbalanced dataset, and enrich them towards the minority group. Here, a deeper knowledge is required about the nature of forecasters and the reasons of their defeat in detecting the minority group. The cost-sensitive methods are able to use data correction (by adding a certain cost to the wrong classification) and correcting learning algorithms for making them compatible with the possibility of wrong classification. The higher cost of the wrong classification, which is dedicated to the classification of the minority class, reduces the overall cost. The solutions are based on the cost-sensitive learning combine data methods and the algorithm level.

3.3. Cost-sensitive trees
The induction of a decision tree is an important and active topic in data mining and machine learning. Major algorithms in inducing decision trees such as ID3, CART, and C4.5 are widely and successfully used in different applications [30]. The existing algorithms optimize the classifying decision trees with the objective of maximizing precision in classification or minimizing wrong

classifications. The traditional methods of decision trees are designed under the supposition that all the classification mistakes are considered as equal costs. In fact, in actual applications, different classification errors usually lead to different costs. For example, false negative costs are very different from false positive costs in medical diagnoses. Thus it leads to the creation of cost-sensitive learning (CSL) search area [32].

3.4. Ensemble methods
Ensemble methods are very compatible with unbalanced areas, and have demonstrated a great performance [19]. The Accuracy of the fraud detection model is a critical factor for a proper categorization of fraudulent or legal case [33]. Advancements in machine learning suggest using a classifier ensemble instead of a single forecaster. Many researches indicate that an ensemble of classifiers will have better results than a single classifier. Bagging, boosting, and random forests are the most well-known examples of these methods. Random forests are very efficient for the classification and regression problems [34]. A random forest is a collection of decision trees. The reputation of random forest is due to its high performance compared with the other algorithms [29].

4. Proposed method
As Figure 2 suggests, the proposed method consists of two main parts, namely feature selection and decision forest construction. The first part of the proposed method includes division of the datasets and an extended wrapper method that leads to selecting the best and the most efficient features. The second part of the suggested method consists of dividing the dataset to several parts, making a decision tree for each part, scoring each tree, and choosing the best tree with the highest score in the decision forest.

4.1. Extended wrapper-based feature selection
In this stage, to provide stability on the best features for the final experiments, different subsets of training dataset are created. Thus first, the training dataset is divided into 5 different subsets, which include different percentages of the available data (i.e. 80%, 85%, 90%, 95%, and 100%). First, the features are ranked based on the Chi-squared filter, gain ratio, and ReliefF. These filters are known as appropriate and efficient filters for feature rankings [20]. The Chi-squared filter is based on the χ^2 statistics, and evaluates each feature based on the class labels separately. The objective of the gain ratio filter is to

maximize information gain. ReliefF is a sample-based filter that determines the volubility of a feature by repeated sampling and considering the value of a feature for discriminating a sample from a neighboring sample of a similar or a different class. Equations (1), (2), and (3) denote the Chi-squared, gain ratio, and ReliefF filters, respectively [35]:

$$X^2 = \sum_{i=1}^{r} \sum_{j=1}^{c} \frac{\left(O_{ij} - E_{ij}\right)^2}{E_{ij}} \tag{1}$$

$$GR = \frac{IG}{H(X)} \tag{2}$$

$$W[A] = W[A] - \sum_{j=1}^{k} \frac{diff\left(A, R_i, H_j\right)}{m.k}$$

$$+ \sum_{C \neq class(R_i)} \frac{P(C)}{1 - P\left(class\left(R_i\right)\right)} \sum_{j=1}^{k} diff(A, R_i, M_j(C)) \tag{3}$$

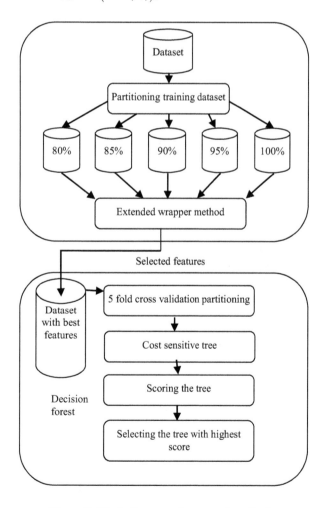

Figure 2. Block diagram of proposed method.

In (1), O_{ij} is the resulting output when E_{ij} is the target output. In (2), IG denotes the information gain [35]. The ReliefF measure, as denoted in (3), randomly selects an instance R_i and its k same-class nearest neighbors, denoted by H_j and k different-class nearest neighbors denoted by

$M_j(C)$. Then the ReliefF measure is updated for attribute A using the above-mentioned subsets. The contribution for each class is weighted with the prior probability of that class $P(C)$. The second term is to ensure that the contribution of each class is in the range of [0, 1] and sums to 1 [35].

Then the feature sets created by the Chi-squared, gain ratio, and ReliefF filters are integrated, and for each training subset, a candidate feature set is made. Form the feature sets made by the three filters, a feature with the highest rank is selected. In order to choose the best features of different subsets, the candidate features of each subset that are selected based on their rank, are, respectively, classified by the C4.5 decision tree. Then the accuracy of the classifier is determined. In case the accuracy of the classifier does not decrease, the feature is selected. However, if the feature being studied decreases the accuracy of the classifier, the feature is not selected, and the next feature is investigated (pseudo-code 1).

Pseudo code 1: Selecting best features for each phase

Input: Data set selected from candidate feature set;
Output: Selecting the best features

1. Steps 2 to 6 are repeated until all of candidate features are investigated.
2. Classifier (C4.5) is made for each feature in candidate feature set.
3. Classifier accuracy is calculated.
4. The feature is selected and added to the best feature set if classifier accuracy does not decrease.
5. Else the next feature is investigated.
6. End.

In the last stage, the best features that are common between all the subsets are selected. After performing the first part of the proposed method, the irrelevant features are discarded. The selected features are expected to include the precise features that enhance the accuracy of the classifier.

4.2. Decision forest

In this phase, the dataset with the selected features is divided into several parts in order to make a decision forest (the number of parts in each decision tree is different) and with no overlap. Then for each part, a cost-sensitive decision tree is made; each tree is ranked (based on precision and F-Measure). In the decision forest, the tree with the highest score is selected as the best one. For creating a cost-sensitive tree, the cost of each feature is calculated using CS-Gini [11]. The false negative and false positive decision costs are calculated using (4) and (5), respectively:

$$C_N = \left(\sum_{i=1}^{f} \left(C_{FN} \right)_i \right) * \left(\frac{f}{n+f} \right)^2 \qquad (4)$$

$$C_P = n * C_{FP} * \left(\frac{n}{n+f} \right)^2 \qquad (5)$$

In (4), C_N is the total cost of wrong classification of legal transactions (non-fraudulent), f shows the number of frauds, n is the number of non-fraudulent transactions, and the cost of a wrong classification of fraudulent transactions (C_{FN}) is equal to 1. In (5), C_P is the total cost of a wrong classification for determining the transaction known as fraudulent. Also the cost of a wrong classification of legal transactions (C_{FP}) is 1.

After calculating the total cost of wrong classifications, the least cost of a wrong classification is selected as the feature cost using (6) [11]:

$$Cost(A) = \min(C_N, C_P) \qquad (6)$$

Then the gain ratio is calculated for each feature A using (7) [36]. In this equation, W shows the importance level of the feature:

$$Rate(A) = 2^{Gain(A)} - 1 / \left(Cost(A) + 1 \right)^W \qquad (7)$$

By calculating the gain ratio of each feature, the feature with the highest gain ratio is selected as the root of the tree. In the next stage, using the algorithm of the cost-sensitive decision tree, children of the root node are created. The algorithm is repeated for each child as well (pseudo-code 2).

Pseudo code 2: Decision forest

Input: Credit card dataset with best features
Output: The best cost-sensitive decision tree for fraud detection

1. Steps 2-6 are repeated until a tree with a high score is selected.
2. Training dataset is divided into several parts.
3. Cost-sensitive decision tree is made for each part of dataset.
4. Each tree made in the decision forest is ranked based on precision and F-Measure.
5. The tree with a high score between trees of decision forest is selected.
6. End

---

5. Evaluations

To evaluate the proposed method, the dataset from the second robotic & artificial intelligence festival of Amirkabir University was applied (http://araif2013.aut.ac.ir/index/). Table 1 shows the characteristics of the dataset. In this dataset, 3.75% of instances are fraudulent transactions, and 96.25% are non-fraudulent. As seen, the fraudulent and non-fraudulent classes are obviously imbalance.

Table 1. Characteristic of dataset.

Non-fraudulent	Fraudulent	Features	Instance
28012	1092	20	29104

5.1. Assessment measures

In the presented article, four assessment measures were used, namely recall, precision, F-measure, and accuracy. Regarding that the mentioned measures are calculated based on the confusion matrix, this matrix is depicted in table 2. The confusion matrix shows the performance of the classification algorithm when assigning input data to different classes [11].

Table 2. Confusion matrix.

	Positive (Fraud)	Negative (Non-Fraud)
Positive (Fraud)	True Positive (TP)	False Negative (FN)
Negative (Non-Fraud)	False Positive (FP)	True Negative (TN)

The recall measure (8) shows the efficiency of the classifier in detecting the actual fraudulent transactions.

$$Recall = \frac{TP}{FN + TP} \qquad (8)$$

The precision measure (9) shows how much the output of the classifier is reliable.

$$Precision = \frac{TP}{TP + FP} \qquad (9)$$

Finally, the F-measure (10) is the harmonic mean of recall and precision measures.

$$F - Measure = \frac{2 * Recall * Precision}{Recall + Precision} \qquad (10)$$

Also accuracy (as in (11)) denotes the total performance of a classifier. It shows that how many of the total experimental records have been classified correctly by the designed classifier.

$$Accuracy = \frac{TP + TN}{TP + FP + TN + FN} \qquad (11)$$

However, the F-measure is a more trustable measure for evaluating the data mining systems with imbalance classes because it is the harmonic mean of Recall and Precision measures. Therefore, using the F-measure, both the TP and TN measures are equally important when we have an unbalanced dataset. We used a 5-fold cross scheme approach to evaluate the proposed approach.

5.2. Efficiency of decision forest

The efficiency of the decision forest with different numbers of trees and based on the F-measure and precision is depicted in figures 3 and 4. In these experiments, increasing the number of trees in the decision forest continued up to the level that both the F-measure and accuracy approach their maximum value and become stable.

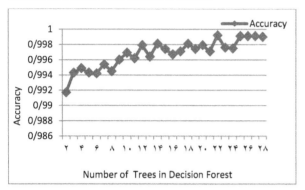

Figure 3. Assessing decision forest with different number of trees using accuracy.

Figure 4 denotes the changes in F-measure with increasing the number of trees in the decision forest. F increases to 0.9975 with increasing the number of trees in the decision forest from 2 to 4. This measure decreases from 0.9975 to 0.9971 when the number of trees rises to 6. Then by increasing the number of trees from 6 to 23, changes in the F-measure has a growth-decline process and it is repeated. This measure reaches a constant level of 0.9988 in a decision forest with 23 and 24 trees, and increases with 25, 26, and 27 trees and reaches 0.9996.

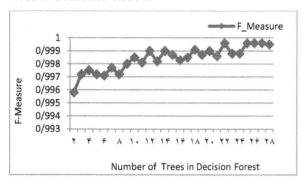

Figure 4. Assessing decision forest with different numbers of trees using F-measure.

Similarly, regarding figure 3, it is obvious that the accuracy increases to 0.9949 by increasing the number of trees from 2 to 4. This measure decreases from 0.9949 to 0.9942 by the increment of the trees from 4 to 6. Then by increasing the trees from 6 to 23, the changes in accuracy become a growth-decline process. This measure increases to 0.9991 in a forest with 25, 26, and 27 trees, and becomes stable.

5.3. Comparison with other classification approaches

The results of the proposed method (with 27 trees with maximum precision and F-measure) was

compared with some basic classifiers including ID3 tree, J48 tree, Naive Bayesian, Bayesian network, and NBT tree using recall, precision, and F measure, as depicted in figures 5, 6, and 7.

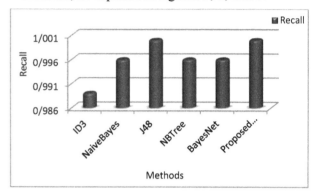

Figure 5. Comparison between proposed method (with 27 trees in decision forest) and basic classification algorithms based on recall.

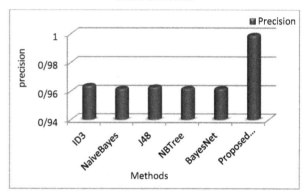

Figure 6. Comparison between proposed method (with 27 tees in decision forest) and basic classification algorithms based on precision.

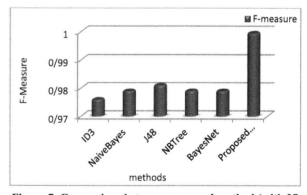

Figure 7. Comparison between proposed method (with 27 tees in decision forest) and basic classification algorithms based on F-measure.

These figures show that the proposed approach (with 27 trees in the decision forest) is superior to the mentioned algorithms. Based on the F-measure, the proposed method had 2.4%, 1.8%, 2%, 2%, and 2% absolute advantage over ID3 tree, J48 tree, Naive Bayesian, Bayesian network, and NB Tree, respectively.

Also, as depicted in figure 7, the error rate of the proposed approach was about 0.2%, while the error rate of ID3, NaïveBayes, J48 tree, NB Tree, and BayesNet approaches are 2.6%, 2.2%, 2.0%, 2.2%, and 2.2%, respectively. Therefore, the relative error rate of the proposed approach decreased by 92.3%, 90.9%, 90%, 90.9%, and 90.9% as compared with the above-mentioned approaches. This shows a considerable decrement in the detection error, which is mainly due to the precision of the approach resulting from a cost-sensitive paradigm.

6. Conclusion

Along with the recent advances of technology, credit cards have been accepted as one of the most important cases of pay systems. Due to the deficiencies in the security of credit card systems, fraud is increasing, and millions of dollars are lost every year. Thus, credit card fraud detection is a highly important issue for banks and credit card companies. The sooner the fraudulent transaction is detected, the more damages can be prevented. The proposed approach benefited from the extended wrapper method for selecting good features that are efficient for decreasing the run time and increasing the accuracy of the classifier. Then using the decision forest that consists of cost-sensitive decision trees, each tree was scored regarding accuracy and F-measures, and later, the tree with the highest score was chosen. The results obtained indicated that the proposed method is superior to the basic classification algorithms including ID3 tree, J48 tree, Naive Bayesian, Bayesian Network, and NB tree. The precision of the proposed method was 99.96 percent based on the F-measure.

Further works are suggested on using other methods such as majority voting for selecting features and applying other cost-sensitive learning approaches. One can study approaches such as sampling methods to overcome the class imbalance problem. In addition, since it is claimed that the distance metric learning (DML) approaches are robust against class imbalance, their applicability can be studied as a future work.

References

[1] Humpherys S. L., et al. (2011). Identification of fraudulent financial statements using linguistic credibility analysis, Decision Support Systems, vol. 50, no. 3, pp. 585-594.

[2] Kim J., et al. (2012). Classification cost: an empirical comparison among traditional classifier, cost-sensitive classifier, and meta-cost, Expert Systems with Applications, vol.39, no.4, pp. 4013-4019.

[3] Aral K. D., et al. (2012). A prescription fraud detection model. Computer Methods and Programs in Biomedicine, vol. 106, no. 1, pp. 37-46.

[4] Duman, E. & Ozcelik, M. H. (2011). Detecting credit card fraud by genetic algorithm and scatter search. Expert Systems with Applications, vol. 38, no. 10, pp. 13057-13063.

[5] Jha, S., Guillen, M. & Westland, J. C. (2012). Employing transaction aggregation strategy to detect credit card fraud. Expert Systems with Applications, vol. 39, no. 16, pp. 12650-12657.

[6] Ngai E. W. T., et al. (2011). The application of data mining techniques in financial fraud detection: a classification framework and an academic review of literature. Decision Support Systems, vol. 50, no. 3, pp. 559-569.

[7] Bhattacharyya S., et al. (2011). Data mining for credit card fraud: a comparative study. Decision Support Systems, vol. 50, no. 3, pp. 602-613.

[8] Hilas, C. S. & Mastorocostas, P. As. (2008). An application of supervised and unsupervised learning approaches to telecommunications fraud detection. Knowledge Based Systems, vol. 21, no.7, pp. 721-726.

[9] Panigrahi S., et al. (2009). Credit card fraud detection: a fusion approach using Dempster–Shafer theory and Bayesian learning. Inform Fusion, vol. 10, no. 4. pp. 354-363.

[10] M. Thampi S., et al. (2013). Hybrid approach for improvising credit card fraud detection based on collective animal behavior and SVM. Security in Computing and Communications, Mysore, India: Springer, pp. 293-302.

[11] Sahin, Y., Bulkan, S. & Duman, E. (2013). A cost-sensitive decision tree approach for fraud detection. Expert Systems with Applications, vol. 40, no. 15, pp. 5916-5923.

[12] Wei W., et al. (2012). Effective detection of sophisticated online banking fraud on extremely imbalanced data. 21st International World Wide Web Conference, Lyon, France.

[13] Soltani Halvaiee, N. & Akbari, M. K. (2014). A novel model for credit card fraud detection using Artificial Immune Systems. Applied Soft Computing, vol. 24, pp. 40-49.

[14] Santiago, G. P., Pereira, A. C. M. & Hirata, R. (2015). A modeling approach for credit card fraud detection in electronic payment services. 30th Annual ACM Symposium on Applied Computing, New York, USA.

[15] Kulkarni, P. & Ade, R. (2016). Logistic regression learning model for handling concept drift with unbalanced data in credit card fraud detection system. 2th International Conference on Computer and Communication Technologies.

[16] Bahnsen A. C., et al. (2016). Feature engineering strategies for credit card fraud detection. Expert Systems with Applications, vol. 51, pp.134-142.

[17] Sadatrasoul, S. M., Gholamian, M. R., Siami, M. & Hajimohammadi, Z. (2013). Credit scoring in banks and financial institutions via data mining techniques: A literature review. Journal of AI and Data Mining, vol. 1, no.2, pp. 119-129.

[18] Chandrashekar, G. & Sahin, F. (2014). A survey on feature selection methods. Computers & Electrical Engineering, vol. 40, no. 1, pp. 16-28.

[19] Dal Pozzolo A., et al. (2014). Learned lessons in credit card fraud detection from a practitioner perspective. Expert Systems with Applications, vol. 41, no. 10, pp. 4915-4928.

[20] Chang, W. H. & Chang, J. S. (2012). An effective early fraud detection method for online auctions. Electronic Commerce Research and Applications, vol. 11, no. 4, pp. 346-360.

[21] Tabakhi, S., Moradi, P. & Akhlaghian, F. (2014). An unsupervised feature selection algorithm based on ant colony optimization. Engineering Applications of Artificial Intelligence, vol. 32, pp. 112-123.

[22] Zhang Y., et al. (2014). Binary PSO with mutation operator for feature selection using decision tree applied to spam detection. Knowledge-Based Systems, vol. 64, pp. 22-31.

[23] Xue, B., Zhang, M. & Browne, W. N. (2014). Particle swarm optimization for feature selection in classification: Novel initialization and updating mechanisms. Applied Soft Computing, vol. 18, pp. 261-276.

[24] Feng, D., Chen, F. & Xu, W. (2014). Supervised feature subset selection with ordinal optimization. Knowledge-Based Systems, vol. 56, pp. 123-140.

[25] Bouaguel, W., Mufti, G. B. & Limam, M. (2013). A fusion approach based on wrapper and filter feature selection methods using majority vote and feature weighting. International Conference on Computer Applications Technology (ICCAT), Sousse.

[26] Wang, G., Ma, J. & Yang, S. (2014). An improved boosting based on feature selection for corporate bankruptcy prediction. Expert Systems with Applications, vol. 41, no. 5, pp. 2353-2361.

[27] Zhao, H. & Qin, K. (2014). Mixed feature selection in incomplete decision table. Knowledge-Based Systems, vol. 57, pp. 181-190.

[28] López V., et al. (2012). Analysis of preprocessing vs. cost-sensitive learning for imbalanced classification, open problems on intrinsic data characteristics. Expert Systems with Applications, vol. 39, no. 7, pp. 6585-6608.

[29] del Río S., et al. (2014). On the use of MapReduce for imbalanced big data using random forest. Information Sciences, vol. 285, pp. 112-137.

[30] Krawczyk, B., Woźniak, M. & Schaefer, G. (2014). Cost sensitive decision tree ensembles for effective imbalanced classification. Applied Soft Computing, vol. 14, pp. 554-562.

[31] Kotsiantis, S. B. (2011). Decision trees: a recent overview. Artif Intell Rev, vol. 39, pp. 261-283.

[32] Zhang, S. (2012). Decision tree classifiers sensitive to heterogeneous costs. Journal of Systems and Software, vol. 85, no. 4, pp. 771-779.

[33] Louzada, F. & Ara, A. (2012). Bagging k-dependence probabilistic networks: An alternative powerful fraud detection tool. Expert System Applications, vol. 39, pp. 11583-11592.

[34] Elghazel, H., Aussem, A. & Perraud, F. (2011). Trading-off diversity and accuracy for optimal ensemble tree selection in random forests. Ensembles in Machine Learning Applications, Chennai, India, pp. 169-179.

[35] Robnik-Šikonja, M. & Kononenko, I. (2003). Theoretical and empirical analysis of ReliefF and RReliefF. Machine Learning, vol. 53, no. 1, pp. 23-69.

[36] Jiawei, H., Micheline, K. & Jian, P. (2012). Data Mining concepts and techniques. 3nd ed. USA, Elsevier.

20

Expert discovery: A web mining approach

M. Naeem*, M. Bilal Khan, M. Tanvir Afzal

Mohammad Ali Jinnah University Isalamabad Pakistan

*Corresponding author: naeems.naeem@gmail.com (M. Naeem)

Abstract

Expert discovery is a quest in search of finding an answer to a question: "Who is the best expert of a specific subject in a particular domain within a peculiar array of parameters?" Expert with domain knowledge in any fields is crucial for consulting in industry, academia and scientific community. Aim of this study is to address the issues for expert-finding task in real-world community. Collaboration with expertise is critical requirement in business corporate, such as in fields of engineering, geographies, bio-informatics, and medical domains. We have proposed multifaceted web mining heuristic that results into the design and development of a tool using data from *Growbag*, *dblpXML* with Authors home pages resource to find people of desired expertise. We mined more than 2,500 Author's web pages based on the credibility of 12 key parameters while parsing on each page for a large number of co-occurred keyword and all available general terms. It presents evidence to validate this quantification as a measure of expertise. The prototype enables users easily to distinguish someone, who has briefly worked in a particular area with more extensive experience, resulting in the capability to locate people with broader expertise through large parts of the product. Through this extension to the web enabling methodology, we have shown that the implemented tool delivers a novel web mining idea with improved results.

Keywords: *Web mining, multifaceted, social computing, expert discovery, high profile, higher order co-occurrence.*

1. Introduction

In any corporate entity, the knowledge of expertise is a non-trivial resource. Although, critical projects in corporate sector have been observed with focus on design and implementation issues, the success of any project and research problem also involves careful selection of right experts. Collaboration cannot be effective unless one can identify the person with whom communication might be required. Previous research has helped clarify the amount of engineering effort devoted to communication. Particularly in engineering, one classic study spent around 16% of their time in communicating with experts [1]. Interestingly, Allen [1] reported a tendency for high-performing engineers to consult much more with experts outside their own discipline as compared to low-performing engineers, although both groups spent almost the same proportion of time for communication.

People with work locations separated by 30 meters have been observed to communicate as infrequently as people whose workplaces are located in different continents [2], which show importance of consultancy with concerned experts. So, if any organization expects projects with members spread across multiple floors of a single building, it might experience much-reduced communication among more widely separated members. Previous work suggested an approach for solving the expertise-finding problem. In an empirical study of finding experts in a software development organization, Ackerman et al., [3] pointed out that experience was the primary criterion, engineers ordinarily used to show expertise. In fact, developers often used change history to identify those who had experience with a particular file, generally assuming that the last person to change it was most likely to be "the expert". This strategy had several shortcomings, including the inability to determine if s/he is the person who carried out the change had made a large or small change, and whether the person had made many or only a few alterations in the relevant code. Additionally, when someone with capabilities in depth was deemed, it was quite difficult to identify such a person from the changing information stored in individual files.

There are also expertise detection systems based entirely on an analysis of user activity and behaviour while being engaged in an electronic environment. Krulwich et al., [4] have analyzed the number of interactions of an individual within a discussion forum as a means of online structuring an expert's profile. Although such an approach is useful in monitoring user participation, measures such as number of interactions on a particular topic, which in itself is not reflective of knowledge levels of individuals. Knowledge can be categorized into two classes: Tacit and explicit knowledge. Management systems focus on explicit knowledge because it can be articulated in written language. However, according to the Delphi Group's study carried out on more than 700 US companies, a large portion of corporate knowledge (42%) was revealed to be tacit knowledge.

Expertise, a major component of tacit knowledge, is the most valuable knowledge because it defines an organization's unique capabilities and core competencies [5]. The great value of expertise can only be exploited when an individual's expertise can be shared with others [5]. Recently Li et al., [6] discussed the importance of expert reviewer in the field of marketing. They argued to find the potential influential nodes for effectively and quickly spreading product impressions within a marketing network. However, codifying expertise is difficult and expensive [7]. One effective method of sharing expertise is to enhance people to communicate with each other. Expertise matching – the process of finding experts with a specific expertise – plays an important role in connecting people.

The topic facets efficiently organize one particular facet, using such metadata with respect to user-provided keywords [8]. The main difference to existing (static) facet organizations is that this topic facet is sensitive with respect to time and user community. This provides a motivation for exploiting the currently available metadata from *Growbag* and *dblpXML* collection for computer science. The great value of expertise can be exploited only when an individual's expertise can be shared with others. Generalized processes to find experts are expensive whereas automatic expert finding systems already have delivered ambiguous results. Manual approaches are limited to specific projects only because of costly resources.

However, the fundamental question still remains. How can a person be identified as an expert in a domain? Kajikawa et al. [9] pointed out that deluge of publications has raised a problem of achieving a comprehensive view even on a topic with limited scope. Zainab et al. [10] argued over the objectivity and functionality of the research publications by showing a detailed statistical data about research publications. In this study, we have relied on two reference models. The first model is Academia Europaea [11]. They have focused on prestigious awards, especially Nobel Laureates, in their membership nomination form. The importance of publications and citations was no doubt considered but it was not the only criteria. The second reference model is Pakistan Academy of Sciences [12]. The page for the fellowship has again focused on numerous local/international awards. We can draw conclusion from careful examination of the two reference models that number of publications and citations does play a role but there are still other factors that organizations consider while selecting an individual as an eminent expert in a specific field.

This study explores the discovery of expertise within the context of a digital electronic journal; the *Growbag* an updated *dblpXML* has very large number of articles covering all topics of computer science. A reference work related to the journal-ranking problem has recently been drawn [13]. Our work handles the problems of finding experts using automatic multifaceted approach, which handles automation errors using multi-feature extraction. We justified results by multiple facets using different metrics and find appropriate intensive experts. Presented work mines different metrics from *Growbag* dataset resulting in weighted constrains while calculating expert score. Facets offer different dimensions. Such facets can be considered a way to categorize content or document collections for intuitive user interaction. We shall summarize the main contributions of this work as below.

- To the best of our knowledge, the proposed technique to dig out the web-based faceted ranks is very important in the area of finding experts in academics.
- Our main contributions center around a context-sensitive web mining based on approach heuristic is inspired by the concept of finding automated and manual approach as described by Afzal et al. [7].
- The technique is aimed at rendering help to journal editors and conference organizers to assign score to mark any authors for their potential role in reviewing.

2. Related work

Discovery of expertise is a crucial task. Many people and organizations are working on it to fairly find an expert. Both autonomous system and manual efforts have been exercised to the purpose of discovery of expertise. In manual approach persons have to perform huge amount of effort but in the end quality of output is very fine. Many measuring factors are used to find the pertinent information in finding experts. An expert is a major member (either a software agent or a human expert), with the knowledge of the agent world in a complex multi-agent domain but with focused expertise for a particular problem solver in a special field [14].

Finding an expert may vary from field to field, such as for academia profile, projects, publication and many other factors (herein called weights) could be used to find the exact expert. If we talk about finding a reviewer for an expert work, *Most Expert Finder* systems will be based on highly localized, privatized and specialized datasets, and the systems are beneficial only in narrow margin with small settings [15]. By facilitating the task of finding suitable reviewers, we anticipate that the quality of an overall conference could improve, since both the number of reviewers available for consideration would be larger and the extent of their expertise would be determined and useful in the selection process. If we delve into the application of expert discovery, then there is a potential possibility to fulfil the requirement of fair distribution of staff in an enterprise and all together the same can be applied into projects, awards, publications. Unfortunately, active

experts do not have enough time to preserve sufficient descriptions of their continuously changing and specialized skills [16]. One notable example is MITRE database where it was pointed out that quickly maintaining and updating previous experience databases are not considered a trivial job.

Expert finder fills this gap by mining information and activities related to experts while providing it is an intuitive fashion to end-users [16]. A specific example is university that is considered a well knowledge-based organization. The authorities at universities have also realized that effective development and management of their organizational knowledge base is critical for survival in today's competitive service industry. The knowledge and expertise of a university staff involved in teaching and research in various areas is the major asset that a university holds [17]. When the user searches using a specific term, the system ranks employees by the mentioned term or phrase and its statistical association with the employee name resulting into the realization that one of the most important problems in developing expert systems is knowledge acquisition from experts [18, 16]. In order to mechanize this problem, many techniques and inductive learning methods, such as induction of decision trees [19, 20], rule induction methods [19, 21, 22] and rough set theory [23, 24] were introduced and performed. These learning methods have shown reasonable suitability to extract knowledge from databases. Other researchers investigated the discovery of communities of practicing experts via a prototype called XperNet [16]. XperNet is designed to extract expertise networks. It uses statistical clustering techniques and social network analysis to glean networks or affinity groups consisting of people having related skills and interests [16, 25].

Mockus et al. [26] applied a technique over data from a software project's change management records to find people with desired expertise in a large organization [26]. In literature, some other systems have been reported which detect experts entirely on an analysis of user activity, behaviour, likes and dislikes while being engaged in an electronic environment. A notable example in a past decade is the analysis of number of interactions of an individual within a discussion forum as a means of constructing an expert's profile [4]. Even though this kind of approach is helpful in monitoring user contribution, the measures, such as number of interactions on a particular topic in itself requires significant insightful knowledge levels of individuals. Another approach discussed in literature was related to use of semantic structure Expert/Expert-Locator (EEL) pair requests for technical information in a large study and development company [27]. The system automatically constructs a semantic space of organizations and terms, using a statistical matrix decomposition technique (singular value decomposition) to represent semantic similarity present in large text sources. McDonald et al. [28] reported on a system that uses various files organizationally closest to the requester, and how well the requester knows the expert (based on a previous analysis of the social network in the organization). The problem of finding experts is not limited to widely distributed teams, however. In fact, people whose offices are separated by 30 meters communicate about as infrequently as people who are located on different continents [29].

S. D Neil et al. [30] analysed quality filter in scientific communication process and proposed information analyst is used as a filter to identify quality research papers, especially using the validity criterion, fact lead to our author research work quality phenomena to extract legendary in field. Awang Ngah Zainab et al. [31] measured trends for expert systems in library and information services based upon authorship patterns and expressiveness of published titles. He identified the total, trends, focus of studies, authorship pattern and expressive quality of publications covering Expert System (ES) applications in the broad or sub-domain of Library Information System (LIS). Robert P. Vecchio et al. [32] raised issue of particularistic bias, agreement, and predictive validity in manuscript review process. He applied his study process on 853 manuscripts and an initial study shows the majority of the reviewed papers rejected after initial review (603, or 81.6%), whereas the remainder (136, or 18.4%) received an invitation to revise and resubmit, which leads research quality. Anne S. Tsui et al. and John R. Hollenbeck et al. [33] suggest that conversation should be about addressing the large gap between the demand for effective reviewers and the supply of individuals who are both successful authors and effective reviewers. Towards parallelism in a

structural scientific discovery Gehad M. Galal et al. [34] investigated approaches for scaling particular knowledge discovery in databases (KDD) system to discover interesting and repetitive concepts in graph-based databases from a variety of domains.

A similar approach proposed by Mockus et al. [26] could be adopted to compute expertise for researchers across different topics. Studies indicate that engineers and scientists instinctively do not communicate much with colleagues whose offices are distant to each other, so there are fewer opportunities to find out whoever holds expertise in various areas when teams are distributed [26]. Cameron et al [15] collected the expertise of a subset of researchers who have published papers in World Wide Web and Semantic Web Conferences. This dataset includes more than 1,200 researchers and 1,504 relationships to about 100 unique topics. Expertise, a major component of tacit knowledge, is the most valuable knowledge because it defines an organization's unique capabilities and core competencies [5]. The most widely used approach for expertise matching within academia is to build an expertise database where individuals specify their expertise using several keywords or short sentences resulting in empowering the users to search these databases to find an expert [17]. A prototype system has been implemented based on the architecture with the aim to help PhD applicants find potential supervisors [17]. The literature details a number of systems that undertake a fully automatic approach to locate experts including Who Knows [27], Agent Amplified Communications [35], Contact Finder [4], Yenta [2], MEMOIR [35], Expertise Recommender [28], Expert Finder [36], SAGE [37] and the KCSR Expert Finder [38]. This is reflected by wide variety of expertise evidence, such as emails [35], electronic messages on bulletin boards [4], program codes [39, 40], Web pages [2, 35], and technical reports [41, 38] used in expert finder systems. Sim et al [41] proposed that the heterogeneity of information sources should be used as an indicator for reflecting experts' competencies. Expert finder systems can be integrated into other organizational systems, such as information retrieval systems, recommender systems and Computer Supported Cooperative Work systems [41].

XML is accepted as the standard for data interchange [42]. Heterogeneous data structures can be represented in a uniform syntax (nested tagged elements). On the other hand, in XML, user can add tags and the same information can be represented differently by different XML structures. Recently Razikin et al. [43] carried out an important work investigating the effectiveness of tags in facilitating resource discovery by means of machine learning and user-centric approaches. They showed that all of the tags are not useful for content discovery. Their research was limited to only 100 frequent tags extracted from a corpus of 2,000 documents. Lu et al. [44] reported importance of tagging in social computing within the domain of digital library science. They highlighted the difference and connections between expert-assigned subject terms and social tags in order to uncover the potential obstacles for implementation of social tagging in the domain of digital libraries. Researchers as well as an organization designs different systems, tools for expert discovery whether their techniques are different but the purpose is the same to find the expert quickly so that time could be saved. Chen et al. [13] argued that previous studies addressed the problem of journal ranking through expert survey metrics, or use an objective approach such as citation-based metrics. They suggested integrating both of these approaches. However, their work focused only on journal ranking problem [13].

By virtue of the complexity of temporary nature of transient information available on the web, it has been a challenge to find out the right actor in mixed service-oriented systems. [45]. Daniel et al., [45] presented an approach Human-Provided Services (HPS) with the argument of necessitating automated inference of knowledge and trust in an environment of distributed collaboration. They illustrated that the skill and capabilities of experts is treated as a service. Recently, Lopez et al., [46] has reported the importance of coordination of expertise based upon crowd sourcing so that the corporate services, including IT Service Delivery, IT Inventory Management and End-User Support, can benefit from the knowledge network.

3. Research questions

The two research questions are as follows:

1. Can an expert (E) in an academic environment be ranked (R) by its web weights (W) alongside the conventional ranking Scores (S), such as citations, co-author network and publication count?

$$E^R < - \bigcup_{s_i \in s} s_i + \bigcup_{w_i \in w} w_i$$

2. Is any correlation found between web weights and non-web weights?

$$\bigcup_{s_i \in s} s_i <-> \bigcup_{w_i \in w} w_i$$

To respond to the research questions, we need to find expert weight from *Growbag* dataset, *dblpXml* and author's homepage. This leads to our focus on mining web for author's homepages to identify multifaceted parameters to rank and build expert profile. Authors profile required building with highly concerned parameters to identify highly ranked authors on a specific domain.

4. Web mining for expert discovery

In order to achieve the optimized utilization of the expertise held by individuals within an organization, various organizations have reportedly adopted the searching system: Expert Recommender Systems (ERS). Usually, the prime interest of an inquirer is to find out an expert to address a specific problem [47]. Although ERS permits quick searching of experts, the inquirers may notice the absence of capability of system for informing accurate usefulness. Fully automated systems have been reported as an alternative to these self-reporting recommender systems, such as SAGE [37], bulletin boards [4], systems with email as input [48], Web pages [2], software coding system [28, 36], technical reports [38] and the artefacts of social software systems, such as Wikis and Weblogs and also social networks e.g. Lin and Griffiths-Fisher et al. [48]. However, Crowder et al. [38] found that systems mimic like ERSs have been found to prone the problems of concerning expertise analysis support, heterogeneous information sources, reusability and interoperability. Ehrlich et al. [48] illustrated the social impact of finding and contacting domain experts. They discussed Small Blue and ERS developed for IBM for mapping each staff member's social network for providing the information of "who is connected to whom and where social networks overlap". Competent expert discovery systems in the past have been innovatively applied in helping PhD scholars and research community in finding germane supervisors [17]. Peer-reviewers identification for conferences and the former made use of a manually derived expertise profile database and employed reference mining for all papers submitted to a conference [49]. Later on, co-authorship network was constructed for each submitted paper making use of a measure of conflict-of-interest to ensure that associates did not review papers. Manually constructed taxonomy in which manually crafted taxonomy employed for 100 topics in DBLP covering the research areas of a small sample of researchers appearing in DBLP [15].

We enhanced the work towards topics identification and considered co-occurred keywords as well as general term as Topics for Growbag dataset. Our technique efficiently finds credible results for which we developed a tool. We retrieved authors from each topic with their publication analysis. Moreover, we employed technique of web mining for author's homepages to get their profiles in different aspects. Our proposed work and implemented tool considerably delivered results of more than 2,500 experts' homepages analysis on behalf of multifaceted parameters.

Algorithm 1.   Expert Profile Algorithm

Input: Topic T. Year x. WebfactorCount k

Output: Collection of Authors with their ranks

---

for *each Topic do*

  get 'authors'

  for each *'author' do*

    get *'author's co-author network size'*

    get *'author's publication'*

    get *'publication'* in last x years

        get_auth_home-Page

        for each *"Home Page" do*

          get *Bool P_Score*

                {" 'Project' , 'Awards' , 'Honorarium' , 'Affiliations' , 'RFCs' , 'Supervision' , 'Collaboration' , 'Relevance' , 'Keynote_Speaker' , 'Reviewer' , 'Protocol Design' , 'Distinctions' "

                }

        end

  non_web_wt ← (citations/size(publications));

  non_web_wt ← non_web_wt +(size(publications/size(co.auth.net));

  non_web_wt ← non_web_wt +(size(publications/last_x_years_publication);

  non_web_wt ← non_web_wt +(size(publications in relevant field /publication);

  $web\_wt \leftarrow \sum_{i=1}^{k} web\_factor$

  Expert Profile ← non_web_wt + web_wt;

end

return *expert profile;*

end

---

5. Proposed methodology

We employed and focused our work on dblpXML for mining home pages to build an expert profile. In this aspect we sorted out different facets like contribution of a particular domain expert, authors project contribution. In this view we parsed her/his online homepage to search out whether s/he majorly contributed in well-known project or supervision? Whether s/he received any awards and other achievements? *Growbag* database provided by DBLP has been reported as a very imperfect database for researcher in the domain of computer science [50]. In this study, we have endeavoured to identify the reviewers behind the research papers in the margin of qualifying scoring weights. We have precisely classified the weights into two categories, *Grwobag* weights (or non-web weights) and web weights. Incomplete as well as inconsistent information were not treated at all. The model in which we acquired different weights to fill expert profile building blocks is shown in the Figure 1.

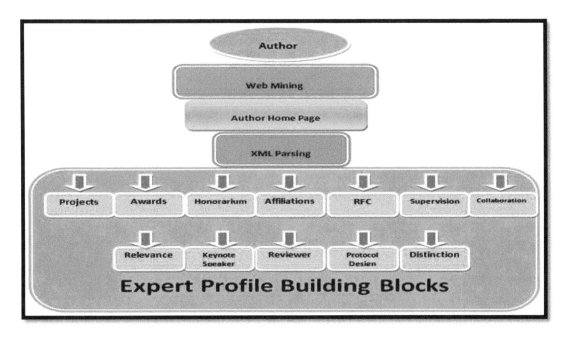

Figure 1. Expert profile building blocks

We shall describe each of them below:

- **Projects:** We employed parameter of a Project on Authors homepage while using text mining techniques and XML parsers to find whether there is any role of author in any technical project. At first level we used Boolean values to take decision of this parameter.
- **Awards:** An award is a key weight to find out an author's credibility. This leads to our examination whether there are any reputed awards won by authors.
- **Honorarium:** Honorariums deliver the benchmark values of author's contribution showing his/her contribution in his domain in well-formed way.
- **Affiliations:** It shows an author's significant influential role in his field because multiple affiliations build the portfolio. This indicates the versatile proficiency of authors in various domains of knowledge.
- **RFCs:** Request for Comments (RFCs) is popular in the domain of computer networks and communication. RFC is produced as the result of a large number of experimentations in a specific field. Usually, RFC is not ranked, but we were impressed by the reality that author's practical experimentation knowledge in a specific area based on a large-scale handshaking methodologies demands lot of expertise. Consequently, if an author has a profile with contribution in RFC, then it is a positive and a loud indication of his/her expertise in a particular domain.

- **Supervision:** A PhD scholar needs supervisor, and a researcher needs guidance in project supervision. Supervisor plays a vital role in the success of any projects or scholars' research deliverables, which are included as weights in our expert profile.
- **Collaboration:** Experts in every field play a role of collaboration in different versatile features, which impact better on community considered as a weight.
- **Relevance**: Basically for the domain expert, it is necessary to find an expert relevant to the field. So an expert belonging to the B-Topic is not meant for C-Topic within a scope of consideration for B-Topic, so we evaluated the relevance.
- **Keynote Speaker**: A keynote speaker in any domains of knowledge demonstrates the gist of a theme. Not only in corporate but also in commercial environments, a keynote speaker enjoys a significant importance. Prime functionality of the keynote speaker is to lay down the framework associated with the central dogma of a theory or discussion. In other words, we can say that a keynote speaker can play a role in the capacity of convention moderator whether it is the process of reviewing research articles or examining any experimental evaluation. The crucial importance of the keynote speaker has motivated us to include this status in our web weights.
- **Reviewer:** A reviewer is an expert who evaluates a product. The product may be a scholarly publication or an industrial/commercial service or hardware. In an academic journal or conference, a reviewer decides and measures the strength of contributed knowledge diffusion. A person who is already involved in the capacity of reviewing indicates that s/he is trusted by an organization. So we consider this measure considerably for building blocks of expert profile.
- **Protocol Design:** Protocol standards are the patent resource of communication and processing within heterogeneous environment which necessarily build upon

an intelligence strategy of handshaking or other protocol requirements demonstrating an author's value and hands on expertise in relevant domain. These reasons were sufficient to consider it in one of web weights in this research work.
- **Distinctions:** If an author A is significantly different from his/her peers, then this difference indicats his/her credibility towards expertise profile building.

6. Experimental validation

This section will elaborate our results with their validation in detail. The performance of the system is measured on standard statistical measures including sensitivity, specificity and selectivity. The performance measures of implemented system are given by equation from 1 to 5. These measures are defined formally below.

$$Accuracy = \frac{TP + TN}{TP + TN + FP + FN} \qquad (1)$$

$$Error = \frac{FN + FP}{TP + TN + FP + FN} \qquad (2)$$

$$Sensitivy\ (\mathrm{Re}\,call) = \frac{TP}{TP + FN} \qquad (3)$$

$$Selectivit\ y(\mathrm{Pr}ecision) = \frac{TP}{TP + FP} \qquad (4)$$

$$F - measure = 2 \times \frac{\mathrm{Pr}ecision \times \mathrm{Re}\,call}{\mathrm{Pr}ecision + \mathrm{Re}\,call} \qquad (5)$$

In the domain of information retrieval, the accuracy is described as the degree of closeness of measurements towards its real quantitative value. Conventionally, experts are measured in terms of number of publications and citations. S.D. Neil [30] pointed out that judgment of quality of the produced research articles is of great importance. They proposed that the information analysis be used as a gauge filter of a research paper's quality. As shown in Figure 2, the error rate for all of the web weights ranges from 5% to 14%. The highest error rate we encountered is in RFC. The precision which is equivalent to selectivity is also described as the degree of closeness, but with repeatability experiment. It was discussed in the literature that accuracy-cum-error rate alone is not sufficient to describe any measurement values but presision is also a mandatory requirement. In the literature, two kinds of erros have been reported: error of accuracy or error of precision.

A close examination of Figure 2 and 3 shows that the errors encountered in retrieving the results are of precison. This statement can be validated by the fact that the error of accuracy is always biased in some specific direction and usually delivers a specific pattern. However, this is not true in our case where no significant pattern is observed conforming our statement that this is an error of precison in nature. Yet again it was pointed out that precision alone is not enough rather recall is also an important measure for the presentation of the estimation of the results. Another measure which encompasses both precison and recall is known in the name of F-measure. It has been exploited significantly in scientific experiments for the validation of the results. Figure 3 illustrates the detail of the F-measure of each of the web weights. A careful examination highlights that "RFC", "Protocol Design" received very low F-meaure followed by "Honorarium". On the other hand, "Awards", "Affiliations", "Project", "Distinction" and "Collaboration" exhibit high F-measure value which shows the strenth of results used in our methodology. The rest of the web weights deliver intermediate values of F-measure. This analysis shows that more than 50% web weights yield reliable results.

An expected relation R between S and W is a subset of Cartesian product (S x W). If $(s, w) \in R$ or $s R w$. When R holds a relationship on a set S, which means that R is a subset of SxS. This arise the investigation into the reflexive, symmetric and transitive relationship.

Lemma-1

Web Scores S and web scores W both does not hold reflexive, symmetric and transitive relation such that the relationship $R \subseteq S \times S$ exists if $s R w$ such that $s \in S$.

Proof:

It is evident from the experimental validation depicted from Figure 3 that for every member of the conventional non-web score, a positive or negative relationship exists. Figure 3 shows that a positive relationship exists for every member of S towards every member of web scores. This relationship indicates that no strong relationship exists between members of both of the sets. In general, only some of the factors have tight relationship towards the web scores. But

nevertheless a monotonic relationship is found. It corroborates that class of empty pair-wise disjoint sets are found. Hence, it is proven that both of the sets have no reflexive, symmetric or transitive relationship.

Lemma-2:

No equivalent relationship exists between both conventional scores and web scores such as:

$$\bigcup_{s_i \in s} s_i <-> \bigcup_{w_i \in w} w_i$$

Proof:

We must show that the relationships of both set S and W are tied into a relationship such as E^R. In order to prove it, we need to show that E^R is non-empty set. However, as R does not possess any reflexive, symmetric and transitive properties and it is already known that if a set holds these properties then members of each pair of this set exhibit equivalent classes in connection to their respective domain and range. In our case, the domain and range are non-web conventional scores (S) and web scores (W), respectively. This converges into the fact that both of these sets exhibit non-equivalent relationship.

7. Experimental evaluation

In previous sections, we first argued sufficiently over the importance of identification of experts in any domain; second, we presented our results with their statistical analysis. However, the identification and ranking of these experts is a debatable issue. We concluded that numbers of citations, size of co-author network or publication count alone are not sufficient for ranking experts. But other web factors, which we termed as multifaceted web parameters or web weights are also important. We cited an example of a notable professor at Nanyang Technological University Singapore. Dr. Sun Chengzheng is a Professor at School of Computer Engineering. According to record set retrieved from *Growbag*, his publication count is 20 with citations count of 33 making a size of co-author network only 15 during period of 1996 to 2002. Apparently, these statistics show that the professor is not a high expert in the field. However, the actual facts are quite different. Professor Sun Chengzheng earned double PhD in two distant fields of computing. Since in the last two decades, he has been vigorously active in projects related to computer networks and its allied technologies. He has been an editor of many reputed journals as well as conference reviewers. He has collaboration with Australian and various Chinese universities. He worked in capacity of keynote speaker at various international industrial seminars. He runs half dozen research projects and the same number of research prototype systems. Moreover, he supervised 11 postgraduate students out of which seven hold PhD degree and are working in reputed organizations. This short example is enough to

validate the fact that the conventional parameters of citations, publication counts are not enough but other more robust parameters should also be incorporated while ranking an expert. In support of this analogy, we cited a sentence from Academia Europaea Membership Nomination Form which states that *"mention Honours and Awards (Only mention major awards; max. 20; do not mention best paper awards or fellowships that one gets if one just pays a membership fee"*[11].

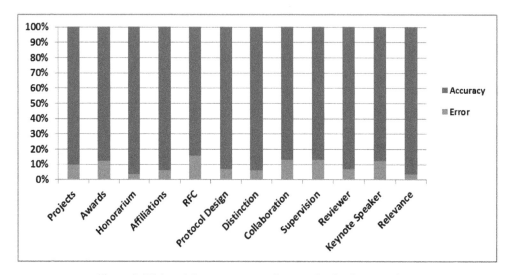

Figure 2. Web weights accuracy and error obtained comparison

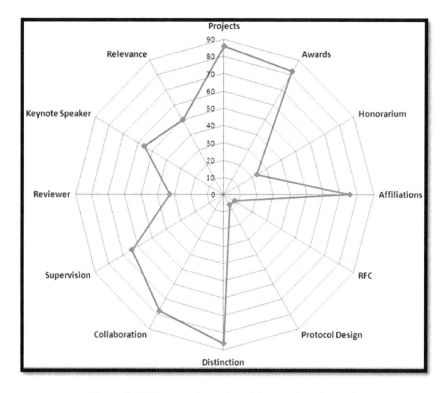

Figure 3. F-Measure for web weights used in the study

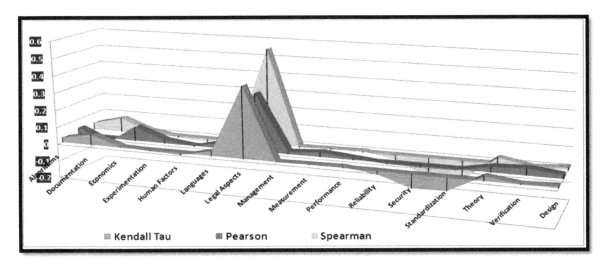

Figure 4. Correlation between non parametric values (web and non-web weights)

Another question that needs to be tweaked is: What is the relationship between both sets of parameters? The answer lies in the statistical correlation measure for non-parametric features shown in Figure 4. If we assume that there are two features: One is a web faceted score and the other is a non-web faceted score. A careful examination of both of these features indicates that these features observe no probability distribution in general. There are a lot of correlation ranking measures for non-parametric features. However, considering the nature of scoring result set generated, we employed Kendall's tau-b, Pearson Correlation rank Spearman's rank correlation coefficient [51, 52]. Figure 4 indicates probabilistic existence of causation between the two kinds of parameters. While applying these correlation measures, we considered non-web-weights as criterion feature whereas the web weights were considered as a predictor feature. We can conclude that a correlation was observed in case of general term "legal aspect". However, in case of security and standardization, a weak or negligible correlation was found between both ranking weights.

8. Conclusions and future research domains

It has always been a desire for every organization to contact the most suitable and right person in time to do what???. This study has addressed the issue of finding a better expert defined within several parameters. The study investigates the problem of topic's expert finding in *Growbag* dataset while using *dblpXML* to access author's homepages. A framework was developed which

was used in the context of identifying computer science topics experts and assigning reviewers. Prime contribution of this study is the introduction and implementation of novel idea of web mining with 12 web faceted parameters. For shrewd reader, complete result dataset can be asked from authors of this research. Our framework mined more than 2,500 Author's web pages on basis of 12 key parameters while parsing on each page for a large number of co-occurred keyword and all available general terms. Results presented evidence to validate our quantification measures of expertise in which we extracted most relevant experts in a growbag dataset.We delivered a credible and remarkable multi-facets mining technique, which considerably enhance and helped research community to get their required domain expert.

In future research domains, we have positive intention to tweak the peculiarities related to other domain converging into solution for building up a system in order to categorize the domain experts in the same way as we perceived and implemented in this study. Future work is aimed toward more robust, saleable and efficient optimization methodology in multi-objective direction focusing on complex expert judgments.

References
[1] Allen, T. J. (1977). Managing the Flow of Technology. Cambridge, MA: MIT Press.

[2] Foner, L. and Yenta, N. A. (1997). Multi-Agent Referral-Based Matchmaking System. In Proceedings of the First International Conference on Autonomous Agents, Marina del Rey, CA, 301-307.

[3] Ackerman, MS. and Halverson, C. (1998). Considering an Organization's Memory. Computer Supported Collaborative Work. Seattle, WA: ACM Press 39-48.

[4] Krulwich, B. and Burkey, B. (1996). The ContactFinder Agent: Answering Bulletin Board Questions with Referrals. Proc. 13th Nat. Conf. on AI . Vol 1, Portland, Oregon, 10-15.

[5] Olson, L. and Shaffer, R. (2002). Expertise Management – and Beyond. White paper in RGS Associates.

[6] Li, YM., Lin, CH. and Lai, CY. (2010). Identifying influential reviewers for word-of-mouth marketing. Electronic Commerce Research and Applications. 9, 294–304

[7] Afzal, MT. and Maurer, H. (2011). Expertise Recommender System for Scientific Community, Journal of Universal Computer Science. 17(11), 1529-1549.

[8] Balke, WT. and Mainzer, K. (2005). Knowledge Representation and the Embodied Mind: Towards a Philosophy and Technology of Personalized Informatics. K.D. Altho et al. (Eds.): WM 2005, LNAI 3782, 586 - 597, Springer-Verlag Berlin Heidelberg

[9] Kajikawa, Y., Abe, K. and Noda, S. (2006). Filling the gap between researchers studying different materials and different methods: a proposal for structured keywords. Journal of Information Science. 32 (6), 511–524

[10] Zainab, AN. and Silva, SMD. (1998). Expert systems in library and information services: publication trends, authorship patterns and expressiveness of published titles, Journal of Information Science. 24 (5), 313–336.

[11] Academia Europea, [WWW document] http://www.aeinfo.org/ae/Acad_Main/Sections/Informatics, (Accessed 1 Feb 2012).

[12] PAS (Pakistan Academy of Science), http://www.paspk.org/indexa.htm, (2003, Accessed Feb 2012).

[13] Chen, YL. and Chen, XH. (2011). An evolutionary PageRank approach for journal ranking with expert judgements. Journal of Information Science. 37(3), 254–272.

[14] Minjie, Z., Xijin, T., Quan, B. and Jifa, GU. (2007). Expert Discovery and Knowledge Mining In Complex Multi-Agent Systems. J Syst Sci Syst Eng. 16(2), 222-234.

[15] Cameron, D., Aleman-Meza, B. and Arpinar, IB. (2007). Collecting Expertise of Researchers for Finding for Relevant Experts in Peer-Review Setting. Proc. of 1st International Expert Finder Workshop (Berlin, Germany, Jan 16 2007).

[16] Mark, T. and Mitre, M. (2006). Technical Report "Expert Finding Systems"

[17] Liu, P. and Dew, P. (2004). Using Semantic Web Technologies to Improve Expertise Matching within Academia. Proceedings of I-KNOW '04 Graz, Austria, June 30 - July 2, 2004.

[18] Buchanan, BG. and Shortliffe, EH. (1984). Rule-Based Expert Systems. Addison-Wesley.

[19] Quinlan, JR. (1993). C4.5 "Programs for Machine Learning" Morgan Kaufmann, CA.

[20] Breiman, L., F'reidman, J., Olshen, R. and Stone, C. (1984). Classification and Regression trees, Belmont, CA: Wadsworth International Group.

[21] Michalski, RS., Carbonell, JG. and Mitchell, TM. (1983). A Theory and Methodology of Machine Learning– An Artificial Intelligence Approach. Morgan Kaufmann, Palo Alto.

[22] Michalski, RS., Mozetic, I., Hong, J. and Lavrac, N. (1986). The Multi-Purpose Incremental Learning System AQ15 and its Testing Application to Three Medical Domains, Proceedings of the fifth National Conference on Artificial Intelligence, 1041-1045, AAAI Press, Palo Alto.

[23] Pawlak, Z., Rough, Sets. (1991). Kluwer Academic Publishers, Dordrecht.

[24] Ziarko, W. (1993). Variable Precision Rough Set Model. Journal of Computer and System Sciences. 46, 39-59.

[25] Maybury, M., D'amore, R. and House, D. (2001). Expert finding for collaborative virtual environments. Commun. ACM. 44(12), 55–56.

[26] Mockus, A. and Herbsleb, JD. (2002). Expertise Browser: A Quantitative Approach to Identifying Expertise, In Proceedings on the International Conference on Software Engineering (Florida, USA, May 19-25 2002). ICSE'02. 503-312.

[27] Streeter, L. and Lochbaum, K. (1988). An Expert/Expert-Locating System Based on Automatic Representation of Semantic Structure. Proceedings of the Fourth Conference on Artificial Intelligence Applications, Computer Society of the IEEE, San Diego, CA, pp. 345-349.

[28] Mcdonald, DW. and Ackerman, MS. (2000). Expertise recommender: a flexible recommendation system and architecture. In Proc. of the 2000 ACM Conference on Computer Supported Cooperative Work (CSCW '00). December 2-5 2000, Philadelphia, Pennsylvania, USA, 231-240.

[29] Allen, TJ. (1977). Managing the Flow of Technology. Cambridge, MA: MIT Press.

[30] Neill, SD. (1989). The information analyst as a quality filter in the scientific communication process. Journal of Information Science. 15- 3.

[31] Awang Ngah Zainab, Sharon Manel De Silva. (1998). Expert systems in library and information services. Journal of Information Science. 24- 313.

[32]Robert, P. (2006). Vecchio. Journal Reviewer Ratings. Bulletin of Science Technology & Society. 26- 228.

[33] Anne, S. Tsui, and John, R. (2008). Hollenbeck. Successful Authors and Effective Reviewers. Journal of Information Science. 05- 6.

[34] Gehad, M. Galal Diane, J. Cook, and Lawrence, B. Holder. (1999). Exploiting Parallelism in a Structural Scientific Discovery System to Improve Scalability Journal of the American Society for Information Science. 50(1), 65–73.

[35] Kautz, HA., Selman, B. and Shah, M. (1997), Referral Web: Combining Social Networks and Collaborative Filtering. Communications of ACM. 40(3, 63-65.

[36] Vivacqua, A., (1999). Agents for Expertise Location. In Proc. AAAI Spring Symposium on Intelligent Agents in Cyberspace, Stanford. CA, 9-13.

[37] Becerra-Fernandez, I., (2006). Searching for experts on the Web: A review of contemporary expertise locator systems. ACM Trans. Internet Technol. 6(4), 333-355.

[38] Crowder, R., Hughes, G. and Hall, W. (2002). An agent based approach to finding expertise. In Proceedings of 4th International Conference on Practical Aspects of Knowledge Management. Berlin Heidelberg. 179-188.

[39] Sebastiani, F. (2002). Machine Learning in Automated Text Categorization. ACM Computing Surveys. 34(1), 1-47.

[40] Kraut, RE., Egido, C. and Galegher, J. (1990). Patterns of Contact and Communication in Scientific Research Collaboration, in Intellectual Teamwork: Social and Technological Foundations of Cooperative Work, J. Galegher, R.E. Kraut, and C. Egido, Editors. Lawrence Erlbaum Associates. Hillsdale.149-171.

[41] Sim, Y., Crowder, R. and Wills, G. (2006). Expert Finding by Capturing Organizational Knowledge from Legacy Documents. In Proc. Int.l Conf. on Comp. & Comm. Eng. (ICCCE '06) KL, Malaysia.

[42] Bray, T., Paoli, J., Sperberg-McQueen, CM. and Maler, E. (2000). Extensible Markup Language (XML) 1.0 (Second Edition), W3C Recommendation.

[43] Razikin, K., Goh, DH., Chua, AYK. and Lee, CS. (2011). Social tags for resource discovery: a comparison between machine learning and user-centric approaches. Journal of Information Science. 37(4) 391–404.

[44] Lu, C., Park, J. and Hu, X. (2010). User tags versus expert-assigned subject terms: A comparison of LibraryThing tags and Library of Congress Subject Headings. Journal of Information Science. 36 (6), 763–779.

[45] Daniel, S., Florian, S. and Schahram, D. (2012). Expert Discovery and Interactions in Mixed Service-oriented Systems. IEEE Transactions on Services Computing. 00- 1-00.

[46] Lopez, M., Vukovic, M. and Laredo, J. (2010). PeopleCloud Service for Enterprise Crowdsourcing. IEEE International Conference on Services Computing, 5-10 July 2010 Miami, Florida.

[47] Yimam-Seid, D. and Kobsa, A. (2003). Expert Finding Systems for Organizations: Problems and Domain Analysis and the DEMOIR approach. Jrnl of Org.l Comp. & Electronic Commerce. 13,1-24.

[48] Ehrlich, K., Lin, CY. and Griffiths-Fisher, V. (2007). Searching for experts in the enterprise: combining text and social network analysis. In: GROUP '07: Proc. 2007 Int.l ACM conf. on Supporting group work. ACM, New York, NY, USA, 117-126.

[49] Rodriguez, MA. and Bollen, J. (2006). An algorithm to determine peer-reviews (Technical Report). Los Alamos National Laboratory.

[50] Ley, M. DBLP. (2009). Some Lessons Learned. Proc. VLDB Endow. 2(2), 1493–1500.

[51] Bagdonavicius, V., Kruopis, J. and Nikulin, MS. (2011). Non-parametric tests for complete data. ISTE&WILEY: London & Hoboken. ISBN 9781848212695.

[52] Corder, GW. and Foreman, DI. (2009). Nonparametric Statistics for Non-Statisticians: A Step-by-Step Approach. Wiley ISBN 9780470454619.

Credit scoring in banks and financial institutions via data mining techniques

S. M. Sadatrasoul[1*], M.R. Gholamian[1], M. Siami[1], Z. Hajimohammadi[2]

1. Department of Industrial engineering, Iran University of Science and technology, Tehran, Iran
2. Department of Computer Science, Amirkabir University of technology, Tehran, Iran

Corresponding author:sadatrasoul@iust.ac.ir (S. M. Sadatrasoul)

Abstract

This paper presents a comprehensive review of the studies conducted in the application of data mining techniques focus on credit scoring from 2000 to 2012. Yet, there isn't adequate literature reviews in the field of data mining applications in credit scoring. Using a novel research approach, this paper investigates academic and systematic literature review and includes all of the journals in the Science direct online journal database. The studies are categorized and classified into enterprise, individual and small and midsized (SME) companies credit scoring. Data mining techniques are also categorized to single classifier, Hybrid methods and Ensembles. Variable selection methods are also investigated separately because there is a major issue in a credit scoring problem. The findings of this literature review reveals that data mining techniques are mostly applied to an individual credit score and there is inadequate research on enterprise and SME credit scoring. Also ensemble methods, support vector machines and neural network methods are the most favorite techniques used recently. Hybrid methods are investigated in four categories and two of the frequently used combinations are "classification and classification" and "clustering and classification". This review of literature analysis provides scope for future research and concludes with some helpful suggestions for further research.

Keywords: *Credit scoring, Banks and financial institutions, Literature review, Data mining.*

1. Introduction

Credit scoring consists of the assessment of risk associated with lending to an organization or a consumer (an individual). There are so many papers used intelligent and statistical techniques since the 1930s. In that decade, numerical score cards were first introduced by mail-order companies [1]. It seems that since then, although statistical techniques are used in some papers especially in hybrid techniques which mainly combine different techniques strengths to overcome their weaknesses, the usage of data mining techniques in the area of research has increased and become the dominant area in the field.

When assessing the credit, according to the context we can roughly summarize the different kind of scoring as follows [2]:

- **Application (credit) scoring:** It refers to the assessment of the credit worthiness for new applicants. It quantifies the default, associated with credit requests, by questions in the application form, e.g., present salary, number of dependents, and time at current address. Usually, a credit score is a number that quantifies the creditworthiness of a person;

- **Behavioral scoring:** It involves principles that are similar to application scoring, with the difference that it refers to existing customers. In fact, the decision about that how the lender has to deal with the borrower is in this area. Behavioral scoring models use customer's historical data, e.g., account activity, account balance, frequency about past due, and age of account to predict the time to default;

- **Collection scoring:** It is used to divide customers with different levels of insolvency into groups, separating those who require more decisive actions from those who don't need to be attended to immediately. These models are distinguished according to the degree of delinquency (early, middle, late recovery) and allow a better management of delinquent customers, from the first signs of delinquency (30–60 days) to subsequent phases and debt write-off;

- **Fraud detection:** fraud scoring models rank the applicants according to the relative likelihood that an application may be fraudulent.

This paper investigates credit scoring problems used data mining techniques. Over the past few years, a number of review articles have appeared in different publications. Hand and Henely reviewed several statistical classification models in consumer credit scoring [3]. They concluded that there is not a best method for scoring and selecting the best method depends on parameters like data structure, and the variables used other contextual characteristics. They concluded that when the data is not structured, it's better to use flexible intelligent methods like neural networks.

Thomas surveys the statistical and operational research techniques used to support credit and behavioral scoring decisions. He also discusses the need for Profit scoring, in terms of the profit, a consumer will bring to the lending organization. He explained that Profit scoring would allow organizations to have a tool that is more aligned to their objective of profitability than the present tools to measure customer's delinquency. The paper concludes that developing more quality information systems credit and behavioral scoring area are going to have more studies in new areas like profit scoring [4].

Kamleitner and Kirchlerpresent a conceptual process model, and stress the character of credit use, and review credit literature with regard to the three major parts of the consumer credit process, which are processes before, processes at, and processes after credit takes up [5]. They conclude their study with nine findings and two major gaps about credit process.

Abdou and Pointon reviewed articles based on credit scoring applications in various areas especially in finance and banking based on statistical techniques [6]. Their study also include

some of data mining techniques, and comparison of different techniques accuracy for different UCI datasets, they conclude that there is no overall best statistical technique in building scoring models.

This paper is an up to date review, which is defined in the new area and has new objectives. First, it is to develop a framework for classifying data mining application in the credit scoring and provides a comprehensive review of new articles in the area based on the framework. Second, it is to provide a guideline for new researchers and practitioners in credit scoring area especially for those who want to use data mining techniques. Third, it is to investigate the pre-process and especially variable selection techniques used in the area.

The rest of the paper is organized as follows: Section 2 presents review methodology, section 3 gives the classified articles based on section 2 methodology, in section 4 the discussions are represented and the important insights of the research is analyzed and bolded. Section 5 concludes the research and future directions in the field are suggested.

2. Methodological framework

As there are many previous works in the area of credit scoring, the literature review was based on the descriptor, "credit scoring". Full text of articles reviewed and the ones that were not actually related to the data mining techniques are excluded. Other selection criteria are as follows:

- Only Science direct online journal database were used;

- Only those articles that were in published journals and used the data mining techniques are included;

- Masters and doctorial theses, conference papers, working papers and internal reports, text books are excluded from the review mainly because academics prefer journals to acquire and disseminate information.

Figure 1 shows the methodological framework of the research.

The primary databases have about 110 articles and with further investigations and refining the results 44 articles were remained and other 66 articles were eliminated because they were not related to the application of data mining techniques in credit scoring. Each of the 44remaining articles was studied and reviewed carefully and classified in 5 tables according to their type of study.

3. Classification method
In this section, a graphical conceptual framework shown in Figure 2 is used for classifying credit scoring and data mining techniques. The conceptual framework is designed by literature review of current researches and books in credit scoring area [1]. As shown in Figure 2, the given framework consists of two levels. The first level includes three types of credit scoring problem comprising Enterprise credit score, individual's credit score and small and midsized credit score.

(i) **Individual (consumer) credit score:** The individual credit score, scores people credit using variables like applicant age, marital status, income and some other variables and can include credit bureau variables.

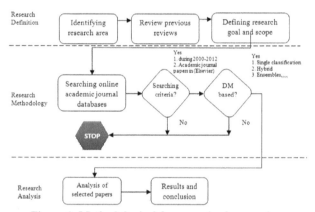

Figure 1. Methodological framework of research

(i) **Enterprise credit score:** using audited financial accounts variables and other internal or external, industrial or credit bureau variables, the enterprise score is extracted.

(ii) **SME credit score:** For SME and especially small companies financial accounts are not reliable and it's up to the owner to withdraw or retain cash, there are also other issues, for example small companies are affected by their partners and their bad/good financial status affects them, so monitoring the SMEs counterparts is another way of scoring them [1]. As a matter of fact, small businesses have a major share of the world economy and their share is growing, so SME scoring is a major issue which is investigated in this paper.

Although some differences can be found for scoring of export guarantees, EXIM banks and other

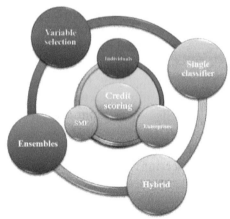

Figure 2. Classification framework for intelligent techniques in credit scoring

institutions which have not the profit as their main goal, they are excluded because of their low literature [1].

The second layer, comprised from three types of solutions and variable selection, they are presented below.

- **Variable selection:** Selecting appropriate and more predictive variables is fundamental for credit scoring [7]. Variable selection is the process of selecting the best predictive subset of variables from the original set of variables in a dataset [8]. There are many different methods for selecting variables include Stepwise regression, Factor analysis, and partial least square.

- **Single classifier:** Credit scoring is a classification problem and mainly classified applicant to good or bad. There are many data mining techniques for classification including support vector machine, and decision tree.

- **Hybrid approaches:**
  The main idea behind the hybrid approaches is that different methods have different strengths and weaknesses. This notion makes sense when the methods can be combined in some extent. This combination covers the weaknesses of the others. There are four different hybrid methods [9].
  - **Classification + Clustering**
    Clustering is an unsupervised learning technique and it cannot distinguish data accurately like supervised techniques. Therefore, a classifier can be trained first, and its output is used as the input for the cluster to improve the clustering results.

In the case of credit scoring, one can cluster good applicants in different groups.

- **Clustering + Classification**

In this approach, clustering technique is done first in order to detect and filter outlier. Then the remained data, which are not filtered, are used to train the classifier in order to probably improve the classification result.

- **Classification + Classification**

In this approach, the aim of the first classifier is to 'pre-process' the data set for data reduction. That is, the correctly classified data by the first classifier are collected and used to train the second classifier. It is assumed that for a new testing set, the second classifier could provide better classification results than single classifiers trained by the original dataset [9].

- **Clustering + Clustering**

For the combination of two clustering techniques, the first cluster is also used for data reduction. The correctly clustered data by the first cluster are used to train the second cluster. Finally, for a new testing set, it is assumed that the second cluster could provide better results.

- **Ensemble approaches:**

Ensemble methods aggregate the predictions made by multiple classifiers to improve the overall accuracy. They construct a set of classifiers from the training data and predict the classes of test samples by combining the predictions of these classifiers [10]. There are several types of Ensembles include bagging and boosting.

Table 1. Distribution of articles according to the proposed classification model

Credit scoring categories	Data mining application class	Data mining techniques	Prescreening/Variable selection	References
Enterprises	Ensemble	NN cross validation, bagging, and boosting Ensemble strategies compared with multilayer perceptron neural network	-	[11]
		Bagging, Boosting (adaboost), staking ensembles based on Logistic Regression, Decision Tree, Artificial Neural Network and Support Vector Machine compared with each other	-	[12]
		Subagging compared with 5 other methods	Manually based on strong correlation	[13]
Individuals	Single classification	Genetic programming compared with weight of evidence and Probit analysis	-	[14]
		Back-propagation artificial neural network compared with logistic regression	genetic algorithm and principle component analysisfor variable selection	[15]
		Neural networks(multilayer perceptron, mixture-of-experts, radial basis function, learning vector quantization, and fuzzy adaptive resonance) compared to linear discriminate analysis, logistic regression, k nearest neighbor, kernel density estimation, and decision trees	-	[16]
		Probabilistic neural nets and multi-layer feed-forward nets are compared with conventional techniques (discriminant analysis, probit analysis and logistic regression)	-	[17]
		Rule base	-	[18]
		Expert system compared with ٣٧ techniques include intelligent and statistical	-	[19]
		Multi-Layer Perceptrons compared with other 14 methods	principal component analysis (PCA) and different treatment methods of experiences	[20]
		Artificial neural network (RBF) compared with SVM and logistic regression	New feature selection based on rough set and tabu search	[21]
		Two evolutionary rule learners compared with neuro fuzzy classifier, Fisher discriminant analysis, Bayes' classification rule, Artificial neural networks, C4.5 decision trees	-	[22]
		Two staged MARS and NN hybrid compared with discriminant analysis, logistic regression, artificial neural networks and MARS	multivariate adaptive regression splines (MARS)	[23]
		SVM compared with neural networks, genetic programming, and decision tree classifiers	Genetic algorithm	[24]
		SVM compared with Multilayer Perceptrons (MLP)	No variable selection/include data encoding and discritization	[25]
		Genetic programming compared with ANN, decision trees, rough sets, and logistic regression.	No variable selection/ include discritization	[26]
		SVM(RBF Kernel , KGPF Kernel) compare with logistic regression	-	[27]
		SVM compare with logistic regression, discriminant analysis and k-Nearest neighbors	Feature selection by SVM	[28]
		Three link analysis algorithms compared with traditional SVM	SVM prescreening	[29]
		Clustering-launched classification(CLC) compared with SVM , SVM +GA	-	[30]
		SVM grid search compared with CART and MARS	CART and MARS	[31]
		Different feature selection for SVM compare with original SVM	discriminate analysis, decision tree, Roughs set and Fscore	[32]

Credit scoring categories	Data mining application class	Data mining techniques	Prescreening/Variable selection	References
		Random subspace method compared with Bagging, Class Switching, Rotation Forest and stand-alone classifiers	-	[33]
		CART and MARS compared with discriminant analysis, logistic regression, neural networks, and support vector machine	-	[34]
		rule extraction techniques for SVM compared with Trepan, G-REX and three other methods	-	[35]
		Genetic algorithm compared with logistic and linear regression	pre-process categorical and continuous variables to code them as a set of dummy variables	[36]
		using grid search to optimize RBF kernel parameters of SVM compared with linear discriminant analysis, logistic regression and neural networks	neighborhood rough set compared with t_Test, Correlations, Stepwise, CART, MARS, Pawlak's rough set	[37]
		Support vector machine with variable selection compared with genetic programming, neural network, SVM based genetic algorithm	F score	[38]
		Radial bases function with feature selection compared with J48 and logistic regression	based on rough set and scatter search	[39]
		Decision tree chi-square automatic interaction detector (CHAID), compared with logistic regression and weight of evidence and scorecard	Manual data preprocessing and cleaning	[40]
		Random forest and gradient boosting compared with 8 other methods	-	[41]
		Multi layer perceptron and Classification and regression trees compared with discriminant analysis and logistic regression	categorizing the data using dummy variables	[42]
	Classification + Classification	Back propagation neural networks combined with discriminant analysis	Discriminant analysis also works as a variable selection	[43]
		Hybrid neural networks (NNs) and genetic algorithms compared with discriminant analysis and CART	-	[44]
		Two-stage genetic programming compared with other 6 methods	-	[45]
		ANN and case based reasoning(CBR) compared with discriminant analysis, Logistic regression, CART and ANN	MARS	[46]
	Clustering + Classification	Self organizing map and k-means for clustering and neural network for classification	-	[47]
		Self organizing map and fuzzy k-nn rule compare with fuzzy rule base	-	[48]
	Ensemble	Three layer back-propagation neural network single classifier compared with multiple classifier	-	[49]
		Vertical bagging decision trees model(VBDTM) compared with other 10 methods	Rough set	[50]
		Least squares support vector machines (LSSVM) compared with 19 other individual classification models	-	[51]
		Hybrid clustering using Two-step and k-means, Ensembles and association rules	Discretization of continuous values with Optimal associate binning and Rank important features with Pearson chi-square test)	[52]
		Two-bagged and the three-bagged based on decision tree compared with different bagging based on logistic regression	-	[53]
		Random subspace(RS)-Bagging decision tree(DT) and Bagging-RS DT compared with single DT and four other methods	-	[54]
SME	Single classification	Classification and Regression Tree (CART) compared with 5 different variables selected	-	[55]

4. Analysis of credit scoring research based on Classification method

This paper provides a new review of literature on the application of data mining in credit scoring based on Figure 2. The distribution of 44 articles was classified by using the proposed classification method shown in Tables 1-5. The following subsections present analysis of data mining techniques in credit scoring.

4.1. Distribution of articles by data mining application classes

The 44 classified articles and their techniques are analyzed and shown in Table 1. All articles were read carefully and categorized based on the type of credit and type of the main data mining techniques. Also other Techniques which are used as the benchmark are mentioned obviously and separated using "compared with" statement. Any

preprocessing or especially variable selection techniques in each article are extracted and determined in Penultimate column. Some articles include both enterprise and individual credit scoring, They are categorized in enterprise level because they have mainly used datasets which haven't seen in previous works, and have more contributions to the knowledge in the field [11]. There are no articles in some categories for example in Enterprise credit scoring using hybrid methods, so no room was specified in this regard. It can be seen that the most of the publications were in the individual's credit scoring with 40 articles (91%). After that, Enterprise credit scoring had the second step (3 with 7%) and SME credit scoring had the third step (1 with 2%). About 22 articles (50%) used a preprocessing method and 17 articles (39%) use variables selection methods some of them manually and others with known techniques. It is clear that data preprocessing and variable selection is used credit scoring research especially for those who used datasets other than UCI benchmark datasets.

4.2. Articles by their main contribution

Table 2 comprises a complete list of the 44 articles in the review; the "main idea" column of the table shows the main idea and objective of each research.

Table 2. Distribution of articles by their main contribution

Ref #	MAIN IDEA
[11]	Ensembles of NN predictors provide more accurate generalization than a single model.
[12]	Comparative assessment of the performance of three popular ensemble methods (Bagging, Boosting, and Stacking).
[13]	The main objective is to build and validate robust models able to handle missing information, class unbalancedness and non-iid data points.
[14]	Investigate the ability of GP in the analysis of credit scoring models in Egyptian public sector banks.
[15]	Using a new method for variable selection because of high correlation between them and evaluating the results using ANN on the newly introduced data.
[16]	Comparing different neural networks versus traditional commercial techniques.
[17]	To investigate the ability of neural nets and conventional techniques in evaluating credit risk in Egyptian banks.
[18]	Giving a complementary view of redundancy in rule bases based on the contribution of individual rules to the overall system's accuracy.
[19]	Machine learning methods haven't any statistically significant advantage over the expert system's accuracy when problems were treated as a classification.
[20]	Solving the problem of imbalanced class distributionscan lead the algorithms to learn overly complex models and can over fit the data.
[21]	A new feature selection based on rough set and tabu search has been proposed.
[22]	Proposing two evolutionary fuzzy rule learners.
[23]	Introducing a new two-stage hybrid modeling procedure using MSRS and NN.
[24]	Increase SVM accuracy by hybrid method and feature reduction.
[25]	To develop a useful visual decision-support tool Using SVM.
[26]	Proposing genetic programming as a more sophisticated model to significantly improving the accuracy of the credit scoring.
[27]	To present a novel and practical adaptive scoring system based on incremental kernel methods.
[28]	To show that support vector machines are competitive against traditional methods on a large credit card database.
[29]	Three link analysis algorithms based on preprocess of support vector machine proposed to estimate an applicant's credit.
[30]	Using a new classifier named clustering-launched classification (CLC) for credit scoring.
[31]	To show that hybrid SVM has better capability of capturing nonlinear relationship among variables.
[32]	Using different feature selection methods for SVM.
[33]	"Random Subspace" method outperforms the other ensemble methods tested in the paper.
[34]	Explore the performance of credit scoring using two commonly discussed data mining techniques CART and MARS.

Ref #	MAIN IDEA
[35]	Extracting rules from SVM to overcome its complexity.
[36]	Seeks to determine the impact of in correct problem specification on performance that results from having different objectives for model construction and assessment.
[37]	To constructs a hybrid SVM-based credit scoring models to evaluate the applicant's credit score.
[38]	A new strategy to reduce the computational time for credit scoring using SVM incorporated with F score for feature reduction.
[39]	A novel approach, called RSFS, to feature selection based on rough set and scatter search is proposed.
[40]	Constructions of credit scoring model based on data mining technique and compare it to a scorecard.
[41]	Compare several techniques that can be used in the analysis of imbalanced credit scoring data sets.
[42]	To make a practical contribution in instance sampling to model building on credit scoring datasets.
[43]	Using NN and discriminant analysis Hybrid models to improve the performance.
[44]	Using GA-based inverse classification to conditional acceptance of rejected customers classified sooner with NN.
[45]	An improvement in accuracy might translate into significant savings, so a more sophisticated model based on Two-stage genetic programming is introduced.
[46]	Introduce a reassigning credit scoring model (RCSM) involving two stages to decrease the Type I error.
[47]	Presents a hybrid mining approach in the design of an effective credit scoring model based on clustering and neural network.
[48]	Introduce a "soft" classifier to produce a measure of support for the decision that provides the analyst with a greater insight.
[49]	Comparing classifier NN ensembles versus single NN classifiers and best single classifier.
[50]	A novel credit-scoring model called vertical bagging decision trees model (abbreviated to VBDTM) is proposed.
[51]	Several ensemble models based on least squares support vector machines (LSSVM) are used to reduce bias.
[52]	Introducing the concept of class-wise classification as a preprocessing step in order to obtain an efficient ensemble classifier.
[53]	A new bagging-type variant procedure called poly-bagging is proposed.
[54]	Random subspace (RS)-Bagging decision tree (DT) and Bagging-RS DT, to reduce the influences of the noise data and redundant attributes.
[55]	A decision tree-based technology credit scoring introduced for start-ups and SMEs.

4.3. Distribution of articles by data mining techniques

Table 3 shows the distribution of articles by the main data mining techniques used in different credit scoring domains and benchmark techniques used for comparison are excluded. The variable selection techniques are also included in Table3 [32]. Some articles used data mining techniques other than the main issue of classification or clustering in credit scoring, for example [14] Kohnenused map for analysis of the overall sample and tested sub-sample. These techniques used for issues other than classification are excluded because they are not concerned with the main objective of the review. In some articles, different types of techniques are used and discussed all of those different types add a single value to the number of technique used [16,17]. Some articles use meta-heuristics or search algorithms to find or tune data mining algorithms parameters. For example, an article used grid search to optimize model parameters, and these algorithms are also included [31]. Ensembles mainly used one (with different parameter settings) or more classification techniques, and in these situations, the data mining technique is reported only in ensemble raw and techniques behind and the ensembles are not reported and computed [12].

The analysis shown that 23 different techniques are used 79 times and artificial neural networks are mostly used and ranked first (12 with 15.2%). Following techniques are Ensemble methods with 11articles (14%) and support vector machines with 9 articles (11.4%).

Because of robustness, transparency needs and also regulators on the credit scoring in some countries do the auditing process. Banks cannot use many of above mentioned methods [56].By using rule bases, decision trees banks can easily interpret the results and explore the rejecting reasons to the applicant and regulatory auditors. Therefore rule based techniques, and other types of decision tree methods are used in 14 articles (17.7%). This shows that these types of techniques are also one of the favorite techniques in credit scoring problems.17 articles used different variable selection techniques, among them rough sets are the most favorite 5 articles (29.4%) used, and are followed by MARS from which 4 articles (23.5%) used.

A brief description of the three most used techniques are as follows:

Neural networks: Artificial Neural Networks (ANNs) are non-linear techniques that imitate the human brains functionality. They are used broadly in classification, clustering and optimization problems[10]. ANNs are able to recognize the complex and non-linear patterns between input and output variables in credit scoring which then predict the creditworthiness of a new applicant. They can also use for clustering applicants.

Support vector machines: SVM is the state-of-the-art technology based on statistical learning, it is designed for binary classification and aims to develop an optimal hyper plain in way that maximizes the margins of separation between the negative and positive data sets [57]. Because in many cases, the used datasets are linearly non-separable, and a non-linear transformation of the

data set into a higher dimensional space in done[10]. In the case of credit scoring, SVM is used to classify the applicants usually based on non-linear input variables.

Ensemble methods:
Ensemble methods combines the predictions of different classifiers [10]. An ensemble method can use a unique classifier with different parameters tuned or different classifiers combined. There are several types of Ensembles include bagging, boosting, random forests. In the case of credit scoring, different classifiers classify an applicant and using a voting mechanism the final decision is kept for an applicant.

4.4. Distribution of articles by journal

Table 5 shows distribution of articles by journal. Articles related to credit scoring publications are from 10 different journals. Most of the publications are dedicated to the "Expert system with applications" journal (32 with 72.7%).European Journal of Operational Research and Computers and Operations Research are followed (6 with 13.5%totally).

5. Conclusion and future directions

Application of data mining techniques is an emerging and growing trend in credit scoring. This paper gathered and analyzed 44 articles, which applied data mining techniques to credit scoring between 2000 and 2012. The aim of this paper is to develop a framework for classifying data mining application in the credit scoring, and provides a guideline for new researchers. Practitioners in credit scoring area especially for those who want to use data mining techniques lastly investigate preprocesses and especially variable selection technique which is used in the area. The findings of the paper are:

- Individuals (consumer) credit scoring has dedicated the most articles from three area of credit scoring research.
- Only one article from Korea focused on SME credit scoring and the reason is that Korean government valued a knowledge-based economy.
- Although there are few literature on SME credit scoring, research on the application of data mining in credit scoring will increase significantly in future in the area of small and midsized companies as they are the companies of future which are more knowledge based.

- The majority of articles especially those who built their models based on real non UCI datasets used variable selection in their model building process.
- Decision trees, rule based classifiers, expert system and any other rule extraction techniques from different data mining techniques are welcomed to the credit scoring and banking industry because of their explicit conditions in accepting/rejecting applicants, and that they are easily understandable by business people compared to other techniques.
- Policy making and evaluating in credit scoring in banks are mainly done with using rules, so the reason is of the importance of new ways through effective rule design and implementation in credit industry.
- "Classification + Clustering" methods are a type of hybrid methods which is not used in reviewed articles but it can identify and extracts potential good and bad applicants groups. Identifying good customer groups helps banks and financial institutes know their customers better and plan their marketing strategies based on different customer clusters.
- With respect to the world financial crises, SMEs are financially weak and easily affected and are bankrupted by fluctuations. Papers focusing on extracting and financially clustering self sufficient silos of business groups are welcomed in the industry to prevent defaults domino effect. This issue applies other data mining techniques in the area of creditworthy business social networks.
- With respect to the research findings, some key papers focused on the area of profit scoring is suggested that profit concept versus default concept developed more financial gains for banks.
- In the field of credit scoring, imbalanced data sets frequently occur as the number of non-worthy applicants is usually much lower than the number of worthy. Some Academics and practitioners reported that non-worthy applicants are usually ten times lower than worthy applicants. So sampling issues on real world credit datasets focused on field of work in the area of credit scoring and there are few researches in the area.

Table 3. Statistics of articles on credit Scoring and data mining techniques.

NO.	Interpretation	Individual credit scoring	Enterprise credit scoring	SME credit scoring	Total
1	Artificial neural networks	12			12
2	Ensembles	8	3		11
3	Support vector machine	9			9
4	Genetic Algorithm	5			5
5	rule based (Fuzzy/non Fuzzy)	5			5
6	Rough set theory	5			5
7	Classification and regression trees	3	1		4
8	multivariate adaptive regression splines	4			4
9	Genetic programming	3			3
10	Grid search	3			3
11	Decision Tree	2			2
12	Discriminant analysis	2			2
13	F score	2			2
14	k-means	2			2
15	Principle component analysis	2			2
16	K nearest neighbor	1			1
17	Expert system	1			1
18	clustering-launched classification	1			1
19	Tabu search	1			1
20	Case-based reasoning	1			1
21	Two-step clustering	1			1
22	Scatter search	1			1
23	Chi-square automatic interaction detector	1			1
Total		75	3	1	79

Table 4. Distribution of articles by journal title.

Journal title	Number	Percentage (%)
Expert Systems with Applications	32	72.7
European Journal of Operational Research	4	9
Computers & Operations Research	2	4.5
Nonlinear Analysis: Real World Applications	1	2.2
Applied Mathematics and Computation	1	2.2
Procedia Computer Science	1	2.2
Advanced Engineering Informatics	1	2.2
Computational Statistics & Data Analysis	1	2.2
Knowledge-Based Systems	1	2.2
International Journal of Forecasting	1	2.2
Total	44	100

- There are so many validation and test methods in the area and accuracy rate, Type I and II errors, Areas under ROC curve are mostly used in the research. These methods are mainly done on "in sample" and "out of sample" records of applicants and "Out of time" and back testing issues are ignored in the reviewed articles. It's another area but it mainly needs the records of applicant's statues at least more than three years.

- The area of collection scoring is rather new in academic publications although there are so much research and software products in the outside market.

- One of the main reasons for limited research in other areas of credit scoring, which includes behavioral scoring, collection scoring, and profit scoring is the lack of appropriate data. So, bridging the gap between academics and Practitioners is of interest. This gap helps practitioners to use data mining techniques better and easier in their works. Establishing benchmark databases like UCI credit databases in other areas of credit research help to develop data mining applications in credit industry research.

This study has some limitations. First, it is limited to the science direct online database and there is a wild variety of online databases. Second, the articles are selected with "credit scoring" keyword and articles that used data mining techniques are selected based on reading articles one by one. Finally, articles which noted above on credit scoring don't use the keywords which are not included.

References

[1] Edelman, D.B. and J.N. Crook. (2002). Credit scoring and its applications. Society for Industrial Mathematics.

[2] Van Gestel, T. and B. Baesens. Credit Risk Management: Oxford University Press.

[3] Hand, D.J. and W.E. Henley. (1997). Statistical classification methods in consumer credit scoring: a review. Journal of the Royal Statistical Society: Series A (Statistics in Society). 160(3), 523-541.

[4] Thomas, L.C. (2000). A survey of credit and behavioural scoring: forecasting financial risk of lending to consumers. International Journal of Forecasting. 16(2), 149-172.

[5] Kamleitner, B. and E. Kirchler. (2007). Consumer credit use: a process model and literature review. Revue Européenne de Psychologie Appliquée/European Review of Applied Psychology.57(4), 267-283.

[6] Abdou, H.A. and J. Pointon. (2011). Credit scoring, statistical techniques and evaluation criteria: a review of the literature. Intelligent Systems in Accounting, Finance and Management.

[7] Leung, K., et al. (2008). A comparison of variable selection techniques for credit scoring.

[8] Cios, K.J., et al. (1998). Data mining methods for knowledge discovery. Kluwer Academic Publishers.

[9] Tsai, C.F. and M.-L. Chen. (2010). Credit rating by hybrid machine learning techniques. Applied Soft Computing. 10(2), 374-380.

[10] Tan, P.N., M. Steinbach, and V. Kumar. (2006). Introduction to data mining. Pearson Addison Wesley Boston.

[11] West, D., S. Dellana, and J. Qian. (2005). Neural network ensemble strategies for financial decision applications. Computers & Operations Research. 32(10), 2543-2559.

[12] Wang, G., et al. (2011). A comparative assessment of ensemble learning for credit scoring. Expert Systems with Applications. 38(1), 223-230.

[13] Paleologo, G., A. Elisseeff, and G. Antonini. (2010). Subagging for credit scoring models. European Journal of Operational Research. 201(2). 490-499.

[14] Hussein A, A. (2009). Genetic programming for credit scoring: The case of Egyptian public sector banks. Expert Systems with Applications. 36(9), 11402-11417.

[15] Šušteršič, M., D. Mramor, and J. Zupan. (2009). Consumer credit scoring models with limited data. Expert Systems with Applications. 36(3, Part 1), 4736-4744.

[16] David, W. (2000). Neural network credit scoring models. Computers & Operations Research. 27(11–12),1131-1152.

[17] Abdou, H., J. Pointon, and A. El-Masry. (2008). Neural nets versus conventional techniques in credit scoring in Egyptian banking. Expert Systems with Applications. 35(3), 1275-1292.

[18] Arie, B.D. (2008) Rule effectiveness in rule-based systems: A credit scoring case study. Expert Systems with Applications. 34(4), 2783-2788.

[19] Ben-David, A. and E. Frank. (2009). Accuracy of machine learning models versus "hand crafted" expert systems – A credit scoring case study. Expert Systems with Applications. 36(3, Part 1), 5264-5271.

[20] Huang, Y.M., C.M. Hung, and H.C. Jiau. (2006). Evaluation of neural networks and data mining methods on a credit assessment task for class imbalance problem. Nonlinear Analysis: Real World Applications. 7(4), 720-747.

[21] Wang, J., K. Guo, and S. Wang. (2010). Rough set and Tabu search based feature selection for credit scoring. Procedia Computer Science. 1(1), 2425-2432.

[22] Hoffmann, F., et al. (2007). Inferring descriptive and approximate fuzzy rules for credit scoring using evolutionary algorithms. European Journal of Operational Research. 177(1), 540-555.

[23] Lee, T.S. and I.F. Chen. (2005). A two-stage hybrid credit scoring model using artificial neural networks and multivariate adaptive regression splines. Expert Systems with Applications. 28(4), 743-752.

[24] Huang, C.L., M.C. Chen, and C.J. Wang. (2007). Credit scoring with a data mining approach based on support vector machines. Expert Systems with Applications. 33(4), 847-856.

[25] Li, S.T., W. Shiue, and M.-H. Huang. (2006). The evaluation of consumer loans using support vector machines. Expert Systems with Applications. 30(4), 772-782.

[26] Ong, C.S., J.-J. Huang, and G.-H. Tzeng. (2005). Building credit scoring models using genetic programming. Expert Systems with Applications. 29(1), 41-47.

[27] Yingxu, Y. (2007). Adaptive credit scoring with kernel learning methods. European Journal of Operational Research. 183(3), 1521-1536.

[28] Bellotti, T. and J. Crook. (2009). Support vector machines for credit scoring and discovery of significant features. Expert Systems with Applications. 36(2, Part 2), 3302-3308.

[29] Xu, X., C. Zhou, and Z. Wang. (2009). Credit scoring algorithm based on link analysis ranking with support vector machine. Expert Systems with Applications. 36(2, Part 2), 2625-2632.

[30] Luo, S.T., B.-W. Cheng, and C.-H. Hsieh. (2009). Prediction model building with clustering-launched classification and support vector machines in credit scoring. Expert Systems with Applications. 36(4), 7562-7566.

[31] Chen, W., C. Ma, and L. Ma. (2009). Mining the customer credit using hybrid support vector machine technique. Expert Systems with Applications. 36(4), 7611-7616.

[32] Chen, F.L. and F.C. Li. (2010). Combination of feature selection approaches with SVM in credit scoring. Expert Systems with Applications. 37(7), 4902-4909.

[33] Nanni, L. and A. Lumini. (2009). An experimental comparison of ensemble of classifiers for bankruptcy prediction and credit scoring. Expert Systems with Applications. 36(2, Part 2), 3028-3033.

[34] Lee, T.S., et al. (2006). Mining the customer credit using classification and regression tree and multivariate adaptive regression splines. Computational Statistics & Data Analysis. 50(4), 1113-1130.

[35] Martens, D., et al. (2007). Comprehensible credit scoring models using rule extraction from support vector machines. European Journal of Operational Research. 183(3), 1466-1476.

[36] Steven, F. (2009). Are we modelling the right thing? The impact of incorrect problem specification in credit scoring. Expert Systems with Applications. 36(5), 9065-9071.

[37] Ping, Y. and L. Yongheng. (2011). Neighborhood rough set and SVM based hybrid credit scoring classifier. Expert Systems with Applications. 38(9), 11300-11304.

[38] Hens, A.B. and M.K. Tiwari. (2012). Computational time reduction for credit scoring: An integrated approach based on support vector machine and stratified sampling method. Expert Systems with Applications.

[39] Wang, J., et al. (2012). Rough set and scatter search metaheuristic based feature selection for credit scoring. Expert Systems with Applications.

[40] Yap, B.W., S.H. Ong, and N.H.M. Husain. (2011). Using data mining to improve assessment of credit worthiness via credit scoring models. Expert Systems with Applications. 38(10), 13274-13283.

[41] Brown, I. and C. Mues. (2012). An experimental comparison of classification algorithms for imbalanced credit scoring data sets. Expert Systems with Applications. 39(3), 3446-3453.

[42] Crone, S.F. and S. Finlay. (2012). Instance sampling in credit scoring: An empirical study of sample size and balancing. International Journal of Forecasting. 28(1), 224-238.

[43] Lee, T.-S., et al. (2002). Credit scoring using the hybrid neural discriminant technique. Expert Systems with Applications. 23(3), 245-254.

[44] Chen, M.-C. and S.-H. Huang. (2003). Credit scoring and rejected instances reassigning through evolutionary computation techniques. Expert Systems with Applications. 24(4), 433-441.

[45] 45. Huang, J.-J., G.-H. Tzeng, and C.-S. Ong. (2006). Two-stage genetic programming (2SGP) for the credit scoring model. Applied Mathematics and Computation. 174(2), 1039-1053.

[46] Chuang, C.-L. and R.-H. Lin. (2009). Constructing a reassigning credit scoring model. Expert Systems with Applications. 36(2, Part 1), 1685-1694.

[47] Nan-Chen, H. (2005). Hybrid mining approach in the design of credit scoring models. Expert Systems with Applications. 28(4), 655-665.

[48] Arijit, L. (2007). Building contextual classifiers by integrating fuzzy rule based classification technique and k-nn method for credit scoring. Advanced Engineering Informatics. 21(3), 281-291.

[49] Tsai, C.-F. and J.-W. Wu. (2008). Using neural network ensembles for bankruptcy prediction and credit scoring. Expert Systems with Applications. 34(4), 2639-2649.

[50] Zhang, D., et al. (2010). Vertical bagging decision trees model for credit scoring. Expert Systems with Applications. 37(12), 7838-7843.

[51] Zhou, L., K.K. Lai, and L. Yu. (2010). Least squares support vector machines ensemble models for credit scoring. Expert Systems with Applications. 37(1), 127-133.

[52] Hsieh, N.-C. and L.-P. Hung. (2010). A data driven ensemble classifier for credit scoring analysis. Expert Systems with Applications. 37(1), 534-545.

[53] Louzada, F., et al. (2011). Poly-bagging predictors for classification modelling for credit scoring. Expert Systems with Applications. 38(10), 12717-12720.

[54] Wang, G., et al. (2012). Two credit scoring models based on dual strategy ensemble trees. Knowledge-Based Systems. 26(0), 61-68.

[55] Sohn, S.Y. and J.W. Kim. (2012). Decision tree-based technology credit scoring for start-up firms: Korean case. Expert Systems with Applications. 39(4), 4007-4012.

[56] Thomas, L.C. (2009). Consumer credit models: pricing, profit, and portfolios. Oxford University Press, USA.

[57] Vapnik, V.N. (2000). The nature of statistical learning theory. Springer Verlag.

Permissions

All chapters in this book were first published in JAIDM, by Shahrood University of Technology; hereby published with permission under the Creative Commons Attribution License or equivalent. Every chapter published in this book has been scrutinized by our experts. Their significance has been extensively debated. The topics covered herein carry significant findings which will fuel the growth of the discipline. They may even be implemented as practical applications or may be referred to as a beginning point for another development.

The contributors of this book come from diverse backgrounds, making this book a truly international effort. This book will bring forth new frontiers with its revolutionizing research information and detailed analysis of the nascent developments around the world.

We would like to thank all the contributing authors for lending their expertise to make the book truly unique. They have played a crucial role in the development of this book. Without their invaluable contributions this book wouldn't have been possible. They have made vital efforts to compile up to date information on the varied aspects of this subject to make this book a valuable addition to the collection of many professionals and students.

This book was conceptualized with the vision of imparting up-to-date information and advanced data in this field. To ensure the same, a matchless editorial board was set up. Every individual on the board went through rigorous rounds of assessment to prove their worth. After which they invested a large part of their time researching and compiling the most relevant data for our readers.

The editorial board has been involved in producing this book since its inception. They have spent rigorous hours researching and exploring the diverse topics which have resulted in the successful publishing of this book. They have passed on their knowledge of decades through this book. To expedite this challenging task, the publisher supported the team at every step. A small team of assistant editors was also appointed to further simplify the editing procedure and attain best results for the readers.

Apart from the editorial board, the designing team has also invested a significant amount of their time in understanding the subject and creating the most relevant covers. They scrutinized every image to scout for the most suitable representation of the subject and create an appropriate cover for the book.

The publishing team has been an ardent support to the editorial, designing and production team. Their endless efforts to recruit the best for this project, has resulted in the accomplishment of this book. They are a veteran in the field of academics and their pool of knowledge is as vast as their experience in printing. Their expertise and guidance has proved useful at every step. Their uncompromising quality standards have made this book an exceptional effort. Their encouragement from time to time has been an inspiration for everyone.

The publisher and the editorial board hope that this book will prove to be a valuable piece of knowledge for researchers, students, practitioners and scholars across the globe.

List of Contributors

A. Mosavi
University of Debrecen, Faculty of Informatics, Hungary

P. Shahsamandi Esfahani and A. Saghaei
Department of Industrial engineering, Science and Research Branch, Islamic Azad University, Tehran, Iran

Sh. Rafieian
Computer Engineering Department, Sheikh Bahaii University, Isfahan, Iran

A. Braani Dastjerdi
Computer Engineering Department, University of Isfahan, Isfahan, IranG. Özdağoğlu
Dept. of Business Administration, Faculty of Business, Dokuz Eylül University, Tınaztepe Campus, Buca, İzmir, Turkey A. Özdağoğlu
Dept. of Business Administration, Faculty of Business, Dokuz Eylül University, Tınaztepe Campus, Buca, İzmir, Turkey

Y. Gümüş
Dept. of Tourism Management, Reha Midilli Foça Tourism Faculty, Dokuz Eylul University, Foça, İzmir, Turkey

G. Kurt-Gümüş
Dept. of International Business and Trade, Faculty of Business, Dokuz Eylül University, Tınaztepe Campus, Buca, İzmir, Turkey

A. Mousavi and A. Hunter
Department of Geomatics, University of Calgary, Calgary, Canada

A. Sheikh Mohammad zadeh
Department of Geomatics, Civil Engineering Faculty, Shahid Rajaee Teacher Training University, Tehran, Iran

M. Akbari
Department of Civil Engineering, University of Birjand, Birjand, Iran

F. Karimian and S. M. Babamir
Department of Computer Engineering, University of Kashan, Kashan, Iran

A. Zarei, M. Maleki, D. Feiz and M. - A. Siahsarani Kojouri
Faculty of Economic, Management and Administrative Sciences, Semnan University, Semnan, Iran

E. Azhir
Department of Computer Engineering, Qazvin Azad University, Qazvin, Iran

N. Daneshpour
Department of Computer, Shahid Rajaee Teacher Training University, Tehran, Iran

S. Ghanbari
IRIB Technical Research Center, Tehran, Iran

F. Zahedi
Department of Engineering, College of Computer Engineering, Yazd Science and Research Branch, Islamic Azad University, Yazd, Iran

M. R. Zare-Mirakabad
School of Electrical and Computer Engineering, Department of Computer Engineering, Yazd University, Yazd, Iran

S. Shoorabi Sani
Faculty of Electrical and Computer Engineering, Hakim Sabzevari University, Iran

M. Sakenian Dehkordi and M. Naderi Dehkordi
Department of Computer Engineering, Najafabad Branch, Islamic Azad University, Najafabad, Isfahan, Iran

A. Telikani
Department of Electronic & Computer Engineering, Institute for Higher Education Pouyandegan Danesh, Chalous, Iran

A. Shahbahrami
Department of Computer Engineering, University of Guilan, Rasht, Iran

R. Tavoli
Department of Mathematics, Chalous Branch, Islamic Azad University, Chalous, Iran

M. Lashksri
Department of Computer Engineering, Ferdows Branch, Islamic Azad University, Ferdows, Iran

M.- H. Moattar
Department of Computer Engineering, Mashhad Branch, Islamic Azad University, Mashhad, Iran

A. Khazaei and M. Ghasemzadeh
Electrical & Computer Engineering Department, Yazd University, Yazd, Iran

S. Miri Rostami and M. Ahmadzadeh
Faculty of computer and IT Engineering, Shiraz University of Technology, Shiraz, Iran

A. Pouramini, S. Khaje Hassani and Sh. Nasiri
Department of Computer Engineering, University of Sirjan Technology, Sirjan, Iran

Z. Sedighi and R. Boostani
Electrical & Computer Department, Shiraz University, Shiraz, Iran

F. Fadaei Noghani and M.- H. Moattar
Department of Computer Engineering, Mashhad Branch, Islamic Azad University, Mashhad, Iran

A. Khazaei and M. Ghasemzadeh
Electrical & Computer Engineering Department, Yazd University, Yazd, Iran

S. Miri Rostami and M. Ahmadzadeh
Faculty of computer and IT Engineering, Shiraz University of Technology, Shiraz, Iran

A. Pouramini, S. Khaje Hassani and Sh. Nasiri
Department of Computer Engineering, University of Sirjan Technology, Sirjan, Iran

Z. Sedighi and R. Boostani
Electrical & Computer Department, Shiraz University, Shiraz, Iran

M. Naeem, M. Bilal Khan and M. Tanvir Afzal
Mohammad Ali Jinnah University Isalamabad Pakistan

S. M. Sadatrasoul, M.R. Gholamian and M. Siami
Department of Industrial engineering, Iran University of Science and technology, Tehran, Iran

Z. Hajimohammadi
Department of Computer Science, Amirkabir University of technology, Tehran, Iran

Index

Printed in the USA
CPSIA information can be obtained
at www.ICGtesting.com
JSHW051432221024
72173JS00006B/1445

9 781639 871506